D0549027

Hispanic Literature of the United States

Hispanic Literature of the United States

A Comprehensive Reference

Nicolás Kanellos

An Oryx Book

GREENWOOD PRESS
Westport, Connecticut • London

Library of Congress Cataloging-in-Publication Data

Kanellos, Nicolás.
    Hispanic literature of the United States : a comprehensive reference / Nicolás Kanellos.
      p. cm.
    "An Oryx book."
    Includes bibliographical references (p.   ) and indexes.
    ISBN 1–57356–558–X (alk. paper)
    1. American literature—Hispanic American authors—History and criticism. 2. Hispanic
Americans—Intellectual life. 3. Hispanic Americans in literature. I. Title.
    PS153.H56K36 2003
    810.9'868—dc21   2003048542

British Library Cataloguing in Publication Data is available.

Library of Congress Catalog Card Number: 2003048542
ISBN: 1–57356–558–X

First published in 2003

Greenwood Press, 88 Post Road West, Westport, CT 06881
An imprint of Greenwood Publishing Group, Inc.
www.greenwood.com

Printed in the United States of America

∞™

The paper used in this book complies with the
Permanent Paper Standard issued by the National
Information Standards Organization (Z39.48–1984).

10 9 8 7 6 5 4 3 2 1

All images are copyright Arte Público Press unless otherwise noted in the caption.

In memory of mi mamá Inés, Pop, Titi Provi, and all of the Latino authors whose
pens have been idled in the last few years.
May they rest in peace.

As always, for my son Miguel and my wife Cris.

And for Titi Aurea, in case you aren't around to see this book
published.

CONTENTS

PREFACE

Today, we are increasingly aware of Latino culture on the national scene. After centuries of evolution, growth and unacknowledged influence on Euro-American culture in the United States, the Hispanic presence seems suddenly to have burst upon the national scene, contributing greatly to our national diet, music, and entertainment and sports, as well as to our paranoia of becoming overwhelmed by hungry, dark-skinned neighbors speaking a foreign tongue. In time, Pulitzer-prize-winning and best-selling authors of Hispanic background will come to dominate the pages of magazines, textbooks, and the large and small screens in both the English- and Spanish-speaking worlds. The grand diversity and bilingualism of Latinos, authors in particular, will make them cultural mediators, able to cross borders at will and transcend cultures.

Hispanic literature has existed in the area that is now the United States since the first explorers and missionaries began to document their travels in these lands in the sixteenth century. The areas from present-day South Carolina and Florida all the way west to California were once claimed and administered by the Spanish Crown, and later some of those lands—from Texas west to Northern California—were part of the Republic of Mexico. Today, the legacy of those Spanish-Mexican-mestizo times survives not only in stone architecture, urban planning, and commercial exploitation of natural resources and agriculture, but also as the living, breathing legacy of thought and expression that has come down to us in documents and in the culture of the descendants inhabiting those same lands. Latinos renewed and added to this native, mixed Spanish-Amerindian-African culture during more than two centuries of immigration and exile. And they often did this in response to and in reflection of U.S. economic and political expansionism into Latin American domestic affairs in disregard of the sovereignty of its Spanish-speaking neighbors in the hemisphere.

This guide to Hispanic literature provides an in-depth overview of the evolution of Latino literature in the United States and identifies the major authors, books, trends, and themes that have come to form this literature. The growing integration of Hispanic literature into the curriculum from middle school to college has made this reference guide useful and necessary. Students and interested readers at all levels will benefit from the guide's precise and current information, drawn from the most advanced studies in the field, from its ready reference time-lines, and from its biographical dictionary, indexes, and bibliographies. The major trends that characterize Hispanic literature across the centuries guide the discussion throughout this text, and special attention is given to such important topics as bilingualism, women and feminism, folklore, orality, and children's literature. The genres of poetry, drama, and novel are given independent treatment, as is a section on publishing trends.

In all, the guide will assist teachers, curriculum and textbook writers, students, and the general public in establishing a firm footing in this growing field of study.

CHAPTER 1

OVERVIEW OF HISPANIC LITERATURE OF THE UNITED STATES

INTRODUCTION

In recent years, more and more Hispanic surnames have been appearing on the pages of book reviews and on college syllabi throughout the United States. One tends to associate this rather sudden appearance of what seems to be a body of work to the growing Hispanic presence in all social spheres within the borders of the United States, as well as to the seemingly ubiquitous Hispanic influence on popular culture in the United States. In fact, because of the lack of available texts, most scholars have limited the study and teaching of Chicano, Puerto Rican, and Cuban literature in the United States to works published within the last forty years, furthering the impression that U.S. Hispanic literature is new, young, and exclusively related to the immigrant experience.

A systematic and thorough examination of Hispanic life in the United States, however, reveals a greater and richer contribution to U.S. literature and culture than previously has been understood. Historically, the diverse ethnic groups that we conveniently lump together as "Hispanics" or "Latinos" created a literature in North America even before the founding of the United States. The sheer volume of their writing over four hundred years is so overwhelming that it would take thousands of scholars researching for many years to fully recover, analyze, and make accessible all that is worthy of study and memorializing. And, in its variety and multiple perspectives, what we will call "U.S. Hispanic" literature is far more complex than the mere sampling of the last forty years would lead us to believe. This literature incorporates the voices of the conqueror and the conquered, the revolutionary and the reactionary, the native and the uprooted or landless. It is a literature that proclaims a sense of place in the United States while it also erases borders and is transnational in the most postmodern sense possible. It is a literature that transcends ethnicity and race, while striving for a Chicano, Nuyorican, Cuban American, or a more generic Hispanic or Latino identity.

THE HISTORICAL BACKGROUND

The introduction of western culture to the lands that eventually would belong to the United States was accomplished by Hispanic peoples: Spaniards, Hispanicized Africans and Amerindians, mestizos, and mulattos. For better or worse, Spain was the first country to introduce a written European language into an area that would become the mainland United States. Beginning in 1513 with Juan Ponce de León's diaries of travel in Florida, the keeping of civil, military, and ecclesiastical records eventually became commonplace in what would become the Hispanic South and Southwest of the United States. Written culture not only facilitated the keeping of the records of conquest and colonization, maintaining of correspondence, planting the rudiments of commerce, and standardizing social organization, but it also gave birth to the first written descriptions and studies of the fauna and flora of these lands new to the Europeans, mestizos, and mulattos. It made possible the writing of laws for their governance and commercial exploitation and for writing and maintaining a history—an official story and tradition—of Hispanic culture in these lands. From the very outset, a literature was created by the explorers, missionaries, and colonizers, as well as the mixed-blood offspring of the Europeans, Amerindians, and Africans.

Ponce de León was followed by numerous other explorers, missionaries, and colonists. Among the most important was Alvar Núñez Cabeza de Vaca, whose *La relación* (*The Account*), published in Spain in 1542, may be considered the first anthropological and ethnographic book in what became the United States, documenting his eight years of observations and experiences among the Indians. Some scholars have treated his memoir as the first book of "American" literature written in a European language. Other chroniclers, memoirists, playwrights, and poets followed in the Floridas and the area that would become the southwestern United States.

Literate culture spread northward through New Spain and into the lands that by the mid-nineteenth century would become part of the United States through conquest, annexation and purchase. All of the European institutions of literacy—schools, universities, libraries, government archives, courts, and others—were first introduced by Hispanic peoples to North America by the mid-sixteenth century. The importation of books to Mexico was authorized in 1525, the printing press was introduced in 1539, and newspapers began publishing in 1541. During the colonial years, Spain founded some twenty-six universities in the Americas, in addition to numerous theological seminaries. In the seventeenth century, the University of Mexico achieved great distinction in the Americas, in everything from canon law and theology to medicine and the Aztec and Otomí languages. The first naturalist to study and write about Texas and the Gulf Coast regions was a University of Mexico professor: Carlos de Sigüenza y Góngora (1645–1700). In 1693, this scholar, in the tradition of the Renaissance man, accompanied Admiral Andrés de Pez on a scientific expedition into what is today the southeastern United States to study the local topography, fauna, and flora.

As for communications and publishing, the populations on the northern frontier of New Spain fared better after independence from Spain, during the Mexican

Title page of the first edition of Cabeza de Vaca's *La relación* (*The Account*), 1542.

period of government, when the missions were secularized and the responsibility for education shifted into the hands of a liberal government struggling to establish a democracy. During the Mexican Period, printing presses were finally introduced into these frontier areas, with both California and New Mexico housing operating presses by 1834. The California press was a government press while the New Mexican press was held privately by Father Antonio José Martínez, who printed catechisms and other books—as well as New Mexico's first newspaper, *El Crepúsculo* (The Dawn)—beginning in 1835. The printing press had already made its way into Texas in 1813 as part of the movement for Mexico's independence from Spain. Thus, considerable progress had been made toward the establishment of a literate population before northern Mexico became part of the United States.

Hispanics settling in the thirteen British colonies had immediate access to printing. In the mid-seventeenth century, the first Spanish-speaking communities were established by Sephardic Jews in the northeast portion of what would become the United States. They were followed by other Hispanics from Spain and the Caribbean who, by the 1800s, were issuing through early American printers and their own presses hundreds of political and commercial books, as well as many works of creative literature written principally by Hispanic immigrants and political refugees. In Louisiana and later in the Southwest and to some extent the Northeast, bilingual publications often became a necessity for communicating, first with the Hispano and Francophone populations and later the Hispano and Anglophone populations, as publications, including literary publications, increasingly reflected bicultural life in the United States.

Hispanic literate culture in the United States, however, has existed quite beyond the need to communicate with non-Spanish speakers and non-Hispanics. By the beginning of the nineteenth century, Hispanic communities in the Northeast, South, and Southwest were substantial enough to support trade among themselves and, thus, require written and printed communications in the Spanish language. Spanish-language newspapers in the United States date from the beginning of the nineteenth century. *El Misisipí* was published in 1808 and *El Mensagero Luisianés* in 1809, both in New Orleans; *La Gaceta de Texas* and *El Mexicano* were issued in 1813 in Nacogdoches, Texas/Natchitoshes, Louisiana. These were followed by the first Spanish-language newspaper in Florida, *El Telégrafo de las Floridas* (1817), the first in the Northeast (Philadelphia), *El Habanero* (1824), and numerous others in Louisiana, Texas, and the Northeast. Throughout the nineteenth century, despite the existence of Spanish language publishers and printers, the principal publishing enterprises in the Spanish-language in the United States and northern Mexico (most of the West and Southwest as we know it today) were the hundreds of newspapers that existed from New York to New Orleans, Santa Fe, San Francisco, and elsewhere. Literally hundreds of newspapers (Recovering the U.S. Hispanic Literary Heritage Project has documented and described some 1,700 Spanish-language periodicals, out of possibly 2,500 that were issued between 1808 and 1960; see Kanellos and Martell, 1999) carried news of commerce and politics as well as poetry, serialized novels, stories, essays, and commentary both from the pens of local writers as well as reprints of the works of the most highly regarded writers and intellectuals of the entire Hispanic world, from Spain to Argentina. And when northern Mexico and Louisiana were incorporated into the United States, this journalistic, literary, and intellectual production, rather than abating, intensified. The newspapers took on the task of preserving the Spanish language and Hispanic culture in territories and states where Hispanic residents were becoming rapidly and vastly outnumbered by Anglo and European migrants, or "pioneers," if one prefers—although they were hardly pioneers since Hispanics, Amerindians and mestizos had already lived in those areas and had established institutions there. The newspapers became forums for discussions of rights, both cultural and civil; they became the libraries and memories of the small towns in New Mexico and the "defensores de la raza" (defenders of Hispanics) in the large cities. Quite often they were the only Spanish-language textbook for learning to read and write Spanish in rural areas—and they were excellent textbooks at that, providing the best examples of written language drawn from the greatest writers in the Hispanic world, past and present. Many of the more successful newspapers grew into publishing houses by the end of the nineteenth century and beginning of the twentieth.

Since the founding of *El Misisipí* in 1808, the Spanish-language newspaper in the United States has had to serve functions never envisioned in Mexico City, Madrid, or Havana. Most of the newspapers, if not functioning as a bulwark of immigrant culture, have at least had to protect the language, culture, and rights of an ethnic minority within the framework of a hegemonic culture that was in the best of times unconcerned with the Hispanic ethnic enclaves and in the worst of times openly hostile to them. The immigrant newspapers reinforced the culture of the homeland and its relationship with the United States; newspapers that saw their communities as minorities in the United States reinforced a native identity, protected the civil rights of their communities and monitored the community's economic, educational, and cultural development. Whether serving the interests of immigrants or an ethnic minority community, it was always incumbent on the press to exemplify the best writing in the Spanish language, to uphold high cultural and moral values and, of course, to maintain and preserve Hispanic culture. Furthermore, Hispanic-owned newspapers and the literature that they published often took on the role of contestation, challenging and offering alternative views to those published in the English-language press, especially on issues that concerned their own communities and homelands.

From the beginning of the nineteenth century, the literary culture of Hispanics began assuming the expressive functions that have characterized it to the present day. These have been predominantly three distinctive types of expression: that of exiles, immigrants, and natives. These categories relate to the sociohistorical processes Hispanics have experienced in the United States. Thus, not only do these categories reveal the three general identities of Hispanics in the United States across history, they also allow us to understand the literary expression of Hispanics. On the foundation of the written and oral legacy of Hispanic exploration and colonization of vast regions that became the United States, these three historical processes and patterns of expression planted firm roots. This foundational base of exploration and settlement included descriptions of the flora and fauna, encounters with the Amerindians and their evangelization, and daily life on the frontier as perceived by the Spanish and Hispanicized peoples (including Africans, Amerindians, mestizos, and mulattoes) in chronicles, journals, ethnographies, letters, and oral lore. The first texts were written by the explorers who charted this territory and its peoples, such as Alvar Núñez Cabeza de Vaca and Fray Marcos de Niza; epic poems were composed by soldiers, such as Gaspar Pérez de Villagrá in his *History of the Conquest of New Mexico*, and missionaries, such as Alonso Gregorio de Escobedo in his *La Florida*. Later, settlers and missionaries, including Fray Gerónimo Boscana and the anonymous authors of the folk dramas *The Texans* and *The Comanches* and the *indita* and *alabado* songs, developed a distinctive mestizo literature, exhibiting many of the cultural patterns that persist to the present. All of this literary ferment, whether written or oral, took place in the northern territories of New Spain and Mexico that did not have access to the printing press. Although the world of books, libraries, and education had been introduced by the Spanish to North America, the strict banning of the printing press by the Royal Crown in its frontier territories impeded the development of printing and publishing among the native Hispanic population, the strongest base of Hispanic native culture in what would become the Southwest of the United States. Instead, there is a strong legacy that still persists of oral or folk expression in these lands, reinforced as well by the overwhelmingly working-class nature of Hispanics over the last two centuries. Ironically, the earliest widespread use of printing and publishing by Hispanics in the United States took place in an English-speaking environment. In the northeastern United States at the turn of the nineteenth century, it was the Spanish-speaking exiles and immigrants who were the first to have access to the printing press.

Thus, by the beginning of the nineteenth century, Hispanic immigrants and political refugees in the newly founded American Republic began creating a body of literature that added new dimensions and perspectives to the writing in Spanish that already existed in the Southeast and Southwest of what would become the United States. Over time, as immigrants and their descendants remained in the United States, their literary production would make the transition to a native literature, as well, to reflect their sense of history, sense of place, and entitlement in the United States. The three categories of U.S. Hispanic literature—native, immigrant and exile—are not rigid; but rather, they indicate the dynamic inter-action in Hispanic communities that have, throughout the last two centuries, continually received new waves of Hispanic immigrants and refugees. The culture and expression of the newcomers often enriched and updated that of the Hispanic residents, whose pre-existing culture and expression have evolved in this place that became the United States for at least four centuries. Furthermore, it is possible to trace the evolution of writers who may have produced texts of exile upon arriving on these shores but over the course of time made the transition to permanent immigrants and even citizens of the United States; their texts register these transitions. This reference work is an intent to identify these texts and tendencies as a means of understanding the development of Hispanic literature in the United States.

NATIVE HISPANIC LITERATURE

Native Hispanic literature first developed out of the experience of colonialism and racial oppression. Hispanics were subjected to more than a century of "racialization" through such doctrines as the Spanish Black Legend and Manifest Destiny (racist doctrines which justified the appropriation of lands and resources by the English and Anglo-Americans). The Hispanics were subsequently conquered and/or incorporated into the United States through territorial purchase and then treated as colonial subjects—as were the Mexicans of the Southwest, the Hispanics in Florida and Louisiana, the Panamanians in the Canal Zone and in Panama itself, and the Puerto Ricans in the Caribbean. (I would also make the case that in many ways Cubans and Dominicans also developed as peoples under United States colonial rule during the early twentieth century.) Adding to the

Gaspar Pérez de Villagrá.

base of Hispanics already residing within the United States was the subsequent migration and immigration of large numbers of people from the Spanish-speaking countries to the continental United States over a period of 100 years. Their waves of emigration were directly related to the colonial administration of their home-lands by the United States. Their children's subsequent U.S. citizenship created hundreds of thousands of new natives with cultural perspectives on life in the United States that differed substantially from those of immigrants and exiles.

Hispanic native literature developed as an ethnic minority literature first among Hispanics already residing in the Southwest when the U.S. appropriated it from Mexico. There are very few extant Hispanic texts from Louisiana and Florida from U.S. colonial and early statehood days. Native Hispanic literature has specifically manifested itself in an attitude of entitlement to civil, political, and cultural rights. From its very origins in the nineteenth-century the editorials of Francisco Ramírez, the novels of María Amparo Ruiz de Burton, and Hispanic native literature in general, have been cognizant of the racial, ethnic, and/or minority status of its readers within U.S. society and culture. Making use of both Spanish and English, Hispanic native literature has also included immigrants in its readership and among its interests, and it has maintained a relationship with the various "homelands," such as Cuba, Mexico, Puerto Rico, and Spain. But the fundamental reason for existence of native Hispanic literature and its point of reference has been and continues to be the lives and conditions of Latinos in the United States. Unlike immigrant literature, it does not have one foot in the homeland and one in the United States; it does not share that double gaze of forever contrasting experience in the United States with experience in the homeland. For native Hispanic peoples of the United States, the homeland *is* the United States; there *is* no question of a return to their ancestors' Mexico, Puerto Rico, or Cuba.

Thus, this literature exhibits a firm sense of place, often elevated to a mythic status. Chicanos in the 1960s and 1970s, for example, referenced Aztlán, the legendary place of origin of the Aztecs supposedly in today's Southwest, which gave them, as mestizo people, priority over Euro-Americans. This sense of place, which for the immigrants often was the "Trópico en Manhattan" or the "Little Havana," in the 1960s and 1970s became transformed into a place where new, synthetic, or syncretic cultures reigned supreme, as in the Nuyoricans' "Loisaida" (the Lower East Side of New York), so eulogized by poet-playwright Miguel Piñero, and "El Bronx" as in Nicholasa Mohr's *El Bronx Remembered*. This sense of belonging to a region or place or just the barrio, where their culture has transformed the social and physical environment, is only one manifestation of the general feeling of newness, that is, of a new culture derived from the synthesis of the old Hispanic and Anglo cultures that had initially opposed each other.

The "Chicanos" and "Nuyoricans" appeared in the 1960s along with the civil rights movement to claim a new and separate identity from that of Mexicans (even from Mexican Americans) and Puerto Ricans on the island. They proclaimed their bilingualism and biculturalism, and mixed and blended the English and Spanish in their speech and writing, creating a new esthetic that was interlingual and transcultural—one that to outsiders at times seemed inscrutable because of the outsiders' own linguistic limitations. The construction of this new identity was often explored in literary works that examined the psychology of characters caught between cultures, pondering the proverbial existential questions, as in four foundational works on coming of age: Piri Thomas' autobiography *Down These Mean Streets* (1967), Tomás Rivera's novel written in Spanish . . . *And the Earth Did Not Devour Him* (1971), Rudolfo Anaya's *Bless Me, Ultima* (1972), and Nicholasa Mohr's *Nilda* (1973). But the process of sorting out identity and creating a positive place for themselves in an antagonistic society was at times facilitated only by a cultural nationalism that, as in immigrant literature, promoted a strict code of ethnic loyalty; the *vendido* (sell-out) stereotype replaced those of the *pocho, agringado*, and *renegado* as negative models. No other artist explored the question of image and identity more than playwright Luis Valdez throughout his career, but most certainly in his allegory of stereotypes *Los Vendidos* (1976), in which he revisited the history of Mexican stereotypes, the products of discrimination and culture clash.

Many of the Hispanic newspapers, books, and other publications which appeared in the Southwest after the Mexican War (1846–1848) laid the basis for U. S. Hispanics shaping themselves as an ethnic minority within this country. While the origins of their literature date to a time well before the crucial signing of the peace treaty between the United States and Mexico, it was the immediate conversion to colonial status of the Mexican population in the newly acquired territories of California, New Mexico, Texas, and other acquired territories that first made their literature a sounding board for their rights as colonized and later as "racialized" citizens of the United States. There was a nascent, native Spanish-language literature in Florida and Louisiana, but the Hispanic population was not large enough to sustain it at the time of their takeover by the United States; only later in the twentieth century does one emerge again in such Florida authors as José Rivero Muñiz, Jose Yglesias, and Evelio Grillo.

While the printing press was not introduced to California and New Mexico until 1834, the society there, as in Texas (where the press appeared in 1813), was sufficiently literate to sustain a wide range of printing and publishing once the press was allowed. When Anglos migrated to these new territories after 1848, they made printing and publishing more widespread; later they also introduced the telegraph, the railroads, and improved communications, thus facilitating the ability of the native populations to associate over distances and solidify their cultures. Despite attempts to form public opinion and exert social control over the Hispanics through bilingual newspapers and publications, the Anglo-American colonial establishment ironically brought the means for Hispanics to effect their own self-expression and creativity, which led to development of alternative identities and ideologies. Subsequently, Hispanic intellectuals founded an increasing number of Spanish-language newspapers to serve the native Hispanic populations. By the 1880s and 1890s, books were also issuing from these presses, although it should be noted that books written in Spanish were printed from the very inception of the printing press in 1834. A native oral literature and a literature in manuscript form had existed since the colonial period as a pre-native base for later expression, and when the printing press became available, this literature made the transition to print. When the railroad reached the territories, dramatic changes occurred as a consequence of greater access to machinery and technology, as well as a better means of distribution for print products. Thus, the last third of the century saw an explosion of independent Spanish-language publishing by Hispanics in the Southwest. It was during this period that an Hispanic native literature helped to solidify a sense of ethnic and regional identity for Hispanics in the Southwest. Autobiographies, memoirs, and novels appeared, specifically treating the sense of dislocation and uprootedness, the sense of loss of patrimony and, given their status as a racial minority in the United States, the fear of persecution and discrimination.

In 1858, Juan Nepomuceno Seguín published his *Personal Memoirs of John N. Seguín*, the first memoir written by a Mexican American in the English language. Seguín was the embattled and disenchanted political figure of the Texas Republic, who ultimately experienced great disillusionment in the transformation of his Texas by Anglo-Americans. In 1872, the first novel written in English by an Hispanic of the United States was published by María Amparo Ruiz de Burton. Her romance *Who Would Have Thought It?* reconstructed antebellum and Civil War society in the North and engaged the dominant U.S. myths of American exceptionalism, egalitarianism, and consensus, offering an acerbic critique of northern racism and U.S. imperialism. In 1885, Ruiz de Burton published another novel, this from the perspective of the conquered Mexican population of the Southwest, called *The Squatter and the Don*, which documents the loss of lands to squatters and banking and railroad interests in southern California shortly after statehood. Even Californios, such as Platón Vallejo and Angustias de la Guerra Ord, who tended to romanticize the Hispanic past in their writings and dictations, were ambivalent and circumspect about the American takeover. In 1881, the first Spanish-language novel written in the Southwest was Manuel M. Salazar's romantic adventure novel *La historia de un caminante, o Gervacio y Aurora* (The History of a Traveler on Foot, or Gervasio and Aurora), which created a colorful picture of pastoral life in New Mexico at that time, perhaps as a means of contrasting this idyllic past with the colonial present. During this territorial and early statehood period in the Southwest, there were also various oral expressions not only of resistance but of outright rebellion. Examples are found in the proclamations of Juan Nepomuceno Cortina and in the *corridos fronterizos*, or border ballads, about such social rebels as Joaquín Murieta, Catarino Garza, and others. Cortina, himself the leader of a massive rebellion known as the "Cortina War," was also a subject of these ballads.

But the real cauldron in which an Hispanic ethnic-minority consciousness fermented was the Spanish-language newspaper. When Francisco P. Ramírez founded *El Clamor Público* (The Public Clamor, 1855–1859), he created a landmark awareness that Hispanics in California had been and were being treated as a race apart from the Euro-Americans who had immigrated into the area. Even the wealthy Californios who had collaborated in the Yankee takeover saw their wealth and power diminish under statehood. In addition to covering California and U.S. news, *El Clamor Público* also maintained contact with the Hispanic world outside California and attempted to present an image of refinement and education that demonstrated the high level of civilization achieved throughout the Hispanic world. This, in part, was a defensive reaction to the negative propaganda of Manifest Destiny, which had cast Mexicans and other Hispanics as unintelligent and uneducated barbarians incapable of developing their lands and the natural resources of the West in order to justify these lands and resources being wrested from their hands by the superior newcomers. Ramírez and his paper were staunch supporters of learning English; not only was it important for business, but also for protecting the Californios' rights. Ramírez from the outset assumed an editorial stance in defense of the native population; on June 14, 1856, he wrote: ". . . it has been our intent to serve as an organ for the general perspective of the Spanish race as a means of manifesting the atrocious injuries of which they have been victims in this country where they were born and in which they now live in a state inferior to the poorest of their persecutors." Only seventeen years old when he took the helm of *El Clamor Público*, Ramírez was a partisan of statehood and of the United States Constitution; however, his indignation became greater and greater as the civil and property rights of the Californios remained unprotected by that Constitution that he loved so much. He became a consistent and assiduous critic, attempting to inspire the Hispanics to unite in their defense and the authorities to protect the Hispanic residents of California who were being despoiled, even lynched.

Ramírez was instrumental in building a consciousness that this injustice and oppression were not isolated and local phenomena by reprinting news and editorials from around the state. It was in *El Clamor Público* that southern Californians could read the speeches of Pablo de la Guerra, decrying the loss of lands and rights by the Californios. In his own editorials, Francisco P. Ramírez laid the basis for the de-

Francisco Ramírez, editor of *El Clamor Público*.

velopment of an Hispanic ethnic minority consciousness in the United States; his influence in disseminating that point of view in the native population and raising their consciousness as a people cannot be underestimated. Ramírez seems to have been the first Mexican-American journalist of the West and Southwest to consistently use the press to establish an Hispanic native perspective and to pursue civil rights for his people.

In the years to come, there were many successors to *El Clamor Público* and Ramírez who insisted on integration into the American education and political system and promoted learning the English language for survival. In doing so, they created a firm basis for the development not only of an ethnic minority identity but also for biculturation, that is, a bicultural and bilingual citizenry for Mexican-Americans—precisely what Hispanics advocate today in the United States.

In Texas, again in the post-statehood period, the numerous journalists and writers included the famed and persecuted Catarino Garza—mentioned above as the subject of *corridos*—who helped to foster a sense of identity among the native Hispanic population. Born on the border in 1859 and raised in or around Brownsville, Garza worked on newspapers in Laredo, Eagle Pass, Corpus Christi, and San Antonio. In the Brownsville-Eagle Pass area, he became involved in local politics and published two newspapers, *El Comercio Mexicano* (Mexican Commerce, 1886–?) and *El Libre Pensador* (The Free Thinker, 1890–?), which criticized the violence and expropriations suffered by Mexican Americans. Beginning in 1888, when he confronted U.S. Customs agents for assassinating two Mexican prisoners, Garza became more militant and struck out at authorities on both sides of the border, leading a band of followers that included farmers, laborers, and former Texas separatists. A special force of Texas Rangers eventually broke up his force of raiders and Garza fled in 1892 to New Orleans and from there to Cuba and Panama, where he was reportedly killed fighting for Panamanian independence from Colombia. Garza's exploits were followed in detail in the Spanish-language newspapers of the Southwest and helped to coalesce feelings of exploitation and dispossession among the Mexican American population. This process was also abetted by the reprinting of Garza's articles in Spanish-language newspapers throughout the Southwest.

While Garza reverted to militantly striking out at authorities, the Idar family of journalists and labor organizers brought both natives and Mexicans together in the pursuit of rights at the turn of the century and concentrated on the consistent year-in-year-out power of editorials and political organizing. Laredo's *La Crónica* (The Chronicle, 1909–?), written and published by Nicasio Idar and his eight children, became one of the most influential Spanish-language periodicals in Texas. Like many Hispanic newspaper publishers and editors who spearheaded social and political causes for their communities, Idar and his eight children led many liberal causes. His daughter Jovita Idar was at the forefront of women's issues and collaborated in a number of women's periodicals. *La Crónica* decried everything from racism and segregation in public institutions to negative stereotypes in tent theaters and movie houses. Of a working-class and union-organizing background, Nicasio Idar's overriding theme was that man in general, and specifically Mexicans in Texas, needed to educate themselves. Only through education would social and political progress come about, and it was the special role of newspapers to guide the way and facilitate that education. Only through education would Mexicans in Texas lift themselves from their poverty and misery and defend themselves from the abuse of the Anglo-Texans. Mexican families were exhorted to maintain their children in school so that gradually the situation of Mexicans in the state would improve from one generation to the next (11 October 1910). The Idar family and their publications were as good as their words: they headed up a successful statewide drive to import Mexican teachers, find them places in which to teach children, and support them financially. Through this strategy, two social ills began to be addressed: non-admittance of Mexican children to many schools and the stemming of the loss of the Spanish language and Mexican culture among the young.

In New Mexico, which received far fewer immigrants than California and Texas, a native press flourished. Because of drawing comparably fewer Anglo settlers and entrepreneurs than California and Texas and because of its proportionately larger Hispanic population—only in New Mexico did Hispanics maintain a demographic superiority in the late nineteenth and early twentieth centuries—New Mexico was the first territory to develop a widespread independent native Hispanic press, which it sustained well into the twentieth century. Not only did more Hispanics than Anglos live there, but they resided in a more compact area and with comparably less competition and violence from Anglo newcomers. The *Nuevomexicanos* were able to hold onto more lands, property, and institutions than did the Hispanics of California and Texas. Control of their own newspapers and publications became essential in the eyes of Hispanic intellectuals and community leaders in the development of Nuevomexicano identity and self-determination in the face of adjusting to the new culture that was foisted upon them during the territorial period. Nuevomexicanos were living under a double-edged sword. On the one hand, they wanted to control their own destiny and preserve their own language and culture while enjoying the benefits and rights of what they considered the advanced civilization the United States had to offer through statehood. On the other hand, they immediately became aware of the dangers of Anglo-American cultural, economic, and political encroachment. According to Gabriel Meléndez, many of the intellectual leaders, especially newspaper publishers, believed that the native population would only advance, learn to protect itself, and merit statehood through education. They saw the newspapers as key to the education and advancement of the natives as well as to the protection of their civil and property rights (Meléndez 1997, 24–5). Nuevomexicanos felt the urgency of empowering themselves in the new system and retaining some of the power they had under Mexican rule, while Washington was delaying statehood for more than fifty years in expectation, most historians agree, of Anglos achieving a numerical and voting superiority in the territory (Gómez-Quiñones, 1994, 232–8).

In the decade following the arrival of the railroad in 1879, native Hispanic journalism and publishing increased dramatically in the New Mexico territory, and a true flowering of Nuevomexicano periodicals followed in the 1890s, when some thirty-five Spanish-language newspapers were being published. It was in these periodicals that native Hispanic literature took hold in New Mexico. From 1879 until New Mexico was admitted as a state of the Union in 1912, more than ninety Spanish-language newspapers were published in New Mexico (Meléndez, 29). How and why did this occur? Meléndez posits the political exigency of preserving their language, culture, and civil rights (30). The new technology that Nuevomexicanos adopted did not represent fundamental cultural change; rather, it empowered cultural expression that was long-held and deeply rooted in the area. As Doris Meyer put it, "The Spanish-language press, as a bridge between tradition and modernity and as an advocate of its people in Hispanic New Mexico, served as a counter discourse contesting the Anglo myth of the frontier and claiming a space for otherness in American society. In its pages one finds the multivocal reality of Neomexicano cultural identity that resists monolithic definition" (110).

In his book, Meléndez proceeds to amply document how the Nuevomexicano journalists set about taking control of their social and cultural destiny by constructing for themselves what they saw as a "national" culture, which consisted of using and preserving the Spanish language and formulating their own version of history and their own literature to ensure their self-confident and proud entrance as a state of the Union. From within the group of newspaper publishers and editors sprung a cohesive and identifiable corps of native creative writers, historians, and publishers who were elaborating a native and indigenous intellectual tradition, which is the basis of much of the intellectual and literary work of Mexican Americans today. Thus, the development of the New Mexican Hispanic press at that time followed a very different pattern from that of New York's Hispanic press, which received publishers, writers, and journalists who had been trained in their homelands and who saw themselves as exiles or immigrants. This same pattern of an immigrant press would also emerge in the major cities of the Southwest with the massive arrival of economic and political refugees of the Mexican Revolution after 1910.

The cultural nationalism of these native journalists sprang from the necessity to defend their community from the cultural, economic, and political onslaught of the "outsiders." To counter the American myth of civilizing the West—i.e., subduing the barbarous and racially inferior Indians and Mexicans—that empowered the United States and its "pioneers" to encroach and dispossess Indians and Hispanics of their lands and patrimony, the Nuevomexicano writers began elaborating a myth of their own, that of the glorious introduction of European civilization and its institutions by the Spanish during the colonial period. Prior achievement legitimized their claims to land as well as to the protection and preservation of their language and culture. In their rhetoric the Nuevomexicano editorialists were able to turn the tables on the Anglo-American settlers and businessmen who had "invaded" the territory; the Nuevomexicanos claimed their own higher breeding and Catholic religion over the low morality, vicious opportunism, and hypocrisy of the Anglo-Protestant interlopers and adventurers. In the construction of their history, the editors included historical and biographical materials regularly, even in weekly columns, covering the full gamut of Hispanic history—from the exploration and colonization of Mexico, including what became the U.S. Southwest, to the life histories of important historical figures such as Miguel de Hidalgo y Costilla, Simón Bolívar, and José de San Martín. They also began to publish history books and biographies documenting their own evolution as a people. Even in their newspapers, biographies became standard fare as they documented the contributions of their own forebearers and their contemporaries in New Mexico and the Southwest.

This "fantasy heritage" of Spanish superiority was carried on long into the twentieth century by essayists, storytellers, poets, and a cadre of women writers who sought to remember and preserve the culture and folkways of their Hispanic ancestors before Anglo culture had begun transforming life in New Mexico. When English became the language of widespread publication in the twentieth century, Nina Otero Warren, Fabiola Cabeza de Vaca, and Cleofas Jaramillo cultivated this idealized heritage in attempts at retaining a grandiose past that reminded them, and supposedly their Anglo readers as well, of the high culture and privilege that anteceded the transformations brought on by the migrants from the East. Even the religious poet and historian Fray Angélico Chávez memorialized the Hispanic past and previously unaltered landscape of New Mexico. In Texas, too, Adina de Zavala and Jovita González plumbed history and folklore in an effort to preserve the Hispanic heritage of their state, lest all forget that there was life and culture there before the arrival of the Anglos. Despite all of these writers' emphasis on validating, some would say romanticizing, life on ranches and missions, their study and preservation of folklore translated to respect for the culture of common men and women, not just the privileged landowners. This perspective differed from that of the nineteenth-century Californios such as Platón Vallejo, Brígida Briones, Angustias de la Guerra Ord, and María Amparo Ruiz de Burton—who had elevated the pastoral and mannered life on ranches and missions to an elite status superior to that of the rough and rowdy forty-niners and "pioneers" who purportedly had civilized the West.

Ironically, during the early twentieth century, while a number of immigrant authors and refugees such as María Cristina Mena, Salomón de la Selva, and Luis Pérez found their way into the mainstream English-language publishing houses in the United States, most of the works of these native writers were issued by small, regional presses or remained unpublished. While Miguel Antonio Otero,

Adina de Zavala, and Amparo Ruiz de Burton had the resources to self-publish and underwrite their books, an important native writer, Américo Paredes of Brownsville, was unsuccessful in placing his early works in English (he had previously published in Spanish in Texas newspapers); his 1936 novel *George Washington Gómez* did not make it into print until 1990. Even as late as 1953, when his manuscript novel *The Shadow* won a national contest, Paredes was unsuccessful in locating a publisher. Similarly, Jovita González in her lifetime never saw her two novels, in print *Caballero* and *Dew on the Thorn*, which sought to preserve the Hispanic cultural past of Texas. It was not until the 1960s that such writers as Puerto Ricans Piri Thomas and Nicholasa Mohr, Cuban American Jose Yglesias, and Chicanos José Antonio Villarreal (actually Doubleday issued his *Pocho* in 1959) and Floyd Salas, a descendant of the original Hispanic settlers in Colorado, saw their works issued by the large commercial houses in New York—although most of their works fit into that melting-pot genre par excellence: ethnic autobiography. The Hispanic civil rights movements and the entrance of a broad sector of Hispanics into universities helped to usher in a flourishing period of Hispanic literature in the English language that began in the 1970s and persists today.

Jovita González.

The Hispanic civil rights movement that emerged in the 1960s had inherited a legacy of resistance against colonialism, segregation, and exploitation; this legacy was expressed in the writings of editorialists, union organizers, and defenders of the culture in the early twentieth century. At the turn of the century, Nicasio and Jovita Idar used their Laredo newspaper *La Crónica* to raise the level of consciousness about the cultural and political struggles, as well as to organize communities of both natives and immigrants. From the 1920s through the 1940s, Alonso Perales published hundreds of letters and editorials in newspapers in defense of civil rights of Mexicans in the Southwest long before he came together with others to found the League of United Latin American Citizens (LULAC), which is still fighting civil rights battles today. New Mexico's Aurora Lucero and

Américo Paredes.

Eusebio Chacón delivered an untold number of speeches in defense of the Spanish language and cultural rights. In San Antonio, the firebrand of the 1938 pecan shellers' strike, Emma Tenayuca, moved thousands with her passionate speeches in the first large, successful strike in that industry; she and Isabel González created in their essays a firm, ideological base for the civil rights struggles of Mexican Americans. But it was Américo Paredes, writing in English in the mid-1930s, who best articulated the cultural and economic devastation felt by his generation of bilingual-bicultural natives of the Southwest. In poems, novels, and short stories, this native of Brownsville, Texas, was able to capture the nuances of language and the ethos of an oppressed people that he would transmit during the Chicano Movement of the 1960s and 1970s through his leadership as a scholar and teacher at the University of Texas. Indeed, a broad range of writers, scholars, and even singer-songwriters such as Tish Hinojosa and Linda Rondstat continue to cite Paredes as their cultural mentor.

Since the late nineteenth century, New York, as the principal port of entry for immigrants from Europe and the Caribbean, has always harbored and nurtured a culture of immigration that facilitated the integration of immigrants into the economy and overall culture. Within this general framework, as we shall see in the section of this book dedicated to immigrant literature, numerous immigrant newspapers flourished, in part to facilitate this transition. Some of those newspapers reflect the awareness of their communities' evolution towards citizenship status or American naturalization, and pronounced the demands for the entitlements and guarantees of citizenship. Even *Gráfico*—which in most respects was a typical immigrant newspaper—began to recognize the American citizenship of its readers, mostly Puerto Ricans and Cubans residing in East Harlem, to demand the rights guaranteed under the Constitution as well as freedom from discrimination. And while the editors of *Gráfico* often made comparisons of their community to those of other immigrant groups, the editors were leveraging the U.S. citizenship of many Hispanics residing in East Harlem. Because of the Jones Act of 1917, extending citizenship to Puerto Ricans, these former islanders did not have to learn English, acculturate, or assimilate to become citizens; citizenship was automatic. Since 1917, this line between immigrant and citizen for Puerto Ricans in New York has been blurred, even accounting for, as we shall see below, highly complex modes of expression that exhibit the confidence and entitlement to the expressive rights of natives while maintaining that double gaze, the dual perspective that is characteristic of immigrant culture.

With the advent of the Depression, New York did not experience the massive repatriation of Hispanics that occurred in the Southwest. Instead, the opposite was true. Hard economic times on the island brought even more Puerto Ricans to the city, a trend that would intensify during World War II as northeastern manufacturing and services industries experienced labor shortages and recruited heavily in Puerto Rico. The massive return of Puerto Ricans who served in the war further intensified the community's identity as a native citizenry. In addition, community members were appealed to as citizens by their local newspapers to organize politically and vote. In 1941, a new newspaper, *La Defensa* (The Defense) appeared in East Harlem specifically to further the interests of the Hispanics in the area who, it stated, were there to stay—"no somos aves de paso" (we are not here as temporary birds).

Front page of *Gráfico* newspaper.

In 1927, a league was formed in New York City to increase the power of the Hispanic community by unifying its diverse organizations. Among the very specific goals of the Liga Puertorriqueña e Hispana (The Puerto Rican and Hispanic League) were representing the community to the "authorities," working for the economic and social betterment of the Puerto Ricans, and propagating the vote among Puerto Ricans. The Liga founded a periodical in 1927 entitled *Boletín Oficial de la Liga Puertorriqueña e Hispana* (The Official Bulletin of the Puerto Rican and Hispanic League) to keep its member organizations and their constituents informed of community concerns. However, the *Boletín* evolved into much more than a newsletter, functioning more like a community newspaper and including essays and cultural items as well as news items in its pages. The periodical provided needed information and education to the Hispanic community and especially promoted suffrage among Puerto Ricans. While cultural items were front and center in the early years, later in its run under the directorship of Jesús Colón coverage of working-class issues and ideology was emphasized. Like Américo Paredes in the Southwest, Jesús Colón was a figure who made the transition from Spanish to English and laid the basis for a more militant literature during the 1960s and 1970s among Nuyoricans. In fact, Colón must be considered one of the most important immigrant writers in the early twentieth century; by the time he was writing in English for the *Daily Worker* and published his first collection of essays, *A Puerto Rican in New York*, in 1963, he had already articulated many of the perspectives on race, class, and esthetics that Nuyoricans would soon adopt.

The Chicano and Nuyorican generations were fortunate to have these models of working-class esthetics available as they began to define their bilingual-bicultural ethnopoetics. These models did not only come from educators like Américo Paredes and journalists like Jesús Colón, but from community poets and activists raised in the oral tradition, such as Abelardo Delgado of El Paso and Jorge Brandon of the Lower East Side of New York City. Historians date the beginning of the Chicano Movement to the mid-1960s effort to organize the United Farm Workers Union, led by César Chávez. The farm worker struggle served as a catalyst for a generation of Mexican Americans inspired by the African American civil rights movement and the protest against the Vietnam War. This was the first generation of U. S. Hispanics to have greater access to college, largely due to the Kennedy-Johnson initiatives to democratize education. For Chicano literature, the decade of the 1960s was a time of questioning all the commonly accepted truths in the society, foremost of which was the question of equality. The first writers of Chicano literature committed their literary voices to the political, economic, and educational development of their communities. Their works were frequently used to inspire social and political action, quite often with poets reading their verses at organizing meetings, at boycotts, and before and after protest marches. Of necessity, many of the first writers to gain prominence in the movement were the poets who could tap into the Hispanic oral tradition of recitation and declamation. Rodolfo "Corky" Gonzales, Abelardo Delgado, Ricardo Sánchez, and Alurista (Alberto Baltasar Urista) stand out in this period. They created works to be performed orally before groups of students and workers to inspire them and raise their level of consciousness. The two most important literary milestones kicking off the movement were both related to grass-roots activism. In 1965, actor-playwright Luis Valdez organized farm workers from the nascent union into an improvisational agit-prop theater company, El Teatro Campesino. In 1967, the epic poem *I Am Joaquín* was written and self-published by "Corky" Gonzales, the founder of the militant Chicano civil rights and social service organization, the Crusade for Justice.

Under the leadership of Valdez and the powerful example of El Teatro Campesino, a full-blown grass-roots theater movement emerged and lasted for almost two decades, with hundreds of community and student theater companies dramatizing the political and cultural concerns of the communities while crisscrossing the nation on tours. The movement, largely student- and worker-based, eventually became professionalized, producing works for Broadway and Hollywood and fostering the creation of Chicano theater at universities. By 1968, Valdez and El Teatro Campesino had left the vineyards and lettuce fields in a conscious effort

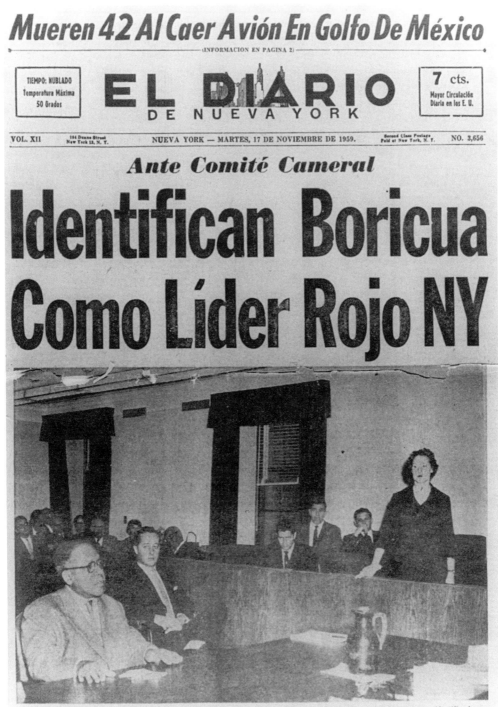

TIEMPO: NUBLADO
Temperatura Máxima
50 Grados

EL DIARIO
DE NUEVA YORK

7 cts.
Mayor Circulación
Diaria en los E. U.

VOL. XII   164 Deane Street New York 13, N. Y.   NUEVA YORK — MARTES, 17 DE NOVIEMBRE DE 1959.   Second Class Postage Paid at New York, N. Y.   NO. 3,656

Ante Comité Cameral

Identifican Boricua Como Líder Rojo NY

IDENTIFICACION POSITIVA. — La detective Mildred Blauvelt (de pie, a la derecha) señala hacia Jesús Colón para identificarlo como líder rojo, mientras éste declaraba ayer ante el Comité de Actividades Anti-Americanas de la Cámara Federal que investiga las actividades del Partido Comunista en la comunidad puertorriqueña e hispana en Nueva York. Colón y otro testigo, identificado como Félix Ojeda Ruiz, rehusaron responder a las preguntas que les fueron formuladas, cobijándose en la Quinta Enmienda Constitucional. — (Inf. en la Pág. 4)
(Foto: EL DIARIO).

Newspaper red-baiting of Jesús Colón as he testified before the House Un-American Activities Committee in 1959.

to create a theater for the Chicano nation, a people which Valdez and other Chicano organizers and ideologues envisioned as exclusively working-class, Spanish-speaking or bilingual, rurally oriented and with a very strong heritage of pre-Columbian culture. Indeed, the word "Chicano" was a working-class derivation and abbreviation of the indigenous-based pronunciation of the name of the Aztec tribes, "Mechicano," from which the name of Mexico is also derived. Through extensive touring of El Teatro Campesino, the creation of a national organization for Chicano theaters and annual conventions and workshops, and through publication of a *teatro* magazine and the company's *Actos*, along with Valdez's guidelines on creating plays about emergent Chicano nationalism, Valdez was able to broadcast and solidify the movement, which eventually gave rise to a generation of theaters and actors and bilingual-bicultural playwrights, directors, producers, and theater educators who are still very active today.

Gonzales' *I Am Joaquín* followed a similar trajectory in disseminating not only a nationalist esthetic, but also in providing a model for poets, both at the grass roots and at universities. The poem, which summarized Mexican and Mexican American history, shaped a nationalist ideological base for activism in that it reviewed the history of exploitation of the mestizos from colonial times to the present and called for an awakening to activism, using the model of the nineteenth-century social rebel Joaquín Murieta. The short bilingual pamphlet edition of the poem was literally passed from hand to hand in communities, read aloud at rallies, dramatized by Chicano theaters, and even produced as a slide show on a film with a dramatic reading by none other than Luis Valdez. The influence and social impact of *I Am Joaquín* and works of the other poets who wrote for and from the grass roots in the militant stage of the Chicano Movement are inestimable. This period was one of euphoria, power, and influence for the Chicano poet, who was sought after, almost as a priest, to give his or her blessings in the form of readings at all Chicano cultural and movement events.

The grass-roots movement was soon joined by one in academe, with university-based magazines and publishing houses formed and Chicano studies and bilingual education departments institutionalized. Sharing the nationalist/indigenist esthetic of Valdez and Gonzales were scholars Octavio Romano and Herminio Ríos, the publishers of the most successful magazine, *El Grito* (The Shout—a title harkening back to the Mexican declaration of independence from Spain), and its affiliate publishing house, Editorial Quinto Sol (Fifth Sun—a title based on the renascence of Aztec culture). Besides introducing Alurista's bilingual poetry and Miguel Méndez's trilingual (Yaqui, in addition to English and Spanish) prose to a broad audience through its magazine and its first anthology, Quinto Sol consciously set about constructing a Chicano canon with its publication of the first three award-winning literary works, all of which have become fundamental Chicano prose fiction: Tomás Rivera's . . . *Y no se lo tragó la terra* (. . . *And the Earth Did Not Devour Him*, 1971), Rudolfo Anaya's *Bless Me, Ultima* (1972), and Rolando Hinojosa's *Estampas del Valle y otras obras* (*Sketches of the Valley and Other Works*, 1973).

This predominantly male canon belatedly admitted a feminist writer of stories and plays in 1975, with the publication of Estela Portillo Trambley's *Rain of Scorpions*. Her influence has not been as lasting as that of other women writing from the mid-1970s, who by the 1980s had taken the reins of Chicano literature,

Cover of first edition of Rodolfo "Corky" Gonzales' *I Am Joaquin* (sometimes spelled *Joaquín*).

making up the first crossover generation of writers to mainstream publishing in English. Most of these writers—including Ana Castillo, Lorna Dee Cervantes, Denise Chávez, Sandra Cisneros, Pat Mora, Helena María Viramontes, Evangelina Vigil—had received their first national exposure through *Revista Chicano-Riqueña* (Chicano-Puerto Rican Review), founded in 1973, and Arte Público

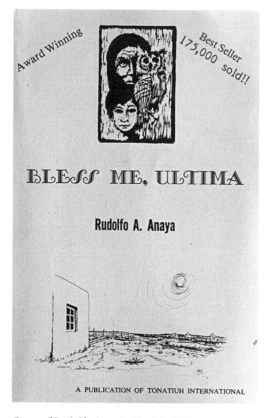

Cover of Rudolfo Anaya's *Bless Me, Ultima*.

Press, founded in 1979, both published at the University of Houston. In addition to picking up the pieces after the demise of Quinto Sol by publishing works of Alurista, Tomás Rivera, Rolando Hinojosa, and Luis Valdez, Arte Público Press continues to bring newer writers to the fore. But in its pan-Hispanism, the press has also been the major publisher of Nuyorican and Cuban American literature. In fact, Arte Público Press and *Revista Chicano-Riqueña* have been the major and longest-lived promoters of a national Latino culture and literature; they were the first publishing enterprises to open their doors to writers of all Hispanic ethnic groups in the United States. And it was Arte Público Press that launched the "Recovering the U.S. Hispanic Literary Heritage" program to find and make accessible all documents created by Hispanics from the colonial period to the present in every area that is now part of the United States.

Nuyorican writing made its appearance in the United States with a definite proletarian identity, emerging from the working-class, urbanized culture of the children of the migrants. It arose as a dynamic literature of oral performance based on the folklore and popular culture within the neighborhoods of the most cosmopolitan and post-modern city in the United States: New York ("Nuyorican" was derived from "New York Rican"). Piri Thomas's multi-volume autobiography in the poetic language of the streets, Victor Hernández Cruz's urban jazz poetry, and Nicholasa Mohr's developmental novel *Nilda*—all issued by mainstream commercial presses—led the way to the establishment of a new cultural and literary Nuyorican identity that was as hip as salsa and as alienated and seethingly revolutionary as shouts from urban labor camps and from prisons—the prisons in which many of the first practitioners of Nuyorican poetry and drama learned their craft. Ex-con and ex-gang leader Miguel Piñero and the Nuyorican group of poets, some of whom were outlaws in the literal as well as figurative sense, embellished the theme of urban marginalization and repression, and made it the threatening dynamic of their bilingual poetry and drama. Piñero was even successful at taking it to the stages of Broadway and to Hollywood films. These works threatened the very concept of literature cultivated by the academy as highly crafted art based on literary models selected from the classical repertoire of Western civilization.

The Nuyorican writers created a style and ideology that still dominates urban Hispanic writing today: working-class, unapologetic, and proud of its lack of schooling and polish—a threat not only to mainstream literature and the academy but also, with its insistence on its outlaw and street culture elements, to mainstream society. Poets such as Tato Laviera, Victor Hernández Cruz, Sandra María

Esteves, and Pedro Pietri did not seek written models for their work. They were far more attuned to and inspired by the salsa lyrics and the recitations of bards and folk poets who had always performed the news, history, and love songs in the public plazas and festivals of small-town Puerto Rico, often in the form of *décimas* and the refrains of *bombas* and *plenas*, the prevalent folk song frameworks on the island. In capturing the sights and sounds of their "urban pastoral," it was an easy and natural step to cultivating bilingual poetry, to capturing the bilingual-bicultural reality that surrounded them, and reintroducing their works into their communities through the virtuosity that live performance demands in folk culture. El Barrio, the Bronx, Loisaida (the Lower East Side) neighborhood audiences, made exigent by the technical sophistication of salsa records and performance as well as television and film, demanded authenticity, artistic virtuosity, and philosophical and political insight. Laviera, Hernández Cruz, Esteves, and Pietri reigned as masters for almost two decades. That they are accessible to far more people through oral performance than publication is not an accident, nor is it a sign of lack of sophistication; it was their literary mission, their political and eco-

Cover of a 1980 edition of *Revista Chicano-Riqueña*.

nomic stance. In fact, it was Miguel Algarín, a university-educated poet, a professor at Rutgers University also raised in the Puerto Rican barrios, who stimulated through example and entrepreneurial insight the publication of Nuyorican poetry in anthologies, magazines, and through Arte Público Press books. He further showcased Nuyorican performance art at his Nuyorican Poets Cafe in "Loisaida" and took troupes of writers on national tours of poetry slams. Besides authoring outstanding avant garde poetry himself, Algarín helped to solidify the Nuyorican literary identity and foster its entrance into the larger world of contemporary American avant garde poetics.

Beginning in the 1980s, with the assistance of such publishing houses as Arte Público and Bilingual Review Press, a new wave of Hispanic writers emerged, not from the barrios, fields, prisons, and student movements but from university creative writing programs. Almost all are monolingual English-speaking and -writing: Julia Alvarez, Denise Chávez, Sandra Cisneros, Daniel Chacón, Sarah Cortez, Alicia Gaspar del Alba, Judith Ortiz Cofer, Cristina García, Junot Díaz, Dagoberto Gilb, Oscar Hijuelos, Alberto Ríos, Benjamin Saenz, Gary Soto Virgil Suárez, Gloria Vando, and Helena María Viramontes. (The outstanding Chicana poet Lorna Dee Cervantes is a transitional figure who arose in the mid-1970s as part of the Chicano Movement, but after becoming a recognized poet, returned to the university in the 1980s in pursuit of a Ph.D.) Most of them are natives of the

United States, but some arrived as children from Puerto Rico, Cuba, and the Dominican Republic. They cultivate coming-of-age novels and novels of immigrant adjustment to American society, akin to the ethnic autobiography written in the United States by a variety of minorities and ethnic groups—to be distinguished from the literature of immigration that is written in Spanish and promotes a return to the homeland. They and many others continue to explore their identity in U.S. society. Some authors, such as Gloria Anzaldúa, Cherríe Moraga, and Aurora Levins Morales, have furthered feminist positions in their literature, exploring the relationship between gender and ethnic identity, and entering realms considered taboo by earlier generations of Hispanic writers, such as those concerning sexual identities. And from the ranks of the new wave, Hispanic literature in the United States produced its first Pulitzer Prize winner, Oscar Hijuelos' *The Mambo Kings Play Songs of Love*.

The literature of this generation is the one that is most known by a broad segment of readers in the United States today and has the greatest possibility of entering and influencing mainstream culture. However, this is also the Hispanic literature that has emerged from and been influenced most by mainstream culture and its institutions; therefore, it is the most accessible to a broad segment of English speakers and has the greatest access to commercial publishing. On the other hand, this literature is the literature of a minority of Hispanic writers, and often tends to distance itself from its indigenous communities. This is a contemporary manifestation of a longstanding heritage; it is the very tip of an iceberg whose body is made up of writing in Spanish from the three literary traditions: native, immigrant, and exile.

HISPANIC IMMIGRANT LITERATURE

While the roots of immigrant literature were planted in nineteenth-century newspapers in California and New York, it was not until the turn of the twentieth century that a well-defined immigrant expression emerged from New York to the Southwest. Although New York had been the port of entry for millions of Europeans and hundreds of thousands of Latin Americans, major cities in the Southwest received an outpouring of approximately one million dislocated working-class Mexicans during the Mexican Revolution of 1910. Los Angeles and San Antonio received the largest number of Mexican immigrants and consequently supported most writing and publication efforts. San Antonio became home to more than a dozen Spanish-language publishing houses, more than any other city in the United States. In New York, Los Angeles, San Antonio, and many other cities, an entrepreneurial class of refugees and immigrants came with sufficient cultural and financial capital to establish businesses of all types to serve the rapidly growing Hispanic enclaves. They constructed everything from tortilla factories to Hispanic theaters and movie houses, and through their cultural leadership in mutual aid societies, the churches, theaters, newspapers, and publishing houses, they were able to disseminate a nationalistic ideology that ensured the solidarity and isolation of their communities, or market, if you will. In addition to the obvious reason of being the location of important pre-existing Hispanic communities, these cities were chosen by both the economic and political refugees because their urban industrial bases were expanding, undergoing rapid industrialization and modernization, and work and opportunities were available. New York offered numerous opportunities in manufacturing and service industries, while Los Angeles and San Antonio were good bases for recruitment of agricultural and railroad workers.

Since their arrival in the United States, Hispanic immigrants have used the press and literature in their native language to maintain a connection with the homeland while attempting to adjust to a new society and culture here. Hispanic immigrant literature shares many of the distinctions that Park identified in 1922 in a study on the immigrant press as a whole. Included among these distinctions were: (1) the predominant use of the language of the homeland, in (2) serving a population united by that language, irrespective of national origin, and (3) solidifying and furthering nationalism (9–13). The literature of immigration serves a population in transition from the land of origin to the United States by reflecting the reasons for emigrating, recording the trials and tribulations of immigration, and facilitating adjustment to the new society, all the while maintaining a link with the old society.

Underlying Park's distinctions and those of other students of immigration are the myths of the American Dream and the Melting Pot—the belief that the immigrants came to find a better life, implicitly a better culture, and that soon they or their descendants would become Americans and there would no longer be a need for literature in the language of the "old country." These myths and many of Park's opinions and observations about European immigrants do not hold true for the literature of Hispanic immigration, which was *not* about being assimilated or "melting" into a generalized American identity. In fact, the history of Hispanic groups in the United States has shown an unmeltable ethnicity, and, as immigration from Spanish-speaking countries has been almost a steady flow since the founding of the United States to the present, there seems no end to the phenomenon at this juncture in history or in the foreseeable future.

In general, the literature of Hispanic immigration displays a double-gaze perspective: forever comparing the past and the present, the homeland and the new country, and only seeing the resolution of these double, conflicting points of reference when the author, characters, and/or the audience can return to the *patria*. The literature of immigration reinforces the culture of the homeland while facilitating the accommodation to the new land. While fervently nationalistic, this literature seeks to represent and protect the rights of immigrants by protesting discrimination, human rights abuses, and racism. As much of this literature arises from or is pitched to the working-class, it adopts the working-class and rural dialects of the immigrants; today, earlier immigrant literature may be seen as a museum of orality during the time period of its writing.

Among the predominant themes in the literature of immigration are the description of the Metropolis, often in satirical or critical terms, as seen in essays by José Martí, Francisco "Pachín" Marín, and Nicanor Bolet Peraza; the description of the trials and tribulations of immigrants, especially in their journey here and, once here, in their being subjected to exploitation as workers and discrimination as foreigners and racial others, as in Daniel Venegas and Conrado Espinosa; the conflict between Anglo and Hispanic cultures, ubiquitous in this literature; and the expression of gender anxieties in nationalist reaction against assimilation into mainstream culture. Highly politicized authors, including those of the working class, often cast their literary discourse in the framework of an imminent return to the homeland or a warning to those back home not to come to the United States and face the disillusionment that the writers and their protagonists had already experienced. This stance of writing to warn their compatriots, when in actuality they were speaking to their immigrant enclave or community here in the "belly of the beast," to use Martí's term, helped authors find common cause and solidarity with their audiences; both writers and readers were rendering testimony to the uninitiated, the potential greenhorns destined in the future to suffer as had the protagonists of these immigrant genres. Of course, these formulae and themes depended on the underlying premise of immigrant literature—the return to the *patria*—which necessitated the preservation of language and culture and loyalty to the *patria*. Almost invariably, the narratives of immigration end with the main characters returning to the home soil; failure to do so resulted in death, the severest poetic justice, as illustrated in the first novel of immigration, Alirio Díaz Guerra's *Lucas Guevara* (1914) and, almost half a century later, in René Marqués' play *La carreta* (The Oxcart, 1953).

Because of the massive migrations of working-class Mexicans and Puerto Ricans during the first half of the twentieth century, much of immigrant literature is to be found in oral expression, folk songs, vaudeville, and other working-class literary and artistic expression. The anonymous Mexican corrido "El lavaplatos" (The Dishwasher) reproduces the same cycle as Daniel Venegas' working-class novel *Las aventuras de Don Chipote, o cuando los pericos mamen* (*The Adventures of Don Quixote or When Parrots Breast Feed*, 1928)—leaving home to find work in the United States, disillusionment in laboring like a beast of burden here, and eventual return home. The immigrants' songs of uprootedness and longing for the home-land can be heard in the *décima* (a song with ten-line stanzas and a sonnet-like rhyme scheme) "Lamento de un jíbaro" (Lament of the *Jíbaro*). But the ultimate disillusionment and disgrace for the immigrant was being deported, as docu-mented in the plaintive refrains of the *corrido* "Los deportados" (The Deportees) and the outraged newspaper editorials by Rodolfo Uranga. Quite often the setting for this literature is the workplace, be that on the streets walked by Wen Gálvez's door-to-door salesman in his *Tampa: impresiones de un emigrado* (Tampa: Im-pressions of an Emigree, 1897), in the factory of Gustavo Alemán Bolaños' *La factoría* (The Factory, 1925), or under the burning sun in the agricultural fields, as in Conrado Espinosa's *El sol de Texas* (The Texas Sun, 1926). But domestic settings are also frequent, even in contemporary plays such as René Marqués's *La carreta* and Iván Acosta's *El super* (The Superintendent, 1977), both depicting the intergenerational conflict splitting U.S.-acculturated children from their im-migrant parents.

In fact, culture conflict of all sorts typifies this work, and from this conflict arise some of its most typical characters, such as the *agringados* (Gringoized), *renegados* (renegades), and *pitiyanquis* (petit Yankees), who deny their own cul-ture to adopt "American" ways. More than any other archetype of American culture, the predominantly male authors chose the American female to personify the eroticism and immorality, greed, and materialism that they perceived in Amer-ican society. What was an amoral Eve in a metropolis identified as Sodom for Alirio Díaz Guerra evolved into the 1920s flapper in works by Jesús Colón, Daniel

Venegas, and Julio B. Arce ("Jorge Ulica"); this enticing but treacherous Eve led unassuming Hispanic Adams into perdition. These authors placed the responsibility for preserving Hispanic customs and language, for protecting identity, in the hands of their women, and subsequently levied severe criticism at those who adopted more liberal American customs or even dared to behave like flappers themselves.

Despite this conservative, even misogynist propaganda, from these very same communities emerged a cadre of Hispanic women journalists and labor leaders who rejected circumscribed social roles even if draped in nationalist rhetoric fashioned in the lofty and elegant prose of Nemesio García Naranjo's "México de afuera" (Mexico on the Other Side, 1923) or the mordant satire of Jorge Ulica's *Crónicas diabólicas* (The Stenographer, 1925). In word and deed, such political activists and labor organizers as Leonor Villegas de Magnón and Sara Estela Ramírez inspired social action through their speeches, poems, and journalism. Teacher Ramírez was renowned for inspiring predominantly male workers to unionize through her eloquently passionate speeches; a sister teacher in Laredo, Villegas organized Anglo and Mexican/Mexican-American women to enter the Mexican Revolution as nurses, and then sought

Julio G. Arce, who wrote under the penname of Jorge Ulica.

to record their contributions for posterity in her memoir, *The Rebel*. María Luisa Garza, as a *cronista* writing under the pseudonym of Loreley, took on the defense of women in numerous unflinching and elegantly well-reasoned articles. They did this despite having to negotiate the hostile environment of an all-male editorial staff at San Antonio's *La prensa* in the 1920s.

Consuelo Lee Tapia sought to document the history of activism and contributions to Puerto Rican nationhood by women. On the same pages of Tapia's *Pueblos Hispanos* (Hispanic Peoples), one of the greatest lyric poets of the Americas, Julia de Burgos, wed her intimate verses to the movement for Puerto Rican nationhood. And on the very grass-roots but subtle level of vaudeville tent performances, Netty Rodríguez through her *agringada* (Anglicized) persona vigorously resisted her mate's exhortations to conform to the feminine role as prescribed by working-class Mexican culture. But the clearest example of Hispanic feminism dates back to the beginning of the twentieth century, when again in deed and practice Puerto Rican labor organizer Luisa Capetillo disseminated her spirited break with all social constraints on women in her treatises, plays, and poems. All of these women writer-activists presented powerful models of thought and expression that continue to inspire their spiritual descendants today.

For the Hispanic immigrant communities, defense of civil and human rights extended to protecting their enclaves from the influence of Anglo-American culture and the very real dangers present in the workplace, in the schools, and in public policy. Editorial discontent has dominated the publications of Hispanic immigrants in the major cities since the beginning of the century. Joaquín Colón, president of the Puerto Rican and Latin League and brother of Jesús Colón, used the bully pulpit in the Liga's newspaper during the 1930s to chastise the Hispanic community for its failings. His memoir, *Pioneros puertorriqueños en Nueva York* (Puerto Rican Pioneers in New York City), is a chronicle of the struggles, against political and economic odds, of the community to organize for its defense and progress. The editorial pages of most Hispanic newspapers resounded with cries for equality and freedom from discrimination and segregation; defense of the community was not just a theme to be displayed on their mastheads. Editorialists in the Southwest, from Nemesio García Naranjo to the Idar family and Rodolfo Uranga, were also vigilant of abuses of the immigrant and native communities and often lodged protests through their columns. Uranga decried one of the greatest injustices perpetrated on Mexican immigrants (and on numerous natives, as well): widespead deportations during the Depression. Today's Spanish-language newspapers continue in the same tradition, repeatedly criticizing discrimination and deportations by the Immigration and Naturalization Service. And immigrant authors—in editorials, poems, essays, and stories—continue to erect a bulwark of vigilance and defense of their communities. However, because Puerto Ricans have been citizens since 1917, deportation for their political or labor-organizing activities, as well as for being "burdensome" to the welfare system, has not been part of their psyche. Once again, there is a clear distinction between the "immigrant" legal status and the "immigrant" cultural experience. Puerto Ricans in the continental United States have immigration and migration deeply imbedded in their collective experience, but the fear of deportation as a form of discrimination and oppression has for the most part been absent.

Since the beginning of Hispanic immigrant literature, authors have felt it their duty to insulate the community from the influence of Anglo-American culture and the Protestant religion. This explains in part Díaz Guerra's moralistic attack on the big city (New York) and his depiction of the American Eve as representing all of the ills of American society. Mexican publishers and writers in the Southwest, moreover, were almost unanimous in developing and promoting the idea of a "México de afuera" or Mexican colony existing outside of Mexico, in which it was the duty of individuals to maintain the Spanish language, keep the Catholic faith, and insulate their children from what community leaders perceived as the low moral standards practiced by Anglo-Americans. Such expatriate writers and editorialists as the Mexican intellectual Nemesio García Naranjo emphasized continually that not only immigrants and exiles were part of this "México de afuera," but so was the native Hispanic population of the Southwest. However, this ideology promoted an objective that was not held by natives: a return to Mexico as a premise for its nationalism. This premise maintained that Mexican national culture was to be preserved while in exile in the midst of iniquitous Anglo-Protestants, whose culture was seen as immoral and aggressively discriminatory against Hispanics. The ideology was expressed and disseminated by immigrant and exile writers alike, some of whom were the political and religious refugees from the Mexican Revolution. They represented the most conservative segment of Mexican society in the homeland. In the United States, their cultural leadership was exerted in all phases of life in the *colonia*, solidifying a conservative substratum for Mexican American culture for decades to come. While many of the writers were educated and came from middle to upper class backgrounds, the largest audiences for the plays, novels, and poems were made up of the working-class immigrants crowded in urban barrios, an audience hungry for entertainment and cultural products in their own language. Thanks to the expanding American economy, they had the greenbacks to pay for these cultural representations of their lives.

Among the various types of literature that were published in the Hispanic immigrant newspapers, there was a genre that was more traditionally identified with and central to Hispanic newspapers everywhere and was essential in forming and reinforcing community attitudes. It was the *crónica*, a short, weekly column that humorously and satirically commented on current topics and social habits in the local community. Rife with local color and inspired by oral lore of the immigrants, the crónica was narrated in the first person from the masked perspective of a pseudonym. *Cronistas* surveyed life in the enclave and served as witnesses to the customs and behavior of the colony, whose very existence was seen as threatened by the dominant Anglo-Saxon culture. Influenced by popular jokes, anecdotes and speech, their columns registered the surrounding social environment. It was the cronista's job to fan the flames of nationalism and to sustain "México de afuera" and "Trópico en Manhattan" ideologies, the latter signifying the transformation of the metropolitan landscape into home by Caribbean Latinos, as proclaimed by such writers as Bernardo Vega and Guillermo Cotto-Thorner. Cronistas harped on the influence of Anglo-Saxon "immorality" and worried about the erosion of the Spanish language and Hispanic culture with equally religious fervor. Sometimes their messages were delivered from the bully pulpit through direct preaching, as in crónicas signed by Jesús Colón as "Miquis Tiquis." But Alberto O'Farrill, under the guise of "O'Fa," and Julio B. Arce, under the mask of "Jorge Ulica," often employed a self-deprecating humor and a burlesque of fictional characters in the community to represent general ignorance or adoption of what their characters believed to be superior Anglo ways. While these two writers entertained their audiences with the misadventures of working-class immigrants, the autodidact Colón seriously set about elevating the level of education and culture in the Hispanic community. Colón reigned as one of the most important Hispanic columnists and intellectuals in the New York Hispanic community for more than fifty years. A cigar worker from an early age in Cayey, Puerto Rico, he moved to New York as a teenager and eventually became one of the most politicized members of the community of cultural workers and union organizers. Colón made the transition to writing in English and in the mid-1950s became the first Puerto Rican columnist for *The Daily Worker*, the newspaper published by the Communist Party of America. Colón was a life-long progressive thinker and later in his career, in the 1950s, even penned feminist-type essays.

As mentioned previously, Puerto Ricans had been citizens of the United States since 1917 and legally and politically were not immigrants, at least not in the traditional sense. Nevertheless, the texts of most of the working-class writers who had migrated to the city during the twentieth century exhibit many of the classic patterns of Hispanic immigrant literature, including the emphasis on returning to the island. Even non-working class artists whose residence in New York was not as prolonged as Vega's and Colón's—for example, René Marqués, José Luis González, and Pedro Juan Soto—nevertheless employed the dual gaze and culture conflict in their works. The whole object of Marqués's *La carreta* was to construct an argument for the return of the Puerto Rican working classes to the island. And while José Luis González and Pedro Juan Soto identified themselves politically and sympathized with the uprooted working-class Puerto Ricans, their texts nevertheless repeated the trope of the metropolis as an inhuman, inhospitable place for Latinos. Even the title of González's book *En Nueva York y otras desgracias* (In New York and Other Disgraces, 1973) announced the trope that has persisted since Díaz Guerra's turn-of-the-century writing. Thus, while Puerto Ricans are not immigrants in the legal sense of the word, the characteristics exhibited in much of their writing—particularly the authors' profound sense of uprootedness and desire to return to the homeland—justify, although not transparently nor free of contradiction, their inclusion in this category.

Whether the immigrant texts stress a return to the homeland or concentrate on registering life in the immigrant enclaves, contact and conflict with other cultures in the metropolis is the stuff of immigrant literature, from the texts of Alirio Díaz Guerra and Daniel Venegas to those of more cotemporary writers, such as Ernesto Galarza, Guillermo Cotto-Thorner, Wilfredo Braschi, Roberto Fernández, and Mario Bencastro. While Bencastro focuses on the interaction of Central American immigrants with their foremen, bosses, and authority figures today in Washington, DC, Roberto Fernández satirizes the double gaze of residents in Miami's Little Havana—their obsession with reproducing and continuing life as it once was for them in Cuba, not realizing how they are truly living culturally hybrid lives. In fact, because of the political status of Cuban refugees in the United States, return to Cuba is for the near future, and has been for more than forty years, impossible. Thus, writers like Iván Acosta, Roberto Fernández, Dolores Prida, Cristina García, Virgil Suárez, and Gustavo Pérez Firmat find ways for the community to accommodate itself here in the United States. For Acosta in *El super*, it is accepting Miami as an imperfect copy of the homeland. For Dolores Prida in *Botánica* (The Herb Shop, 1990) and Pérez Firmat, the secret lies in accepting and sustaining hybridization; for others, it lies in tropicalizing the environment or otherwise transforming the urban landscape, as had been done earlier in the "México de afuera" and "Trópico en Manhattan" generations. But even in today's writers there are cries of desperation, as in Suárez's pro-

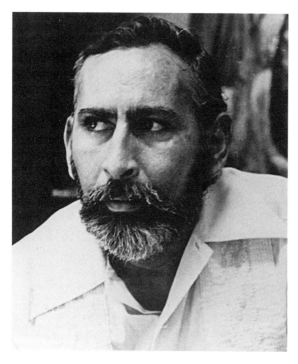

Pedro Juan Soto.

tagonist, who at the end of his novel *Going Under* (1996) jumps into the ocean to swim back to Cuba.

Another trend that began in the early twentieth century was the sporadic and intermittent acceptance of works by Hispanic authors in English-language mainstream publications. Mexican immigrant author María Cristina Mena saw her old-country-based stories published in *Century* and *Harpers,* among others. Luis Pérez, another Mexican immigrant, saw his novel *El Coyote: The Rebel* published by Holt in 1947 (Pérez's other literary works remain unpublished to date). Today, there is a notable cadre of immigrant writers, who like Mena, relocated as children to the United States and have been able to write and publish their works in English, quite often in mainstream, commercial houses: Cristina García, Virgil Suárez, Julia Alvarez, Judith Ortiz Cofer, Gustavo Pérez Firmat, and a handful of others. Each of them is part of a generation educated in American colleges and, for the most part, embarked on professional writing careers; indeed Cofer, Suárez, and Alvarez were trained in university creative writing programs. Although each has made the immigrant experience the grist of their well-crafted literary art, their audience is not the im-

José Luis González.

migrant enclave of many a Spanish-language writer, past or present, but the general English-speaking reader more likely to purchase their works in a chain bookstore than through a mail order catalog in a Spanish-language newspaper. Acculturated in the United States from youth and preferring to write in English for a broad general public, these authors assume many of the stances of native writers, but their predominant theme and their double gaze are distinctly immigrant in nature.

THE LITERATURE OF HISPANIC EXILE

The study of Hispanic exile literature in the United States is the examination of the great moments in the political history of the Hispanic World, from the beginning of the nineteenth century on: the Napoleonic intervention in Spain, the movements of the Spanish American colonies for independence from Spain, the French intervention in Mexico, the War of 1898, the Mexican Revolution, the Spanish Civil War, the Cuban Revolution, the recent wars in Central America, and the numerous struggles in Spanish America against autocratic regimes and foreign interventions, including the many incursions into the domestic affairs of these countries by the United States. The very act of U.S. partisanship in the internal politics of the Spanish American republics at times directed the expatriate streams to these shores. All of these struggles contributed hundreds of thousands of political refugees to the United States throughout its history. Because of U.S. territorial expansion and Hispanic immigration, the United States gradually became home to large communities of Spanish speakers that continually received the expatriates. Thus, the refugees found familiar societies where they could conduct business and eke out a living while they hoped for and abetted change in the lands that would someday welcome their return. Much of the literary expression of the exiles has traditionally emerged from their hopes and desires for the political and cultural independence of their homelands, be that from the Spanish empire or from U.S. imperialism. Much of this literature, particularly that of the nineteenth century, is highly lyrical and idealistic in its poetry and often elegant in its prose. However, it is also characterized by its aggressive and argumentative tone because of its commitment to political change in the homeland.

Printing and publication by Hispanics began at the turn of the nineteenth century in three cities: New Orleans, Philadelphia, and New York. Judging from the number of political books published at the beginning of the nineteenth century, the overwhelming motive for the Spaniards, Cubans, Puerto Ricans, and other Spanish Americans in the United States to bear the cost of printing and distributing their written matter was their desire to influence the politics in their homelands. Spanish-speaking political refugees from both Spain and the Spanish American countries have as part of their political culture repeatedly taken up exile in the United States to gain access to a free press and thus offer their compatriots uncensored news and political ideology, even if their writings had to be smuggled on and off ships and passed surreptitiously hand-to-hand back home. In many cases, the exile press also engaged in political fund raising, community organizing, and revolutionary plotting to overthrow regimes in their countries of origin. The raison d'être of the exile press has always been to influence life and politics in the homeland by providing information and opinion about the homeland, changing or solidifying opinion about politics and policy in the *patria*, and assisting in raising funds to overthrow the current regime.

The freedom of expression available in exile was highly desirable in light of the repression that existed in the homelands. The historical record is rife with examples of the prison terms, torture, and executions of writers, journalists, publishers, and editors during the struggles to establish democracies in Spanish America in the wake of Spain's colonialism. Numerous exile authors suffered torture in prisons and death on battlefields in the Americas. Numerous authors, viewing themselves as patriots without a country, were forced to live in exile and/or wander from country to country creating their literary works and spreading their political doctrines. This ever-present base for the culture and literature of Hispanic communities in the United States exemplifies how U.S. Hispanic literature is transnational and cannot truly be understood solely from within the geographical and political confines of the United States. Hispanic communities in the United States have never really been cut off from the rest of the Americas and the world of Hispanic culture and the Spanish language; the influence and impact of Hispanics of the United States, regardless of their language preferences, have never been limited to their immediate ethno-geographic communities. And certainly, the literature written on U. S. soil, even if written by exiles, is part of the U.S. Hispanic literary heritage.

The first political books printed in exile by Hispanics were written by Spanish citizens protesting the installation of a puppet government in Spain by Napoleon; these exiled writers published poetry and novels in addition to their political treatises. For the most part, these early books of protest were typeset and printed in the shops of early American printers. Typical of these titles was the attack on Napoleon in *España ensangrentada por el horrendo corso, tyrano de la Europa . . .* (Spain Bloodied by the Horrendous Corsican, Tyrant of Europe . . .), published in 1808 in New Orleans by an anonymous author. Shortly thereafter, the wars for independence of the Spanish colonies from Spain were supported by numerous ideologues who had assimilated the teachings of Thomas Paine, Thomas Jefferson, and John Quincy Adams and adapted them to the Hispanic world. Dominican filibusterer José Alvarez de Toledo, in his *Objeciones satisfactorias del mundo imparcial* (Satisfactory Objections from the Impartial World), militated from Baltimore as early as 1812 for Caribbean and Mexican independence; in 1813 he was one of the founders of the first newspaper in Texas, *La gaceta de Texas* (The Texas Gazette), as part of the revolutionary movement led by Miguel de Hidalgo for independence from Spain. By 1822, Hispanics began operating their own presses and publishing houses. One of the first to print his revolutionary tracts on his own press was Ecuadorian Vicente Rocafuerte, who issued his *Ideas necesarias a todo pueblo . . .* (Ideas Necessary for All Peoples . . .) in Philadelphia in 1821 as part of an effort to export the liberal ideas of the newly founded American Republic in support of the South American wars of independence against Spain. By 1825, Carlos Lanuza's press (Lanuza, Mendía & Co.) was operating in New York, printing and publishing political tracts as well as creative literature. In the 1830s, they were joined by the Imprenta Española of Juan de la Granja and the press of José Desnoues, both in New York. However, it bears repeating that New York and Philadelphia newspapers, such as *El Mensagero* (The Messenger), *El Reflector* (The Reflector), and *El Mundo Nuevo* (The New World) were also printing and publishing books. Most of these Hispanic printers and publishers were rather short-lived, but eventually two enterprises appeared with strong enough financial bases and business acumen to last for decades and provide some of the most important books by Hispanics in the nineteenth century: the houses of Cubans Nestor Ponce de León and Enrique Trujillo, from whose presses were issued some of the renowned classics of the Spanish-speaking world, authored by exiled authors José María Heredia, José Martí, Lola Rodríguez de Tió, and Pachín Marín, among many others.

The longest lasting independence movement in the hemisphere was that of Spain's Caribbean colonies, Cuba and Puerto Rico, and many of their independence struggles were plotted, funded, and written about from U.S. shores. One of Cuba's first and most illustrious exiles was the philosopher-priest Félix Varela, who founded *El Habanero* newspaper in Philadelphia in 1824 and moved it to New York in 1825. Subtitled "papel político, científico y literario" (political, scientific and literary paper), *El Habanero* openly militated for Cuban independence from Spain. Varela set the precedent for Cubans and Puerto Ricans of printing and publishing in exile and having their works circulated in their home islands. In fact, Varela's books on philosophy and education, most of which were pub-

Félix Varela.

lished in the United States, were said to be the only "best-sellers" in Cuba, and Varela himself the most popular author there in the first third of the nineteenth century—this despite there being in effect a "conspiracy of silence" in which his name could not even be brought up in public on the island (Fornet 1994, 73–4). While still residing in Philadelphia, Varela also authored the first historical novel ever written in the Spanish language, *Jicoténcal* (named after the protagonist), which illustrated the Spanish abuses of the Native Americans in Mexico and thus bolstered the arguments for independence of the Spanish colonies, which now were made up of people who saw themselves as creatures of the New World.

For the most part, the expatriate journalists and writers founded and wrote for Spanish-language or bilingual periodicals, although some politically oriented newspapers were bilingual because they aspired to influence Anglo-American public opinion and U.S. government policy regarding Cuba and Puerto Rico. Very few of the exiled intellectuals found work in the English-language press, except as translators. One notable exception was Miguel Teurbe Tolón, who in the 1850s worked as an editor for Latin America on the *New York Herald*. Teurbe Tolón had been an editor of *La Guirnalda* (The Garland) newspaper in Cuba, where he also had launched his literary career as a poet. In the United States, besides working for the *Herald*, he published poems and commentary in both Spanish- and English-language periodicals, and translated Thomas Paine's *Common Sense* and Emma Willard's *History of the United States* into Spanish. One of the most important pioneers of Hispanic journalism in the United States, Tolón was also one of the founders of the literature of Hispanic exile, not only because of the exile theme in many of his poems, but also because his works figure most prominently in the first anthology of exile literature ever published in the United States, *El laúd del desterrado* (The Exile's Lute, 1856), issued a year after his death.

Since the writings of Heredia, Varela, and Teurbe Tolón and their colleagues, exile literature has been one of the continuing currents in Hispanic letters and culture in the United States. Many of the writers to follow in the next century and a half became steeped in that tradition, building on the work of their predecessors, who used their literary art to promote their political causes. Exile writers also influenced immigrant and native writers. To this date, some of the commonplace aspects of exile literature remain, even among the most recent exile writers from Central America and Cuba. In general, the literature of exile is centered on the homeland, *la patria*, rather than on the fate of the exile community in the United States. Always implicit is its premise of return to *la patria*, leaving no question of assimilating into the culture during the temporary sojourn in the States.

Despite this desire, the historical fact is that throughout history many exiles and their families have taken up permanent residence, never to return. As return is always impending, however, there is a static vision of the homeland culture that oftentimes does not reflect the evolution of culture in the homeland during the exiles' absence; this literature is nostalgic for the *patria* as remembered before the authors left, and on foreign soil these authors seek through their writing to preserve the language and culture in their communities to facilitate the easy reintroduction into the home culture. The writing does not support the mixing of Spanish and English, as it seeks to emulate the best cultural forms in the elevation of their political ideologies. The stories tend to be epic in nature and the heroes larger than life, even in their tragic downfalls. Often, the metaphors that characterize their lives far from home relate to the Babylonian captivity and to "paradise lost"; their fiction and non-fiction writings emphasize the strangeness of the new social environment and the dangers it poses for cultural survival. The nineteenth-century authors engaged in the movements for independence from Spain, often cultivating the "Spanish Black Legend" (propaganda about the Spanish abuses of the Amerindians spread by the English and Dutch in their competition with Spain for New World colonies) and identifying themselves with the native Americans suffering the inhuman abuses of the Spanish conquistadors; these exile writers sought to construct their own New World identity. Thus, the literature was not only nationalistic culturally, but often politically as well, in attempting to construct the nation and its identity; the impact of this literature is affected by the fact that many of these writers were actually engaged in armed revolutionary and political struggles.

In the world of literature and journalism, the creative and publishing activity of exiled Cubans and Puerto Ricans rivaled the productivity of writers in the homeland. Many of the leading writers and intellectuals of both islands produced a substantial corpus of their works in exile rather than in the repressive environment of Spanish colonial rule. Their substantial legacy includes not only political thought in a remarkable collection of elegant and exquisite essays—such as those of José María de Hostos, Lorenzo Allo, Enrique José Varona, and José Martí—but also books on pedagogy, natural sciences, technology, and, of course, history. Some of the most important Cuban and Puerto Rican literary figures were to follow the examples of Heredia, Varela, and Teurbe Tolón, writing, publishing, and militating from exile in Philadelphia, New York, Tampa, Key West, and New Orleans until the outbreak of the Spanish-American War in 1898. Many of them were journalists and publishers, as well as prolific poets of exile: Bonifacio Byrne, Pedro Santacilia, Juan Clemente Zenea, and, later, but most important, José Martí. They all studied the works of their model, José María Heredia, whose wandering far from his native soil is recorded in some of the most evocative romantic verse of the nineteenth century. In fact, in *El laúd del desterrado*, homage is paid to Heredia by opening with his poems.

In 1887, José Martí, publisher Nestor Ponce de León, and Colombian immigrant poet Santiago Pérez Triana founded the influential literary club Sociedad Literaria Hispano-Americana de Nueva York that brought together all Hispanic literary enthusiasts and writers from throughout the city. This club was separate from the political clubs that were organized to raise funds to support the armed revolution. From the late nineteenth century to the present, Hispanics have sus-

Arturo Alfonso Schomberg.

tained literary societies in all the major cities of their residence in the United States. These clubs offered an intellectual environment in which literary works could be read and discussed, speeches made, and authors visiting from out-of-town received and celebrated.

Puerto Rican intellectuals joined the expatriate Cubans who established revolutionary clubs and supported book and newspaper publication. In clubs such as Las Dos Antillas (The Two Antilles), co-founded by the Afro-Puerto Rican bibliographer Arturo Alfonso Schomberg, they pronounced the eloquent speeches that would be printed in the newspapers that circulated throughout the exile communities and were smuggled back into Puerto Rico. Serving as an important convener of the group at her home in New York was the thrice-exiled Doña Lola Rodríguez de Tió, whose nationalistic verse appeared frequently in local periodicals. In addition to the illustrious philosophers, essayists, and poets that made up this group of expatriate Puerto Ricans, there were two craftsmen whose work was essential to the revolutionary cause and to the literature of exile: typesetters Francisco Gonzalo "Pachín" Marín and Sotero Figueroa, who were also exponents of exile poetry.

Marín brought his revolutionary newspaper *El Postillón* (The Postilion) from Puerto Rico, where it had been suppressed by the Spanish authorities, to New York in 1889. In the print shop he set up in New York, Marín published his paper, as well as books and broadsides for the Cuban and Puerto Rican expatriate communities. His shop became a meeting place for intellectuals, literary figures, and political leaders. In New York, Marín published two volumes of his own verse that are foundational for Puerto Rican letters: *Romances* (1892) and *En la arena* (c.1895). Sotero Figueroa was the president of the Club Borinquen and owner of the print shop, Imprenta América, which provided the composition and printing for various revolutionary newspapers and other publications, including *Borinquen* (the indigenous name of the island of Puerto Rico), a bimonthly newspaper issued by the Puerto Rican section of the Cuban Revolutionary Party. More important, Figueroa worked closely with José Martí on both his political organizing (Figueroa was the board secretary for the Cuban Revolutionary Party) and his publishing projects; Figueroa provided the printing for one of the most important organs of the revolutionary and literary movements, New York's *Patria*, which, after being founded by Martí, became the official organ of the Cuban Revolutionary Party and in which Martí and Figueroa published essays, poems, and speeches. In addition, Figueroa's Imprenta América probably prepared the books and pamphlets that were issued for *Patria*'s publishing house.

Sotero Figueroa also printed books for the Cuban exile newspaper *El Porvenir*, appropriately entitled "The Future." One product of the press was the *Album de "El Porvenir"* (issued beginning in 1890), a monumental five-volume biographical dictionary memorializing the expatriate community and providing it a firm sense of historical mission. There were many other publications that indicate the exiled Cubans were actively engaged in the process of nation building. One of the most important was the extensive biographical dictionary *Diccionario biográfico cubano* (Cuban Biographical Dictionary), compiled by Francisco Calcagno, published in part in New York by printer Nestor Ponce de León in 1878. The 728-page text was a veritable storehouse of information about accomplished Cubans in all fields of endeavor, many of whom resided in exile. The dictionary complemented the efforts of newspapermen and creative writers who were actively writing their nation's colonial history and independent future. Writers such as Francisco Sellén not only attacked Spaniards in their prose and poetry, but also lay down a mythic and ideological background on which to construct their nation's culture. In his published play *Hatuey* (1891), Sellén (like Varela in *Jicoténcal*) identified Cubans with the indigenous past by writing about the last rebel Amerindian chief in Cuba and building on Bartolomé de Las Casas' documentation of Spanish inhumanity during the Conquest. This work not only attempted to create a mythological base for Cuban ethnicity and nationhood but also indicted the immorality of the Spanish colonialists.

While Cubans and Puerto Rican expatriates had to endure passage by ship and inspections by customs authorities to enter as refugees into the United States, Mexican exiles crossed the border with relative ease to establish their press in exile. Given that there was no Border Patrol until 1925, they simply walked across what was an open border for Hispanics—as opposed to Asians, who were barred by various exclusionary laws—and installed themselves in the longstanding Mexican-origin communities of the Southwest. In fact, the relatively open border had served as an escape route for numerous criminal and/or political refugees from both the northern and southern sides of the dividing line for decades. The Mexican exile press began around 1885, when the Porfirio Díaz regime in Mexico became so repressive that scores of publishers, editors, and writers were forced north into exile. Publishers such as Adolfo Carrillo, who had opposed Díaz with his *El Correo del Lunes* (The Monday Mail), crossed the border, hoping to smuggle their papers back into Mexico. Carrillo ended up in San Francisco, where he established *La República* (The Republic) in 1885, and remained there for the rest of his life. Carrillo became so identified with the Hispanic tradition in California that he set his short stories in California's Hispanic past. Notwithstanding Carrillo's example, most of the exiled Mexican literati of the late nineteenth and early twentieth centuries eventually returned to Mexico when the environment was once again safe for their respective political ideologies.

By 1900, the most important Mexican revolutionary journalist and ideologue, Ricardo Flores Magón, had launched his newspaper *Regeneración* (Regeneration) in Mexico City. An anarchist militant, Flores Magón was jailed four times in Mexico for his radical journalism. Following a sentence of eight months in jail, during which he was prohibited from reading and writing, Flores Magón went into exile in the United States and, by 1904, had again begun publishing *Rege-*

neración in San Antonio, in Saint Louis in 1905 and in Canada in 1906; in 1907, he founded *Revolución* in Los Angeles, and once again in 1908 revived *Regeneración* there. Throughout these years, Flores Magón and his brothers employed any and every subterfuge possible to smuggle their writings from the United States into Mexico, even stuffing them into cans or wrapping them in other newspapers sent to San Luis Potosí, where they were then distributed to sympathizers throughout the country. They also became leaders of labor union and anarchist movements among minorities in the United States. For their revolutionary efforts, they were persistently repressed and persecuted by both the Mexican and U.S. governments.

Numerous Spanish-language periodicals in the Southwest echoed the ideas of Flores Magón and were affiliated with his Mexican Liberal Party, which was promoting revolution. Among them were *La Bandera Roja* (The Red Flag), *El Demócrata, La Democracia, Humanidad, 1810, El Liberal, Punto Rojo* (Red Point), *Libertad y Trabajo* (Liberty and Labor), and *La Reforma Social* (Social Reform). These periodicals were located along the border from the Rio Grande Valley in South Texas to Douglas, Arizona, and west to Los Angeles. Among the most interesting newspapers were those involved in articulating labor and women's issues as part of the social change that should be implemented with the triumph of the revolution. Notable among the early writers and editors associated with the PML and Flores Magón was school teacher Sara Estela Ramírez, who emigrated from Mexico to teach in Mexican schools in Laredo, Texas, in 1898. With her passionate and eloquent speeches and poetry performed at meetings of laborers and community people, she spread the ideas of labor organizing and social reform in both Mexico and Texas. Ramírez wrote for two important Laredo newspapers, *La Crónica* (The Chronicle) and *El Demócrata Fronterizo* (The Border Democrat), and in 1901 began editing and publishing her own newspaper *La Corregidora* (The Corrector), which she printed in Mexico City, Laredo, and San Antonio. In 1910, Ramírez founded a literary magazine, *Aurora*, which was short-lived; she died that same year from a long-time illness. Other periodicals under the direction of women not only furthered the revolutionary cause but also articulated gender issues within that cause: Teresa Villarreal's *El Obrero* (The Worker, 1909), Isidra T. de Cárdenas' *La Voz de la Mujer* (The Woman's Voice, 1907), Blanca de Moncaleano's *Pluma Roja* (Red Pen, 1913–1915), and Teresa and Andrea Villarreal's *La Mujer Moderna* (The Modern Woman), affiliated with the feminist Club Liberal "Leona Vicario." Unfortunately, we have not been able to find extant copies of their writing.

The Mexican exile press flourished into the 1930s, with weekly newspapers siding with one faction or another, and publishing houses, often affiliated with newspapers, issuing political tracts as well as novels of the revolution. In fact, more than any other literary genre published in book form, the novel of the Mexican Revolution flourished during this time, as more than one hundred of them poured forth from the presses of newspapers and their affiliated publishing houses, such as Casa Editorial Lozano in San Antonio. Through the novel of the revolution, such expatriate authors as Teodoro Torres and Manuel Arce sought to come to terms with that cataclysm that had disrupted their lives and had caused so many of their readers to relocate to the southwestern United States. The authors represented the full gamut of revolutionary factions in their loyalties and

La Voz De La Mujer

● SEMANARIO LIBERAL DE COMBATE ●

Defensor de los Derechos del Pueblo y Enemigo de las Tiranías.

La mujer forma parte integrante de la gran familia humana; luego tiene el deber y el derecho de exigir y luchar por la Dignificación de su Patria

AÑO I.   EL PASO, TEXAS, SEPTIEMBRE 6 DE 1907.   NÚM. 9

LABOR DE FIGAROS.

El flagelo de nuestra fusta ha sangrado los escamosos morrillos de la burguesía altanera. Nuestras rebeldías no han conocido valladar que contenga las justas iras emanadas contra el sistema atentatorio con que los impunes sueñan en reivindicar su historia de oprobio; por que, impotentes para combatir con razonamientos, son tenaces, también para reicidir, enfangados en el estercolero que les sirbe de lecho.

Á nuestra mesa de redacción nos llegan distintas quejas de los atentados que cometen en la ínsula de los contrabandos los bandidos caciques investidos de autoridad.

El primer fustazo que nuestro semanario asestó al contrabandista en funciones de Jefe Político, Silvano Montemayor, lo hizo convertirse en réptil, se enroscó, y dió un chillido, le robó a nuestro papelero unos ejemplares y lo amagó con hospedarlo en el *hotel de su propiedad*, si volvía a vender "La Voz de la Mujer." Nuestra protesta cargó sobre el cacique vulgar, castigando su insolencia como lo merecía.

Un Castrado ascendido y cornamentado ha tomado a su encargo molestar a los abonados y repartidores de nuestro periódico, amagándolos con cárcel ¿Con qué derecho lo hace este Moisa?

¡Tales son los méritos de los bandidos de uniforme!

Hoy nos visita una nueva querella: Un paquidermo que *ruge* de cobrador en el mercado de C. Juárez, y de eunuco de antesala, se opone a viva fuerza á que circule "La Voz de la Mujer," en la cafrería donde cree tener, en símil el derecho de usufructo.

Éste estulto cuadrúpedo no está conforme con andar en cuatro remos, sino que, persiste en escarbar con la trompa.

La impudicia de tales moluscos los congestiona, padecen sonambulismo y sueñan en el exterminio de la prensa independiente. ¡Falsa creencia! para que los ideales mueran, se necesita destrozarnos, ya que odiados somos; sólo que ese odio nos eleva por que prueba nuestra honradez, desde el momento en que los tiranos no nos estiman. Por esto los flagelamos para despertar su encono, seguras de que si sucumbimos debe ser levantando ámpula; nuestra vacante será substituida con nuevas energías, con plumas viriles empapadas en luz fevea.

Nuestros carácteres están enteramente trocados: nosotras, rebeldes, ellos serviles; nosotras honradas, ellos bandidos; nuestro medio no es el de ellos; el espíritu de rebeldía tonifica nuestros cerebros y es el talismán que nos hace prepotentes en los azares políticos, en la cruenta lucha que sostenemos con los burgueses; somos pobres y la pobreza es maga cuando va emparejada con honradez y abnegación; porque en los mayores infortunios, el porvenir nos sonríe, nos da fuerza y nos acaricia. Esto no pasa con los tiranos criminales: su existencia es mezquina y ruin; sus espíritus siempre están emponzoñados por el crimen y la maldad; sus morbosos y enfermisos cerebros a diario se sienten atacados por la misma ruindad que los deprime; no tienen convicciones propias y viven en continuo asecho de víctimas que aseguran sus canonjías; sus almas siempre sarnosas sólo piensan en el mal; jamás se preocupan por nada loable.

¡Horrible torcedor para los tiranos, pensar en día de las represalias! ¡La hora suena, inexorable y justiciera contra los autores de tanto crimen! ¡Oidlo, bien, tiranos y bandidos y si es que lo olvidáis, nosotras os lo recordaremos!

¡Vivid tranquilos!

DEFUNCION.

En San Antonio, Texas, rindió tributo á la Natraleza el rebelde liberal Aurelio N. Flores, dejando un vacío en las filas liberales.

¡La muerte se engalanó al apoderarse de alma tan noble! El Partido Liberal perdió un valiente luchador. ¡Paz á sus restos! ¡Consuelo á sus deudos!

Int. Institut.
Sec. Geschiedenis
Amsterdam

Front page of *La Voz de la Mujer* newspaper.

ideologies, but for the most part the genre was characterized by a conservative reaction to the socialistic change in government and community organization that the Revolution had wrought. One of the first to establish this genre was the now classic work of Latin American literature, Mariano Azuela's *Los de abajo* (The Underdogs), which was not counterrevolutionary. *Los de abajo* appeared as a serialized novel in an El Paso Spanish-language newspaper and was later published in book form in that city in 1915. From that time on, literally scores of these novels were published from San Diego to San Antonio. By no means were the press and the publishing enterprise at that time as liberal as the exile press prior to the outbreak of the Revolution. On the contrary, many of these novels were typical of the exile culture promoted by conservatives dislodged from Mexico by the socialist revolution; they came with resources in hand to well-established Mexican American communities and became entrepreneurs in cultural as well as business enterprises. Some of them founded newspapers, magazines, and publishing houses to serve the rapidly expanding community of economic refugees, and their newspapers eventually became the backbone of an *immigrant* rather than an *exile* press, as their entrepreneurial spirit overtook their political commitment to change in the homeland. Indeed, the large Hispanic communities in the United States could reproduce the culture of the homeland for enclaves of working people who had the financial resources to sustain business and culture. Most of these people were economic refugees—i.e., immigrants whose ethos differed from that of the political exiles.

With the Cristero War (1926–1929), resulting from the government attempting to limit the power of the Catholic Church, based on the anticlerical tenets of the 1917 Mexican constitution, a fresh batch of political refugees founded newspapers and publishing houses to attack the Mexican government and to serve the needs of the religious community in exile. During the buildup of conflict between church and state in Mexico, numerous religiously based periodicals and publishing houses were founded in El Paso, Los Angeles, and elsewhere in the Southwest. In fact, El Paso became a publishing center for many Hispanic religious presses—not just for the Catholics but for the Mexican Baptists, Methodists, and others who took refuge from the persecution in Mexico. The influence of the Cristero refugees was felt in many secular publications and in much of the religious—and secular—literature. The already conservative counterrevolutionary papers naturally focused on the religious persecution in Mexico and the atrocities committed by the government of *bolcheviques*. Numerous memoirs by expatriate religious, preachers, and bishops issued from presses in El Paso, Los Angeles, Kansas City, and San Antonio. Also, memoirs of Mexicans and Mexican Americans who achieved religious conversion became popular, such as José Policarpo Rodríguez's memoir of his path to becoming a Presbyterian minister, *The Old Trail Guide*, first published in 1898 but reprinted various times in the twentieth century. This religious, conservative background has left an indelible mark on the Mexican American literary tradition in the United States.

The next large wave of Hispanic political refugees to reach these shores came from across the Atlantic: the liberals defeated by Spanish fascism. Hispanic communities across the United States embraced the refugees and sympathized with their cause; many were the Cuban, Mexican, and Puerto Rican organizations that held fund raisers for the Republicans during the Spanish Civil War. The Spanish expatriates themselves were fast to establish their own exile press. Their efforts hit fertile soil in Depression-era communities that were hotbeds for union and socialist organizing. Manhattan and Brooklyn were centers of Hispanic anti-fascist fervor and contributed such titles as *España Libre* (Free Spain, 1939–1977), *España Nueva* (New Spain, 1923–1942), *España Republicana* (Republican Spain, 1931–1935), *Frente Popular* (Popular Front, 1937–1939), and *La Liberación* (The Liberation, 1946–1949). Many of the Hispanic labor and socialist organizations, in which Spanish immigrant workers were prominent, published newspapers that also supported the Republican cause: the long-running anarchist paper *Cultura Proletaria* (Proletarian Culture, 1910–1959), *El Obrero* (The Worker, 1931–1932), and *Vida Obrera* (Worker Life, 1930–1932). During this period and the years of the Francisco Franco regime that followed, some of Spain's most famous writers took refuge in the United States and Puerto Rico. Among their number were novelist Ramón Sender and poet Jorge Guillén, as well as poet Juan Ramón Jiménez, who while living in Puerto Rico would win the Nobel Prize.

The focus of protest writing shifted somewhat during the twentieth century to attacking modern dictatorships and authoritarian regimes, as well as to criticizing the repeated intervention of the United States in the Latin republics' domestic politics, quite often on the side of dictators and their repressive regimes. The pseudonymous writer Lirón was one of the most outrageously graphic in his attacks on Spanish dictator Francisco Franco, while Salvadoran Gustavo Solano, who used the pseudonym of "El Conde Gris" (The Grey Count), consigned Manuel Estrada Cabrera, the Guatemalan dictator to Hell in his play *Sangre* (Blood, 1919). Before residing for many years in exile in the United States, Solano had been incarcerated for his revolutionary activities in Mexico and had become persona non grata in almost all of the Central American republics for his pursuit of a united and democratic Central America. From their distant perspective in the United States, other Central American writers, such as Nicaraguan Santiago Argüello, reinvigorated Simón Bolívar's ignored vision of a united Spanish America, not only to stave off the imperialist threats of the United States but to fully integrate the economies and cultures of Central and South America. Puerto Ricans Juan Antonio Corretjer and his wife Consuelo Lee Tapia militated through their newspaper *Pueblos Hispanos* (Hispanic Peoples) and their individual writings for Puerto Rican independence from the United States. Corretjer, who had been imprisoned in an Atlanta federal penitentiary for his nationalist activities on the island, took up residence in New York after being prohibited by federal authorities from returning to Puerto Rico. The U.S. military administration of the island colony was far more repressive than authorities in New York and other cities on the continent. The Puerto Rican dissidents enjoyed greater freedom of association and were less noticed writing in Spanish and organizing in the Hispanic communities of New York, Tampa, and Chicago than in full view of their vigilant government at home. Corretjer and Tapia were at the center of a cadre of Puerto Rican nationalist writers in New York, while many of their compatriots, even the more radical ones, such as Jesús Colón also writing in *Pueblos Hispanos*, were staking out claims on New York as their rightful home. But while Corretjer and Tapia indicted the U.S. military government of Puerto Rico, Dominican journalist Carmita Landestoy eloquently unmasked the Rafael Trujillo regime in her homeland, a regime that was also supported by the United States, which had administered a military government in the Dominican Republic for most of the early twentieth century. Thus the ironic situation in which the Caribbean and Central American writers found themselves was that of being exiled in the belly of the beast that they accused of causing many of the ills in their homeland.

Exiles and political refugees have continued to make up an important segment of Hispanic immigrants to the United States. With the Cuban Revolution and the United States fighting much of the Cold War through involvement in the civil wars in Central America and Chile, large-scale immigration of political refugees has continued to the present day, and the dictatorships in these countries and Argentina have arisen as themes in the literature of Hispanic exile. Beginning in 1959, a new wave of refugees from the Cuban Revolution established a widespread exile press, as well as a more informal network of hundreds of newsletters. Chileans, Salvadorans, Nicaraguans, and other Spanish-American expatriates have all contributed to a literature of exile. What is different today is that many of these exiled voices have been readily translated into English, and the works of such liberal writers as Argentines Luisa Valenzuela, Manuel Puig, and Jacobo Timmerman; Chileans Emma Sepúlveda and Ariel Dorfman; and Guatemala's Arturo Arias are published alongside the more conservative voices of Cuban exiles, such as those of Heberto Padilla and Reinaldo Arenas. As the Hispanic population of the United States continues to grow—estimated to be one-fourth of the total population by 2050—and as the economy of the United States becomes more integrated with those south of the border through such alliances as the North American Free Trade Agreement (NAFTA), United States culture will become even more directly linked to the internal politics of Spanish America. The culture of Hispanic exile will continue to be part of the overall culture of the United States in the foreseeable future; the United States will continue to be a preferred base from which political refugees will use the press, the electronic media and U.S. popular culture, the Internet, and recent film hits such as *Death and the Maiden* and *The Kiss of the Spider Woman* to express their opposition to governments in their homelands.

More than that, Hispanic political refugees, through their use of the press and their leadership in community organizations and churches, have left indelible marks on the ethos and philosophy of Hispanic communities within the United States. Their knowledge and perspectives live on in Hispanic culture today, regardless of whether refugees returned or not to their homelands. Many of those that remained here, as well as their children, intermarried with other Hispanic natives and immigrants and eventually blended into the grand community that is recognizable today as a national ethnic minority.

SIN FRONTERA: BEYOND BOUNDARIES

Much of the preceding has substantiated that Hispanic literature of the United States is transnational in nature, that it emerges from and remains intimately related to the crossing of political, geographic, cultural, linguistic and racial boundaries. Hispanic peoples in the United States are the result of the United States expanding its borders, of conquering, incorporating and importing peoples from the Hispanic world—a world that has not only existed immediately outside of the United States but within its ever-expanding geographic and economic borders. Hispanic culture in the United States exists on a continuum with the Hispanic world through family relationships, ethnic bonds, travel, and communications. Hispanic peoples in the United States have never severed or felt the need to sever their ties to the rest of the Hispanic world. Likewise, life in the United States has transformed Hispanic culture within and influenced Hispanic culture beyond U.S. borders; U.S. Hispanics have created their own cultural patterns, which, in turn, have influenced the rest of the Hispanic world through travel and communications.

Our paradigm of native, immigrant, and exile cultures and literatures is meant to be dynamic: it allows for the ebbs and flows of new cultural inputs into U.S. Hispanic culture and for culture change from one generation to another. It allows for entrances and exits from Hispanic U.S.A. and for evolving cultural stances, language preferences, and identities of individuals such as Jesús Colón, Américo Paredes, Adolfo Carrillo and many others, who in one moment saw themselves as immigrants or exiles and in another as naturalized citizens or natives identifying greatly with the long history of Hispanic culture in the United States. Given that immigration and exile are still very much part of the daily life of Hispanic communities in the United States, and promise to remain so for a long time, the transnational and borderless nature of Hispanic culture in the United States will become only more apparent and characteristic as media also continue to cement the relationship of Latinos in the United States to the rest of the Spanish-speaking world. The three U.S. Spanish television networks function hemispherically by satellite; Spanish-language book and magazine distribution is everyday more hemispheric; some forty years of bilingual education in the United States, often imparted by immigrant teachers, has solidified cultural bonds with nearby Spanish American countries; moves towards the economic integration of the Americas through such agreements as NAFTA will further consolidate the interdependence of the nation states of the Americas and of the Spanish-speaking populations; air travel is cheaper and more accessible to all populations and will continue to contribute to a borderless America/América.

Among the many writers who have been able to identify the transnational and borderless nature of Latino culture are the visionaries Luis Rafael Sánchez and Guillermo Gómez Peña. Sánchez—responding to the cultural circumstances of Puerto Ricans being defined by their colonial status on the island and migrant-citizen status on the continent and to the third of the population that lives on the continent and the high number of Puerto Ricans that has at some point lived on the continent—chose *La guagua aérea* (The Airbus) as the symbol of Puerto Rican culture. It is a patent symbol of migratory status and culture engendered from that existential condition. It proclaims borderlessness and intercultural fluidity; it does not abandon Puerto Rican ethnicity but acknowledges its dynamism, its ability to evolve and incorporate and, most of all, to survive. Writer and performance artist Gómez Peña sees the cultural dynamism of borders—ie., hybridity, fluidity, syncretism, and synthesis—overtaking and becoming the common communication style not only for the United States and Spanish America, but for the entire world. True post-modernity for the United States and much of the world—we must consider the European Union here—will bring the erasure of borders and the disappearance of separate political and economic systems, more synthesis of language and cultural ways, and more racial blending. In fact, this may be the overriding lesson and example of Hispanic literature of the United States.

WORKS CITED

Fornet, Ambrosio. *El libro en Cuba*. Havana: Editorial Letras Cubanas, 1994.

Gómez-Quiñones, Juan. *Roots of Chicano Politics, 1600–1940*. Albuquerque: University of New Mexico Press, 1994.

Kanellos, Nicolás, with Helvetia Martell. *Hispanic Periodicals in the United States, Origins* to 1960: A Brief History and Comprehensive Bibliography. Houston: Arte Público Press, 2000.

Meléndez, Gabriel. So All Is Not Lost: The Poetics of Print in Nuevo Mexicano Communities, 1834–1958. Albuquerque: University of New Mexico Press, 1997.

Meyer, Doris. Speaking for Themselves: Neo-Mexicano Cultural Identity and the Spanish-Language Press, 1880–1920. Albuquerque: University of New Mexico Press, 1996.

Park, Robert E. The Immigrant Press and Its Control. New York: Harper & Brothers, 1922.

CHAPTER 2

CHRONOLOGY OF HISPANIC LITERATURE AND CULTURE OF THE UNITED STATES

1492: Christopher Columbus arrives at an island he calls San Salvador in the Caribbean and encounters Amerindian culture.

1493: During his second voyage, Columbus discovers the Virgin Islands and Puerto Rico.

1509: Juan Ponce de León explores and settles the island of San Juan Bautista (Puerto Rico) after subduing the native population.

1513: Juan Ponce de León explores Florida.

1519: Alonso Alvarez de Pineda discovers the coast of the Gulf of Mexico and claims Texas for Spain.

1521: The Aztec Empire falls to the Spaniards.

1528: Pánfilo de Narváez sails into Tampa Bay and takes possession of the land; later Núñez Cabeza de Vaca becomes shipwrecked and begins his nearly ten years of wandering the South and Southwest of the North American continent above the Rio Grande River.

1533: The printing press is brought to the Americas, to Mexico City.

1538: The first university in the Americas is founded: St. Thomas Aquinas in the city of Santo Domingo.

1539: Hernando de Soto begins his explorations of the current states of Florida, Mississippi, Tennessee, North Carolina, Arkansas, and Louisiana; he describes the Mississippi River.

1540: Francisco Vásquez de Coronado begins his expedition in search of Cíbola or Quivira, the famed cities of gold in the Southwest. He encounters the Grand Canyon, Pike's Peak, and the Rio Grande River.

1542: Juan Rodríguez de Cabrillo discovers the Bay of San Diego in California.

1551: Universities are founded in Mexico City and Lima.

1560: The Spanish found the first European settlement in what later becomes the continental United States: Santa Elena, in South Carolina.

1565: Saint Augustine, Florida, the oldest permanent European settlement on the mainland United States, is founded by Pedro Menéndez de Avilés.

1598: In the mission to colonize New Mexico led by Juan de Oñate are literary men who import the first European-style drama and poetry into what will become the

Southwest of the United States. Among Oñate's men is an amateur playwright, Capfán Marcos Farfán de los Godos, author of a play that the soldiers perform based on their colonizing adventure. This is the first play in a European language written and performed in what will become the present-day United States. The soldiers also have in the repertoire the folk play, often performed on horseback, entitled *Moros y cristianos* (The Moors and the Christians), which dramatizes the re-conquest of the Spanish peninsula from the Moors during the Crusades. Also, the poet Gaspar Pérez de Villagrá pens a long, epic poem memorializing the expedition, *La conquista de la Nueva Méjico* (The Conquest of New Mexico), which is later published in Spain.

1600:   By 1600, the Spaniards establish the first schools in what will become the continental United States, in Florida, New Mexico, and Georgia.

1602:   With three ships, Sebastián Vizcaíno explores and charts the coast of California, and identifies Monterey as an ideal place for major Spanish settlement.

1610:   Santa Fe, New Mexico, is founded.

1654:   The first Spanish-speaking community in the Northeast of what will become the United States is the colony of Sephardic Jews, who establish an oral and literary tradition that remains unbroken to this day.

1690:   San Francisco de los Tejas is founded, the first permanent European settlement in Texas.

1691:   Father Eusebio Kino makes his first missionary inroads into Arizona.

1716:   San Antonio is founded in 1716 by Alonso de Alarcón; it becomes the most important and most prosperous settlement in Texas.

1722:   The first newspaper appears in the Americas: *La gaceta de México* (The Mexico Gazette).

1732:   Miguel de Quintana, a New Mexico peasant, becomes the first writer in the history of the Southwest to be tried by the Inquisition. The poet's verses come under suspicion and, on March 17, 1732, formal charges are made against Quintana to the Holy Office in Santa Fe, whereupon depositions and evidence are collected and sent to Mexico City. On May 22, 1734, the Inquisition office in Mexico City rules that it does not have enough evidence to prosecute Quintana, although it advises Quintana be "examined for lesions of the head and questioned intensively regarding his claim to a divine inspiration behind his writing."

1760:   France cedes to Spain's claims to lands west of the Mississippi.

1761:   The province of Alta, California, is founded.

1769:   The mission at San Diego, California, is established and the colonization of California begins.

1776:   Probably the first documented library (other than private libraries) in New Mexico and much of the Southwest is in existence and use by this date at the Santo Domingo mission, according to a report by Fray Anastacio Domínguez, who is studying the schools and churches in New Mexico. The catalog lists some 256 titles, but this number does not include sets and duplicates, which are extensive.

1779:   Ignacio de Arteaga sails to the mouth of Prince William Sound in Alaska, names the port Santiago de Apóstol and claims it for Spain; this is the northernmost point ever taken possession of by Spanish subjects.

1781:   Los Angeles, California, is founded.

1783:   Spain regains Florida.

1789:   The first plays to be performed by subscription in what will become the U.S. Southwest are performed in Monterey, California. By the 1840s, itinerant troupes of players will be performing in the major urban areas up and down the California coast. A professional Spanish-language stage is functioning in New Orleans by the 1830s.

1800:   Spain cedes Louisiana to France through the Treaty of San Ildefonso.

1803:   The French sell Louisiana to the United States.

1803:   The first literary work in the Spanish language published in the United States is José Agustín Caballero's *Sermón fúnebre en elogio del excelentísimo señor Don Cristóbal Colón* (Funereal Sermon in Eulogy of that Excellent Gentleman Don Christopher Columbus), issued in Philadelphia by printers Eaken & Mecum.

1804:   President Thomas Jefferson funds the expedition of Lewis and Clark, which prepares the United States for expansion westward.

1807:   Napoleon Bonaparte invades Spain and Portugal. Ferdinand VII abdicates the Spanish throne and Napoleon names his brother as the successor. Creoles begin plotting the independence of their Spanish American countries.

1808:   The first book of exile literature, a popular Hispanic genre in the United States during the next two centuries, is *España ensangrentada* (Bloodied Spain), written anonymously by "Viejo castizo español" (an old Spaniard of pure blood). Published in New Orleans, it is a protest against the French invasion of Spain and Napoleon's puppet, Francisco Godoy. This same year marks the birth of the first Spanish-language newspaper in the United States: *El Misisipí*.

1810:   Under the leadership of Father Miguel de Hidalgo y Costilla, Mexico declares its independence from Spain.

1811:   The first Spanish-language novel published in the United States is Atanasio Céspedes y Monroy's *La paisana virtuosa* (The Virtuous Countrywoman), issued by Mathew Carey in Philadelphia. That same year, Carey issues another novel by Céspedes: *La presumida orgullosa* (The Presumptuously Proud Woman).

1813:   Filibuster José Alvarez de Toledo is responsible for the introduction of the printing press to Texas as part of the movement for independence of Mexico from Spain. As part of this movement, the first newspaper in the Southwest is published, *La gaceta de Texas*, in Nacogdoches, Texas.

1821:   Mexico gains its independence. After exerting much pressure on the Spanish crown, the United States buys Florida from Spain for five million dollars.

1821:   The first great eulogy by an Hispanic recorded in history is that of Captain Jacob de la Motta, a Sephardic Jewish doctor residing in Charleston. He gives the speech in New York on the death of the famed Reverend Gershom Mendes Seixas, also a Sephardic Jew. The eulogy is of particular relevance to Hispanic Jews in that it compares the freedom that Jews encounter in the United States with their persecution in Europe. Many of Charleston's Jews are immigrants or descended from immigrants who had to leave Spain and Portugal when they were persecuted by the Inquisition. Like de la Motta, a medical doctor and Army surgeon who had served with distinction in the War of 1812, many of the Sephardics become founding and leading citizens in South Carolina and Georgia (which had originally belonged to Spain). So effective and moving is de la Motta's eulogy that two former U.S. presidents congratulate him in writing: James Madison and Thomas Jefferson.

1822:   The first anthology of Spanish literature, *Extractos de los más célebres escritores y poetas españoles* (Excerpts from the Most Celebrated Spanish Writers and Poets), is published in Baltimore for use as a textbook in St. Mary's School.

1823:   President James Monroe of the United States announces the Monroe Doctrine.

1824:   In Philadelphia, the first philosophical work is published by the great Cuban patriot, novelist, journalist, and Catholic priest Félix Varela: *Lecciones de Filosofía* (Lessons in Philosophy). Varela is the first Catholic vicar of New York and one of the leaders of the Cuban independence movement.

1825:   The first collection of poems by an Hispanic writer is published in New York: *Poesías de José María Heredia*, by Cuban exile José María Heredia. Heredia is considered to be one of the greatest poets of Spanish America and one of the founders of the literature of Hispanic exile in the United States. The first Spanish-language play by a resident playwright is published in the United States: Félix Mejía's *Lafayette in Mt. Vernon*; the play is also published in English translation. Both versions were published in Philadelphia.

1826:   The first Hispanic novel written and published in the United States, *Jicoténcal*, attributed to Cuban philosopher Félix Varela, is issued in Philadelphia. The novel relates the wars of Spanish conquest over the Indians of Mexico and, thus, indirectly supports the Cuban independence movement by equating Spanish Americans with the Indians. The novel, first published anonymously, is also the first historical novel ever written in the Spanish language; the historical genre enters Hispanic literature through the influence of Sir Walter Scott and James Fenimore Cooper.

1828:   The first collection of poetry by a Mexican author is published in the United States: *Poesías de un mexicano* (The Poems of a Mexican), by Anastasio María de Ochoa y Acuña, in New York.

1828:   The first collection of Spanish Golden Age plays to be read and studied as literature in U.S. colleges and universities is compiled and published in Boston by Francis Sales. *Selección de obras maestras dramáticas por Calderón de la Barca, Lope de Vega y Moreto* (A Selection of Dramatic Master Works by . . .) includes plays by three of the greatest playwrights of Spain's theatrical flowering in the seventeenth century. This anthology and others that follow help to canonize these authors in the American college curriculum. During the 1820s, Sales publishes a number of anthologies and collections of Spanish literature.

1831:   The first Spanish-language theatrical company of record in the South is the Compañía Española de Teatro, which performed for a season in New Orleans at the New Orleans Theater. Included in its repertoire were five-act Spanish melodramas and three-act tragicomedies.

1834:   The printing press is finally introduced to the provinces of Alta, California, and to New Mexico—to California by the government and to New Mexico by Father Antonio José Martínez, who uses it to print catechisms, school books, and New Mexico's first newspaper, *El Crepúsculo* (The Dawn).

1836:   Texas declares its independence from Mexico and is victorious over the forces led by General Antonio López de Santa Anna.

1845:   President John Tyler of the United States signs the resolution to annex Texas to the Union.

1846:   The Bear Flag Revolt takes place in California. The United States declares the war against Mexico, which brings into the Union territories that form the current states of New Mexico, Colorado, Arizona, and California.

1848:   The Treaty of Guadalupe Hidalgo is signed by the United States and Mexico, bringing a close to the war. President James K. Polk of the United States offers Spain $100 million for Cuba.

1848: The first Spanish-language theater house of record in the Southwest is Antonio Coronel's, built as an addition to his house in Los Angeles. Before then theater companies performed in halls and billiard parlors or in the open air.

1849: The Gold Rush lures thousands of Anglo-Americans and Europeans to California. For the first time, a state constitution, California's, defines citizenship based on the inclusiveness of all races, as was practiced in Mexico.

1852: President Franklin Pierce offers Spain $130 million for Cuba.

1853: The United States obtains Mexico's Mesilla Valley through the Gadsden Purchase.

1858: The first autobiography written by a Mexican-American in the English language is Juan Nepomuceno Seguín's *The Personal Memoirs of John N. Seguín*. Seguín is an embattled and disenchanted political figure of the Texas Republic and former mayor of San Antonio. As a figure caught between two cultures, Seguín is considered a forerunner of the bilingual and bicultural literature, as well as one of the first Mexican Americans to express the disillusionment that many Mexican American writers felt after the Anglo-American takeover of the Southwest.

1858: The first anthology of Hispanic exile literature, *El laúd del desterrado* (The Lute of the Exiled) is published in New York by a group of Cuban exile poets and includes the works of José María Heredia, Miguel Teurbe Tolón, Juan Clemente Zenea, and others. The anthology is an important indication that these writers are aware of the whole tradition of Hispanic literary exile; it establishes political exile as one of the bases for literary creation by Hispanics in the United States to the present.

1859: The first man to organize an armed protest by Texas Mexicans against the abuses of Anglos and the power structure they had instituted after the Mexican War is Juan Nepomuceno Cortina. His exploits are celebrated in such oral literature as the *corrido*, or ballad.

1862: The U.S. Congress passes the Homestead Act.

1863: Puerto Rican intellectual Eugenio María de Hostos publishes his attack on Spanish colonialism, *La peregrinación de Bayoán* (The Pilgrimage of Bayoán), which supports a growing independence movement.

1864: The French intervene in Mexico, with Napoleon III placing the puppet Emperor Maximilian on the throne of Mexico.

1867: After expelling the French, President Benito Juárez marches triumphantly into Mexico City.

1868: President Ulysses S. Grant attempts to annex the Dominican Republic, but the treaty is rejected by the Senate.

1868: Cuban independence from Spain is proclaimed at Yara, thus precipitating the Ten Years' War. Puerto Rican independence is proclaimed at Lares, Puerto Rico, but is a short-lived insurrection.

1868: The Fourteenth Amendment to the Constitution of the United States is adopted, declaring all people of Hispanic origin born in the United States to be U.S. citizens.

1872: The first novel written and published in English by a Hispanic of the United States is María Amparo Ruiz de Burton's domestic romance *Who Would Have Thought It?* Originally published anonymously, the novel reconstructs antebellum and Civil War society in the North and engages the dominant U.S. myths of American exceptionalism, egalitarianism, and consensus, offering an acerbic critique of opportunism and hypocrisy as it represents northern racism and U.S. imperialism. The novel is the first by a U.S. Hispanic to address the disenfranchised status of women.

1876:   Porfirio Díaz leads a military takeover of the Mexican government and assumes the presidency.

1881:   The first Spanish-language novel written and published in the Southwest is Manuel M. Salazar's romantic adventure novel, *La historia de un caminante, o Gervacio y Aurora* (The History of a Traveler on Foot, or Gervasio and Aurora), which creates a colorful picture of pastoral life in New Mexico at the time.

1883:   An early fight, possibly the first in the Southwest, against segregation in Texas takes place when Army veteran Juan Cárdenas organizes a successful protest against prohibiting the use of a dance floor in San Pedro Park, San Antonio, to Mexicans. The first Hispanic labor-organizing activity recorded in United States history is Juan Gómez's organizing of cowboys in the Panhandle of Texas.

1885:   The first fictional narrative, written and published in English from the perspective of the conquered Mexican population of the Southwest is María Amparo Ruiz de Burton's *The Squatter and the Don*; it is self-published in San Francisco under the pseudonym of C. Loyal. The novel documents the loss of lands to squatters and banking and railroad interests in southern California shortly after statehood. Ruiz de Burton was a member of the landed gentry in southern California, and she witnessed the disintegration of the old order, shifts in power relations, and the rapid capitalist development of the California territory, all of which led to the disruption of everyday life for the Californios. In *The Squatter and the Don*, an historical romance, Ruiz de Burton laments land loss and calls for justice and redress of grievances. The novel questions United States expansionism, the rise of corporate monopolies, and their power over government policy.

María Amparo Ruiz de Burton pictured on the cover of her collected letters.

1886:   The first transfer of a whole industry from Latin America to the United States and the building of a company town occurs with the founding of Ybor City in Florida, which becomes a cigar manufacturing center.

1887:   Writer José Martí, publisher Nestor Ponce de León, and Colombian immigrant poet Santiago Pérez Triana establish the influential literary club Sociedad Literaria Hispano-Americana de Nueva York that brings together all Hispanic literary enthusiasts and writers from throughout the city. From the late nineteenth century to the present, Hispanics have sustained literary societies in all of the major cities in the United States in which they reside. These clubs offer an intellectual environment in which literary works can be read and discussed, speeches made, and authors visiting from out of town received and celebrated.

1889:   Spanish-born philosopher George Santayana becomes the first Hispanic philosopher, and writer to receive a Ph.D. from Harvard. He goes on to become a noted poet, philosopher and professor in the United States and Europe. He publishes his first book on esthetics, *The Sense of Beauty*, in 1896. In 1890, he is named assistant professor in the Philosophy Department of Harvard and in 1890 publishes his first book of poems, *Lucifer: A Theological Tragedy*.

1891:   José Martí is successful in launching a new independence movement for Cuba.

1891:   The cigar workers in Ybor City, Florida, construct the first of six mutual aid societies, Centro Español, each of which is equipped with a theater to house performances by the local amateurs and by professionals on tour or residing in Ybor City. Eventually, the theatrical culture among the cigar workers evolved, launching performers, companies, and material for the professional stage in New York and the Caribbean.

George Santayana. Reproduced from the Collections of the Library of Congress.

1894:   The Alianza Hispano Americana, one of the first important Hispanic civil rights organizations, is founded.

1898:   The United States declares war on Spain and as a result of its victory obtains dominion over Cuba, Puerto Rico, the Virgin Islands, Philippines, and Guam through the Treaty of Paris.

1900:   Mexican revolutionary Ricardo Flores Magón founds his ideological newspaper *Regeneración* in Mexico City. When he reestablishes it in exile in Los Angeles in 1904, it serves as a model for exile and revolutionary newspapers throughout the Southwest.

1901:   The U.S. Congress passes the Platt Amendment, which allows for U.S. intervention in Cuba, and forces it into the Cuban constitution. Tomás Estrada Palma is elected president of a nominally independent Cuba.

1902:   The U.S. Congress passes the Reclamation Act, dispossessing many Hispanics in the United States of their lands.

1903:   Panama rebels against Colombia to gain its independence and negotiates separately with the United States for the construction of the canal. The Hay-Bunau-Varilla Treaty is signed by the United States and Panama, allowing for U.S. building of the canal and for intervention in Panama.

1904:   President Theodore Roosevelt announces his "Corollary" to the Monroe Doctrine.

1905:   Upon the assassination of dictator Ulises Hiereaux, the U.S. intervenes in the Dominican Republic.

1906:   United States troops occupy Cuba for three years.

1910:   The Mexican Revolution breaks out and has the effect of precipitating the largest exodus of Mexicans to the United States during the shortest period of time: some 1 million by 1920.

1911:   The regime of Mexican dictator Porfirio Díaz is defeated and the dictator takes flight to Europe after thirty years in power. Francisco Madero is elected to the presidency. Emiliano Zapata fights for the Plan of Ayala during the Mexican Revolution.

1911:   The first large convention of Mexicans for action against social injustice, El Primer Congreso Mexicanista (The First Mexicanist Congress) is held in Laredo.

1912:   New Mexico achieves statehood.

1913:   General Victoriano Huerta, with U.S. backing, has President Madero of Mexico assassinated and seizes the presidency.

1914:   The Panama Canal goes into operation.

1914:   U.S. Marines invade Veracruz, Mexico. Huerta's army surrenders unconditionally to Carranza's Constitutionalists, who come to power in Mexico.

1914:   Colombian expatriate author Alirio Díaz Guerra publishes *Lucas Guevara*, the first novel of Hispanic immigration to the United States. The novel introduces many of the formulas and much of the style that will characterize the literature of immigration during the entire twentieth century. *Lucas Guevara* is the story of a young South American student who immigrates to the grand metropolis of New York, becomes disillusioned, and commits suicide.

1915:   *Los de abajo* (The Underdogs), by Mariano Azuela, is the first and most important of a new genre: the novel of the Mexican Revolution. A long line of novels of the revolution are to follow its example, most of them published in exile in the United States.

1915:   The first widespread plot at overthrowing United States rule of the territories taken from Mexico and creating a separate republic is uncovered: the Plan de San Diego.

1916:   The United States installs its own military government in the Dominican Republic.

1916:   General Francisco Villa's forces raid the town of Columbus, New Mexico.

1916:   The first literary book to be published by a Dominican author in the United States is Pedro Henríquez Ureña's *El nacimiento de Dionisos* (The Birth of Dionysus). At the time, Henríquez Ureña is the editor of the New York newspaper *Las novedades* (The News); he also is a brilliant teacher and literary critic.

1917:   Through the Jones Act, the United States Congress confers U.S. citizenship on all Puerto Ricans; nevertheless, they may only vote in national elections as residents of the continental states, not the island, nor may the island have congressional representation.

1917:   The Mexican Revolution is officially over when Venustiano Carranza is elected to the presidency. Under Carranza's leadership, Mexico passes a reform constitution that is the basis for the modern Mexican state.

1919:   The first Spanish-language theater house opens in New York City, El Teatro Español. It is run and leased by leading man Manuel Noriega, who formed a stock company to perform in the house: Gran Compañía de Opera y Zarzuela.

1925:   The Border Patrol is created by the U.S. Congress.

1926:   In riots in Harlem, Puerto Ricans are attacked by non-Hispanics.

1926:   The Mexican government suspends the practice of Catholicism in Mexico. This leads to the Cristero War, which lasts until 1929, and a further exodus of political refugees from Mexico to the United States.

1927:   Poet-philosopher George Santayana is the first U.S. Hispanic to be awarded the Gold Medal from the Royal Society of Literature in London.

1929:   The largest and longest lasting Hispanic civil rights organization, League of United Latin American Citizens (LULAC), is founded in Texas.

1929:   Poet-philosopher George Santayana becomes the first U.S. Hispanic poet to be offered a chair at a major university: the prestigious Norton Chair of Poetry at Harvard. However, he does not accept the chair because he has given up teaching.

1930:   Dictator Rafael L. Trujillo comes to power in the Dominican Republic. He reigns until his assassination in 1961.

1930:   *Independent School District (Texas) v. Salvatierra* finds that Mexican Americans have been segregated.

1931:   Between 1931 and 1938, during the Depression, authorities at various levels of government conduct a mass repatriation program of Mexicans from the United States.

1933:   President Franklin Delano Roosevelt announces his "Good Neighbor Policy."

1933:   Farm workers establish the El Monte Berry Strike in Los Angeles County, California.

1933:   In a revolt by sergeants in the Cuban army, Fulgencio Batista comes to power and rules through a series of puppet leaders until his election in 1940.

1934:   President Franklin Delano Roosevelt annuls the Platt Amendment as a show of goodwill during his Good Neighbor Policy.

1935:   The first novel written by a U.S. Hispanic to be nominated for the Pulitzer Prize is George Santayana's *The Last Puritan: A Memoir in the Form of a Novel*.

1936:   The Spanish Civil War breaks out, and thousands of Spanish refugees become part of Hispanic communities of the United States, especially on the east coast.

1936:   The Tampa Hispanic unit of the Federal Theater Project, under the Works Progress Administration, is the only Hispanic company involved in the effort to save the American stage during the Depression.

1938:   A national congress of Hispanic peoples is organized in Los Angeles, California.

1939:   Brother Angélico Chávez publishes his first book of poetry, *Clothed with the Sun*, and eventually becomes the greatest religious poet among Hispanics in the United States.

1940:   Fulgencio Batista is elected president of Cuba.

1941:   Hispanics in the United States enthusiastically support the involvement of the United States in World War II and become the most decorated ethnic group of soldiers.

1942:   The Mexican Farm Labor Supply Program or "Bracero Program" is established in the United States. It lasts until 1964.

1943:   The "Zoot Suit Riots" begin in southern California as U.S. servicemen attack Mexican American teenagers as foreigners. This and other events become memorialized in Luis Valdez's 1978 play, *Zoot Suit*.

1945:   Chilean Gabriela Mistral becomes Latin America's first Nobel Prize-winner, for poetry. After becoming a Nobel laureate, she spends many years in the United States as Chilean ambassador to the League of Nations and the United Nations. Mistral's first book, *Desolación* (Desolation), was published in New York by the Hispanic Institute in 1922. Of her twenty-some books of poetry, *Desolación* and

Tala are considered her best works. She dies in Hempstead, New York, on January 10, 1957.

1945:   Mexican-American parents in Orange County, California, win a lawsuit (*Méndez et al. v. Westminster School District*) alleging segregation of their children.

1947:   The American G.I. Forum, a civil rights organization, is established by Mexican American veterans.

1949:   Luis Muñoz Marín serves as the first Puerto Rican governor elected by the citizens of Puerto Rico.

1950:   The U.S. Congress upgrades Puerto Rico's status from protectorate to commonwealth. Puerto Rican nationalists attack President Harry S. Truman's residence at Blair House.

1952:   The Commonwealth of Puerto Rico is instituted—the official status of the island to this date.

1952:   The record-breaking sitcom, "I Love Lucy" is the first television comedy to feature an Hispanic as a star: Desi Arnaz. This important popular culture phenomenon is later memorialized in Gustavo Pérez Firmat's book, *Life on the Hyphen: The Cuban-American Way.*

1953:   Puerto Rican René Marqués' play of dislocation and migration, *La carreta (The Oxcart)*, makes its debut in New York.

1954:   Puerto Rican nationalists shoot up the U.S. House of Representatives.

1954:   Through "Operation Wetback," more than one million Mexicans are deported from the United States.

1954:   *Hernández v. Texas* is the first Mexican American discrimination case to reach the U.S. Supreme Court.

1957:   The National Puerto Rican Forum is founded in New York City.

1957:   The Civil Rights Act is the first passed by the U.S. Congress since the end of the Civil War.

1958:   Novelist Floyd Salas becomes the first U.S. Hispanic writer to receive a Rockefeller Foundation Fellowship to study creative writing at the prestigious Centro Mexicano de Escritores in Mexico City. Upon returning to California from Mexico, Salas works on Bay Area campuses as a creative writing instructor and publishes his first novel, *Tatoo the Wicked Cross,* in 1967.

1959:   José Antonio Villarreal publishes what is considered to be the first Chicano novel in contemporary times: *Pocho*, a developmental novel in which the protagonist has a classic identity crisis. It is also the first Chicano novel to be published by a major commercial house: Doubleday.

1959:   Fidel Castro's Cuban Revolution triumphs, sending dictator Fulgencio Batista into exile. In the years that follow, hundreds of thousands of Cubans go into exile in the United States.

1960:   Cuba's Fidel Castro establishes diplomatic relations and trade with the Soviet Union. The Cuban government expropriates and nationalizes all property and businesses owned by U.S. citizens and interests.

1961:   A U.S. backed counterrevolutionary invasion at Cuba's Bay of Pigs fails.

1961:   President John F. Kennedy announces the creation of the Alliance for Progress, a program that hopes to stem the spread of Communism in Latin America.

1961:   ASPIRA Inc., the first organization promoting higher education and providing counseling services for Puerto Ricans in the United States, is founded.

1962:   President John F. Kennedy brings the United States to the brink of nuclear war when he forces the Soviet Union to remove its missiles from Cuba. In return for their removal, he promises the United States will not invade or support others who invade Cuba.

1962:   Nuyorican writer Piri Thomas is the first Hispanic writer to receive a grant from the Louis M. Rabinowitz Foundation, which enables him to finish writing his groundbreaking autobiography, *Down These Mean Streets* (1967). The basic work that launches Nuyorican literature, *Down These Mean Streets* is also the first agonizing tale of the search for identity among conflicting cultural, racial, ethnic, and linguistic alternatives presented to Latinos in general, and Afro-Hispanic peoples in the United States, in particular. It is such a milestone that the Nuyorican and Latino literature that follows it either continues its themes or totally rejects its poetic melange of street language and psychodrama as a naive and unsophisticated cry stemming from the culture of poverty.

Piri Thomas.

1963:   Jose Yglesias becomes the first Cuban American creative writer to be published by a mainstream press, with the publication of his *A Wake in Ybor City*, based on the Cuban-Spanish community in Tampa, Florida.

1963:   Reies López Tijerina organizes the Alianza Federal de los Pueblos Libres (Federal Alliance of Free Towns) in New Mexico, a movement to regain land grants for the *Nuevomexicanos*. It is a precursor to the Chicano Movement. This self-educated minister later writes a passionate memoir of his movement leadership, *They Called Me "King Tiger": My Struggle for the Land and Our Rights*.

1963:   The first play that can be called "Chicano" is Luis Valdez's *The Shrunken Head of Pancho Villa*, which he writes as his M.A. thesis play while he is a student at San Jose State University. The drama department produced the play and he was graded on it.

1964:   The first literary magazine founded by Cuban exiles from the Cuban Revolution, *Cuadernos desterrados* (Exiled Notebooks), is established in Miami, Florida.

1965:   President Lyndon Baines Johnson sends the Marines to the Dominican Republic to prevent another Cuban-style Communist takeover.

1965:   César Chávez begins to lead the United Farm Workers through a series of strikes and national boycotts in the creation of a farm workers' union. Scholars today acknowledge this as the beginning of the Chicano Movement.

1965:   Luis Valdez founds El Teatro Campesino as part of the farm worker movement and as one of the first creative institutions in the Chicano Movement. Cuban American playwright María Irene Fornés becomes the first Hispanic playwright to win an Obie for distinguished playwriting of *The Successful Life of Three*.

1965:   The first publishing house to serve the Cuban refugee community, Ediciones Universal, is founded in Miami by Juan Manuel Salvat, and has remained the largest publisher of Cuban emigré scholars and literary figures. It is not until the 1970s and 1980s that other Cuban and Cuban-American publishing houses begin to appear: Editorial SIBI, Editorial Persona, Editorial Arcos, Linden Lane Press, among others.

1966:   San Antonio poet Angela de Hoyos becomes the first U.S. Hispanic poet to gain international recognition by winning the Bronze Medal of Honor (poetry), Centro Studi e Scambi Internazionale (CSSI), Rome, Italy.

1966:   Puerto Rican youths riot in Chicago.

1966:   Rodolfo "Corky" Gonzales, a boxer and author of the Chicano epic poem *I Am Joaquín*, founds the Crusade for Justice in Denver, Colorado. It is one of the most militant Chicano civil rights organizations.

1967:   The most influential Chicano magazine, *El grito* (The Shout), is founded in Berkeley, California, by two University of California professors: Octavio Romano and Herminio Ríos. *El grito* and the publishing house, Editorial Quinto Sol (Fifth Sun Publishers), which they establish in 1968, launch the careers of the most important writers of the Chicano Movement, such as Alurista, Tomás Rivera, Rudolfo Anaya, and Rolando Hinojosa. They also define Chicano literature and establish the canons of that literature by publishing works that best exemplify Chicano culture, language, themes, and styles. The very name of the publishing house emphasizes its Mexican/Aztec identity, as well as the Spanish language; the "quinto sol" refers to the Aztec belief in a period of cultural flowering that will take place some time in the future, in a fifth age that conveniently coincides with the rise of Chicano culture. In their publications there is a definite insistence on working-class and rural culture, as exemplified in the works of Rivera, Anaya, and Hinojosa, as well as the promotion of works written bilingually or in dialect.

1967:   Rodolfo "Corky" Gonzales, founder of a militant Chicano civil rights organization, the Crusade for Justice, writes and self-publishes the first Chicano epic poem, *I Am Joaquín/Yo Soy Joaquín*, which influences the development of Chicano literature and its nationalist ideology. The poem, widely read and emulated, becomes the basis of a film created by El Teatro Campesino and narrated by Luis Valdez.

1967:   Broadway and Hollywood actress Miriam Colón founds the Puerto Rican Traveling Theater in New York. With the exception of El Teatro Campesino, it is the longest lasting Hispanic theater in the country.

1968:   The first federal law mandating bilingual education—the Bilingual Education Act, which became Title VII of the Elementary and Secondary Education Act—is passed.

1968:   Luis Valdez and El Teatro Campesino become the first Hispanic theater company to win an Obie. Valdez and the company establish a national Chicano theater association, Teatro Nacional de Aztlán (TENAZ), that organizes yearly festivals, workshops, and publications.

1969:   The first National Chicano Youth Liberation Conference is held in Denver, Colorado.

1969:   Nuyorican poet Victor Hernández Cruz becomes the first Puerto Rican poet to be published by a mainstream publishing house when Random House issued his *Snaps*.

1969:   Editorial Quinto Sol publishes the first (or one of the first) anthologies of Chicano literature: *El Espejo* (*The Mirror*), edited by Octavio Romano-V. It includes the works of such notable and still-studied authors as Alurista, Miguel Méndez, and Tomás Rivera.

1970:   Editorial Quinto Sol establishes the first national award for Chicano literature: Premio Quinto Sol. The Premio includes a $1000 prize and publication of the winning
book manuscript. For the first three years the prize goes to books that are still seen
as foundational Chicano novels: Tomás Rivera's . . . *Y no se lo tragó la tierra* (. . .
And the Earth Did Not Devour Him), Rudolfo Anaya's *Bless Me, Ultima*, and
Rolando Hinojosa's *Estampas del Valle y otras obras* (*Sketches of the Valley and Other
Works*).

1970:   Herman Badillo becomes the first Puerto Rican ever elected as a voting member
of Congress.

1971:   The Mexican-American political party, La Raza Unida Party, is born.

1971:   Mexican American author Tomás Rivera publishes his foundational novel of migrant farm labor . . . *Y no se lo tragó la tierra* (. . . *And the Earth Did Not Devour
Him*).

1971:   Celedonio González becomes the first writer in exile from Castro's Cuba to change
the focus from the political situation in Cuba to the development of Cuban culture in
the United States in his novel *Los primos* (The Cousins). In this and following
novels, he not only examines culture shock and conflict between Cubans and Americans, but also treats a very taboo topic: criticism of the economic system of the
United States, especially in its exploitation of Cuban workers. González is the first
writer to present readers with Cubans who do not see themselves as Americans but
who are also conscious that Cuba is no longer theirs. This represents an interme-
diate step to the development of a Cuban-American literature in the English language.

1971:   *Floricanto en Aztlán* (Flower and Song in Aztlán), by Alurista, becomes the first
Chicano poetry book to be published by a university, the Chicano Studies
Publications of the University of California, Los Angeles. The book is highly influential in integrating pre-Columbian culture and symbolism into rising Chicano
nationalism. It is also an exemplary model of bilingualism in poetry.

1971:   Cuban American playwright Iván Acosta's play *Abdala-José Martí* is the first Hispanic play featured at the Lincoln Center Theater Festival in New York.

1972:   Rudolfo Anaya's novel, *Bless Me, Ultima*, the second winner of the Premio Quinto
Sol, becomes the best-selling Chicano novel, selling more than one million copies
over a twenty-year period, according to the publishers. Written in a straightforward
narrative, the novel is about a boy's coming of age and having to mediate the
competing Indian and Spanish traditions of his maternal and paternal heritages in
rural New Mexico.

1972:   The first journal for the study and promotion of Puerto Rican culture of the mainland
United States, *The Rican Journal*, is founded and published by a Northeastern Illinois
University sociology professor, Samuel Betances, in Chicago. In addition to pub-
lishing social science articles, the journal publishes original literature by Nuyoricans.

1972:   Festival Floricanto, the first national Chicano literature festival, is held in Los Angeles.

1973:   The first national magazine of U.S. Hispanic literature, *Revista Chicano-Riqueña*
(The Chicano Puerto Rican Review), is founded at Indiana University Northwest
in Gary, Indiana, by co-editors Nicolás Kanellos and Luis Dávila. Over the years,
the magazine, which changes its title to *The Americas Review* while published at
the University of Houston, promotes a pan-Hispanic culture in the United States
and launches the careers of many important writers of Hispanic literature, including
Lorna Dee Cervantes, Sandra Cisneros, Ana Castillo, and many others. In 1979,
the magazine founds its own literary press, Arte Público Press, which grows to be
the largest non-commercial publisher of literature in the United States.

Nicholasa Mohr.

1973:   Nicholasa Mohr becomes the first U.S. Hispanic woman in modern times to have her literary works published by the major commercial publishing houses—and develops a longer career as a creative writer for these publishing houses than any other Hispanic female writer. Only Jose Yglesias publishes more works than she—and during a longer period of time. Ricardo Sánchez becomes the first Chicano writer to have a book of poetry published by a mainstream commercial publishing house when Anchor/Doubleday issues his *Canto y grito mi liberación* (I Sing and Shout for My Liberation). Poet-novelist Floyd Salas becomes the first Hispanic writer to serve as the statewide coordinator of poetry in the schools of California.

1973:   Actress Carmen Zapata launches the Bilingual Foundation for the Arts, a theater to serve as a showcase of Hispanic acting and play writing for Hollywood.

1974:   Estela Portillo Trambley becomes the first woman to win the national award for Chicano Literature, Premio Quinto Sol, for her collection of short stories, *Rain of Scorpions*. Her winning marks the ascendancy of Mexican-American women into the Chicano literary movement, which had been so dominated by males.

1974:   A group of young and radical Cuban emigrés founds the first pro-Cuban Revolution magazine in the United States: *Areíto*. Headed by Lourdes Casal, the magazine supports the Cuban government, which they believe has created a more egalitarian society. Their stance prompts the defection of various sponsors of the magazine and continued hostile reaction from the Cuban refugee press and intellectuals. Despite the hostility, *Areíto* survives well into the 1980s.

1974:   The U.S. Supreme Court, in *Lau v. Nichols*, holds that the San Francisco unified School District discriminates by not providing programs for limited English-speaking students.

1974:   Puerto Rican Miguel Piñero wins the New York Drama Critics' Circle Award for Best American Play, an Obie, and a Drama Desk Award for *Short Eyes*.

1975:   The first anthology of Nuyorican literature is compiled by Miguel Algarín and Miguel Piñero: *Nuyorican Poetry: An Anthology of Puerto Rican Words and Feelings*. (Algarín owned and administered the Nuyorican Poets Cafe, which promoted the distinct identity of Puerto Ricans born and/or raised on the mainland, and Piñero was the first Nuyorican playwright to gain national acclaim with his play *Short Eyes*). New York Puerto Rican novelist Nicholasa Mohr's second book, *El Bronx Remembered*, is awarded the New York Times Outstanding Book Award in teenage fiction and receives the Best Book Award from the *School Library Journal*. *El Bronx Remembered* is also a National Book Award finalist in children's literature.

1975:   Alejandro Morales becomes the first Chicano novelist to have a book published in Spanish in Mexico: *Caras viejas y vino nuevo* (Old Faces and New Wine). The event is an important landmark in Mexico's recognition of Mexican-Americans and their culture. Gary Soto becomes the first Hispanic poet to win the Academy of American Poets Prize. That same year, he wins the *Nation*-Discovery Award.

1976:   The first literary magazine founded by Cuban exile writers outside of Miami is founded: *Exilio*. It is published in New York until 1973 by Víctor Batista Falla and Raimundo Fernández Bonilla.

1976:   Rolando Hinojosa becomes the first U.S. Hispanic writer and the first American to win the prestigious international award, Premio Casa de las Américas (House of the Americas Prize) from Cuba for his novel *Klail City y sus alrededores* (Klail City and Surroundings). He is the first Chicano novelist to win an international award.

1977:   Nicholasa Mohr's third book, *In Nueva York* is the first Hispanic title to be named Notable Trade Book in the Field of Social Studies by the joint committee of the National Council for Social Studies and the Children's Book Council.

1977:   San Antonio poet Evangelina Vigil-Piñón became the first Hispanic writer to win the National Literary Contest of the Coordinating Council of Literary Magazines for work published in a small magazine.

1977:   Henry G. Cisneros becomes the first Hispanic mayor of San Antonio in modern times.

1978:   The Sandinista Front for National Liberation begins its revolution to topple the dictatorship of Anastasio Somoza Debayle in Nicaragua.

1978:   Tomás Rivera, the renowned scholar and creative writer, becomes the first Hispanic chancellor in the University of California system.

1978:   Luis Valdez becomes the first Mexican American playwright to break into mainstream theater, with Los Angeles' Mark Taper Forum's production of *Zoot Suit* and the 1980 Broadway production of the same play.

1978:   The group of young Cuban emigrés publishing the pro-Cuban Revolution magazine *Areíto* in New York publishes the first émigré anthology, *Contra viento y marea* (Against Wind and Waves), in Cuba. The writings of these refugees, forced to accompany their parents into exile from Cuba at an early age, recounted their experiences as refugees in a foreign culture and their allegiance to communist Cuba. In 1978, the anthology is awarded Cuba's highest literary award: Premio Casa de las Américas (House of the Américas Prize).

1978:   Puerto Rican novelist and short story writer José Luis González becomes the first U.S. Hispanic writer to win Mexico's most prestigious literary award, the Xavier Viallurrutia Prize for Fiction, for his novel *Balada de otro tiempo* (Ballad of Another Time), which is set to the background of the U.S. invasion of Puerto Rico during the Spanish-American War.

1978:   Poet Gary Soto's book *The Tale of Sunlight* becomes the first book by a Chicano poet to be nominated for the Pulitzer Prize. It is also the first Hispanic poetry book to be nominated for the National Book Award.

1979:   The oldest and largest publisher of U.S. Hispanic literature, Arte Público Press, is founded by Nicolás Kanellos, a professor and founder/editor of *Revista Chicano-Riqueña*, the oldest and most established Hispanic literary magazine in the United States. Over the years, the press wins numerous awards and launches the careers of most of the prominent U.S. Hispanic writers. By the early 1990s, the press becomes

Nicolás Kanellos.

the largest non-commercial publisher of literature in the United States, issuing more than thirty titles per year. The first book published by Arte Público Press is Tato Laviera's groundbreaking collection of poems *La Carreta Made a U-Turn.*

1979: Arte Público Press organizes the First National Latino Book Fair in Chicago, Illinois. In addition to exhibiting and selling books by the few Hispanic presses and magazines that exist in the United States at that time, the book fair features readings by some of the most important writers of the period, such as Ana Castillo, Lorna Dee Cervantes, Sandra Cisneros, Abelardo Delgado, Sandra María Esteves, Miguel Algarín, Tato Laviera, and Rolando Hinojosa.

1979: Nicolás Kanellos, editor of *Revista Chicano-Riqueña* literary magazine, becomes the first Hispanic to receive the $5000 award for Outstanding Editor from the Coordinating Council of Literary Magazines.

1979: A military junta takes power in El Salvador just as the leftist guerrilla movement gains enough power to throw the nation into civil war.

1979: The Sandinista revolution is triumphant in Nicaragua.

1979: Julián Nava becomes the first Mexican American to serve as an ambassador to Mexico. In 2002, he publishes an autobiography, *Julián Nava: My Mexican American Journey.*

1980: Ronald Reagan begins his two terms as president of the United States, during which time he considers Latin American affairs solely within the context of the Cold War and the East-West struggle. A flotilla of boats assists 125,000 Cubans escaping from the Castro regime through Mariel Harbor. Many writers and artists escape Cuba for the United States during this exodus. The U.S. Congress passes the Refugee Act, which redefines the category of "refugee" for immigration purposes.

1980: Prize-winning novelist Rudolfo Anaya is the first Hispanic novelist to receive a gubernatorial award, the New Mexico Governor's Award for Excellence.

1980: Mexican American poet Luis Omar Salinas becomes the first Hispanic writer to win the Stanley Kunitz Poetry Prize and the Earl Lyon Award for his collection, *Afternoon of the Unreal.*

1981: Jesús Abraham "Tato" Laviera becomes the fist Hispanic author to win the American Book Award of the Before Columbus Foundation, which recognizes and promotes multicultural literature.

1981: Lorna Dee Cervantes's *Emplumada* (Plumed) becomes the first poetry book by a Chicana to be published by a university press—the University of Pittsburgh Press in its prestigious Pitt Poetry Series.

1981: Two Chicana lesbian writers, Cherríe Moraga and Gloria Anzaldúa, become the first to compile an anthology of the literature and thought of women of color,

This Bridge Called My Back: Writings by Radical Women of Color. The book becomes the most famous and best-selling anthology of its kind and has inspired a movement of Hispanic feminist and lesbian writers.

1981:   New York poet Sandra María Esteves's *Yerba buena* is the first Hispanic book to win the award for Best Small Press Publication.

1981:   Victor Hernández Cruz becomes the first U.S. Hispanic poet to be canonized as one of the few great American poets when the April 1981 issue of *Life* magazine proclaims him a national and includes him among a handful of outstanding American poets—without making reference to his race or ethnicity.

1982:   Cuban-American playwright María Irene Fornés becomes the first Hispanic to win an Obie for sustained achievement in theater. This adds to the numerous Obies she has received for individual plays.

1983:   The first magazine published by Cuban refugees from the Mariel Boatlift is founded: *Revista Mariel.* Established in Miami initially by Reinaldo Arenas, Roberto Valero, and Juan Abreu, it later is moved to New York and specializes in publishing the works of authors who have been silenced by the Castro regime, including its leading editor and literary figure, Reinaldo Arenas.

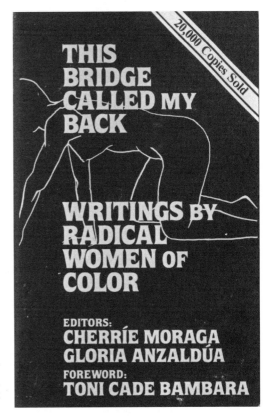

Cover of *This Bridge Called My Back.*

1983:   Playwright-director Luis Valdez is the first Hispanic to be awarded the National Medal for the Arts. Texas Mexican American writer Lionel G. García is the first Hispanic to win the PEN Southwest Award, for his novel, *Leaving Home.* Poet Evangelina Vigil-Piñón becomes the first Hispanic female writer to win the American Book Award from the Before Columbus Foundation for her *Thirty an' Seen a Lot.* Luis Omar Salinas is the first Hispanic writer to win the General Electric Foundation Younger Writers Award, based on poems he published in the literary magazine *Revista Chicano-Riqueña.* Nicolás Kanellos, founder and publisher of Arte Público Press, is the first Hispanic publisher to be inducted into the international writers organization PEN.

1984:   El Paso poet Pat Mora's first collection of poems, *Chants,* is the first Hispanic book to win the Southwest Book Award, given by the Border Regional Library Association.

1984:   A draft for Lionel García's first novel, *Leaving Home,* becomes the first Hispanic book to win the PEN Southwest Discovery Prize.

1985:   Miami elects its first Cuban-born mayor: Xavier Suárez.

1985:   Nicholasa Mohr's collection of feminist short stories, *Rituals of Survival: A Woman's Portfolio,* becomes the first Hispanic book to receive a legislative commendation, from the New York State Legislature.

1985:   Future Pulitzer prize winning author Oscar Hijuelos becomes the first U.S. Hispanic writer to win the prestigious American Academy in Rome Fellowship from the American Academy and the Institute for Arts and Letters.

1986:   *The Americas Review* (formerly *Revista Chicano-Riqueña*) becomes the first and only Hispanic magazine to win the Citation of Achievement from the Coordinating Council of Literary Magazines. The magazine goes on to win the Citation again in 1987.

1986:   Dominican-American novelist and poet Julia Alvarez becomes the first Hispanic female writer to win the General Electric Foundation Award for Young Writers.

1986:   The United States Congress enacts the Immigration Reform and Control Act, which creates an alien legalization program.

1987:   Bob Martínez becomes the first Catholic and first Hispanic to be elected governor of Florida.

1988:   Poet Pat Mora is the first Hispanic writer to be named to the *El Paso Herald Post* Writer's Hall of Fame. An El Paso native and winner of Southwest Book Awards, Mora is also inducted into the Texas Institute of Letters the same year.

1988:   Nicolás Kanellos, the founder and publisher of Arte Público Press, becomes the first and only Hispanic publisher to be honored with the Hispanic Heritage Award for Literature, presented at the White House by President Ronald Reagan.

1989:   The United States invades Panama in its war against the illicit drug trade.

1989:   Poet Carolina Hospital compiles the first anthology of Cuban American literature, *Los Atrevidos: The Cuban American Writers*, thus announcing the birth and acceptance of Cuban-American literature as being other than a literature of exile and immigration. Short story writer and novelist Helena María Viramontes becomes the first Hispanic to win the Storytelling Award of the Sundance Institute, the famed workshop for screenwriters.

1989:   The first Hispanic book to win the title of Outstanding Book in the Humanities is *European Perspectives on Hispanic Literature of the United States*, edited by Genvieve Fabre and published by Arte Público Press.

1989:   The first television documentary on Hispanic literature of the United States is aired by the Public Broadcasting Service: *Birthwrite: Growing Up Hispanic*, directed by Jesús Salvador Treviño.

1989:   Nicolás Kanellos, publisher of Arte Público Press books, becomes the first publisher to be honored with the American Book Award in the Publisher-Editor category of the Before Columbus Foundation.

1990:   Recovering the U.S. Hispanic Literary Heritage Project is founded at the University of Houston, a ten-year effort by scholars, librarians, and archivists from throughout the United States, Mexico, Puerto Rico, Cuba and Spain to reconstitute the written legacy of Hispanics until 1960 in what became the United States. Funded by the Rockefeller Foundations and other national funders and agencies, the extensive project's goals include finding all of the texts, preserving them, and making them accessible to scholars, students, and the general public. The project achieves bibliographic control of more than 18,000 written and published works by Hispanics in the United States before 1960, 1700 periodicals, and hundreds of manuscript archives, much of which is being digitized for distribution over the Internet. Among the titles recovered and published in book form by the Recovery Project are María Amparo Ruiz de Burton's novel; Alirio Díaz Guerra, Félix Varela, and Daniel Venegas' novels; the stories of María Cristina Mena; Jovita González's stories, and Jesús Colón's *crónicas*—all of which find immediate acceptance in the college curriculum.

1990:   The first major textbook of Chicano literature for high schools, *Mexican American Literature*, edited by Charles Tatum, is published by the educational publishing giant Harcourt Brace Jovanovich. The publication marks not only the institutionalization of Chicano literature, but also the growth of the Mexican American school population.

1990:   Poet-novelist Judith Ortiz Cofer becomes the first Hispanic writer to receive a Special Citation from the PEN Martha Albrand Award for *Silent Dancing: A Partial Remembrance of a Puerto Rican Childhood* (1990), which is a collection of autobiographical essays and poems. The book is also awarded the Pushcart Prize in the essay category and is included in the New York Public Library System List of Best Books for the Teen Age. The title essay was chosen by Joyce Carol Oates for *The Best American Essays* (1991).

1991:   Mikhail Gorbachev announces the withdrawal of Soviet troops from Cuba. President George Bush signs the Cuban Democracy Act, which further bans trade with Cuba.

1991:   Oscar Hijuelos becomes the first Hispanic writer to win the Pulitzer Prize for Fiction, for his book *The Mambo Kings Play Songs of Love*. Victor Villaseñor's family autobiography, *Rain of Gold*, becomes the first book published by an Hispanic press, Arte Público Press, to make it on to the bestseller lists in the United States. Publishing giant Random House issues a collection of essays and short stories—Sandra Cisneros's *Woman Hollering Creek and Other Stories*—and then also reissues her two previous titles: *The House on Mango Street* and *My Wicked Wicked Ways*. Cisneros thus becomes the first Chicana to be supported by the commercial publishing establishment. *Intaglio: A Novel in Six Stories*, by Roberta Fernández, becomes the first Hispanic book to win the Minority Publishers Exchange Award for fiction.

1992:   Mexican American Jungian psychologist Clarissa Pinkola Estés becomes the first U.S. Hispanic author to have her book, *Women Who Run with Wolves: Myths and Stories of the Wild Woman Archetype*, make the *New York Times* bestseller list, just five weeks after its publication; the book remained on the list longer than any other book written by an Hispanic to date. *Women Who Run with the Wolves* contains original stories, folktales, myths, and legends by Estés, along with psychoanalytic commentary based on women's lives. *Hispanic* magazine hailed it as a "feminine manifesto for all women, regardless of age, race, creed, or religion, to return to their wild roots. . . ." Estés founds and directs the C.P. Estés Guadalupe Foundation, which has as one of its missions the broadcasting of strengthening stories, via short wave radio, to trouble spots around the world. In 1994 Estés was awarded the Associated Catholic Church Press Award for Writing and, in 1995 the National Association for the Advancement of Psychoanalysis Gradiva Award.

1992:   Mexican American novelist Lucha Corpi becomes the fist Hispanic writer to win the PEN Oakland Josephine Miles Award, for her *Eulogy for a Brown Angel*, in which Corpi creates the astute Chicana detective, Gloria Damasco, who unravels the mysterious assassination of a young boy during the protest activities of the 1970 Chicano Moratorium against the Vietnam War. Described as a feminist detective novel, *Eulogy* is fast-paced, suspenseful, and packed with an assortment of interesting characters. Her feminist protagonist, Gloria Damasco, is somewhat of a clairvoyant who is able to use more than reason and logic in solving a very puzzling crime. In addition to PEN Oakland Award, *Eulogy* also receives the Multicultural Publishers Exchange Best Book of Fiction award. Corpi has subsequently written two more Gloria Damasco mysteries.

1992:   Mexican American poet Lorna Dee Cervantes is the first Hispanic writer to win the prestigious Paterson Poetry Prize, for her second book, *From the Cables of Genocide: Poems of Love and Hunger*. It is also awarded the Latin American Writers Institute Award that same year. Cristina García is the first Cuban American woman to experience mainstream success as a novelist in the United States, through the publication of her first novel *Dreaming in Cuban*, issued by Knopf.

1993:   Mexican-American poet Luis Rodríguez's memoir of life on the streets, *Always Running*, is the first Hispanic book to win the Carl Sandburg Award for Non-Fiction. It also wins the *Chicago Sun-Times* First Prose Book Award in 1994. *Heartbeat Drumbeat*, by Irene Beltrán Hernández, is the first Hispanic book to win the Benjamin Franklin Award for Juvenile-Young Adult Fiction. Novelist Sandra Benítez becomes the first Hispanic writer to win the Barnes & Noble Inc. Discovery Great New Writers Award for her first novel, *A Place Where the Sea Remembers*.

1994:   El Salvador holds its first free elections in sixty-four years. The North American Free Trade Agreement is instituted to integrate the economies of the U.S., Canada, and Mexico.

1994:   Puerto Rican novelist, short story writer, and poet Judith Ortiz Cofer is the first U.S. Hispanic to win the O. Henry Prize for the short story. That same year, she also wins the Anisfield-Wolf Award in Race Relations for her novel *The Latin Deli*. Graciela Limón's novel *In Search of Bernabé* and José Bareiro's novel *The Indian Chronicles* become the first U.S. Hispanic literary works to be chosen as finalists for the *Los Angeles Times* Book Award. Puerto Rican poet Gloria Vando's book *Promesas: A Geography of the Impossible* becomes the first Hispanic book to win the Thorpe Menn Award for literary achievement.

Alba Ambert.

1995:   Mexican-American poet Sandra Cisneros is the first Hispanic writer to win the prestigious MacArthur Award. Lionel G. García becomes the first Hispanic writer to win first place in the Texas Playwright Festival for his play *An Acorn on the Moon*, produced by Houston's Stages Repertory Theatre in 1995. Tina Juárez's historical novel *Call No Man Master* is the first Hispanic book to win the Austin Writer's League Violet Crown Book Award and the Presidio La Bahía Award, the latter presented by The Sons of the Republic of Texas. *El desierto es mi madre* (*The Desert Is My Mother*), by Pat Mora with illustrations by Daniel Lechón, is the first Hispanic children's picture book to win the Skipping Stones Book Award for children's literature.

1996:   Puerto Rican novelist Alba Ambert wins the first Carey McWilliams Award for Multicultural Literature, presented by the *Multicultural Review*, for her novel *A Perfect Silence*. Novelist Isabel Allende, an immigrant from Chile, becomes the first Hispanic writer to win the prestigious Harold Washington

Award for Literature, presented in Chicago on May 3. The next day, she receives an honorary doctorate from Columbia College in Chicago.

1996:   New York's Teatro Repertorio Español receives an honorary Drama Desk Award for its excellence in presenting plays in Spanish and English.

1998:   Hollywood actor Edward James Olmos establishes the annual Latino Book and Family Festival, the nation's largest Hispanic book fair, in Los Angeles. As part of the book fair, an annual Latino Book Summit is held yearly at the major book industry trade show, Book Expo. Eventually the participant publishers, distributors, agents and booksellers develop into a Latino book industry trade group. Affiliated with the summit is the Latino Literary Hall of Fame book awards, presented yearly. Winners include Marcos McPeek Villatoro, Lucha Corpi, and Pat Mora.

2000:   Diane Gonzales Bertrand's young adult novel, *Trino's Choice*, is named Best Book of the Year by *Foreword* Magazine in its annual award ceremonies, held at Book Expo. The novel also wins the Austin Writers' League Teddy Award for Best Children's Book, the Latino Literary Hall of Fame and is named to the Lone Star Reading List.

2001:   Cahners Corporation, publishers of magazines and information services for the book industry, launches *Crítica*, the first review magazine of books in Spanish for the United States market. The advent of *Crítica* signifies that the Hispanic population of the United States is finally seen as sizeable enough to support the publishing, importing, and distribution of Spanish-language books, magazines, and information services.

2001:   Arte Público Press and the El Paso Corporation sponsor the national award for Hispanic children's literature, the "Reading with Energy" Award, which offers a $5000 prize and publication. The first winner is Diane Gonzales Bertrand's *El picnic de Tío Chente* (*Uncle Chente's Picnic*).

2002:   Oxford University Press publishes *Herencia: The Anthology of Hispanic Literature of the United States*, the first comprehensive anthology to compile works from the entire historical span of Hispanic culture in North America, including the written culture of all Hispanic ethnic groups that have lived in what is now the United States. Edited by Nicolás Kanellos and a team of scholars from the Recovering the U.S. Hispanic Literary Heritage Project, the anthology is the result of a ten-year effort by hundreds of scholars to find and make accessible hundreds of thousands of literary documents from the colonial period to the present. After collecting, evaluating, translating, and selecting these works for the Oxford anthology, the same team publishes the Spanish-language originals in Arte Público Press's *En otra voz: antología de la literatura hispana de los Estados Unidos* (In Another Voice: Anthology of Hispanic Literature of the United States).

CHAPTER 3

WHO'S WHO OF HISPANIC AUTHORS OF THE UNITED STATES

Iván Mariano Acosta (1943–)

An outstanding playwright and filmmaker, Iván Mariano Acosta was born in Santiago, Cuba, on November 17, 1943. He immigrated to the United States with his parents during the Cuban Revolution. After graduating in film direction and production from New York University (1969), he worked as a playwright and director at the Centro Cultural Cubano and the Henry Street Settlement Playhouse in New York City. His play, *El super* (The Superintendent), first produced at the Centro Cultural Cubano, is probably the most successful Hispanic play to come out of an ethnic theater house; it not only was highly reviewed and won awards, but it was also adapted to the screen by Acosta in a feature film that won twelve awards for best script and best director. *El super* was published in book form in 1982, and four other plays were published in a collection titled *Un cubiche en la luna y otras obras* (A Cuban on the Moon and Other Works) in 1989. Acosta has won various awards, including the Cintas Fellowship (1980), The Ace Award for Best Writer (1980), the Thalia Best Writer Award (1972), and the Ariel Best Writer Award (1971).

Oscar Zeta Acosta (1935–1974)

Oscar Zeta Acosta, lawyer and writer, was born on April 8, 1935, in El Paso, Texas, and raised in southern California. Acosta served four years in the Air Force and upon discharge moved to San Francisco, where he spent years studying law in night school while working as a copy boy on a San Francisco newspaper during the day. After graduating from law school, he was admitted to the California Bar in 1966, and worked at a legal aid clinic in Oakland in 1966. He soon became disenchanted and moved to Los Angeles, where he became a member of the Con Safos literary group, which published the magazine in which his writings first appeared. It was through Con Safos that he became one of the first writers to develop a Chicano aesthetic in literature, and went on to establish some of the

Oscar Zeta Acosta.

perspectives and style that later became common, especially among that first group of socially committed Chicano authors: identification with the working classes, a biting humor, an interest in promoting ethnic identity, rejection of the established order. During this time, Acosta continued his social activism and became the lead attorney in a number of landmark cases, including *Castro v. Superior Court of Los Angeles*, in which he successfully protected the right to free speech of teachers involved in the Los Angeles school walkouts, and *Carlos Montez et al. v. the Superior Court of Los Angeles County*, in which Acosta argued that Spanish-surnamed individuals had been systematically excluded from serving on juries.

Acosta's two books, *Autobiography of a Brown Buffalo* (1972) and *Revolt of the Cockroach People* (1973), represent two parts of a fanciful autobiography of the author in which contemporary events and people are the setting for a picaresque, satirical romp of Acosta's "Brown Buffalo" alter-ego in his tongue-in-cheek sallies to fight for the rights of Chicanos. In reality, the books represent a journey of self-discovery, where the main character seeks to establish his ethnic, cultural, and psychological identity. *The Autobiography of a Brown Buffalo* charts how this confused main character, addicted to drugs, alcohol and psychotherapy, becomes a committed Chicano activist. In *The Revolt of the Cockroach People*, the ethnic pride and activism that "Brown Buffalo" achieved at the end of the first book becomes the basis for his involvement in the political upheavals occurring in Los Angeles during the early 1970s. Here the Chicano lawyer Buffalo Zeta Brown raises a series of challenges to the courts, the schools, and the church. Acosta takes the reader into the midst of guerrilla-movement politics in Los Angeles, describing the plotting of bombings and political demonstrations. In addition to being an engrossing adventure novel, *The Revolt of the Cockroach People* is the Chicano novel that has best and most closely captured the spirit and detail of the militant phase of the Chicano Movement. For all of his ability and insight, and for all of his irreverence, Acosta became a model for Chicano writers who sought to balance their aesthetics with their social commitment. In addition, he also represented that uniquely Chicano/Mexican propensity for self-deprecation and for not taking oneself too seriously.

Mercedes de Acosta (1893–1968)

Mercedes de Acosta, one of the few Hispanic women to develop a successful career as an English-language playwright and screenwriter in New York City and

Hollywood, was born in New York to Spanish parents. On her mother's side she was related to the dukes of Alba; her father, also of Spanish descent, was raised in Cuba. Mercedes was a child prodigy who began writing at the age of twelve and soon became a protégé of a famous Broadway impresario. She published her first book of poems, *Moods*, in 1919. De Acosta followed this collection with two others: *Archways of Life* (1921) and *Streets and Shadows* (1922). She was the author of two novels: *Wind* (1920) and *Until the Day Break* (1928), as well as an autobiography, *Here Lies the Heart* (1960). Four of her five plays—her most famous was *Sandro Botticelli*—were published, if not produced, and led to her transition to Hollywood, where she developed scripts for Paramount and Metro-Goldwyn-Meyer, including for the films *East River*, *Rasputin*, *Desperate*, and *Joan of Arc*. During her career in Hollywood as a scriptwriter, she became a member of the glitterati and one of actress Greta Garbo's most notorious lovers. Despite her intense literary creativity, Acosta's works were not well received—except for her autobiography, which became something of a tell-all sensation during her last years of life.

Miguel Algarín (1941–)

Miguel Algarín is a renowned poet and the founder of the Nuyorican Poets Café on the Lower East Side of Manhattan. A native of Santurce, Puerto Rico, Algarín moved with his working-class parents to New York City in the early 1950s. Algarín is a graduate in English of the University of Wisconsin (B.A. 1963) and Pennsylvania State University (M.A. 1965). After teaching English at Brooklyn College and New York University for a short time, Algarín went on to Rutgers University, where he taught English and Puerto Rican studies until his retirement in 2001. Algarín became a spokesman for the Nuyorican literary movement in the late 1960s and founded a center in which its poets and playwrights could perform their works in a setting reminiscent of the coffee houses of the beat generation.

Algarín played an important leadership role in the definition of Nuyorican literature by compiling, with Miguel Piñero, its first and only anthology, *Nuyorican Poetry: An Anthology of Puerto Rican Words and Feelings* (1975). He also founded a short-lived publishing house, the Nuyorican Press, which issued only one book, his own *Mongo Affair* (1978). One year later, he took part in the launching of Arte Público Press, which became the leading publisher of Nuyorican literature, as well as the leading publisher of Chicano and Cuban-American literature.

Algarín has written plays, screenplays, and short stories, but is principally known as a poet. His books include *Mongo Affair, On Call* (1980), *Body Bee Calling from the 21st Century* (1982), *Ya es tiempo* (*Time's Now*, 1985) and *Love Is Hard Work: Memorias de Loisaida/Poems* (1997). He has also published anthologies of works performed at the Nuyorican Poets Café, including *Aloud: Voices from the Nuyorican Poets Café* (1994). Algarín's poetry runs the gamut from jazz-salsa to the mystical. He is one of the foremost experimenters with English–Spanish bilingualism.

Isabel Allende, pictured on the cover of her biography.

Isabel Allende (1942–)

Born in Lima to Chilean parents, Allende was raised from the age of three by her divorced mother in Santiago, Chile. In Santiago, Allende became a journalist and editor of the magazine *Paula* and also worked in television. Her family's work in politics and diplomacy resulted in her exile after her relative, President of Chile Salvador Allende, was assassinated. Her significant literary career was launched while she resided in exile in Venezuela; it was there that she published her most successful novel, *La casa de los espíritus* (*The House of the Spirits*, 1980), which made her an international literary superstar. Other novels followed, *De amor y sombra* (*Of Love and Shadows*, 1984), and *Eva Luna* (1988), in which her credentials as a feminist were underscored. In 1988, she married her second husband, William Gordon, and made a transition to living in the United States. In the San Francisco Bay Area, she has continued her productivity, also making a transition to immigrant both as an individual and as a writer. Her latest three novels relate to California in one way or another: *El plan infinito* (*The Infinite Plan*, 1991), *Hija de la fortuna* (*The Daughter of Fortune*, 1999) and *Retrato en sepia* (*Portrait in Sepia*, 2000). In 1996, Allende became the first Hispanic writer to win the prestigious Harold Washington Award for Literature, presented in Chicago on May 3. The next day, she received an honorary doctorate from Columbia College in Chicago.

Alurista (Alberto Baltazar Urista, 1947–)

Alurista, born in Mexico City, is considered one of the pioneers of Chicano literature. Alberto Baltazar Urista spent his early years in the states of Morelos and Guerrero. At age thirteen he immigrated to the United States with his family, which settled in San Diego, California. He began writing poetry at an early age, and was a restless and widely read student. He entered Chapman College in 1965 and transferred to and graduated from San Diego State University in 1970 with a B.A. in psychology. He later obtained an M.A. from that institution and a Ph.D. in literature from the University of California at San Diego in 1983. Around 1966 he began writing poetry seriously for publication and assumed the pen name of Alurista, which is virtually the only name he uses to this date.

Alurista, one of the first poets to support the Chicano Movement through his poetry, was the writer and signer of important manifestos of the movement, as well as a founder of the Movimiento Estudiantil Chicano de Aztlán (MECHA, Chicano Student Movement of Aztlán) in 1967. He was also one of the first to establish the concept of Aztlán in literature, which forecasts a return to the glories of Aztec civilization by the Chicanos in the mythic homeland of the Aztecs, what is today roughly the five southwestern states in the United States.

Alurista is a prolific and talented poet, and a pioneer of bilingualism in Chicano poetry. Throughout his career his study of the Nahuatl and Mayan languages and mythology has enriched his poetic works and inspired his promotion of the ideology of Aztlán. But it is his bilingualism that has opened new frontiers in poetry, with his free experimentation in combining the sounds, meanings, and graphic representations of Spanish and English in the same poem, quite often achieving surprising and beautiful effects. Alurista has published the following books of poetry: *Floricanto en Aztlán* (1971), *Nationchild Plumaroja, 1967–1972* (1972), *Timespace Huracán: Poems, 1972–1975* (1976), *A'nque* (Although, 1979), *Spik in Glyph?* (1981), *Return: Poems Collected and New* (1982), *Et Tu . . . Raza* (1997), and *As Our Barrio Turns . . . Who the Yoke Be On?* (2000).

Julia Alvarez (1950–)

Novelist and poet, Julia Alvarez was born in the Dominican Republic to politically connected parents, who had to take the family into exile in New York City when she was ten years old. Alvarez graduated summa cum laude as an English major from Middlebury College in 1971, and in 1975 she earned a master's degree in creative writing from Syracuse University. She went on to develop a career as a poet and fiction writer and became a tenured professor at Middlebury College. Alvarez's narratives are loosely based on growing up between the two cultures of the United States and the Dominican Republic, although her perspective has always been one of growing up in privilege as the daughter of a successful doctor and politically connected exile. When her father became involved in an unsuccessful plot to overthrow the regime of dictator Rafael Leonidas Trujillo, he and his family had to leave the country. Julia Alvarez, thus, finished her education in the United States in English and creative writing and went on to become a professor of creative writing at Middlebury College in Vermont.

As a creative writer, she has received grants from the National Endowment for the Arts and the Ingram Merrill Foundation. After publishing poems and stories in literary magazines, she published a book of verse, *Homecoming* (1984), and her first novel, *How the García Girls Lost Their Accents* (1991); in so doing, she joined a wave of Hispanic writers breaking into mainstream presses with their tales of immigration and growing up within the United States. In 1994, she published the novel *In the Time of Butterflies*, which was later made into a feature film, and, in 1995, another collection of poems, *The Other Side* (*El Otro Lado*). In 1995, Alvarez published a collection of autobiographical essays, *Something to Declare: Essays*. Among Alvarez's other novels are *In the Name of Salomé* (2001) and *Before We Were Free* (2002). Alvarez has also written books for children, including *How*

Tía Lola Came to Visit/Stay (2000) and *Secret Footprints* (2001). In 2002, Alvarez joined many of the leading Hispanic novelists in writing for young readers with the publication of her young adult novel, *Before We Were Free*, centering on a plot to overthrow Dominican dictator Rafael Leonidas Trujillo, as seen through the eyes of a teenager.

Alba Ambert (1946–)

Born and raised in an infamous slum in San Juan, Puerto Rico, novelist and short story writer Alba Ambert was one of those "scholarship" children who through force of will and extraordinary intelligence are able to pull themselves up out of adversity and not only make something of themselves but contribute greatly to humanity. Ambert followed a round-about route to becoming a barrio teacher in Boston, and later a successful creative writer. She studied philosophy at the University of Puerto Rico, graduating with a B.A. in 1974 with great distinction; thereafter Ambert received an M.A. and Ed.D. in psycholinguistics from Harvard University in 1975 and 1980, respectively. Not only was Ambert a bilingual teacher, she also specialized in the teaching of bilingual special education students, curriculum writing, and theory—experiences reflected in the scholarly books that she has written.

In 1986, Ambert began teaching and researching in Europe, which also gave her time to devote to her creative writing. Interested in poetry and writing since her childhood, Ambert began publishing her poetry in Europe and then in the United States. In 1987 she published *Porque hay silencio*, a highly autobiographical novel charting the protagonist's psychological struggle to resolve her previous life of poverty with her present life as a highly successful woman of letters. The book proved to be a milestone for Ambert: It was awarded the Literature Prize of the Institute for Puerto Rican Literature. She later rewrote the book in English as *A Perfect Silence*, for which she won the first Carey McWilliams Award for Multicultural Literature, presented by the *Multicultural Review* in 1996. Alba Ambert creates penetrating psychological narrative in fiction, much of which is based on her rise out of abject poverty in Puerto Rico into the highest realms of academe in the United States and abroad.

A poet and scholarly writer as well, Ambert combines lyrical and rhapsodic narrative style with minute attention to detail. In 1997, Ambert published *The Eighth Continent and Other Stories*, a collection of nine narratives that run the gamut from the realism of underground Puerto Rican revolutionaries to a gloss on the legend of the Chupacabras.

Rudolfo A. Anaya (1937–)

Novelist Rudolfo A. Anaya was born in the village of Pastura, New Mexico, on October 30, 1937, in surroundings similar to those celebrated in his famous novel about growing up in the rural culture of New Mexico, *Bless Me, Ultima*. He attended public schools in Santa Rosa and Albuquerque and earned both his B.A.

(1963) and his M.A. (1968) in English from the University of New Mexico. In 1972 he also earned an M.A. in guidance and counseling from the same university. From 1963 to 1970 he taught in the public schools, and in 1974 he became a member of the English Department of the University of New Mexico.

With the success of his writing career, Anaya rose to become the head of the creative writing program at the University of New Mexico. Included among his many awards are the following: an honorary doctorate from the University of Albuquerque, the New Mexico Governor's Award for Excellence, the President's National Salute to American Poets and Writers in 1980, and the Premio Quinto Sol in 1972 for his novel, *Bless Me, Ultima*. Anaya is also a fellow of the National Endowment for the Arts and the Kellogg Foundation, through whose auspices he has been able to travel to China and other countries for study.

Anaya is very much a believer and promoter of a return to pre-Columbian literature and thought through the reflowering of Aztec civilization in Aztlán, the mythic homeland of the Aztecs that corresponds to the five states of today's Southwest. He sees his role in literature as that of the shaman; his task as a storyteller is to heal and reestablish balance and harmony. These ideas are present throughout his works, but are most successfully represented in his prize-winning novel, *Bless Me, Ultima*, in which the folk healer Ultima works to reestablish harmony and social order in the life of the Mares family and to bring psychological well-being to Antonio, the protagonist who is struggling to understand the roles of good and evil in life. In the rest of his work, Anaya has explored everything from the detective novel to folk legend and the broad epic of the development of the Southwest.

Anaya's other books are: *Heart of Aztlán* (1976), *Tortuga* (1979), *The Silence of the Llano* (1982), *The Legend of La Llorona* (1984), *The Adventures of Juan Chicaspatas* (1985), *A Chicano in China* (1986), *The Farolitos of Christmas* (a children's book, 1987), *Lord of the Dawn: The Legend of Quetzalcoatl* (1987), his sprawling epic novel *Albuquerque* (1992), his detective novel *Zia Summer* (1995), and *Río Grande Fall* (1996).

Gloria Anzaldúa (1942–)

Born on the Jesús María ranch settlement in south Texas, Anzaldúa has become a leading figure in Latina feminism and lesbian literature. Anzaldúa, who grew up doing agricultural field work on large farms and ranches, continued supporting herself in this manner until she graduated from Pan American University with a B.A. in 1969. In 1972, she received an M.A. in English from the University of Texas at Austin, after which she worked as a teacher, often for migrant children. During the late 1970s and early 1980s, Anzaldúa began teaching at colleges in California and studying for a Ph.D. program at the University of California at Santa Cruz, where she concentrated on feminist theory and cultural studies. Anzaldúa's first, highly influential book, *Borderlands/La Frontera: The New Mestiza* (1987), blends literary genres and the English and Spanish languages, as well as memoir and feminist analysis. Anzaldúa is also the editor of *Making Face, Making Soul/Haciendo Caras: Creative and Critical Perspectives by Feminists of Color*

(1990), which won the Lambda Literary Best Small Press Award. In addition, Anzaldúa has written children's books, including *Prietita Has a Friend* (1991), *Amigos del otro lado* (*Friends from the Other Side*, 1993), and *Prietita y La Llorona* (1996). She is the recipient of a National Endowment for the Arts Fellowship, the 1991 Lesbian Rights Award, and the 1992 Sappho Award of Distinction.

Julio G. Arce (1870–1926)

Among the cultural elites who disseminated the ideology of "México de afuera" was one political refugee who, through writing as well as publishing a newspaper, became immensely influential. Julio G. Arce was a newspaper publisher from Guadalajara who took up exile in San Francisco, vowing never to return to Mexico because he was so disillusioned with the Revolution. Arce's series, entitled "Crónicas Diabólicas" (Diabolical Chronicles), published under the pseudonym of Jorge Ulica, became the most widely syndicated *crónica* in the Southwest because of its ability to comment humorously on life in the Mexican immigrant community.

By and large, Ulica assumed the elite stance of satirist observing the human comedy as a self-appointed conscience for the community. Ulica's particular talents lay in caricature, in emulating the colloquialisms and popular culture of the working-class immigrant, and in satirizing the culture conflict and misunderstandings encountered by greenhorn immigrants from the provinces in Mexico. In "The Stenographer," he is not only scandalized but titillated by the Mexican or Mexican-American flapper whom he employs as a stenographer. The flapper was seen by *cronistas* as the most representative figure of American female liberation and loose morality. Hispanic women who adapted their dress and customs were subjected to the harshest censure as men sought to preserve the male prerogatives and power.

Reinaldo Arenas (1943–1990)

Cuban novelist, poet, and memoirist, Reinaldo Arenas is best known as a severely persecuted writer under the Fidel Castro regime who became an exile in the United States and eventually died of AIDS. Born in rural Oriente Province, Arenas was raised in poverty by his mother and a succession of other women; he nevertheless became a poet in childhood and, at age 19, won a scholarship to the University of Havana. While there, he published his first novel, *Celestino antes del alba* (1967; *Singing from the Well*, 1987). When his award-winning biography of Friar Servando Teresa de Mier was refused publication by government authorities, Arenas began sending his works abroad to avoid state-sponsored censorship. After publishing two books in Mexico, his international reputation began to increase and, in 1969, critics in France named him the best foreign novelist.

Arenas was continuously persecuted by Cuban authorities for his homosexuality and his literary work. In 1970, Arenas was sent to a sugar plantation for forced labor. While there he wrote a poem about the sugar mill; the poem was smuggled out of the country to be published in Spain. His next novel, *Otra vez el mar*

(Once again the Sea), went through two editions (1969, 1971) in Cuba, which were taken out of circulation by authorities. It was eventually republished in 1982 and translated to English as *Farewell to the Sea* in 1986. From 1974 to 1976, Arenas was imprisoned on moral charges; he was not allowed to leave prison until he confessed to having conducted counterrevolutionary activities and swearing to write only "optimistic" novels.

In 1980, Arenas went into exile in the United States, eventually ending up in New York, where he was able to publish new work freely and reissue some of his previously proscribed writing. Arenas' writing was supported in 1982 with a Guggenheim Fellowship and in 1987 with a Woodrow Wilson Fellowship. In 1993, Arenas published *Asalto (Assault)*, a passionate attack on Fidel Castro and post-revolutionary Cuba. Arenas' most known work—probably because it was made into an award-winning movie in 2000—was his posthumously published autobiography, *Antes que anochezca* (1993; *Before Night Falls*, 1994), which documented not only his trials in Cuba, but also his continued unhappiness in the United States. The book also announced his imminent suicide.

Ron Arias (1941–)

Born in Los Angeles, California, Ron Arias was raised principally by his maternal grandmother since his parents were constantly on the move because of his father's military career. After becoming interested in journalism in high school, Arias furthered his study of that field at universities in the United States, Argentina, and Spain. Sent to Argentina with an Inter-American Press Association scholarship, Arias began publishing important series of articles in the *Buenos Aires Herald*. After a stint in Peru with the Peace Corps, Arias returned to California in 1967 to continue his education and write for several newspapers. During the 1970s, Arias published short stories in magazines throughout the United States and emerged as an important Chicano author. In 1975, he published his magic realist novel *The Road to Tamazunchale*, which was nominated for a National Book Award. During the 1980s and 1990s, Arias concentrated on his journalism, serving as a senior editor of *People* magazine and writing non-fiction; in 1989, he authored a non-fiction documentary, *Five against the Sea*, about a group of castaways.

Franca de Armiño (dates unknown)

Franca de Armiño (possibly a pseudonym) was a Puerto Rican journalist, essayist, and playwright active during the 1920s and 1930s in New York. While her name is mentioned a number of times in the newspapers of her era, in which her essays appeared sporadically, all we know is that Franca de Armiño was a labor organizer and a columnist for *Gráfico* (Graphic) newspaper. Her major mark on literary history to date was the production and publication of her play, *Los Hipócritas* (The Hypocrites), issued in hardcover in 1937. *Los Hipócritas* debuted in three performances at the Park Palace Theatre in New York on April 15 and 16, 1933, produced by the Compañía Manuel Santigosa. It is a social drama in four acts and eight scenes, which the author dedicated to the oppressed of the world and to those who work for social renovation. Obvious from the play is the fact that she was a socialist, this possibly accounting for her writing under a pseudonym, as well as for the dearth of data on her life.

Mariano Azuela (1873–1952)

Mariano Azuela, one of Mexico's greatest novelists and chroniclers of the Mexican Revolution, was born on January 1, 1873, in Lagos de Moreno, Jalisco, Mexico. Educated as a physician (University of Guadalajara, M.D., 1898), Azuela pursued his career as a writer while practicing medicine until his death of a heart attack on March 1, 1952. Azuela's early career as a writer, in fact, was developed while participating in the Revolution first hand as a physician in the army of Francisco "Pancho" Villa. Azuela wrote more than forty novels, most of them based on Mexico's political life from the point of view of a skeptic and critic bent on reforming social and political life in his native land.

In many of his works, he documents the loss or corruption of the ideals that were fought for during the Revolution. Azuela's keen ear for dialog and deft appropriation of characters from social reality contributed to recognition of grass-roots Mexican culture that had not appeared in Mexican letters before, especially within the context of political analysis through literature.

True to a tradition of Hispanics writing in exile, Azuela's greatest and most renowned novel, *Los de abajo (The Underdogs)*, was written while he was a fugitive in El Paso, Texas. Published in 1915, *Los de abajo* was the first and most important in a long line of novels of revolution published in exile, and is also an important work in the history of Hispanic exile literature. In the novel, Azuela examines the Revolution through the eyes of a common soldier and ultimately condemns the uncontrollable whirlwind of violence that the Revolution had become. Azuela's condemnation was a pointed indictment of the forces of corruption and greed in converting the Revolution into the slaughter of those it was meant to protect and vindicate, including the rural, grass-roots protagonist, who is ultimately killed on the very spot where his involvement in the struggle began.

Throughout his career Azuela was a productive novelist. His other works include *María Luisa* (1907), *Los fracasados* (The Failures, 1908), *Mala yerba* (Bad Weed, 1909), *Andrés Pérez* (1911), *Sin amor* (Without Love, 1912), *Los caciques* (The Bosses, 1917), and many others.

Jimmy Santiago Baca (1952–)

Jimmy Santiago Baca is one of the most successful Chicano poets to come out of the oral tradition, tempered by prison experiences and the Chicano Movement; in this and other aspects, his background is similar to that of Ricardo Sánchez. Baca was born in Santa Fe, New Mexico, in 1952 to Mexican and Apache-Yaqui parents who abandoned him to be raised first by his Indian grandparents and then in an orphanage. In 1973, Baca was sentenced to five years imprisonment for narcotics possession. While in a maximum security prison in Arizona, Baca taught himself to read and write and passed his G.E.D. exam. In prison, Baca discovered poetry and began penning his first compositions. While he was still serving time, *Mother Jones* magazine published his first poems.

By the time of his release in 1978, his first book of poems, *Immigrants in Our Own Land*, had been accepted for publication by the prestigious Louisiana State University Press, which issued the book in 1979. Baca's poems were highly polished but naturalistic, and met with immediate critical approval; the accolades from mainstream critics expanded with his next books: *What's Happening* (1982), *Martin and Meditations on the South Valley* (1987), and *Black Mesa Poems* (1989). In 1993, Baca also published a book of autobiographical essays, *Working in the Dark: Reflections of a Poet in the Barrio*, and, in 1993, wrote a screenplay for a film, *Bound by Honor*, which was released by Disney's Hollywood Pictures. His other books include *A Place to Stand* (2001) and *Healing Earthquakes: A Love Story in Poems* (2001). For *Black Mesa Poems*, Baca became the first Hispanic poet to win the important Wallace Stevens Poetry Award. Baca has served as a poet in residence at Yale University and the University of California at Berkeley.

Pura Belpré (1919–1985)

Born in Cidra, Puerto Rico, Belpré became a pioneering children's librarian in New York City, where she also established a successful career as the author of books for children. In her writing, she often adapted Puerto Rican folk tales to English-language children's book format, always highlighting the moralistic values to be learned from these tales. Belpré came to the United States in 1920 and studied library science at the New York Public Library School and at Columbia University. As a librarian, she began telling stories to children, often illustrating them through puppet shows.

Belpré eventually began writing down her stories and published more than a dozen children's books, first with a small press, Warne, and later with many of the mainstream commercial publishers of children's literature. Her full-length young adult novel, *Firefly Summer*, which recreates life and culture in Puerto Rico at the turn of the twentieth century, was not published during her lifetime, because it was written during World War II, when there was a shortage of paper and a cutback in publishing; it was first issued some fifty years later, in 1997, by the Recovering the U.S. Hispanic Literary Heritage Project.

Among her best-known children's books are *Perez and Martina* (1932), *The Tiger and the Rabbit* (1946), and *Juan Bobo and the Queen's Necklace: A Puerto Rican Folk Tale* (1962). Belpré also had a rewarding career in translating English-language children's books to Spanish for major publishing houses. Reforma, the organization of librarians serving Hispanic communities, annually confers an award for children's literature in her honor.

Mario Bencastro. Photo by Luís Salvatierra.

Mario Bencastro (1949–)

Born in Ahuacapán, El Salvador, Bencastro has become the leading novelist of Salvadoran immigration to the United States. Initially trained as a painter, Bencastro gave up his brushes and canvas when he felt they were incapable of recording and expressing the tragedy of civil wars in his country. He began writing stories about the wars and immigrated to the United States in 1978, the same year he experienced the highest success as a painter in El Salvador when the National Exposition Hall presented twenty-five of his paintings.

From 1979 on, Bencastro has concentrated on writing to reflect the social and political life of his communities, both in El Salvador and here in the United States. In 1989, his first novel, *Disparo en la catedral (A Shot in the Cathedral)*, was a finalist in the Novedades-Diana International Literary Prize and was published in the original Spanish in Mexico. His short fiction collection, *Arbol de la vida: Historias de la Guerra Civil (Tree of Life: Stories of the Civil War)* was published in Spanish in El Salvador in 1993; some of the stories were later transformed into plays and staged and others were chosen for various anthologies. His best known novel, *Odisea del Norte (Odyssey to the North)*, appeared in 1999, is a classical novel of immigration, following economic and political refugees from their homes in Central America and Mexico into poor-paying and hazardous jobs in the Washington, DC, area. All three of his books have been translated into English and published in the United States in both English and Spanish-language editions.

Sandra Benítez (1941–)

Benítez was born Sandy Ables in Washington, DC. She claims midwestern (her father was a diplomat from the American Midwest) and Puerto Rican (her mother was Puerto Rican) descent, but spent ten years of her childhood in El Salvador, where her father was a diplomat. When she was fourteen, Benítez was sent back to the United States to become "Americanized"; she went to high school and college in Missouri, where she received B.S. (1962) and M.A. (1974) degrees from Northeast Missouri State University. Benítez did not start writing until she was 39, when she began attending creative writing courses.

The writings of Sandra Benítez focus on the civil war in El Salvador. She examines this war by writing about the everyday life of people of different classes from the perspective of common folk and their suffering. Her first novel, *A Place Where the Sea Remembers* (1993), which covers five decades of life in El Salvador, received the Barnes and Noble Discover Award and the Minnesota Book Award. Her second novel, *Bitter Grounds* (1997), was awarded the American Book Award. In 2000, she published a third novel, *The Weight of All Things*.

Diane Gonzales Bertrand (1956–)

Bertrand is the most prolific author of Hispanic children's literature, producing books for three age groups: children learning to read, middle readers, and young adults. Born on March 26, 1956, and raised in San Antonio, Texas, where she obtained a bachelor's degree in English from the University of Texas at San Antonio (1978) and a master's in English from Our Lady of the Lake University (1992), Bertrand taught in primary and secondary schools from 1979 to 1988, after which she began teaching creative writing at St. Mary's University. Among her novels are *Sweet Fifteen* (1995), *Alicia's Treasures* (1996), *Lessons of the Game* (1998), *Trino's Choice* (1999) and *Trino's Time* (2001). Her children's picture books include *Sip, Slurp, Soup, Soup/Caldo, Caldo, Caldo* (1997), *Family, Familia* (1999), *The Last Doll* (2000), and *The Empanadas that Abuela Baked* (2003). Among her various awards, *Trino's Choice* was named best book of the year by *Foreword Magazine* in 1999. Bertrand creates characters and plots grounded in Latino barrio life and culture, but always in a positive light that empowers readers to believe in their ability to control life forces and achieve their goals in a multicultural society.

Julia de Burgos (1914–1953)

The most recognized and respected female poet in Puerto Rican history, Julia de Burgos was born in Carolina, Puerto Rico, into an economically disadvantaged family that, despite its poverty, encouraged and supported Julia's education. In 1933, she received her degree in education and became a teacher in rural Puerto Rico, where her love of nature influenced her writing. Here and later in San Juan, she wrote many of the memorable poems that celebrate the Puerto Rican countryside.

Julia de Burgos published her first book, *Poemas exactos a mí misma* (Exact Poems to Myself), in 1937, and wrote children's plays while living and working in San Juan. Also in San Juan in 1938 she published one of her most successful books, *Poemas en veinte surcos* (Poems in Twenty Rows). In 1939, she was awarded the Institute of Puerto Rican Culture poetry prize for *Canción de la verdad sencilla* (The Song of Simple Truth). In 1940, Julia de Burgos moved

Julia de Burgos.

to New York where she became active in the Puerto Rican nationalist movement and was associated with the Juan Antonio Corretjer's liberationist newspaper, *Pueblos Hispanos* (Hispanic Peoples), in which she published many of her most famous poems. She spent somewhat more than a year in Cuba and then returned to New York in 1942, where she experienced isolation, depression, and alcoholism for the next eleven years. In 1946 she received the prize for journalism from the Puerto Rican Literature Institute for an editorial she wrote in *Pueblos Hispanos*. In 1953, her body was found on a New York City street without any identification. Today she is celebrated for her elegant lyricism, her commitment to freedom, women, and her country.

María Amparo Ruiz de Burton. *See* page 144

Fabiola Cabeza de Vaca (1894–1991)

Fabiola Cabeza de Vaca was born into a New Mexico ranch family. She received her teaching degree from New Mexico Normal School in 1921, and later a degree in home economics from New Mexico State University. She became a renowned nutritionist, working on Indian reservations and for the United Nations in Mexico. Cabeza de Vaca took pen to hand to record the culinary heritage of New Mexico, a mission that she accomplished with various unconventional cookbooks such as *The Good Life* (1949), in which she provided stories and descriptions of folk life and ritual in addition to recipes; she thus memorialized the almost forgotten and fast-disappearing culture of the *Nuevomexicanos* and the role that women played in this culture. In *We Fed Them Cactus* (1954), Cabeza de Vaca recreated the life and customs of the first Hispanics to settle on the New Mexico plains and documented how much was lost with the coming of the Anglo-Americans.

Lydia Cabrera (1900–1991)

Short story writer and folklorist Lydia Cabrera was born on May 20, 1900, in Havana, Cuba. She immigrated to the United States in 1960 after the Cuban Revolution triumphed. Throughout her career both in Cuba and in Miami, where she resided after 1960, Cabrera collected, studied, and published Afro-Cuban legends and tales. She also studied and documented Náñigo secret societies and other manifestations of African religious and Catholic syncretism. Most of Cabrera's fiction is also based on the Afro-Cuban folklore that surrounded her when she was growing up. In addition, her narrative style is direct and also owes much to the modes of oral performance and delivery of Afro-Cuban folklore.

In both Cuba and the United States, Cabrera's work has had an enriching impact on literature by introducing the themes and culture of a previously ignored and misunderstood base of Cuban and Caribbean literature and culture. Her groundbreaking first collection, *Cuentos negros de Cuba* (Black Tales from Cuba) was published in Havana in 1940, although it was written and already circulating as early as 1936. Among her most important fiction works are the following: *Ayapá: Cuentos de Jicotea* (Ayapá: Stories from Jicotea) in 1971, *Francisco y Francisca: Chascarillos de negros viejos* (Francisco and Francisca: The Spice Anecdotes of Old Black Folk) in 1976, and *Cuentos para adultos, niños y retrasados mentales* (Stories for Grown-Ups, Children and the Mentally Retarded) in 1983.

Rafael Campo (1964–)

Born in Dover, New Jersey, to an Italian-American mother and a Cuban father, Campo attained a prestigious and privileged education, earning the degree of medical doctor from Harvard Medical School (1992) and serving as a Rhodes Scholar at Oxford University (1986). Since graduating from Harvard, he has served as a researcher and working doctor in Boston-area hospitals. His career as a poet began as an undergraduate at Amherst College, where he created a collection of poems as an honors thesis in creative writing, while also majoring in neuroscience. His career has been replete with writing awards, including a George Starbuck Writing Fellowship to Boston University (1990), the Agni Poetry Prize (1991), and *The Kenyon Review* Writer of the Year award (1992).

Rafael Campo.

Campo has published his poems and belles lettres in numerous magazines, including *The Paris Review*, *The Partisan Review*, and *Prairie Schooner*. His first collection of poems, *The Other Man Was Me: A Voyage to the New World* (1990), explored Latino ethnicity, gay identity, the responsibility of doctors in the age of AIDS, and the meaning of family. It won the National Poetry Series 1994 Open Competition. It was also a finalist for the American Library Association's Gay, Lesbian and Bisexual Book Award (1995), among others. Campo's other poetry collections include: *What the Body Told* (1996), a Lambda Literary Award winner, and *Diva* (1999). In 1996, Campo published a prose collection, *The Poetry of Healing*, also a Lambda Award winner.

Luisa Capetillo (1879–1922)

Puerto Rican labor leader and feminist Luisa Capetillo was born in Arecibo, where she received her early education in a private school and won prizes in grammar, history, and geography. Shortly after graduating, she worked as a journalist and labor organizer. In 1912, she lived in New York City and, in 1913, she moved to Ybor City, Florida, to organize cigar workers. From 1914 to 1915, she lived in Cuba, presumably continuing her organizing among cigar workers. Thereafter, she returned to Puerto Rico and became involved in the labor and feminist movements as a socialist. She was particularly outstanding in militating for women's suffrage. She is known as the first woman in Puerto Rico to dress in pants in public, an exterior sign of her rebellion. She advocated free love, had children out of wedlock, and worked for a society without social classes.

Luisa Capetillo was the founder and editor of the magazine *La mujer* (Woman) and authored various books detailing her philosophy: *Ensayos libertarios* (Libertarian Essays, 1909), *La humanidad en el futuro* (Humanity in the Future, 1910), *Mi opinión sobre las libertades, derechos y deberes e la mujer* (My Opinion on the Liberties, Rights and Duties of Women, 1911), and *Influencia de las ideas modernas* (The Influence of Modern Ideas, 1916). Included in the books are essays, poems, and plays that were published in Hispanic labor newspapers; the plays were presumably performed at labor and political organizations. She died of tuberculosis in Río Piedras, Puerto Rico, in 1922.

Adolfo Carrillo (1865–1926)

A journalist persecuted by the government of Mexican dictator Porfirio Díaz, Adolfo Carrillo settled in San Francisco, California, where in 1885 he founded *La República* (The Republic) newspaper; he lived the rest of his life in the Bay area, where he continued working as a journalist, running his own printing establishment, and writing books. His book *Cuentos californianos* (California Stories), first published in the early 1920s, indicates the degree to which he identified with the Hispanic background of California and the Southwest. In many stories from that book Carrillo evokes the pastoral life on the large haciendas, the adventure and ever-present danger of pirates and bandits, and the rowdy, cosmopolitan atmosphere of San Francisco during early statehood.

Ana Castillo (1953–)

Born in Chicago to working-class Mexican-American parents, Castillo made her way into print during the 1970s as a Chicana feminist poet, first in such magazines as *Revista Chicano-Riqueña* (Chicano-Puerto Rican Review), and later by self-publishing her own chapbooks, *Otro Canto* (Another Song, 1977) and *The Invitation* (1979). In 1984, Castillo published her first full-length collection of poems, *Women Are Not Roses*, with Arte Público Press, which launched her soon-to-be extensive touring career. During the late 1980s, Castillo developed into a respected fiction writer, publishing novels with the independent small press, Bilingual Review Press, and later with W. W. Norton: *The Mixquiahuala Letters* (1986), *So Far from God* (1994), *Loverboys* (1997), and *Peel My Love like an Onion* (2000). In 1995, Castillo published a feminist tract, *Massacre of the Dream-*

ers: Essays on Xicanisma, which is often cited along with her work on the Spanish version of *This Bridge Called My Back*, as a standard text on Chicana feminist and literary perspectives.

As a Chicana feminist, Castillo has stated, "Part of the problem for women, I think all women in this society, but I was focusing on the women of my own culture, has been the taking away of our sense of self on many different levels. One of them is our sense of self psychologically, another one is physically, what we call spiritually. Your soul. Your center. And the history of our selves as sexual beings." In her writing, Castillo strives to restore that sense of self to Chicanas and Latinas.

Lorna Dee Cervantes (1954–)

In 1992, Mexican American poet Lorna Dee Cervantes became the first Hispanic writer to win the prestigious Paterson Poetry Prize, for her second book, *From the Cables of Genocide: Poems of Love and Hunger*. It was also awarded the Latin American Writers Institute Award that same year. Cervantes is the most celebrated Hispanic female poet of the United States. Although she is the author of only two books, the result of some twenty-five years of work, Cervantes' poems are so finely crafted and insightful of Mexican American and women's culture that they are the most reprinted in anthologies and textbooks of any Hispanic woman writer's.

Of Mexican and Amerindian ancestry, poet Lorna Dee Cervantes was born into a very poor family in the Mission District of San Francisco, California. Despite this poverty, she was able to discover the world of books at a very early age. Lorna began writing poetry when she was six years old; poems written when she was fourteen were eventually published in a magazine after Cervantes had established her career as a writer. In 1990, she left her Ph.D. studies in philosophy and esthetics at the University of California, Santa Cruz, before finishing her dissertation. She then went on to teach creative writing at the University of Colorado in Boulder.

Cervantes' early career as a poet achieved recognition in 1974 when her work was published in *Revista Chicano-Riqueña*. She was one of the first Chicana poets to achieve publication and quickly assumed leadership in the literary movement by founding and editing a literary magazine, *Mango*, out of San Jose. Her work was quickly circulated throughout the Chicano literary movement and soon began to appear in anthologies and textbooks nationwide. Many of these early movement poems, dealing with identity and roots, became part of *Emplumada* (Plumed, 1981), Cervantes's first collection of poems, published by the prestigious University of Pittsburgh Press Poetry Series. The predominant themes include culture conflict, oppression of women and minorities, and alienation from one's roots. Cervantes's poetry is very well-crafted and has the distinction of using highly lyrical language while at the same time being direct and powerful. Cervantes's second book, *From the Cables of Genocide: Poems of Love and Hunger*, which is very much the work of a mature poet, deals with the great themes of life, death, social conflict, and poverty.

Eusebio Chacón (1870–1948)

Journalist, poet, and civic leader Eusebio Chacón was known as a great orator, especially when it came to defending the language and cultural rights of the native New Mexicans. Born in Penasco, New Mexico, Chacón moved to Colorado with his family at an early age. He returned to New Mexico to study at the Jesuit Las Vegas College; in 1889, he received a degree in law from the University of Notre Dame, in Indiana. He is the author of two of the earliest Spanish-language novels to be written by native New Mexicans: *El hijo de la tempestad* (Son of the Tempest) and *Tras la tormenta la calma* (Calm after the Storm), both published in 1892 by the newspaper *El Boletín Popular* (The Popular Bulletin). The first deals with a realistic portrait of a bandit, whose crimes seem to be insignificant when compared to those of politicians. The second is a romantic novel about a pair of lovers. The novels have a pastoral setting, perhaps reminding the reader of idyllic life before the coming of the Anglo-Americans to the New Mexico territory.

Felipe Maximiliano Chacón (1873–19??)

Born into a wealthy and powerful New Mexico family, Chacón was the son of Urbano Chacón, the New Mexico superintendent of schools and journalist. Felipe was educated in Santa Fe public schools and at the College of St. Michael. He was a poet, essayist, and prose writer. From 1911 to 1914, he was the associate editor of Las Vegas, New Mexico's *La Voz del Pueblo* (The People's Voice), then went on in 1914 to found *El Faro del Río Grande* (The Rio Grande Beacon), and later served as editor of *El Independiente* (The Independent), *El Eco del Norte* (The Northern Echo), and *La Bandera Americana* (The American Flag). In 1924, Chacón published his *Obras de Felipe Maximiliano Chacón, el cantor neomexicano: poesía y prosa* (Works of Felipe Maximiliano Chacón, the New Mexico Singer: Poetry and Prose), which represents a selection of works created by him over a period of forty years. Part One contains fifty-six original poems and seven poems translated from English and American poets; Part Two contains two stories and a short novel. His works are thematically diverse, running the gamut from love and religion to politics.

Father Angélico Chávez (1910–)

The greatest religious poet among Hispanics in the United States, Father Angélico Chávez was born on April 10 in Wagonmound, New Mexico. He was raised in Mora and attended St. Francis Seminary in Cincinnati, Ohio, and colleges in the Midwest. Chávez was the author of some nineteen books, and was also an historian of his order and of the Catholic Church in New Mexico. What unifies Chávez's large output as a poet and historian is his interest in New Mexico's past and his own Catholicism. Beginning as a religious poet, he later took an interest in historical fiction and, finally, in the history of the region itself, as in his most famous historical essay, *My Penitente Land: Reflections on Spanish New Mexico* (1947). Chávez's reputation as a creative writer rests upon an important body of poetic works that include *Clothed with the Sun* (1939), *Eleven Lady Lyrics and Other Poems* (1945), *The Single Rose; The Rose Unica and Commentary of Fray Manuel de Santa Clara* (1948), and *The Virgin of Port Lligat* (1959). Although Chavez's poetry and all of his works are grounded in New Mexican Catholicism, his poems are not local color pieces celebrating New Mexico's picturesque landscape; instead they depict Chavez's inner life.

Father Angélico Chávez.

Denise Chávez (1948–)

Denise Chávez is a talented actress and a prolific playwright, but it is as a novelist that she has gained a deserved place in Chicano literature. Born on August 15, 1948, in Las Cruces, New Mexico, Chávez was raised principally by her mother, Delphina, a teacher; her father had abandoned the family while she was still young. After attending schools and colleges in Las Cruces, Chávez obtained a master's degree in theater arts from Trinity University in San Antonio, Texas, in 1974, and a master's in creative writing from the University of New Mexico in 1984.

As a playwright and fiction writer, Chávez has received numerous awards and fellowships, including the Steele Jones Fiction Award in 1986, National Endowment for the Arts fellowships in 1981 and 1982, and a Rockefeller Foundation fellowship in 1984. Despite Chávez's high productivity as a playwright, it is her works of fiction that have garnered the most attention. Chávez has published short stories in magazines and three novels: *The Last of the Menu Girls* (1986), *Face of an Angel* (1993), and *Loving Pedro Infante* (2001).

For Chávez, literature is very much the art of writing about lives, about individuals and the stories they have to tell. Her three novels present a series of lives, or characters, talking for themselves in idiosyncratic southwestern dialects, within a loose biographic structure. In the case of her first novel, the unifying structure is the life of Rocío Esquivel who, through a series of interconnected stories, gains maturity by rebelling against the social roles created for her. *Face of an Angel* on the other hand centers on the life of a waitress and the unfortunate and tragicomic amorous relationships that she has with men. In the midst of the narration Chávez brings in various types of unlikely elements, such as a manual on how to become a good waitress that the protagonist is writing. In *Loving Pedro Infante*, Chávez's emphasis is again on the small people and their prosaic lives.

Sandra Cisneros.

Sandra Cisneros (1954–)

Mexican-American poet Sandra Cisneros became the first Hispanic writer to win the prestigious MacArthur Award (1995). Cisneros is the short story writer, essayist, and poet who has brought Chicana writing into the mainstream of literary feminism. She is also the first Chicana writer to be published and promoted by mainstream commercial publishing houses. Born on December 20, 1954, in Chicago into a Mexican American working-class family, Cisneros nevertheless benefited from a private education, graduating with a B.A. in English from Loyola University (1976) and later with an M.F.A. in creative writing from the prestigious Iowa Workshop (1978).

Cisneros's first novel, *The House on Mango Street* (1983), remains her most important contribution in that it captured the hopes, desires, and disillusionment of a young female writer growing up in the city. In *Mango Street*, Esperanza Cordero functions in a similar manner to the unidentified narrator in Tomás Rivera's classic . . . *Y no se lo tragó la tierra* (. . . *And the Earth Did Not Devour Him*), observing the behavior and attitudes of the people who populate their environments. In Esperanza's urban Chicago world, children naively internalize the attitudes about gender and class of their adult Latino models; however, somehow the spirit of independence and creativity grows in Esperanza and leads her to escape the barrio in search of a house of her own—her own personality and identity—presumably through literature. Cisneros was awarded the American Book Award (1985) for *The House on Mango Street* and she began touring college campuses for readings. Her other awards include a Dobie-Paisano Fellowship (1986) and National Endowment for the Arts Writing Fellowships in Fiction and Poetry (1982, 1990).

Cisneros published her first full-length collection of poems, *My Wicked Wicked Ways*, in 1987 with an Hispanic feminist press, Third Woman Press, of Berkeley, California. In 1991, publishing giant Random House issued Cisneros' collection of essays and short stories, *Woman Hollering Creek and Other Stories*; it did not surpass the critical acclaim of *Mango Street*, which had assumed a secure place in college and high school curricula. In 2002, Cisneros published her long-awaited generational novel of Mexican immigration and accommodation in the United States: *Caramelo*. Using a woven Mexican shawl as a trope, Cisneros weaves the intricate tale of the various members of the Reyes family and their generational journey from Mexico City to the United States.

As a celebrated author, Cisneros has often been asked who her models were and for whom she writes. Her answer is: "You know who I think of? I think of a world reader. My standards are very high, and I really think of the writers I love the best. I'm trying to match them. And my favorite writers are, right now Merce Rodoreda, Grace Paley, Juan Rulfo, Manuel Puig, Marguerite Duras—these are my favorite writers. I'm trying to reach that world level. I think that we should always aim for that level."

Uva A. Clavijo (1944–)

Uva A. Clavijo (also known as Uva de Aragón) was born in Havana, Cuba, in 1944. After coming to Miami, Florida, with her refugee parents, Clavijo received her university education and began writing as a journalist for such exile newspapers as *Diario de las Américas* (The Americas Daily). She also published poetry and essays widely in the Cuban exile press and books in Spanish in the United States and abroad: *Eternidad* (Eternity, 1972), *Ni verdad ni mentira y otros cuentos* (Not Truth nor Lies and Other Stories, 1976), *No puedo más y otros cuentos* (I Can't Anymore and Other Stories, 1989), and *Memoria del silencio* (A Memory of Silence, 2002). Her poetry books include *Entre semáforos* (Between Stop Lights, 1980) and *Los nombres del amor* (The Names of Love, 1996), among others. Her books of essays include *El caimán ante el espejo. Un ensayo de interpretación de lo cubano* (The Gator in Front of the Mirror. An Essay Interpreting Cubanness, 1993) and *Alfonso Hernández Catá: Un escritor cubano, salmantino y universal* (Alfonso Hernéndez Catá: a Cuban Writer, Salamancan and Universal, 1996). Clavijo is a professor and adjunct director of the Cuban Research Institute at Florida International University.

Judith Ortiz Cofer (1952–)

Puerto Rican novelist, short story writer, and poet Judith Ortiz Cofer was born in Hormigueros, Puerto Rico, on February 24, 1952, into a family that was destined to move back and forth between Puerto Rico and Patterson, New Jersey, because of her father's career in the Navy. Upon her father's retirement from the Navy, the family moved to Augusta, Georgia, where Cofer attended both high school and Augusta College. After college, Cofer pursued further studies, obtaining an M.A. degree from Florida International University and receiving a fellowship for graduate work at Oxford University in England. Throughout her education, Cofer was a writer and, in 1980, began to receive recognition for her work, first with a fellowship from the Florida Arts Council, then

Judith Ortiz Cofer.

through other awards from the Bread Loaf Writers Conference (1981) and from the National Endowment for the Arts (1989). After a distinguished career as a creative writing professor at the University of Georgia, in 2000 Judith Ortiz Cofer accepted an endowed chair at Vanderbilt University in Nashville.

Cofer became the first Hispanic writer to receive a Special Citation from the PEN Martha Albrand Award for *Silent Dancing: A Remembrance of a Puerto Rican Childhood* (1990), which is a collection of autobiographical essays and poems. The book was also awarded the Pushcart Prize in the essay category, the New York Public Library System List of Best Books for the Teen Age, and its title essay was chosen by Joyce Carol Oates for *The Best American Essays* (1991). Cofer was also the first U.S. Hispanic to win the O. Henry Prize (1994) for the short story. In 1994, she also won the Anisfield-Wolf Award in Race Relations for her novel *The Latin Deli*. Cofer's two major works of poetry are *Reaching for the Mainland* and *Terms of Survival*, both published in 1987.

Cofer's well-crafted poetry reflects her struggle as a writer to create a history for herself out of the cultural ambiguity of a childhood lived between two lands, two cultures, and two languages. Through her poetry and her essays, such as those in *Silent Dancing*, she also explores from a feminist perspective her relationships with her father, mother, and grandmother, while also considering the different expectations for males and females in both Anglo-American and Hispanic cultures. Her novel *Line of the Sun* (1990) is based on her family's gradual immigration to the United States and chronicles the years from the Great Depression to the 1960s. Her young adult story collection, *The Year of Our Revolution* (1999), picks up where *Silent Dancing* left off, examining a young Latina's coming of age in Patterson and beginning to rebel against the old ways of her Hispanic family.

About her identity as a writer and her subject matter, Cofer has stated, "Some people try mightily to forget who they are and where they came from, and those people seem a little lost to me. It's important for the artist to retain some hold on her original self even if it is painful or unattractive. Even if it would be better to forget. How can you inject passion and purpose into your work if it has no roots?"

Jesús Colón (1901–1974)

A noted Puerto Rican journalist and political activist, Jesús Colón was born into a working-class, Afro-Puerto Rican family in Cayey, Puerto Rico. Colón's writings are considered to be landmarks in the development of Puerto Rican literature in the continental United States because he is one of the first writers to become well known through his use of English and because of his identification with the working class and his ideas on race. These three factors in the essays that he was already writing in the 1940s and 1950s make him a clear forerunner of the Nuyorican writers who began to appear two decades later.

Colón actually started writing in Spanish for Hispanic periodicals in New York in the second decade of the twentieth century. Having arrived in the city at age sixteen as a stowaway, Colón worked in a series of jobs that exposed him to the exploitation and abuse of immigrants, lower class, and unskilled workers. He became involved in literary and journalistic endeavors while working as a laborer, trying to establish a newspaper and writing translations of English-language poetry. As he strived to develop his literary and journalistic career, he encountered racial prejudice, mainly because of his dark skin color. Despite discrimination, Colón became active in community and progressive politics. After writing for many years in Spanish, in the late forties Colón became an English-language columnist for the *Daily Worker*, the publication of the national office of the Communist Party. Colón also founded and operated a publishing house, Hispanic Publishers (Editorial Hispánica), which issued history and literary books, as well as political information in Spanish. In 1952 and 1969, Colón ran for public office on the Communist Party ticket, but was unsuccessful.

Colón published a selection of his newspaper columns and essays in 1961 in book form under the title of *A Puerto Rican in New York and Other Sketches.* Two other collections have been published posthumously, *The Way It Was and Other Sketches* (1993) and *Lo que el pueblo me dice* (What the People Tell Me, 2001). In these essays, or sketches, as Colón preferred to call them, his major themes are (1) the creation and development of a political consciousness, (2) the development of Puerto Rican nationalism, (3) advocacy for the working-class poor, and (4) the injustices of capitalist society in which racial and class discrimination are all too frequent and individual worth does not seem to exist. The collections are richly expressive of a socially conscious and humanistic point of view.

Antonio Coronel (1817–1894)

Antonio Coronel, educator, politician, and man of letters and theater, was born in Mexico City. At the age of seventeen he moved with his parents to Los Angeles, Alta, California. Under Mexican rule, he served as a schoolteacher and on various civic commissions and boards. After the Mexican-American War, he continued his public service as an American citizen. During the Gold Rush, Coronel amassed riches, but returned to Los Angeles when faced with considerable discrimination against Mexicans in the gold fields. He returned to teaching and to various elected positions in city government, including that of mayor of Los Angeles. He also was a theatrical impresario and owner of the Teatro de la Merced (Merced Theater). Coronel wrote poetry, sometimes in honor of his theater's leading ladies, and memoirs of his life in California before the coming of the Anglo-Americans; however, some of the most engaging sections of his "Cosas de California" (Californiana, 1877), record the conflict with the Anglo newcomers. In 1867, he was elected state treasurer as a Democrat. He later was elected to the state senate. He died on April 17, 1894.

Lucha Corpi (1945–)

Born in the small tropical village of Jáltipan, Veracruz, Mexico, in 1945, Corpi married young and moved with her husband to Berkeley, California, when he

Lucha Corpi.

began his studies at the University of California. At the time of their emotional divorce in 1970, Corpi, too, was a student at the university and was heavily involved in the Free Speech Movement and the Chicano Civil Rights Movement. Corpi has remained politically active, which is evident in much of her creative writing. She eventually earned both a B.A. and an M.A. in comparative literature, and since 1977 has been a tenured teacher in the Oakland Public Schools Neighborhood Centers Programs, where she specializes in adult education. She is also a founding member of the cultural center, Aztlán Cultural, which later merged with a center for writers, Centro Chicano de Escritores.

During the 1970s, Corpi began publishing Spanish poetry in small magazines; it is a poetry luxuriant and sensual and reminiscent of her tropical upbringing. In 1976, a group of her poems, along with those of two other poets, was issued in book form in *Fireflight: Three Latin American Poets*. By 1980 Corpi's collected poems were published in her first book, *Palabras de mediodía* (*Noon Words*), along with their translations by Catherine Rodríguez-Nieto. In 1990, Corpi published a third collection, *Variaciones sobre una tempestad* (*Variations on a Storm*), again with translations of her poems by Rodríguez-Nieto. In the early 1980s, Corpi made the transition to prose and to writing in English with the publication of various short stories in magazines. In 1984, she published her first novel, *Delia's Song*, based on her involvement in the Chicano Movement and campus politics at the University of California. *Delia's Song* is one of the very few novels that deal with that historical period which is so important in the making of the modern Chicano.

It was not until 1992 that Corpi's writing career took another turn with her creation of an ongoing series of detective novels. In *Eulogy for a Brown Angel*, Corpi introduced the astute Chicana detective, Gloria Damasco, who unravels the mysterious assassination of a young boy during the 1970 Chicano Moratorium against the Vietnam War. Described as a feminist detective novel, *Eulogy* is fast-paced, suspenseful, and packed with an assortment of interesting characters. Her feminist protagonist, Gloria Damasco, is somewhat of a clairvoyant who is able to use more than reason and logic in solving a puzzling crime. *Eulogy* was awarded the PEN Oakland Josephine Miles award and the Multicultural Publishers Exchange Best Book of Fiction award. In 1995, Gloria Damasco returned in *Cactus Blood*, a mystery set against the background of the United Farm Workers Movement in California. *Cactus Blood* opens with a flashback to the 1970s when a young Gloria Damasco's investigation into the disappearance of a young woman begins with the 1973 United Farm Workers strike and boycott in the San Joaquin Valley and continues to an old native American ghost-dancing site in the Valley of the Moon. Historic settings, California panoramas, and Hispanic culture give texture to this suspenseful search for a ritualistic assassin. In 1999, Corpi continued with the series in *Black Widow's Wardrobe*, a mystery inspired in the Mexican rituals of the Day of the Dead, which leads Gloria Damasco once again into the historical past on a trip to Cuernavaca, Mexico, and indigenous culture.

Lucha Corpi's bilingual artistry has manifested itself differently from other writers, who either use Spanish-English code-switching or create two, separate versions of their works (one in Spanish, the other in English). Throughout the body of her highly symbolic, intimate poetry and in her short fiction for children, Corpi uses the language of her early upbringing and education in Mexico: Spanish. Her prose fiction, on the other hand, is written in the language of her professional life and education in California: English.

José Corrales (1937–2002)

Cuban playwright Corrales was the author of some twenty works for the stage, many of which were never performed or published because of the limited resources and facilities available to him in exile. During his long residence in New York, however, some of his more successful plays were produced, including *El espíritu de Navidad* (The Spirit of Christmas), *Juana Machete o la muerte en bicicleta* (Juana Machete or Death on a Bicycle), *Brillo funerario* (Funereal Shine), and *De cuerpo presente* (Present in Body). Corrales left Cuba in 1965 and wrote and published most of his poetry and plays while living in New York. Included among his books are *Razones y amarguras* (Reasons and Bitterness, 1978), and *Los trabajos de Gerión* (The Trials of Gerión, 1980). In 2001, Corrales was awarded the Palma Espinada Award by the Cuban American Cultural Institute in California, thus becoming recognized as one of the most distinguished writers of the Cuban expatriate community.

Juan Antonio Corretjer (1908–1985)

Born in Ciales, Puerto Rico, Corretjer's career as a poet began when he published his first poem at age twelve. By age seventeen, he was publishing verse in Puerto Rico's major magazines. In 1929 he began a career in journalism as a writer for *Democracia* (Democracy). Corretjer was a communist and militant nationalist, for which he was sentenced to federal prison for seven years (1935–1942); he was not allowed to return to Puerto Rico after his release in Georgia after serving five years of his term. He relocated to New York, where he continued his radical activities and published and edited *Pueblos Hispanos* (Hispanic Peoples), an anti-imperialist newspaper in which appeared columns by leading Puerto Rican writers in New York, such as Julia de Burgos and Jesús Colón. Over the years, his politics were softened and he was able to return to Puerto Rico in 1946, but he continued to pursue Puerto Rican independence and socialism. He was a poet of nationalism and Puerto Rican cultural identity, who cultivated such traditional forms as the *décima* with elegance. Among his most celebrated books are: *Amor de Puerto Rico* (Love of Puerto Rico, 1937), *Alabanza en la torre de Ciales* (Praise in the Ciales Tower, 1952) and *Yerba bruja* (Witch's Weed, 1957).

Guillermo Cotto-Thorner (1916–1983)

Born in Puerto Rico and a student for the ministry at the universities of Puerto Rico and Texas and at Columbia University, Cotto-Thorner was ordained a Baptist minister in 1942. Cotto-Thorner ministered to Hispanic populations in Milwaukee and East Harlem in New York City during the 1940s and 1950s. During this time, he also published numerous articles in Baptist and non-sectarian Spanish-language newspapers around the United States. His first two works are of a religious nature: the full-length *Camino de Victoria* (The Road to Victory, 1945) and the pamphlet *Conspiración católica romana contra la democracia* (The Roman Catholic Conspiracy against Democracy, 1948). His novels, *Trópico en Manhattan* (The Tropics in Manhattan, 1951) and *Gambeta* (1971), on the other hand, examine two aspects of immigration: respectively, the Puerto Rican community in East Harlem and Puerto Rico under the influence of Anglo-American immigration.

Victor Hernández Cruz (1949–)

Victor Hernández Cruz, the Nuyorican poet who was discovered as a precocious street poet while still in high school in New York, has become the most recognized and acclaimed Hispanic poet by the mainstream. Despite his early acceptance into creative writing circles, culminating with *Life* magazine's canonizing him in 1981 as one of the twenty-five best American poets, Hernández Cruz has resisted estheticism and academic writing to remain very much an oral poet, a jazz poet, a bilingual poet, a poet of the people and popular traditions, a poet of intuition and tremendous insight.

Victor Hernández Cruz was born on February 6, 1949, in Aguas Buenas, Puerto Rico. He moved with his family to New York's Spanish Harlem at the age of five. Cruz attended Benjamin Franklin High School, where he began writing poetry. In the years following graduation, his poetry began to appear in *Evergreen Review, New York Review of Books*, and many other magazines. Beginning in 1970, he worked with poetry-in-the-schools programs in New York, including the Teachers and Writers Collaborative. In 1973, Cruz left New York and took up residence in San Francisco, where he worked for the U.S. Postal Service and served as a visiting poet at area colleges. From 1973 to 1975, he took up the life of the traveling troubadour, covering the full expanse of the United States from Alaska and Hawaii to Puerto Rico, reading and performing his works while also continuing to write. Thereafter, he alternated living in San Francisco and Puerto Rico, dedicating himself mostly to writing and accepting engagements nationally to read from his works.

Hernández Cruz received fellowships from the National Endowment for the Arts and the Guggenheim Foundation in 1980 and 1991, respectively. His poetry books include *Papo Got His Gun* (1966), *Snaps: Poems* (1969), *Mainland* (1973), *Tropicalization* (1976), *By Lingual Wholes* (1982), *Rhythm, Content and Flavor* (1989), *Red Beans* (1994), *Panoramas* (1997), and *Maraca: New and Selected Poems, 1965–2000* (2001).

Juan Delgado (19??–)

Born in Mexico and raised in Colton, California, Delgado did not become a naturalized citizen until 1989. A graduate in English from California State University in 1983, Delgado received an M.F.A. in creative writing from the University of California at Irvine in 1985 and went on to make a life for himself as a professor and academic administrator. But his first love was poetry, and he has distinguished himself by publishing his poems in magazines throughout the United States and authoring three important collections of poems: *All Too Familiar* (2002), *El Campo* (1998), and *Green Web* (1994). In addition to various fellowships and distinctions, Delgado was the first Chicano to have a manuscript win the Contemporary Poetry Series contest, resulting in *Green Web* being published by the University of Georgia Press.

Abelardo Delgado (1931–)

Abelardo "Lalo" Delgado is one of the most renowned and prolific Chicano poets, a pioneer of bilingualism in Hispanic poetry and a consummate oral performer of his works. Delgado was born in the small town of La Boquilla de Conchos in northern Mexico on November 27, 1931. At age 12 he and his mother immigrated to El Paso, Texas. In El Paso, he lived in a poor Mexican barrio until 1969. Despite early problems in school with the English language, Delgado excelled as a student, and by graduation in 1950 from Bowie High School, he had become vice president of the National Honor Society chapter there. He went on to college while working at a variety of jobs and graduated from the University of Texas, El Paso, in 1962. Since that time he has earned his living as a counselor for migrant workers and as a teacher in Texas and later in Colorado.

During the height of the Chicano Movement in the late 1960s and throughout most of the 1970s, Delgado was also one of the most popular speakers and poetry readers in the Southwest, which translated into a life of frequent tours and engagements. Besides writing numerous poems, essays, and stories that have been published in literary magazines and anthologies nationwide, Delgado is the author of some fourteen books and chapbooks; many of these were published through his own small printing operation known as Barrio Press. Delgado's first book, *Chicano: 25 Pieces of a Chicano Mind* (1969), is his best known, containing many of the poems that were performed personally in the heat of the protest movement and that subsequently received widespread distribution through small community newspapers and hand-to-hand circulation throughout the Southwest. Poems such as his "Stupid America" not only embodied the values of life in the barrio but also called for the types of social reform that became anthems for the Chicano Movement. Other noteworthy titles include *It's Cold: 52 Cold-Thought Poems of Abelardo* (1974), *Here Lies Lalo: 25 Deaths of Abelardo* (1979), and his book of essays, *Letters to Louise* (1982), which ponders the feminist movement and the social roles of women and men, and was awarded the Premio Quinto Sol, the national award for Chicano literature. In all, Delgado is a remarkably agile bilingual poet, an outstanding satirist and humorist, an undaunted and militant protester and pacifist, and a warmhearted and loving narrator and chronicler of the life and tradition of his people.

Junot Díaz (1968–)

Born in the Dominican Republic, short story writer Díaz came to the United States with his parents when he was seven. Raised in a low-income neighborhood in northern New Jersey, he became a mill worker after high school, but soon decided to go on for a college education. He received a B.A. in

English from Rutgers University and a Master of Fine Arts Degree from Cornell University (1995). His short fiction has appeared in noteworthy literary magazines throughout the United States, and his debut collection of stories, *Drown* (1996), received national acclaim. Even before the publication of *Drown*, he had already been hailed as a great discovery based on a short story he published in *Story* magazine. He was soon named one of the "New Faces of 1996" and an "overnight literary sensation" by *Newsweek* because of his excellent short fiction. In *Drown*, his stories recount the immigrant experience with realism and humor, moving from the Dominican Republic to the barrios in New Jersey. Díaz has said of his creative process, "For me, it's like taking all of these different jagged pieces of art and making a really coherent collage, which is coherent but reminds us of where we individually came from."

Junot Díaz. Photo by Ken Schles.

Alirio Díaz Guerra (1862–c.1925)

Born in Sagamoso, Colombia, to a prominent political family, Díaz Guerra became involved in politics at a young age; he also was a creative writer from school age and by his teen years was publishing poetry in Colombian newspapers. By age 20, he published his collection of romantic poetry, *Ensayos literarios* (Literary Essays), and at age 22, he founded his own newspaper, *El Liberal*, which openly opposed the regime in power. Díaz Guerra soon became part of a revolution that resulted in his exile in Venezuela. In Venezuela, he again became involved in politics and was driven back into exile in 1895. This time, he and his family took refuge in New York City, where he would remain for the rest of his life, serving as a salesman of medical supplies and writing for Spanish-language periodicals.

In 1901, Díaz Guerra published two books of poems, *Nuevas poesías* (New Poems) and *Ecce homo* (Behold the Man). The latter book consisted of a long narrative poem of a religious, moralistic, and philosophical nature, and possibly led the way to his greatest contribution, which was the first ever Spanish-language novel of immigration to the United States, *Lucas Guevara* (1914), a moralistic narrative about a young greenhorn who comes to New York and is corrupted by this Sodom. Some scholars have noted that Díaz Guerra published other books before *Lucas Guevara*, but to date they have not been located. It is in *Lucas Guevara* that most of the conventions that will later dominate Hispanic immigrant literature appear: the hopes and then disillusionment of the immigrant, which lead either to his return to the homeland or death in the metropolis; the protest against mistreatment of immigrants; Hispanic nationalism in reaction to the riches and technological advances of the United States; and American women personifying all the ills of the metropolis and serving as temptresses for the Latin males. Among Díaz Guerra's missing books is *May*, a novel about society that arguably continues the trajectory of immigrant literature he began with his first novel.

Martín Espada (1957–)

Poet Martín Espada was born into a Puerto Rican family in Brooklyn, New York. After studying law, passing the bar, and working in the legal profession for some years, Espada gave up the law for poetry. A prolific writer, Espada has published well-received collections of his highly crafted verse, somewhat in the Nuyorican tradition: *A Mayan Astronomer in Hell's Kitchen: Poems* (2000); *Imagine the Angels of Bread* (1996), winner of an American Book Award; *City of Coughing and Dead Radiators* (1993); *Rebellion Is the Circle of a Lover's Hands* (1990); and *Trumpets from the Islands of Their Eviction* (1987). Espada published a prose collection, *Zapata's Disciple: Essays*, in 1998. Among the awards Espada received are the PEN/Voelker Award for Poetry, the Paterson Poetry Prize, and two fellowships from the National Endowment for the Arts. Espada is an associate professor of English at the University of Massachusetts at Amherst.

Conrado Espinosa (1897–1977)

Born in Zapotlán El Grande, Jalisco, Mexico, Espinosa was educated in Guadalajara to go into the teaching profession. As a university student in Mexico City, he shared his ideas about education with the famous rector José Vasconcelos, who as minister of education named Espinosa Mexico's director general of education in 1923. When Vasconcelos went into political exile in 1924, Espinosa fled with him and ended up in San Antonio, Texas, where he became the editor of *El Nacional* newspaper. It was there that in 1926 Espinosa published his most famous novel, *El sol de Texas* (The Texas Sun) through the publishing house of newspaper magnate Ignacio Lozano. *El sol de Texas* is a model novel of immigration, charting the trials and tribulations of a poor family seeking to make ends meet through farm labor under the unforgiving sun of Texas and the equally noxious social environment of exploitation and discrimination facing immigrant laborers.

During the 1920s, Espinosa traveled throughout the United States as a public speaker and writer for various Spanish-language newspapers and magazines, including Lozano's *La Prensa* (The Press) in San Antonio and *Don Quijote* in Santa Barbara, California. Caught up in the fervor of Mexicans fleeing religious persecution in Mexico during the Cristero War, Espinosa often wrote articles on religious topics and published his second novel on this theme: *El Rosal del Tepeyac* (The Rosebush at Mount Tepeyac). He returned to Mexico in 1930 and founded the Centro Escolar del Noroeste in Los Mochis, Sinaloa. His last book, a biography of a sixteenth-century Franciscan missionary, *Fray Sebastián de Aparicio, primer caminero mexicano* (Brother Sebastián de Aparicio, the First Mexican Traveler), was published in Mexico in 1959.

Sandra María Esteves (1948–)

Esteves was born on May 10, 1948, in New York City, the daughter of a Dominican garment worker and a Puerto Rican sailor. She received her early education at a Catholic boarding school, where her Spanish language and Hispanic culture were targeted for obliteration by the strict, Irish-American nuns. But that was on weekdays: her weekends were spent in the warmth and comfort of her Puerto Rican aunt's home. Thus, at an early age she discerned the language and culture conflicts that Hispanics experience in this country. Later in life these conflicts would form the basis for much of her poetry. Esteves studied art at the Pratt Institute in New York City, and when, after various interruptions, she graduated in 1978, her writing career was already firmly established. In the early 1970s, Esteves became part of the Civil Rights Movement and the movement to gain independence for Puerto Rico. In connection with the latter, she sang and recited her poetry with a socialist musical group, simply titled El Grupo, whose recordings became anthems for the independence movement. The recordings also effectively launched Esteves's career as a poet.

In the mid-1970s Esteves became involved in the Nuyorican Poets Cafe and the performance poetry it sponsored under the leadership of writers Miguel Algarín, Tato Laviera, and Miguel Piñero. In a literary movement heavily directed by males, Esteves became a beacon of feminism. Her work as a painter followed a similar course as her writing and she became affiliated with the Taller Boricua (Puerto Rican Workshop), a socially committed collective of graphic artists. After publishing numerous poems in magazines and anthologies, Sandra María Esteves published her first book, *Yerba Buena* (The Good Herb) in 1980 to resounding reviews. *Library Journal* named the book the best small press publication in 1981. The title refers to mint, an herb that in Caribbean culture has medicinal qualities; her tropical and urban poems are meant to heal or mend the rifts of culture and gender conflict among Latinos and Latinas.

Despite widespread interest among publishers in issuing her works, Esteves self-published her next collection of poems, *Tropical Rains* (1984), probably to control distribution herself. The book followed in the bilingual, urban vernacular of *Yerba Buena*, but did not have its impact. Esteves' latest work, *Bluestown Mockingbird Mambo* (1990), is a mature work that is a distillation of jazz and salsa, "sung" in a precisely stylized bilingualism and exuding a deep spirituality and humanism. Like her other works, the line structures and blank verse of the poetry demonstrate that they are meant to be recited and performed. Esteves's incantations come from both *santería* (an Afro-Catholic religion) and the cadences, threats, and caresses of speech heard in the Barrio. Esteves has also had a lateral career in theater, usually related in some way to her poetry as the African Caribbean Poetry Theater director from 1983 to 1990 and the director of The Family Repertory Company, beginning in 1990. Among her awards are the New York State Council on the Arts Poetry Fellowship in 1985; the Award for Outstanding Achievement in the Latino Community from New York University, 1991; and the Edgar Allan Poe Literary Award from the Bronx Historical Society, 1992.

Roberta Fernández (1940–)

Born and raised in Laredo, Texas, Fernández is completely bilingual and has been able to write equally well in English as in Spanish. After obtaining an associate arts degree from Laredo Junior College in 1960, Fernández went on to earn a master's in Spanish from the University of Texas in 1966, and a Ph. D. in romance languages and literature from the University of California in 1990. Since the 1960s, Fernández has taught Hispanic literature at colleges and universities around the United States.

Roberta Fernández.

Fernández is best known for her finely crafted short stories, which she writes in both languages. In 1991, her *Intaglio: A Novel in Six Stories*, based on the lives of six creative women of the border, won the Multicultural Publishers Exchange Award. In 2001, her Spanish re-creation of the same book was published as *Fronterizas: Una novela en seis cuentos*. Fernández is also a critic and literary historian who has edited noteworthy anthologies of Hispanic literature, such as *In Other Words: Literature by Latinas of the United States* (1994). She was also the founding coordinator of the first three issues of *Prisma: A Multicultural, Multilingual Women's Literary Review* (1979–80).

Roberto Fernández (1951–)

Through his novels, Roberto Fernández not only touches upon all of the taboo subjects in the Cuban community of Miami—the counterrevolutionary movement in the United States, racism, acculturation, and assimilation—but he helps the community to take them in a less serious vein and to laugh at itself. Born in Sagua la Grande, Cuba, on September 24, 1951, Fernández went into exile with his family at age eleven. Fernández became interested in writing as an adolescent, and this interest led him to college and graduate school. In 1978, he completed a Ph.D. degree in linguistics at Florida State University and began teaching as an assistant professor; by that time, he had already published two collections of stories: *Cuentos sin rumbo* (Directionless Tales, 1975) and *El jardín de la luna* (The Garden of the Moon, 1976).

Fernández is the author of three novels that have created for him the reputation of being a satirist of the Miami Cuban community. In all three he is a master at capturing the nuances of Cuban dialect in Spanish and English. *La vida es un special* (Life Is on Special, 1982), *Raining Backwards* (1988), and *Holy Radishes!* (1995) are mosaics made up of monologs, dialogs, letters, phone conversations, speeches, and other types of oral performance that, in composite, make up a continuing tale of the development of the exile community and its younger generations of increasingly acculturated Cuban Americans. Through the pages of these books, the author charts the goings-on at social clubs and coming-out parties, follows counterrevolutionary guerrilla movements in the Florida swamps and the emergence of a Cuban pope, plots a mystery novel, discusses a poetry and art contest, and gives many other episodic bits and pieces that create a broad spectrum of a dynamic community caught between two cultures, two languages, two sets of values, and two political systems.

Rosario Ferré (1942–)

Born in Ponce into one of Puerto Rico's leading families (her father was governor for four years), Ferré is one of the island's most successful novelists and one of the very few who has been able to enjoy success through translations to English in major New York publishing houses. After receiving various degrees at the University of Puerto Rico and New York University, Ferré obtained a Ph.D. in Hispanic literature from the University of Maryland in 1986.

Ferré has explored poetry, children's literature, and adult fiction, but it is as a novelist with a critical eye to the governance of Puerto Rico by an elite that furthers its colonial status that she has made her mark. Ferré is also considered one of the leaders of Puerto Rico's literary feminism, since the publication of her first book, *Papeles de Pandora* (Pandora's Papers, 1976, 1979, 2000). Even the story collection *Maldito amor* (Damned Love, 1998, published in English as *Sweet Diamond Dust and Other Stories* in 1996), in which she indicts the United States for the island's colonial condition, employs a feminist analysis. Most of Ferré's books have been published in English, in some cases before their Spanish originals are available. Her most highly acclaimed novel is *A House on the Lagoon* (1996). Ferré is a prolific writer who publishes a book almost yearly.

María Irene Fornés (1930–)

María Irene Fornés is the dean of Hispanic playwrights in New York City, having enjoyed more productions of her works and more recognition, in the form of six Obie awards, than any other Hispanic. Born on May 14, 1930, in Havana, Cuba, she immigrated to the United States in 1945 and became a naturalized citizen in 1951. This sets her off considerably from most of the other Cuban playwrights, who immigrated to the United States as refugees from the Cuban Revolution. Since 1960, Fornés has been a playwright, director, and teacher with Theater for New York City (1973–78) and various other workshops, universities, and schools.

Fornés has had more than thirty plays produced, including adaptations of plays by Federico García Lorca, Pedro Calderón de la Barca, and Chekhov. Her plays have been produced on Hispanic stages, in mainstream Off-Off-Broadway and Off-Broadway, as well as out of town in such cities as Milwaukee, Minneapolis, Houston, London, and Zurich. Fornés' works, although at times touching upon political and ethnic themes, generally deal with human relations and the emotional lives of her characters. Her plots tend to be unconventional, and at times her characters are fragmented, in structures that vary from musical comedy to the theater of ideas to the realistic. Many of her plays have been published in collections of her work: *Promenade and Other Plays* (1971), *María Irene Fornés: Plays* (1986), *Lovers and Keepers* (1987), and *Fefu and Her Friends* (1990).

Ernesto Galarza (1905–1984)

Born in Jalcocotán, Mexico, Galarza immigrated to Sacramento, California, as a child with his mother and two uncles during the Mexican Revolution. Soon after he lost his mother to the influenza epidemic of 1917. Despite poverty and having to work even during his elementary and secondary education, Galarza graduated from Occidental College and later obtained an M.A. from Stanford University in 1929 and a Ph.D. from Columbia University in 1944. Galarza became a renowned expert on labor conditions and practices prevalent in the United States and Latin America, and published pioneering reports for government agencies and books for specialists and the general public in his effort to improve the lives especially of farm workers. In this vein, his most renowned book was his exposé of the Bracero Program, *Strangers in Our Fields* (1956), which helped to put an end to this horribly exploitive program of Mexican guest workers.

From his high school days, Galarza was a creative writer and began publishing his works of poetry and prose in the 1930s. His early publishing included *Thirty Poems* (1935) and *Stegomia, Jr.* (1936?), a play project for junior high school students dramatizing the contribution of the Cuban scientist, Dr. Carlos Finley, to the building of the Panama Canal and the progress of medicine through the discovery of the yellow fever germ carrier. But his most famous and influential literary work, *Barrio Boy* (1971), was not published until the height of the Chicano Movement. It is at the same time a personal autobiography and the epic story of Mexican immigration to the United States; it chronicles both rural life among agricultural workers as well as urban life in immigrant communities. During the 1970s, Galarza became a committed advocate for bilingual education and dedicated himself to writing children's literary materials to be used in the schools to further biliteracy. These include such children's books as *Zoo-risa* (Zoo Laughter, 1968), *Poemas párvulos* (1971), and *Poemas pe-que pe-que-ñitos* (Poems for Ti-Ti-ny Children 1972).

Cristina García (1958–)

Cristina García is the first Cuban-American woman to experience mainstream success as a novelist in the United States, through the publication of her first novel *Dreaming in Cuban*. Her journalistic background and her interest in politics led her into the world of writing and the examination of her Cuban-American circumstances, which have been so shaped by the political history of the United States and Cuba. Cristina García was born in Havana, Cuba, on July 4, 1958, and was brought to the United States when her parents went into exile after the triumph of the Cuban Revolution. García was an excellent student and was able to attend elite American universities; she graduated from Barnard College with a degree in political science in 1979 and from The Johns Hopkins University with a master's in Latin American studies. She was able to land a coveted job as a reporter and researcher with *Time* Magazine, where she was able to hone her writing skills. She quickly ascended to bureau chief and correspondent at *Time*, but left the magazine in 1990 to pursue her career as a creative writer.

García's highly acclaimed *Dreaming in Cuban* was the first novel authored by a woman to give insight into the psychology of the generation of Cubans born or raised in the United States who grew up under the looming myth of the splendors of the island in the past and the evils of Castro—a group, however, that never really had first-hand knowledge of their parents' homeland. In addition, the novel closely examines women's perspectives on the dilemma of living between two cultures. *Dreaming in Cuban* chronicles three generations of women in the Pino family, and in so doing compares the lives of those who live in Cuba with those living in the United States. Celia, a revolutionary and a true believer in the Communist regime, has remained in Cuba with her daughter, Felicia, and her three grandchildren. Celia's equally committed, counterrevolutionary daughter, Lourdes, lives with her own daughter in Brooklyn, where she runs a bakery that also serves as a gathering place for militant exiles. The novel shows how the revolution and the resulting immigration and exile disrupted and fragmented Cuban family life. *Dreaming in Cuban* was awarded the National Book Award in 1992.

García's second novel, *The Agüero Sisters* (1997), is a novel of family history and myth, which contrasts the lives of two sisters, one in Cuba and the other in the United States. The novel explores identity—personal, familial and national—in its rapprochement of the topics that have divided Cubans since the Revolution.

Lionel G. García (1935–)

Texas Mexican American writer Lionel G. García was the first Hispanic to win the PEN Southwest Award (1983), for his novel, *Leaving Home*. García went on to become the first and only Hispanic author to win the two other major awards for fiction in the Southwest: the Southwest Book Award of the Southwest Booksellers Association and the Texas Institute of Letters Award for Fiction for his 1989 novel, *Hardscrub*. García is a novelist who has created some of the most memorable characters in Chicano literature in a style that is steeped in the traditions of the Texas tall tale and Mexican American folk narrative.

Born in San Diego, Texas, on August 20, 1935, García grew up in an environment in which Mexican-Americans were the majority population in his small town and on the ranches where he worked and played. To make a living, García became a veterinarian, but always practiced his first love: storytelling and writing. In 1983 he won the PEN Southwest Discovery Award for his novel in progress, *Leaving Home*, which was published in 1985. *Leaving Home* and his novels, *A Shroud in the Family* (1987) and *To a Widow with Children* (1994), draw heavily on his family experiences and small-town background; both are set in quaint villages very much like San Diego, Texas, where he grew up, and follow the antics of children similar to those friends and family members that surrounded him as a child. These characters reappear in his collection of autobiographical stories, *I Can Hear the Cowbell Ring* (1994). His prize-winning novel *Hardscrub* (1989) is a departure from his for-

Lionel G. García.

mer works; it is a realistically drawn chronicle of the life of an Anglo child in an abusive family relationship.

Nemesio García Naranjo (1883–1962)

A longstanding political exile from Mexico, García Naranjo was one of the best-known leaders of the Mexican expatriate community during the Revolution. Renowned for his eloquence as a speaker and editorialist, García Naranjo's essays and speeches were reproduced in newspapers throughout the Southwest. García Naranjo founded the *Revista Mexicana* (Mexican Review) in 1915 as a forum for the best thought and literary expression in the expatriate community; when the magazine failed in 1920, he went to work as the editorialist for San Antonio's *La Prensa* newspaper, owned and operated by Ignacio Lozano, arguably the most powerful cultural entrepreneur in the Southwest. Both men promoted the nationalistic ideology of "México de afuera" and attempted to bring both expatriates and Mexican-Americans into their culturally nationalist vision. Other political exiles also used the newspapers as employment and as a base from which to pursue their political agendas through organizing, speech-making, and non-fiction agitational writing. Besides commenting and agitating from a conservative perspective on the Revolution—for which he was tried in Laredo for breaking the federal laws of neutrality—García Naranjo also crusaded against racism and discrimination against Mexicans in the United States.

Alicia Gaspar de Alba (1958–)

Born and raised in El Paso, Texas, Gaspar de Alba is the quintessential bilingual/bicultural writer, penning poetry, essays and narrative with equal facility in English and Spanish. Gaspar de Alba earned bachelor's (1980) and master's (1983) degrees in English from the University of Texas at El Paso and a Ph.D. in American Studies from the University of New Mexico (1994). Alicia Gaspar de Alba is an associate professor and founding faculty member of the César Chávez Center for Chicana/Chicano Studies at UCLA. In 2001, she was jointly appointed to the English Department. She is also member of the Lesbian, Gay, Bisexual, and Transgender Studies Faculty Advisory Committee, and is affiliated with the women's studies program.

Gaspar de Alba is the author of a short story collection, *The Mystery of Survival* (1993), which won the Premio Aztlán, and the highly acclaimed historical novel *Sor Juana's Second Dream* (1999), which has been translated into Spanish and German. In addition, her poetry and essays have been published widely in magazines and anthologies. In 1989, she received a Massachusetts Artists Foundation Fellowship Award in poetry, and in the fall of 1999, she held the prestigious Roderick Endowed Chair in English at the University of Texas at El Paso, where she was a Distinguished Visiting Professor for one semester. In all of her work, Gaspar de Alba is one of the most eloquent exponents of a lesbian esthetic and a promoter of the empowerment of women.

Dagoberto Gilb (1950–)

Born in Los Angeles to a Mexican mother and an Irish-American father, Gilb earned a B.A. (1973) and an M.A. (1976) from the University of California, Santa Barbara. Until he became an established writer, Dagoberto Gilb worked as a carpenter, which has lent his fiction writing a common-man perspective. It was not until the mid-1980s that Gilb's stories began to garner the attention of critics and academics for their fine craft and down-to-earth attitude. After publishing noteworthy short story collections in the 1990s, Gilb began taking visiting professorships in creative writing departments at universities, and in 1997 became a tenured associate professor at Southwest Texas State University in San Marcos, Texas. Gilb's short story collections include *Winners on the Pass Line* (1985), *The Magic of Blood* (1993), and *Woodcuts of Women* (2001). In 1994, Gilb published his first novel, *The Last Known Residence of Mickey Acuña*. Some of these books have been translated to French, German, Italian, and Japanese, as well as reprinted in the United Kingdom and Australia. Gilb's awards include the Ernest Hemingway Foundation/PEN Award (1994), a Guggenheim Fellowship (1995), and a National Endowment for the Arts Fellowship (1992).

Isaac Goldemberg (1945–)

Born in Chepén, Peru, to a Russian-Jewish father and a Peruvian mother, Goldemberg was until age eight raised by his Catholic mother, but in 1953 went to live with his father, attended a Jewish school and became immersed in the Jewish metropolitan culture of Lima. At age seventeen, he went to Israel and lived in a kibbutz for almost two years. After marrying a North American and having a child, Goldemberg immigrated to the United States in 1965 and developed into a leading voice of Hispanic immigrant writers as well as Hispanic-Jewish literature. He has been able to develop his literary career while earning a living as a professor in the Spanish Department of New York University. As his own biography demonstrates, one of Goldemberg's major themes is multiple identities or multiple cultural backgrounds; faced with the challenges of identity, Goldemberg searches for an ever-elusive spiritual, if not physical, home. These themes are explored in both his poetry and in his novels: *The Fragmented Life of Don Jacobo Lerner* (1976, 1999, translated by Robert S. Picciotto), *Hombre de paso* (*Just Passing Through*, 1981, translated by David Unger), *Tiempo al tiempo* (Time for Time, 1984), and *En el nombre del padre* (*The Name of the Father*, 2002).

Guillermo Gómez-Peña (1955–)

Interdisciplinary artist and writer Gómez-Peña was born in Mexico City. He immigrated to the United States in 1978 and has become the most renowned experimenter with transculturalism and transnationalism in the arts. His poetry and theater often take place within the context of happenings and installations employing multimedia—including music, video, journalism, and visual arts. Three volumes of his diverse essays, scripts, poetry, and drama have been published: *Mexican Beasts and Living Santos* (1997), *The New World Border* (1996, winner of the American Book Award), and *Warrior for Gringostroika* (1994). Gómez-Peña was the recipient of a Bessie Award, the *Prix de la Parole*, at the 1989 International Theatre of the Americas (Montreal) and a 1991 MacArthur Fellowship. He has performed and exhibited his work internationally at the 1992 Sydney Biennale, as well as the 1993 Whitney Biennale and the Brooklyn Academy of Music's Next Wave Festival, among many others. Gómez-Peña was also the editor of the experimental arts magazine *La Linea Quebrada* (*The Broken Line*, 1985–1990) and was a founding member of The Border Arts Workshop/Taller de Arte Fronterizo (1985–1990).

Adalberto Elías González (dates unknown)

Adalberto Elías González was by far the most prolific and successful playwright in the Hispanic communities of the United States. A native of Sonora, Mexico, who probably immigrated to Los Angeles in 1920 to further his education after graduating from the Escuela Normal in Hermosillo, he is known to have worked as a journalist and professional playwright in Los Angeles at least until 1941. Because of the subject matter of some of his plays, it is assumed that he also had military experience in Mexico before moving to the United States. By 1924, González had steady employment as a movie critic for *El Heraldo de México* (The Mexico Herald) newspaper in Los Angeles and had four new plays debut that year. By 1928, his fame as a playwright was so great that in one year alone his works were staged in Hermosillo, Mexicali, El Paso, Nogales, and, of course, Los Angeles.

González's works ran the gamut from historical drama to dime-novel sensationalism. The most famous of his plays was *Los Amores de Ramona* (The Loves of Ramona), a stage adaptation of the Helen Hunt Jackson novel of early California, which broke all box office records when it was seen by more than 15,000 spectators after only eight performances in 1927. His second most successful work, *La Asesino del Martillo, o La Mujer Tigresa* (The Hammer Assassin, or Tiger Woman), was based on news stories of 1923 and 1924. González also wrote historical drama, based both on Hispanic history in California and on the Mexican Revolution, including *La Conquista de California* (The Conquest of California), *Los Expatriados* (The Expatriates), *La Muerte de Francisco Villa* (The Death of Francisco Villa), and *El Fantasma de la Revolución* (The Phantom of the Revolution). González was the leading winner of playwriting contests in Los Angeles at the height of a playwriting boom never before seen among Hispanics in the United States. In all, González is known to have written some fourteen or fifteen plays that were successfully produced in Los Angeles during the 1920s and 1930s.

Celedonio González (1923–)

Celedonio González has been known as "el cronista de la diáspora" (the chronicler of the Cuban diaspora or flight from Cuba). Of all of the Cuban exile novelists, he is the one who has turned the greatest attention to the trials, tribulations, and successes of the Cuban refugees and their children in the United States. Born on September 9, 1923, in the small town of La Esperanza in central Cuba, González began his education in the neighboring city of Santa Clara at a Catholic school and later graduated from a Protestant high school in the city of Cárdenas. Upon returning to La Esperanza he began working in his family's farming enterprises, which he eventually came to manage. He was a supporter of progressive causes and of Castro's revolution, but by 1960 he had become disillusioned with the revolution and was imprisoned for two months as a counter-revolutionary. Upon release, he immigrated to the United States with his wife and children. In Miami he eked out a living at a number of odd jobs. In 1965, he and his family settled in Chicago in search of a better living. It was there that he began writing, but it was not until his return to Miami at age 41 that he wrote his first successful novel, *Los primos* (The Cousins, 1971), a mirror of Cuban life in Miami during the 1960s. The same year, his short stories depicting the loneliness of Cuban exile life in the United States, *La soledad es una amiga que vendrá* (Solitude Is a Friend Who Will Come), were published in book form. His novel *Los cuatro embajadores* (The Four Ambassadors, 1973) criticizes American capitalism and the dehumanization in American life. His greatest work to date is his *El espesor del pellejo de un gato ya cadáver* (The Thickness of Skin of a Dead Cat, 1978), a call for Cubans to give up their dreams of returning to the island of their birth and to make the best of life in the United States. González's short stories also deal often with American life from the vantage point of the Cuban laboring classes and small-scale shopkeepers.

José Luis González (1926–1996)

Puerto Rico's greatest fiction writer, González was born in Santo Domingo in the Dominican Republic to a Puerto Rican father and a Dominican mother. The family migrated to Puerto Rico when González was four, where he was raised and educated. Before graduating from the University of Puerto Rico in 1946, he had already published two collections of stories, the second of which, *Cinco cuentos de sangre* (Five Bloody Tales, 1945), won the Instituto de Literatura Puertorriqueña Prize. After graduating, González moved to New York City and attended the graduate New School for Social Research; during this time he became involved in the Puerto Rican community and with writer Jesús Colón, who published one of González's books on his small press. In 1948, González returned to Puerto Rico and became politically active in the socialist and independence movements and published *El hombre en la calle* (The Man on the Street), which protested the oppression of the urban poor in Puerto Rico.

In 1950, González published his famous novel *Paisa*, which was a poetic but realistic portrayal of Puerto Rican life in New York City. In 1953, González renounced his American citizenship in protest of American colonialism and moved to Mexico, where he spent the rest of his life, writing and working with some of the leading figures in Latin American fiction. In 1972, González published his short novel *Mambrú se fue a la guerra* (Mambrú Went to War), a remarkable piece of antiwar fiction. In 1978, he became the first Puerto Rican novelist and short story writer to win Mexico's most prestigious literary award, the Xavier Viallurrutia Prize for Fiction, for his novel *Balada de otro tiempo* (Ballad of Another Time, 1978), which is set to the background of the U.S. invasion of Puerto Rico during the Spanish-American War. However, *Paisa* and the short story collection *En Nueva York y otras desgracias* (In New York and Other Disgraces, 1973) remain his most famous works from the perspective of Hispanic immigration to the United States.

Juan Felipe Herrera (1948–)

Born in Fowler, California, Herrera graduated from high school in San Diego (1967) and later received a B.A. in anthropology from the University of California at Los Angeles (1972), despite the interruptions in his education that resulted from his parents' migrant work. Working with the arts, from theater to photography, in the Chicano Movement and afterward, Herrera went on to pursue a Ph.D. in anthropology, which he soon abandoned in favor of literature. In 1990 he received his M.F.A. in creative writing from the University of Iowa and soon began a career as a professor of Chicano and Latin American Studies at Fresno State University. From the late 1960s, Herrera wrote poetry and became one of the most experimental poets during the Chicano Movement, not only basing his work in the pre-Columbian past, but also in other media, such as weaving tapestry, as in his first book *Rebozos of love we have woven sudor de pueblos on our backs* (1974), or photography, as in his *Exiles of Desire* (1983). Included among Herrera's other books are *Facegames* (1987), *Zenjosé: Scenarios* (1988), *Akrílica* (1989), *Border-Crosser with a Lamborghini Dream (Camino del Sol)* (1999), and *Crash Boom Love* (2001).

Oscar Hijuelos (1951–)

Oscar Hijuelos became the first Hispanic writer to win the Pulitzer Prize (1991) for Fiction, for his book *The Mambo Kings Play Songs of Love*. Born to Cuban American working-class parents in New York City, Hijuelos was educated in public schools and obtained a B.A. in 1975 and an M.A. in 1976, both in English, from City College of the City University of New York. Hijuelos is one of the few Hispanic writers to have formally studied creative writing and to have broken into the Anglo-dominated creative writing circles, participating in prestigious workshops such as the Breadloaf Writers Conference and benefiting from highly competitive fellowships, including the American Academy in Rome Fellowship from the American Academy and the Institute for Arts and Letters (1985), the National Endowment for the Arts Fellowship (1985), and the Guggenheim Fellowship (1990). Hijuelos is the author of various short stories and five novels, *Our House in the Last World* (1983), *The Mambo Kings Play Songs of Love* (1989), *The Fourteen Sisters of Emilio Montez O'Brien* (1993), *Mrs. Ives' Christmas* (1995), and *Empress of the Splendid Season* (1999).

While Hijuelos's first book is a novel of immigration cut in the mold of American ethnic autobiography, *The Mambo Kings Play Songs of Love* is more than just a story of immigration; it examines a period in time when Hispanic culture was highly visible in the United States and was able to influence American popular culture—the 1950s during the height of the mambo craze and the overwhelming success of Desi Arnaz's television show, "I Love Lucy." Written in a poetic but almost documentary style, the novel follows two brothers who are musicians trying to ride the crest of the Latin music wave. While providing a picture of one segment of American life never seen before in English-language fiction, the novel also indicts womanizing and alcoholism.

Rolando Hinojosa (1929–)

Rolando Hinojosa is the most prolific and probably the most bilingually talented of Latino novelists, with original creations in both English and Spanish published in the United States and abroad. Born to an Anglo-American school teacher and a Mexican-American policeman father and raised in Mercedes, Texas, Hinojosa has embodied in his life and literature the cultural fusion and conflict that he depicts in his continuing, epic narrative about life in Texas' Rio Grande Valley.

His Quinto Sol Award-winning *Estampas del Valle y otras obras* (*Sketches of the Valley and Other Works*, 1973) is a mosaic of the picturesque character types, folk customs, and speech of the bilingual community in the small towns in South Texas. While his sketches and insights are at times reminiscent of the local color *crónicas* published in Spanish-language newspapers of the 1920s, his experimentation with numerous novelistic forms—ranging from reportage to epistolary to detective fiction—make Hinojosa's art one of the most sophisticated contributions to Hispanic literature. Hinojosa sees students as ideal readers: "My work speaks to students. It is historically based—the people who live and die in my works are part of the history of this country. I think my works say to students, 'Look, this is who all of us are.' "

Estampas was just the beginning phase of a continuing novel that has become a broad epic of the history and culture of the Mexican-Americans and Anglos of the Valley, as centered in the fictitious Belken County and centering on the lives of two fictitious characters and a narrator—Rafa Buenrostro, Jehú Maacara, P. Galindo—all of whom may be partial alter egos of Hinojosa himself. What is especially intriguing

Rolando Hinojosa.

about Hinojosa's continuing novel, which he calls the Klail City Death Trip Series, is his experimentation not only with various forms of narration—derived from Spanish, Mexican, English, and American literary history—but also with English-Spanish language bilingualism.

The respective installments of the continuing novel include: *Klail City y sus alrededores*, (1976; *Klail City*, 1987), which owes much to the picaresque novel; *Korean Love Songs* (1980) written in narrative poetry; *Mi querido Rafa* (1981, *Dear Rafe*, 1985), part epistolary novel and part reportage; *Rites and Witnesses* (1982), mainly a novel in dialogue; *Partners in Crime* (1985), a detective novel; *Claros varones de Belken* (*Fair Gentlemen of Belken*, 1986), a composite, and *Becky y sus amigos* (*Becky and Her Friends*, 1990), which continues the novel in the style of reportage but with a new unnamed narrator, P. Galindo having died; *The Useless Servants* (1993), a highly autobiographical chronicle of his characters' participation in the Korean War; and *Ask a Policeman* (1998), a detective novel about drug smuggling on the border.

Because of his many awards—including the international award for Latin American fiction given in Cuba, Premio Casa de las Américas, 1976—his academic background as a Ph.D. in Spanish and, in particular, the positive response to his sophisticated art from critics and university professors, Hinojosa is one of the few Hispanic writers in the country to teach in creative writing programs at a high level. In holding the distinguished title of Ellen Clayton Garwood Professor of English and creative writing at the University of Texas, Hinojosa is the most recognized and highest ranking Chicano/Hispanic author in academia.

Carolina Hospital (1957–)

Born in Havana, Cuba, Hospital accompanied her family into exile in 1961 and was raised and educated in Florida. Hospital graduated from the University of Florida in 1979 with a B.A. in English and since 1979 has taught English at Miami-Dade Community College. A poet from an early age, Hospital captures in her bilingual verse the transition of her community from exile to and immigration to American identity. In 1989, Hospital compiled the first anthology of Cuban American literature, *Los Atrevidos: Cuban American Writers,* thus announcing the birth and acceptance of Cuban American literature as other than a literature of exile and immigration. Before Hospital's works there was barely a consciousness of the corpus of Cuban American literature—the legacy of exile being so dominant, especially in Miami. The prevailing political sentiment in Miami and other centers of Cuban exile had fought against the

Carolina Hospital. Photo by Phil Roche.

concept of a Cuban *Americanism*, since the exile community's identity depended on remaining distinctively Cuban and someday returning to their home. Hospital braved the opposition, openly embracing English and bilingualism and recognizing the birth of a literature that is firmly planted in American soil and is here to stay. In *Cuban American Writers: Los Atrevidos*, she declared that Cuban American writers were risk-takers, daring to belong to a future made up of a new reality.

Eugenio María de Hostos (1839–1903)

Eugenio María de Hostos, the writer and political figure, was born in Mayagüez, Puerto Rico. Hostos was educated by tutors at home and later attended a Lyceum in San Juan, before being sent to Spain for his secondary and university education. He dropped out of law school to return to Puerto Rico and become involved in its struggle for independence. While still in Spain, he wrote his first book, attacking Spain's colonialism in the Americas—*La peregrinación de Bayoán* (The Pilgrimage of Bayoán, 1863). In 1868, he became the editor of a liberal newspaper, *El progreso* (Progress), in Barcelona, which was shut down by the authorities, who deported Hostos to France. In 1869, Hostos traveled to New York and became involved with other distinguished conspirators for the independence of Puerto Rico and Cuba. It was at this stage of his life that he began to envision the creation of an Antillean Federation, a government of free, united islands of the Caribbean.

In 1870, Hostos began traveling throughout Spanish America to raise support for the cause of independence. In Lima, Hostos founded a newspaper, *La patria* (The Fatherland) and became involved in the struggle to organize labor. In 1872, he moved to Chile, where he was able to write many of his most important works on history, art, politics, and a second edition of his *La peregrinación de Bayoán*. He also worked as a writer for the newspaper *Ferrocarril* (Railroad) and the magazine *Sud América* (South America), and became involved in the struggle for women's rights to education. In 1873, he became a university professor of philosophy in Buenos Aires. In 1874, Hostos returned to New York to join the revolutionary movement there, but, persecuted by the police, he was forced to move to Venezuela in 1876. From 1878 to 1888, he lived in Santo Domingo, where he dedicated himself to organizing primary and secondary schools and teaching constitutional law at the university level. In 1889, he was invited to Chile to become the rector of the Miguel Luis Amunátegui Liceum. He remained there until 1898, when he returned to New York to organize the Liga de Patriotas (League of Patriots) to promote independence. When the United States invaded Puerto Rico, he pleaded his case for independence to the government in Washington and to his compatriots in Puerto Rico, but all of his learned arguments and passion fell upon deaf ears; he ultimately became disillusioned and went into voluntary exile in Santo Domingo to finish out his life as a teacher. There he died on August 11, 1903.

The twenty volumes of his complete works—which include writings on politics, education, biography, law and his own creative writing—were published posthumously in Puerto Rico in 1939. For his internationalist spirit and contribution to education and culture in many countries of Spanish America, Hostos has been called "Citizen of the Americas." His most important literary piece, *La peregrinación de Bayoán*, is a political allegory in the form of a novel, in which his liberal ideas take on flesh and blood. But his best known work is *Moral social* (Social Morality, 1888), a philosophical treatise in which he illustrates the thesis that individual good and social good are always joined. Hostos rejected the notion that man's instinctive or animal nature is inherently evil and in need of constant suppression by reason and will; instead, he saw man's reason as inevitably and indissolubly linked to his social and instinctive nature.

Angela de Hoyos (1940–)

De Hoyos was born into a middle-class family in Coahuila, Mexico, the daughter of a proprietor of a dry-cleaning shop and a housewife who had an artistic bent. After a tragic accident in which she was burned as a young child, de Hoyos was forced to convalesce in bed for many months, during which she entertained herself by composing rhymes. While she was still a child, her family moved to San Antonio and her interest in poetry continued. From her teenage years on, her education was informal but supported by art courses she took in area institutions. In the late 1960s, de Hoyos began publishing poetry and entering her work in international competitions, for which she won such awards as the Bronze Medal of Honor of the Centro Studii e Scambi Internazionale (CSSI), Rome, Italy, 1966; the Silver Medal of Honor (literature), CSSI, 1967; Diploma di Benemerenza (literature), CSSI, 1968; and the Diploma di Benemerenza, CSSI, 1969 and 1970.

During the 1970s, her interest in literature and her awareness of the lack of opportunity for Chicano writers led her to establish a small press, M & A Editions, in San Antonio, through which she issued not only her own work but also that of such writers as Evangelina Vigil-Piñón. During the 1980s, de Hoyos also founded a cultural periodical, *Huehuetitlan*, which is still in existence. In addition to this intense literary life, de Hoyos developed a successful career as a painter. Her works, also inspired by Mexican American culture, are widely exhibited and collected in Texas. De Hoyos has cultivated a free-verse, terse, conversational poetry—which at times takes dialog form—that provides

Angela de Hoyos.

a context for cultural and feminist issues within a larger philosophical and literary framework.

De Hoyos, a student of writing in many languages and cultures, examines themes and issues from cross-cultural perspectives and her work is multi faceted. While her readers are always aware of these larger frameworks, the themes are perceived as being very specific and embodied in the actions and circumstances of real people. De Hoyos' poetry is socially engaged while at the same time humanistic in the best sense of the word. Her particular concerns are poverty, racism, and disenfranchisement, whether of a people, her people, children, or women. Her particular mission is to give voice to those who cannot express themselves. De Hoyos is also a poet of humor and wit, creating piquant exchanges in verse between lovers and enemies, as exemplified in her dialogues between Hernán Cortez and La Malinche.

Her most important book, *Woman, Woman*, deals with the roles that society has dictated for women and their struggle to overcome the limits of those roles. De Hoyos surveys history from Aztec days to the present, and even casts an eye on the image of women in fairy tales, as in her poem "Fairy-Tale: Cuento de Hadas." Throughout *Woman, Woman*, de Hoyos sustains the dynamic tension that both unites and separates male and female. In her poetry, that tension is always erotically charged, always threatening to one or the other, always reverberating in the political. In *Woman, Woman*, de Hoyos has also perfected her bilingual style, innovatively mixing the linguistic codes of English and Spanish to reach beyond the merely conversational to the more philosophical. The choice of language and lexicon is not just a sociolinguistic one; it is also a deeply cultural one.

Jovita Idar (1885–1946)

Born in Laredo, Texas, into a family of journalists and labor leaders, Jovita Idar dedicated herself to journalism, education, and women's issues. After receiving her teaching certificate in 1903, Idar worked as a grammar school teacher in Ojuelos, close to Laredo, but became discouraged by the scarcity of resources and the poor conditions that existed for Mexican-American children in Texas. She returned to Laredo to work on her family's newspaper, *La Crónica* (The Chronicle), in part to campaign for the betterment of educational conditions and to convince parents of the need for education. She became a frequent essayist in newspapers she and her family published. Much of her work appears unsigned in *La Crónica*. She also wrote for Laredo's *El Progreso* (Progress), San Benito's *La Luz* (The Light) and Corpus Christi's *El Eco del Golfo* (The Gulf Echo), which she also edited. When her family spearheaded an effort to unite Mexicans in Texas to protect their civil rights through El Primer Congreso Mexicanista (The First Mexicanist Congress), she assumed leadership as president of the affiliated Liga Femenil Mexicanista (Mexicanist Women's League). One of her greatest contributions as an editor was her founding of the *Evolución* newspaper in Laredo in 1916, which lasted until 1920. Her final stint at the helm of a periodical was as co-editor of the Methodists' *El Heraldo Cristiano* (The Christian Herald). Idar's career as a creative writer really began as a prize-winning child poet and a performer (*declamadora*) of poetry at social and civic events. Despite her love of poetry and the number of poems she published in newspapers, it is Idar's clarity of thought and passionate commitment to progress for women and her people that rings so strongly in her essays and editorials.

Arturo Islas (1938–1991)

Born in El Paso, Texas, to a policeman and a secretary, novelist, poet, and essayist, Islas grew up dealing with the conflict between his homosexuality and the familial and social environment. Early on he developed the discipline to survive and to become an outstanding student, which resulted in his attending Stanford University on a scholarship. In 1960, Islas graduated Phi Beta Kappa from Stanford and went on to study for his Ph. D. in English, also at Stanford. He earned a Ph.D. in 1971 and became a member of the faculty at Stanford, where he won various awards for excellence in teaching. He was a pioneer in teaching Chicano literature and Chicano creative writing courses at that institution. Islas began writing in elementary school and by the time he reached college was already penning excellent stories and essays. At Stanford, he was fortunate to study as an undergraduate and graduate with such outstanding writers as Wallace Stegner.

Despite his excellent prose and academic credentials, Islas had difficulty placing his works with the New York commercial presses; thus his first book, *The Rain God: A Desert Tale* (1984), was issued by a small press in California. Nevertheless, *The Rain God* achieved outstanding reviews and went through twelve printings by the time his next novel, *Migrant Souls*, was ready; it was finally accepted and issued by a mainstream publisher in 1990, a year before his untimely death due to AIDS. In both his novels, Islas examines family relationships, border culture, and the omnipresence of death (Islas had faced death battling intestinal cancer for a number of years). Also embedded in these novels is a critique of partriarchy and traditional views of gender and homosexuality. The larger part of Islas' writings, including a large body of poems and stories, an unfinished novel, and essays, were published posthumously in 2003.

Ofelia Dumas Lachtman (1919–)

Born on July 9, 1919, in Los Angeles of Mexican immigrant parents, Ofelia Dumas Lachtman attended Los Angeles city schools and received an A.A. degree from Los Angeles City College in 1939; she suspended her plans to study further when she married and moved to Riverside, California. There, she raised two children while developing a writing career in her spare time. She had been writing since childhood, and, in fact, her first work was published in an anthology of children's poetry when she was only twelve years old. Little did she know then that as an adult she would become a successful writer for young people. During World War II, Dumas Lachtman worked as a stenographer. Later, after her children were grown and had left home, she became a group worker and eventually rose to the position of executive director of the Los Angeles–Beverly Hills YWCA. She retired from that position in 1974 and devoted herself full time to writing. In addition to her books, she has published personal interest stories and short fiction in major city dailies and magazines throughout the country.

Dumas Lachtman's first young adult novel, *Campfire Dreams*, was published in 1987 by Harlequin and was eventually translated into French, German, and Polish. *Campfire Dreams* is the story of a camp counselor who believes she has found her biological mother and does not know how to break the news to her adoptive mother, whom she loves very much. Despite the success of *Campfire Dreams*, Dumas Lachtman was not able to find another publisher until her agent placed her works with Arte Público Press in the mid-1990s. Thereafter, Dumas Lachtman's productivity seemed boundless and she

Ofelia Dumas Lachtman.

completed many books, including a novel for adults, *A Shell for Angela* (1995), which explores the consequences of rejecting one's heritage. The novel charts a well-to-do Mexican American woman's past and her journey to Mexico to solve the mystery of her father's deportation from the United States and his subsequent murder. But the journey becomes more than just a quest to solve a mystery; it becomes one of finding roots and identity.

Dumas Lachtman is the author of five children's picture books: *Pepita Talks Twice* (1995), *Lupita y La Paloma* (Lupita and the Dove, 1997), *Big Enough* (1998), *Pepita Thinks Pink* (1998), and *Pepita Takes Time* (2000). Her tremendously popular Pepita series charts the misadventures of a precocious young Mexican-American girl, confronting cultural as well as psychological problems in her barrio life. In 1995, Ofelia Dumas Lachtman won the Stepping Stones Award for Children's Multicultural Literature for *Pepita Talks Twice* (*Pepita habla dos veces*). The Pepita series, like Dumas Lachtman's other books, highlights the inventiveness and genius of girls. Initiative, courage, and resourcefulness also win the day in Dumas Lachtman's most important book to date, *The Girl from Playa Blanca* (1996), which received critical acclaim and won the Benjamin Franklin Award for Young Adult Literature. The adventure follows a teenager and her little brother from their Mexican seaside village to Los Angeles in search of their father, who has disappeared while working in the United States. The young protagonist unravels the mystery behind a major crime and succeeds in finding her father in the metropolis, falling in love along the way. Dumas Lachtman followed up with two other mystery novels for young adults: *Call Me Consuelo* (1997) and *The Summer of El Pintor* (2001). Dumas Lachtman has also written a book for middle readers, *Leticia's Secret* (1997), which sensitively—and in the context of the Hispanic family—deals with the subject of death. Leticia is a terminally ill preteen whose family members attempt to keep her illness a secret. Leticia's cousin and close friend, on the other hand, sees Leticia's secret as a mystery to unravel. *Leticia's Secret* is a book that can help preteens and teens deal with death and grief, topics that are deftly, even poetically, handled by Dumas Lachtman.

John Lantigua (1947–)

Born in the Bronx, New York, of Cuban and Puerto Rican parents, Lantigua is the author of mystery novels issued by mainstream publishing houses. Lantigua's first career is that of a journalist, who is known for his coverage of Central America for the *Washington Post* and the *Chicago Tribune*. As a reporter for the *Miami Herald*, Lantigua shared the 1999 Pulitzer Prize for investigative reporting for his articles on voter fraud in the 1997 Miami mayoral election. Often basing his suspense and mystery novels on historical events, Lantigua is the author of *Twister* (1992), *Player's Vendetta: A Little Havana Mystery* (1999), and *Heat Lightning* (1987), his first novel, nominated for the Edgar Prize by the Mystery Writers Association of America. *Player's Vendetta* is one of the very few Hispanic mystery novels translated to Spanish and issued by a publisher in Spain, as *Finca Roja* (2001). In *Player's Vendetta*, a murder mystery, Lantigua penetrates the nocturnal worlds of Havana in 1960 and Miami in 1990. His fifth novel, *The Ultimate Havana*, was published in 2001.

Jesús Abraham "Tato" Laviera (1951–)

Jesús Abraham "Tato" Laviera became the first Hispanic author to win the American Book Award of the Before Columbus Foundation, which recognizes and promotes multicultural literature. Laviera is the best-selling Hispanic poet in the United States and bears the distinction of still having all of his books in print. Born September 5, 1951, in Santurce, Puerto Rico, he migrated to New York City at the age of ten with his family, which settled in a poor area of the Lower East Side. After finding himself in an alien society and with practically no English, Laviera was able to adjust and eventually graduate high school as an honor student. Despite having no other degrees, his intelligence, aggressiveness, and thorough knowledge of his community led to his developing a career in the administration of social service agencies.

After the publication of his first book, *La Carreta Made a U-Turn* (1979), Laviera gave up administrative work to dedicate his time to writing. Since 1980, Laviera's career has included not only writing but also touring nationally as a performer of his poetry, directing plays he has written, and producing cultural events. In 1980, he was received by President Jimmy Carter at the White House Gathering of American Poets. In 1981 his second book, *Enclave*, was the recipient of the American Book Award. Tato Laviera has said, "I am the grandson of slaves transplanted from Africa to the Caribbean, a man of the New World come to dominate and revitalize two old world languages." And, indeed, Laviera's bilingualism and linguistic inventiveness have risen to the level of virtuosity.

Laviera is the inheritor of the Spanish oral tradition, with all of its classical formulas, and the African oral tradition, with its wedding to music and spirituality; in his works he brings both the Spanish and English languages together, as well as the islands of Puerto Rico and Manhattan—a constant duality that is always in the background. His first book, *La Carreta Made a U-Turn* uses René Marqués's *Oxcart* as a point of departure and redirects it back to the heart of New York instead of to Puerto Rico, as Marqués had desired; Laviera is stating that Puerto Rico can be found here, too. His second book, *Enclave* is a celebration of diverse heroic personalities, both real and imagined: Luis Palés Matos and *salsa* composers, the neighborhood gossip, and John Lennon, Miriam Makeba, and Tito Madera Smith, the latter being a fictional, hip offspring of a Puerto Rican and a southern American black. *AmeRícan* (1986) and *Mainstream Ethics* (1988) are surveys of the lives of the poor and marginalized in the United States and a challenge for the country to live up to its promises of equality and democracy.

Tato Laviera. Photo by Georgia McInnis.

Aurora Levins Morales (1954–)

Aurora Levins Morales is an award-winning writer, essayist, and historian of Puerto Rican and Jewish descent. She writes and speaks about multicultural histories of resistance, feminism, the uses of history, cultural activism, and the ways that racism, anti-Semitism, sexism, class, and other systems of oppression interlock. Her most recent works are *Medicine Stories: Writings on Cultural Activism* (1998) and *Remedios: Stories of Earth and Iron from the History of Puertorriqueñas* (1998). The first is a collection of essays on culture and politics; the latter, co-authored with her mother, is like her first mother-daughter collaboration—*Getting Home Alive* (1986)—a dialog in prose and poetry about identity, family, and the immigrant experience. A major theme in Aurora Levins Morales's work is identity as a lesbian of biracial, bicultural and bireligious heritage. In all of her works, language and reading are the keys to remembering to integrate one's history and sense of identity and place in the world.

Graciela Limón (1938–)

Born on August 2, 1938, and raised in Los Angeles by Mexican immigrant parents, Limón began writing prose fiction after achieving success in her career as a professor of Latin American history and culture. With a Ph. D. from the Univer-

Graciela Limón.

sity of California at Los Angeles, Limón developed a long career at Los Angeles' Loyola Marymount University. Only in her forties did she begin to sketch out novels based on Mexico's pre-Columbian history. "My journey as a writer has not been a straight one—it's been roundabout and had lots of obstacles," she has said.

Limón's first critical acclaim was achieved with *In Search of Bernabé*, which was named a New York Times Notable Book for 1993 and a finalist for the Los Angeles Times Book Award. *In Search of Bernabé* won the American Book Award of the Before Columbus Foundation in 1994. Inspired in her official visits to El Salvador during its civil war, the book chronicles a desperate mother's search for her son after being separated from him during the war; both eventually end up in Los Angeles. Limon's second novel, *The Memories of Ana Calderón* (1994) is a novel of immigration that follows the trials and tribulations of a young woman who rises from the working classes to business success but experiences ultimate disillusionment after battling the forces of family, church, and the justice system in the United States. One of her most popular novels, *The Song of the Hummingbird* (1996), finally deals successfully with the pre-Columbian world at the time of the Spanish conquest; Limón successfully portrays this time of conflict and synthesis of cultures through the eyes of an Aztec woman who was captured and forced to deal with Christianity.

Limón updated her chronicling of the conflict between Spanish and Indian cultures, as well as the evolution of racism, in her *The Day of the Moon*, which sets the conflict within a tale of forbidden love. After visiting Chiapas, Mexico, and researching the history of the Mayan conflict that erupted into the 1994 revolt of the Zapatistas, Limón again took on the conflict of indigenous peoples with authorities in her *Erased Faces* (2001), which explores this conflict from the perspective of women and amorous relationships in conflict with ancestral patriarchal traditions. Although Limón has been consistently published by a small press, Arte Público Press of the University of Houston, she is one of the most distinguished and accomplished novelists in Latino literature—prolific and highly literary, but nevertheless able to reach everyday readers beyond academe.

Francisco "Pachín" González Marín (1863–1897)

Francisco González Marín, known affectionately in Puerto Rican history as "Pachín" Marín, was a Puerto Rican patriot and literary figure born in Arecibo, where he received only a rudimentary elementary education. He learned the trade of typesetter and earned his living as such throughout his life. It was this trade that eventually developed him into an intellectual and man of letters. In 1884, "Pachín" Marín published his first book of poems, *Flores nacientes* (Newborn Flowers). While living in Ponce with a journalist uncle during the 1880s, he worked for Puerto Rico's autonomy from Spain and dedicated his second book of poems, *Mi óbolo* (My Little Bit), to the "Apóstol" (apostle) of autonomy, Román Baldorioty de Castro in 1887. In 1887 in Arecibo, he founded the newspaper *El Postillón* (The Postilion), which was an organ for the anti-Spanish group La Torre del Viejo. This led to his exile in Santo Domingo, where he worked as a teacher, and where his ideas led to his becoming persona non grata; he subsequently moved to Venezuela, and from there was deported to Martinique. "Pachín" Marín returned to Puerto Rico in 1890 and resumed publishing his combative *El Postillón*. This again led to exile in 1891, this time to New York, where he also established a print shop and joined the Junta Revolucionaria de Cuba y de Puerto Rico (Revolutionary Junta for Cuba and Puerto Rico) and became an important conspirator and fundraiser for the independence movement. In New York, he published his book of poems, *Romances* (Ballads), in 1892. In 1896, he joined the revolutionary forces in Cuba and died in battle at Turiguanó in 1897. While serving in Cuba, he wrote his last book of poems, *En la arena* (In the Sand), which was published posthumously in 1898. Many of Marín's poems and writings in newspapers have not yet been collected and studied. In his literary corpus, there is also a play, *El 27 de febrero* (February 27), which takes the independence of Santo Domingo as a theme.

René Marqués (1919–1979)

Considered Puerto Rico's foremost playwright and writer of short fiction, René Marqués was born in Arecibo, Puerto Rico, into a family of agrarian background. Marqués studied agronomy at the College of Agriculture in Mayagüez and actually worked for two years for the Department of Agriculture. But his interest in literature took him to Spain in 1946 to study the classics. Upon his return, Marqués founded a little theater group dedicated to producing and furthering the creation of Puerto Rican theater. In 1948 he received a Rockefeller Foundation fellowship to study playwriting in the United States, which allowed him to study at Columbia University and at the Piscator Dramatic Workshop in New York City. After his return to San Juan, he founded the Teatro Experimental del Ateneo (the Atheneum Society Experimental Theater). From that time on, Marqués maintained a heavy involvement not only in playwriting but also in developing Puerto Rican theater. In addition, he produced a continuous flow of short stories, novels, essays, and anthologies.

While Marqués' best known work is still the all-important play, *La Carreta*, which debuted in 1953 and was published in 1961 (*The Oxcart*, 1969), he had been writing since 1944, when he published his first collection of poems, *Peregrinación* (Pilgrimage). His published plays include *El hombre y sus sueños* (Man and His Dreams, 1948), *Palm Sunday* (1949), *Otro día nuestro* (Another of Our Days, 1995), *Juan Bobo y la Dama de Occidente* (Juan Bobo and the Western

Lady, 1956), *El sol y los MacDonald* (The Sun and the MacDonalds, 1957), and a collection, *Teatro* (1959), which includes three of his most important plays: "Los soles truncos" (The Fan Lights), "Un niño azul para esa sombra" (A Blue Child for that Shadow), and "La muerte no entrará en palacio" (Death Will Not Enter the Palace).

There are many other published plays, novels, collections of short stories, and essays. Marqués is one of the few Puerto Rican writers who has had international audiences and impact; his work is truly one of the high points in Latin American drama. The style, philosophy, and craft of his works, as produced in New York, have had long-lasting influence on the development of Hispanic theater in the United States. In particular, his play *La Carreta* is a classic of the theater of immigration, chronicling the uprooting of a rural family from its ancestral lands in the mountains and its wayward pilgrimage to slums in San Juan and then to the metropolis of cement and ice, New York, where disillusionment and the loss of family members send the survivors back to the island.

José Martí (1853–1895)

José Martí (José Julián Martí y Pérez), poet, writer, and lawyer, was born on January 28, 1853, in Havana, Cuba. Martí became the leading figure in the Cuban revolutionary movement for independence from Spain and the most important precursor of the modernist literary movement. In his organizing for the revolution, he served time in prison in Spain (1871) and suffered long exiles in Mexico (1875), Guatemala (1877), Venezuela (1881), and New York City, which he used as a base for organizing there and in Philadelphia, Tampa, Key West, and New Orleans. In New York, he founded the Cuban Revolutionary Party in 1892. After a military assault from the sea at Dos Playitas, Cuba, he was killed in battle at Boca de Dos Ríos, Cuba, on May 19, 1895. Martí is the Cuban national hero, often called a martyr and an apostle of independence.

As a writer, Martí was one of the greatest Spanish American poets of all time; he was also a distinguished essayist (and orator), journalist, and literary critic. Both his prose and poetry are characterized by clarity and simple elegance. His poetry is also known for its nostalgic and sincere tone. One of his most important books of poetry, *Ismaelillo*, was dedicated to his son and, along with his book of *Versos sencillos* (Simple Verses), has contributed many poems to the standard elementary education curriculum throughout the Spanish-speaking world. Martí also published a magazine for children, *La edad de oro* (The Golden Age). Finally, Martí was also celebrated for his epistolary art, as can be seen in his *Cartas a mi madre* (Letters to My Mother), as a dramatist, newspaper columnist, and novelist. His plays include *Abdala, Amor con amor se paga* (Love Is Paid with Love) and *Adúltera* (Adulteress). His one known novel is *Amistad funesta* (Unlucky Friendship). Martí's greatest essay, which he also delivered as a speech, "Nuestra América" (Our America), represents his dream, and that of many Spanish-American thinkers and patriots, of a politically united Spanish America, one able to confront the political and cultural threat of the United States.

Demetría Martínez (1960–)

Martínez was raised in Albuquerque, New Mexico, received a bachelor's degree in public policy from Princeton University in 1982 and began publishing her poems in 1987. The very next year, she was indicted for smuggling refugee women into the United States, and the government attempted to use one of her poems "Nativity for Two Salvadoran Women" against her as evidence. Martínez was acquitted, based on First Amendment rights. In 1990, she became a columnist for the *National Catholic Reporter* in Kansas City, but soon lost interest and returned to poetry and creative writing. Her plan came to fruition as her first novel, *Mother Tongue*, won the Western States Fiction Award. In 1997, Martínez published a book of poems, *Breathing between the Lines*.

Max Martínez (1943–2000)

Born on May 10, 1943, in Gonzales, Texas, a farm town some forty miles from San Antonio, Max (Maximiano) Martínez was raised in a rural agricultural community similar to the one depicted in his three novels, *Schoolland* (1988), *White Leg* (1996), and *Layover* (1997). After graduating high school, he sought to escape the country life, where his lot as a Mexican American was limited, and he went to sea as a merchant marine. He was able to see a good portion of the world, including Spain, which left an indelible impression on his young mind. He returned to San Antonio and studied English and philosophy at St. Mary's University, graduating with a B.AS. in 1972. By December 1973, he had finished a master's degree in comparative literature at East Texas State University in Commerce, but rather than becoming a teacher, he once again experienced wanderlust and went off to New York to work as a stockbroker. This lasted almost no time at all. Having lived the life of a sailor, a stockbroker, and freelance writer, Martínez tried to settle down in 1975 into a more stable intellectual environment by studying for his Ph.D. in English at the University of Denver and, beginning in 1977, pursuing a career as a college professor at the University of Houston. But it turned out that neither was for him; he never finished his dissertation and he abandoned the tenure track at the university by the mid-1980s to dedicate himself to serious writing. He did this until his death in 2000 from a series of strokes.

Aside from numerous stories published in a variety of literary magazines, as well as hundreds of "man-on-the-scene" commentary and thought pieces that he wrote for trade journals, the fruits of Martínez's labors have been five books. In addition to the three novels mentioned above, there are two collections of short stories. In *The Adventures of the Chicano Kid and Other Stories* (1983), he experiments with a variety of styles to depict the variety of Chicano life: a farm worker; a middle-class suburban businessman (what today would be called a yuppie); an educated, self-confident, modern Chicano in a face-off with traditional rural prejudice in the person of a Texas "redneck" (a portrait of blue-collar racism is in most of Martínez's books); an old man snoozing on a park bench and bemoaning how things have changed; and others. The title story is a satire of nineteenth-century dime novels. *Schoolland* (1988), Max Martínez's autobiographical novel, is a young boy's first-person account of the year of the great drought (1953), the same year that his beloved grandfather foretold his own death and began making preparations for it. The novel is a coming-of-age tale, as well as a social protest that details the tragedy of bank takeovers of farmland—both boy and reader lose their innocence. Not only does the grandfather die, so does a Texas-Mexican way of life on the land. Martínez's second collection of stories, *Red Bikini Dream*, also includes some autobiographical tales, but offers stories of non-Chicano experiences as well. The stories' characters include successful lawyers, drunken sailors, and even a middle-aged Jewish American couple on a dude ranch in Texas. The tension between "civilized" behavior and the desire to experience life in an unbridled and wild way holds the varied stories together. Martínez again gives us glimpses of his own life as a struggling writer in New York, as a sailor, and as a child growing up in a fatherless home.

White Leg and *Layover* are well-crafted mystery novels set in the small rural towns of central Texas. Sharing some of the same characters, they are both a powerful portrait of the dangerous politics and culture of small-town life. Martínez's works have been praised for capturing the rhythm and nuance of rural Texas life, for their sensitive evocation of past times in central Texas, and for their array of interesting and diverse characters. They have been censured at times for their scenes of explicit sex and violence and for what has been seen as their victimization of women. Martínez wields a powerfully sharp pen that cuts so close to the bone of the reader that it is often hard to arrive at an objective judgment.

Rubén Martínez (1967–)

Martínez, a non-fiction writer of Salvadoran and Mexican heritage, was raised in Los Angeles. He has distinguished himself as a journalist as well as an author of feature articles and books. An associate editor of the Pacific News Service and a Loeb Fellow of Harvard University's Graduate School of Design, Martínez is also a pioneer in what has been called the "non-fiction novel," a narrative which recreates lives and events based on historical and journalistic research. His most renowned work in this genre is *Crossing Over: A Mexican Family on the Migrant Trail* (2001), which traces the lives of an extended family of migrants during several years and through thousands of miles. Among Martínez's other works are *The Other Side: Notes from the New L.A., Mexico City and Beyond* (1992) and *Eastside Stories: Gang Life in East Los Angeles* (1998). His reportage, opinion pieces, and essays have been published nationwide, from *The New York Times* to the *Los Angeles Times*, as well as in Mexico. Martínez was awarded an Emmy for hosting the politics and culture series, *Life & Times* (1995), on Los Angeles' KCET-TV. He is also the recipient of the Freedom of Information Award from the American Civil Liberties Union (1994) and the University of California at Irvine prize in poetry (1990). As a poet, Martínez has had many spoken performances and participated in public schools as an artist in residence.

Tomás Eloy Martínez (1934–)

Born in Tucumán, Argentina, Martínez is the author of acclaimed novels, essays, and stories, and has been living in exile on and off since 1975 in Venezuela, Mexico, and, ultimately, New Jersey, where he has become a distinguished professor at Rutgers University in New Brunswick. Among his numerous novels, *Sagrado* (Sacred, 1969), *La novela de Perón* (The Perón Novel, 1985), and *Santa Evita* (1995) have also recieved international acclaim and have been translated into more than thirty languages. From his home in New Jersey, Martínez still weighs in on Latin American political issues as a journalist and columnist, the same type of writing that sent him into exile under the Argentine dictatorships.

A graduate of the University of Tucumán, Martínez established a career as a practicing journalist, film critic, and columnist, rising to the directorship of such newspapers and magazines as *Panorama* (1971–72) and the cultural supplement of *La Opinión* (1972–75). While in exile in 1979, he founded the *Diario de Caracas* (Caracas Daily) newspaper. Since 1996, Martínez has been a columnist for both *The New York Times* and Buenos Aires' *La Nación*. From 1984 to 1987, Martínez taught at the University of Maryland, and since then, at Rutgers.

Martínez's most acclaimed novel, *Santa Evita*, explores the death and post mortem worship of Eva Perón, the widow of the dictator Juan Perón, and one-time ruler in her own right. In the novel, Martínez proves of this personage worshipped as a saint by the working class that "Evita's life and death are inseparable." The historical novel weaves together embalmer's notes, newspaper articles, chronicles of political corruption, folkore, etc., as Martínez reshapes and creates an alternative history: "The only thing that can be done with reality, and with history, is to invent it again."

Julio Matas (1931–)

Julio Matas is a playwright, poet, and fiction writer. Born in Havana, Cuba, on May 12, 1931, Matas was encouraged to follow in the steps of his father, a judge, and he thus obtained his law degree from the University of Havana in 1955. But he never practiced as an attorney. He had enrolled in the University School for Dramatic Arts and by the time of his graduation in 1952, he had already organized a drama group, Arena. In his youth he worked on literary magazines and film projects with some of the figures who would become outstanding in these fields, including Roberto Fernández Retamar, Nestor Almendros, and Tomás Gutiérrez Alea. In 1957, Matas enrolled at Harvard University to pursue a Ph.D. degree in Spanish literature; however, he remained active as a director, returning to Cuba to work on stage productions. It was during the cultural ferment that accompanied the first years of the Communist regime in Cuba that Matas saw two of his first books published there: the collection of short stories *Catálogo de imprevistos*

(*Catalog of the Unforeseen*, 1963), and the three-act play *La crónica y el suceso* (*The Chronicle and the Event*, 1964). In 1965, Matas returned to the United States to assume a position in the department of Hispanic languages and literature at the University of Pittsburgh, a position he kept during the remainder of his life. Matas' plays and short stories have been published widely in magazines, anthologies, and textbooks. One of his most popular plays, *Juego de Damas (Ladies at Play)*, has been performed often and has been published in both Spanish and English.

María Cristina Mena (1893–1965)

Born in Mexico City, Mena became a writer after her immigration to New York City at the age of thirteen, one of the few Hispanic writers to break into professional publications in the early twentieth century. With some support from the famous literary circle in which she matured, which included her husband Henry Kellet Chambers and D.H. Lawrence, Mena was able to publish her stories of Mexican rural life and revolutionary Mexico in such mainstream magazines as *American Magazine*, *The Century Magazine*, *Cosmopolitan*, and *The Household Magazine*. Although Mena was a writer of local color who attracted the interest of Anglo readers by highlighting picturesque Mexican customs, today's scholars insist that her works are sensitive to male–female power relationships, international politics, and class differences. During the 1940s, Mena also became a successful children's author, with such books as *The Water Carrier's Secret* (1942), *The Two Eagles* (1943), and *The Three Kings* (1946). In 1997, her short fiction was compiled and edited in a single volume: *The Collected Stories of María Cristina Mena*.

Miguel Méndez (1930–)

Born in Bisbee, Arizona, into a working-class family during the Depression, Méndez's family moved back and forth across the border in search of employment. Méndez received six years of grammar schooling in Sonora, Mexico, the only formal education he received in his entire life. Nevertheless, Méndez loved reading and books and became an omnivorous reader and a self-taught writer while working as a laborer, farm worker, and brick layer, beginning in his pre-teen years in Tucson. By the age of eighteen, he was already outlining novels and trying his hand at writing stories, but his career as a writer did not really take off until the Chicano Movement of the late 1960s. After the publication of his stories in periodicals and anthologies, most notably those issued by Editorial Quinto Sol, Méndez was hired as a teacher of writing at Pima Valley College in 1970. He later became a distinguished professor at the University of Arizona and, in 1984, received an honorary doctorate from that university.

Méndez's greatest work is *Peregrinos de Aztlán* (Pilgrims in Aztlán, 1974), in which he faithfully depicts border culture and class strife in a baroque Spanish style full of neologisms and regional dialects, as well as elevated diction. His most famous story, "Tata Casehua," was written by him in Yqaqui, as well as in Spanish. Among his many other publications are *Los criaderos humanos (épica de los desamparados) y Sahuaros* [Human Flesh Pots (An Epic of the Wretched) and Sahuaro Cacti, 1975], *Tata Casehua y otros cuentos* (Tata Casehua and Other Stories, 1980), and *El sueño de Santa María de las Piedras* (The Dream of Saint Mary of the Stones, 1993). Méndez has had three of his books translated into English and three of them published in Mexico, including his *El circo que se perdió en el desierto de Sonora* (The Circus that Got Lost in the Sonoran Desert, 2002).

Gabriela Mistral
(1889–1957)

Chilean Gabriela Mistral was Latin America's first Nobel Prize winner, for poetry. After becoming a Nobel

Miguel Méndez.

laureate in 1945, she spent many years in the United States as an ambassador to the League of Nations and the United Nations for Chile; she was highly influential in the Hispanic literary and artistic communities of the United States during her extended sojourn here. Mistral was born in Vicuna, Chile, and trained as a teacher. As she became well known in the world of letters, she left teaching to serve as a consul and later an ambassador. As Latin America's first Nobel laureate, she traveled extensively throughout the Americas and became known as a great humanitarian, an active promoter of public education, and a wonderful speaker. In her poetry, Mistral shows she is a great humanitarian of broad erudition in world literature and the classics. But her overriding theme was always love. Her work is also rooted in a deep religiosity and the condition and circumstances of women, spanning the gamut of preoccupations from maternity to sterility. Mistral's first book, *Desolación* (Desolation), was published in New York by the Hispanic Institute in 1922. Of her twenty-some books of poetry, *Desolación* and *Tala* are considered her best works. She died in Hempstead, New York, on January 10, 1957.

Nicholasa Mohr (1935–)

Nicholasa Mohr was the first U.S. Hispanic woman in modern times to have her literary works published by major commercial publishing houses, and she has developed the longest career of any Hispanic female writer. Only Jose Yglesias published more works than she and for a longer period of time. Mohr's books for such publishers as Dell/Dial, Harper & Row, and Bantam, in both the adult and children's literature categories, have won numerous awards and outstanding reviews. Part and parcel of her work is the experience of growing up a female, Hispanic, and part of a minority in New York City. Born in New York City, Nicholasa Mohr was raised in Spanish Harlem. Educated in New York City schools, she finally escaped poverty after graduating from the Pratt Center for Contemporary Printmaking in 1969. From that date until the publication of her first book, *Nilda* (1973), Mohr developed a successful career as a graphic artist.

Nilda, a novel that traces the life of a young Puerto Rican girl confronting prejudice and coming of age during World War II, won the Jane Addams Children's Book Award and was selected by *School Library Journal* as a Best Book of the Year. It was the first book by a U.S. Hispanic author to be so honored. The Society of Illustrators presented Mohr with a citation of merit for the book's jacket design. After *Nilda*'s success, Mohr was able to produce numerous stories, scripts, and the following titles: *El Bronx Remembered* (1975), *In Nueva York* (1977), *Felita* (1979), *Rituals of Survival: A Woman's Portfolio* (1985), *Going Home* (1986), *A Matter of Pride and Other Stories* (1997), and others. In 1975, *El Bronx Remembered* was awarded the New York Times Outstanding Book Award in teenage fiction and received the Best Book Award from the *School Library Journal*. *El Bronx Remembered* was also a National Book Award finalist in children's literature. In both *In Nueva York* and *El Bronx Remembered*, Mohr examines, through a series of stories and novellas, various Puerto Rican neighborhoods and draws sustenance from the common folks' power to survive and still produce art, folklore, and strong families in the face of oppression and marginalization. In five stories and a novella, *Rituals of Survival: A Woman's Portfolio*, she portrays six strong women who take control of their lives, most of them by liberating themselves from husbands, fathers, or families that attempt to keep them confined in narrowly defined female roles. *Rituals* is the book that the mainstream houses refused to publish, wanting to keep Mohr confined to what they saw as immigrant literature and children's literature, as in her *Felita* and *Going Home*.

While not a member of groups and collectives, Mohr has been one of the most influential of the Nuyorican writers because of sheer productivity and accomplishment. She has also led the way to greater acceptance of Nuyorican and Hispanic writers in creative writing workshops, such as the Millay Colony, in PEN, and on the funding panels of the National Endowment for the Arts and the New York State Council on the Arts. About her creative process, Mohr has stated, "I love creating a world that has characters who come to life. I deal with the human condition of love and good things like joy, and then things like treachery, betrayal, life, death, love, and interesting situations of the way people interact. I learn a lot by writing. Every time I write, I learn something about human nature."

Matías Montes Huidobro (1931–)

Matías Montes Huidobro is a prolific writer of drama, fiction, and poetry, as well as a theatrical producer and scriptwriter for television and radio. Born in 1931 in Sagua la Grande, Cuba, Montes was educated there and in Havana. In 1952, he obtained a Ph. D. degree in pedagogy from the University of Havana, and in 1949 he began publishing creative literature and literary criticism. He later served as a professor of Spanish literature at the National School of Journalism in Havana, at which point he had a falling out with the political powers and immigrated to the United States. In 1963, he became a professor of Spanish at the University of Hawaii until his retirement, circa 1998. The dramas of Matías Montes Huidobro vary in style, theme, and format, ranging from expressionism to surrealism, from the absurd to the allegorical and political. His published plays include *Los Acosados* (The Accosted, 1959), *La Botija* (The Jug, 1959), *Gas en los Poros* (Gas in the Pores, 1961), *El Tiro por la Culata* (Ass-Backwards, 1961), *La Vaca de los Ojos Largos* (The Long-Eyed Cow, 1967), *La Sal de los Muertos* (Salt of the Dead, 1971), *La Guillotina* (The Guillotine, 1972), *Hablando en Chino* (Speaking Chinese, 1977), *Ojos para No Ver* (Eyes for Not Seeing, 1979), *Funeral en Teruel* (Funeral in Teruel, 1982), and *La Navaja de Olofé* (Olofé's Blade, 1982). Montes has also published important novels, including *Desterrados al fuego* (Exiled into the Fire, 1979) and *Cegar al los muertos* (To Blind the Dead, 1980).

José Montoya (1932–)

One of the celebrated poets of the early Chicano Movement, José Montoya was born on a ranch outside of Albuquerque, New Mexico, but moved to California in the 1940s when his father followed the migrant farm labor circuit. At Fowler High School in California, he was encouraged to pursue art and writing, but nevertheless became a *pachuco* whose scrapes with the law eventually pushed him into the Navy to serve in the Korean War as an alternative to reform school. After returning home, Montoya studied under the G.I. Bill and received a B.A. in art from California College of Arts and Crafts. After graduating he became an art teacher in 1962 and a respected graphic artist at the time when the Chicano Movement was in need of cultural leadership. In 1971, Montoya earned an M.A. in fine arts from Sacramento State University and began teaching at that university, climbing the ranks to full professor by 1981. In 1971, Montoya cofounded a Chicano art collective, the Royal Chicano Air Force, as a support for the Chicano Movement.

It was also a time when his poetry began to attract attention. He had previously published well-received poems in Editorial Quinto Sol's groundbreaking anthology, *El Espejo* (*The Mirror*, 1969), and he published his first collection of grassroots and *pachuco*-inspired poetry, *El sol y los de abajo and Other R.C.A.F. Poems*, in 1972. His second volume, *Information: Twenty Years of Joda*, did not appear until 1992. In the interim he published in pamphlets, chapbooks, and small press collections. His most famous poem, "El Louie," which memorializes the tragic life of a *pachuco*, was recorded dramatically on a 45 rpm record by Luis Valdez and circulated extensively throughout Chicano Movement circles.

Pat Mora (1942–)

Pat Mora has developed the broadest audiences for her poetry of any Hispanic poet in the United States. Her clean, crisp narrative style and the healing messages in her verse have allowed her poetry to reach out to both adults and young people. Mora's poems have been reprinted in more elementary, middle, and high school textbooks than those of any other Hispanic poet. While Mora has often been considered a regional poet who celebrates life in the desert, or a soft-spoken feminist, in reality she is a lyrical, romantic poet who offers a healing embrace for many diverse segments of the reading public. This universality has led her to write poetry that explores the condition of women in the Southwest and also those in Third World countries; it has led her to pen deeply humanistic essays and even to create a richly diverse literature for children that encompasses Mexican folk traditions (as in *The Gift of the Poinsettia*) and even such modern, perplexing topics as adoption (in *Pablo's Tree*).

Pat Mora was born on January 19, 1942, in El Paso, Texas, and received her higher education in this border city. After graduating from the University of Texas at El Paso in 1963, she worked as an English teacher in public schools and colleges. A writer since childhood, Mora published her first, award-winning book of poems, *Chants*, in 1984. It was followed by other poetry collections: *Borders* (1986), *Communion* (1991), and *Agua Santa* (*Holy Water*, 1995), and *My Own True Name* (2000). Mora is also well known for her children's picture books: *A Birthday Basket for Tía* (1992), *Listen to the Desert* (1993), *Pablo's Tree* (1994), *The Desert Is My Mother* (1994), *The Gift of the Poinsettia* (1995), *Delicious Hullabaloo* (1999), *The Bakery Lady* (2001), and *The Big Sky* (2002), the latter made up of fourteen poems as opposed to the narrative technique used in most of her children's books. In 1993, she published autobiographical essays in *Nepantla: Essays from the Land in the Middle*. Mora's awards include fellowships from the Kellogg Foundation (1986) and the National Endowment for the Arts (1994), Southwest Book awards (1985 and 1987) and the Skipping Stones award (1995).

Pat Mora.

Cherríe Moraga (1952–)

The works of Cherríe Moraga have opened up the world of Chicano literature to the life and aesthetics of feminism and lesbians. Moraga's works are well known in both feminist and Hispanic circles for their battles against sexism, classism, and racism. Born in Whittier, California, on September 25, 1952, to a Mexican American mother and an Anglo father, Moraga was educated in public schools in the Los Angeles area, after which she graduated from college with a B.A. degree in English in 1974. While working as a teacher she discovered her interest in writing, and in 1977 moved to the San Francisco Bay Area, where she became acquainted with the Anglo lesbian literary movement. In part to fulfill the requirements for a master's degree at San Francisco State University, Moraga collaborated with Gloria Anzaldúa in compiling the first anthology of writings by women of color, *This Bridge Called My Back: Writings by Radical Women of Color* (1981), which has become the most famous and best-selling anthology of its kind and has inspired a movement of Hispanic feminist and lesbian writers.

In her writings, Moraga explains that her understanding of racial and class oppression suffered by Chicanas only came as she experienced the prejudice against lesbians. In 1983, Moraga edited another groundbreaking anthology with Alma Gómez and Mariana Romo-Carmona, *Cuentos: Stories by Latinas. Cuentos* attempts to establish a poetics or a canon of Hispanic feminist creativity, a canon where there is room for, and indeed respect for, the insights of lesbianism. In 1983, Moraga published a collection of her own essays and poems dating back to 1976, *Loving and the War Years: (lo que nunca pasó por sus labios)*, in which she explores the dialectical relationship between sexuality and cultural identity. Her conclusion here, as elsewhere, is that women must be put first. Moraga is also an outstanding playwright; among her most famous works are *Giving Up the Ghost*, produced in 1984 and published in 1986, and *The Shadow of a Man*, published in 1991. To date, Moraga remains one of the most militant and controversial of the Hispanic literary figures.

Alejandro Morales (1944–)

Alejandro Morales is one of the leading Chicano novelists, with substantial novels published in both Spanish and English in the United States and Mexico that create a better understanding of Mexican American history, at least from the vantage point of working-class culture. Born in Montebello, California, on October 14, 1944, Morales grew up in east Los Angeles and received his B.A. degree from California State University, Los Angeles. He went on to complete an M.A. (1973) and a Ph.D. (1975) in Spanish at Rutgers University in New Jersey. Today Morales is a full professor in the Spanish and Portuguese department at the University of California, Irvine. Morales is a recorder of the Chicano experience, basing many of his narratives on historical research. He is also an imaginative interpreter of that experience through his memorable and dynamic characters and language.

Morales' first books were written in Spanish and published in Mexico, because

Alejandro Morales.

of the lack of opportunity here in the United States. *Caras viejas y vino nuevo* (1975; *Old Faces and New Wine*, 1981) examines the conflict of generations in a barrio family. *La verdad sin voz* (1979, translated as *Death of an Anglo*, 1988) is a continuation of the earlier novel but is created against the backdrop of actual occurrences of Chicano-Anglo conflict in the town of Mathis, Texas. The novel also includes autobiographical elements in the form of a section that deals with racism in academia, which comes to a head when a Chicano professor goes up for tenure. *Reto en el paraíso* (*Challenge in Paradise*, 1983) is based on more than 100 years of Mexican American history and myth, as it centers on a basic comparison of the decline of the famed Coronel family of Californios and the rise of the Irish immigrant Lifford family. The novel charts the transfer of power and wealth from the native inhabitants of California to the gold- and land-hungry immigrants empowered by Manifest Destiny. *The Brick People* (1988) traces the development of two families connected with the Simons Brick Factory, one of the largest enterprises of its type in the country. Again, Morales uses the technique of comparing the lives of two families, those of the owners of the factory and those of an immigrant laborer's family. Morales' novel *The Rag Doll Plagues* (1991), while still incorporating a historical structure, follows the development of a plague and a Spanish Mexican doctor who is caught in mortal battle with this plague in three time periods and locations: colonial Mexico, contemporary Southern California, and a future country made up of Mexico and California united together.

Morales is a meticulous researcher and a creator of novelistic circumstances that are symbolic of Mexican American history and cultural development. His novels have an epic sweep that is cinematic and highly literary.

Carlos Morton (1947–)

Born in Chicago to Mexican American parents who hailed from Texas (his paternal grandparent was a Cuban newspaper publisher who resided in Corpus Christi), Morton became a journalist, poet, and playwright during his years as a university student at the University of Texas at El Paso during the early Chicano Movement. It was then that he became exposed to Luis Valdez's El Teatro Campesino and began to study with Valdez, emulating his style and, ultimately, earning his MFA in playwriting at the University of California, San Diego (1979) and his Ph.D. in drama at the University of Texas (1987). Known for his experimentation with bilingual dialog based on Chicano argot, Morton articulated a style and esthetic that depends on high satire of Mexican and Chicano history. Focusing on the conflict of culture, first between Spaniards and Indians and later between Chicanos and Anglos, he exploits all of the humor that can be derived from outrageous stereotypes and linguistic and cultural misinterpretation.

As a playwright, Morton has seen his works produced at campuses around the country and by some of the most prestigious Latino theaters, including the Puerto Rican Traveling Theater and New York Shakespeare's Festival Latino, which awarded him first prize in its playwriting contest in 1986 for *The Many Deaths of Danny Rosales*. Morton's plays have also won such awards as the Southwestern Playwriting Contest (1977) and second prize at the James Baldwin Playwriting Contest (1989). Morton has won residencies and fellowships and in 1989 he became a Fulbright lecturer at the National University of Mexico in Mexico City. He is one of the very few Latino playwrights to have his works published in more than one volume: *The Many Deaths of Danny Rosales and Other Plays* (1983, 1987, 1994), *Johnny Tenorio and Other Plays* (1992), and *Rancho Hollywood y otras obras del teatro chicano* (1999). In addition, many of his plays have been anthologized. Morton is a tenured, full professor of drama at the University of California, Riverside.

Elías Miguel Muñoz (1954–)

Born in Cuba and raised in the United States, where he earned a Ph.D. in Spanish from the University of California, Irvine (1984), Muñoz is one of the most accomplished bilingual novelists, penning original works in both English and Spanish, based on accommodation of Cuban immigrants to life in the United States. Within that overarching theme of culture conflict and synthesis is the conflict of homosexual identity with societal norms in Hispanic and Anglo-American cultures. After receiving his Ph.D. and becoming a professor of Spanish at Wichita State University, Muñoz gave up on the restricted world of university teaching in 1988 to become a full-time writer. He has been a prolific writer of poetry, stories, and novels. His books include *Los viajes de Orlando Cachumbambé* (1984), *Crazy Love* (1988), *En estas tierras* (*In This Land*, 1989), *The Greatest Performance* (1991), and *Brand New Memory* (1998).

Achy Obejas (1956–)

Cuban-born Obejas is a widely published poet, fiction writer, and journalist. Before publishing her novels, Obejas published her poetry and short stories widely in small magazines and in anthologies. As a poet, she was the recipient of a National Endowment for the Arts Fellowship in 1986. For more than a decade, Obejas was the author of a weekly column for the *Chicago Tribune* and contributed regularly to other Chicago periodicals, as well as to such national publications as *Vogue* and *The Voice*. In her novels *Memory Mambo* (1996) and *Days of Awe* (2001), Obejas explores the themes of identity conflict from ethnic, religious and sexual perspectives; not only is Obejas Latina and gay, she is also a member of the Jewish minority within the Latino culture. Both of her novels were honored with a Lammy for best lesbian fiction. In addition to her awards for fiction, Obejas has also received a Peter Lisagor Award (1989) for political reporting from Sigma Delta Chi/Society for Professional Journalists.

Alberto O'Farrill (1899–?)

Alberto O'Farrill was born in Santa Clara, Cuba, in 1899 and had begun his career as an actor and playwright in Havana in 1921 before immigrating to the United States. In New York O'Farrill was the ubiquitous *negrito* (black face) of *obras bufas cubanas* (Cuban farce) and Cuban zarzuelas (Spanish-style operettas), who made a career playing all the major Hispanic stages in New York's stock and itinerant companies. O'Farrill was also an intensely literate man who had been the editor of *Proteo*, a magazine in Havana. In 1927 he became the first editor of New York's *Gráfico* newspaper, which under his leadership became the principal organ for the publication and commentary of literature and theatre. In *Gráfico*, O'Farrill also published *crónicas* under various pseudonyms.

Despite his literary interests, as of 1926 none of O'Farrill's dramatic works had been published. O'Farrill debuted two zarzuelas at the Teatro Esmeralda in Havana in 1921: *Un negro misterioso* (A Mysterious Black Man), and *Las pamplinas de Agapito* (Agapito's Adventures in Pamplona). His other known works were all debuted at New York's Apollo Theatre in 1926: *sainete* (a comedy), *Un doctor accidental* (An Accidental Doctor) and four zarzuelas—*Los misterios de Changó* (The Mysteries of Changó), *Un negro en Andalucía* (A Black Man in Andalusia), *Una viuda como no hay dos* (A Widow like None Other), and *Kid Chocolate*. In most of these, as in his acting, he seems to have been concerned with Afro-Cuban themes.

Gonzalo O'Neill (?–1942)

Gonzalo O'Neill was a key figure in the cultural life of the Puerto Rican community in New York in the 1920s and 1930s. While a young man on the island of his birth, Puerto Rico, he began his literary career as a poet and as a founder of a literary magazine, *Palenque de la Juventud* (Young People's Forum), which published the works of many who would become Puerto Rico's leading writers. A graduate of Puerto Rico's Instituto Civil, he moved to New York City and soon became a prosperous businessman; but he also maintained his love of literature, culture, and his drive for Puerto Rican independence from the United States. The latter is evident in almost every one of his published dramatic works: *La Indiana Borinqueña* (The Indians of Puerto Rico, 1922), a dramatic dialog in verse; *Moncho Reyes* (1923), a biting satire of the colonial government in Puerto Rico, named after the fictional governor; and *Bajo una Sola Bandera* (Under Just One Flag, 1929), a full-length drama examining the political options for Puerto Rico as personified by a young girl's choice of a betrothed. O'Neill was also an investor in and sponsor of the Teatro Hispano, one of the leading Latino playhouses in New York. He had various plays staged at this theater, including one that was not published, *Amores Borincanos* (Puerto Rican Loves, 1938). An unpublished one-act farce that comments on New York City politics, *Que Lleven al Muerto* (Take the Dead Man Away, 1928), has also recently come to light. It is certain that O'Neill wrote many other works, including other plays, poetry, and possibly essays, but they are as yet lost to posterity. Most of his plays that have been preserved through time have come down to us because O'Neill had the financial resources to publish them.

Miguel A. Otero, Jr. (1859–1944)

Miguel A. Otero, Jr., governor and businessman, was born in Albuquerque, New Mexico, into the distinguished family of his namesake, an outstanding business and political figure. Educated in St. Louis, Annapolis, and Notre Dame Univer-

Miguel A. Otero, Jr.

sity, he learned his business acumen in the offices of his father's company, Otero, Sellar & Co., which served him well when he took the major role in the firm after his father's death. With significant business interests in mining, ranching, real estate, and banking, Otero entered politics as a Republican. During the course of his early career, he held various elected and appointed positions, and was even a candidate for the Republican vice-presidential nomination in 1894. In 1897, Otero was appointed by President William McKinley to the governorship of the New Mexico Territory. Because he opposed President Theodore Roosevelt's National Forest Project, Otero was not reappointed to a second term as governor. At this point, Otero switched to the Democratic Party. Under President Woodrow Wilson, Otero was appointed United States Marshall of the Panama Canal Zone in 1917. Otero remained active in politics in the twenties. He also found time during his busy career to author various memoirs of historical value: *My Life on the Frontier, 1864–1882* (1935), *My Life on the Frontier, 1882–1897* (1939), and *My Nine Years as Governor of the Territory of New Mexico, 1897–1906* (1940). In 1936, he published a biography of the famous New Mexico outlaw, *The Real Billy the Kid*, in which he constructs William H. Bonney as a defender of the native New Mexicans. Four years after the publication of his last book, he died in Albuquerque at the age of eighty-four.

Heberto Padilla (1932–)

Poet and journalist Padilla was born in Puerta de Golpe, Cuba, the son of a lawyer and a homemaker. After college, Padilla sought to participate in the construction of a new Cuba with the triumph of the Castro Revolution. From 1959 to 1968, he worked for the state-sponsored newspaper, *Revolución*, and then for the government newspaper, *Granma*. As the Castro government progressively restricted and controlled artists, especially writers, Padilla became more and more disillusioned with that government. Padilla was singled out for his resistance to government esthetic and ideological dictums and lost his job with *Granma* in 1969. His poetry fell into relative obscurity without outlets for publication. In 1971, Padilla was imprisoned for one month after reading some of his works in public, which led to hundreds of protests internationally and his example enshrined as the "Padilla Case." In 1980, with the assistance of U.S. author Bernard Malamud and Senator Edward Kennedy, Padilla was exiled to the United States, where he has continued to write poetry and founded a literary magazine, *Linden Lane*. Among his most successful works published in the United States are *Legacies: Selected Poems* (1982), *Heroes Are Grazing in My Garden* (1984), and *Self-Portrait of the Other* (1990). All three have had original Spanish-language editions in Spain.

Américo Paredes (1915–1999)

Américo Paredes was born on September 13, 1915, in Brownsville, Texas. A famed folklorist, writer and teacher, Paredes received his B.A., M.A., and Ph.D. degrees from the University of Texas in 1951, 1953, and 1956, respectively. After working at a variety of jobs, including journalist, and serving in the armed forces, Paredes received an advanced education later in life and became one of the most distinguished Hispanic scholars in U.S. history. Paredes taught English, folklore, and anthropology at the University of Texas from 1951 until his retirement. He was instrumental in the development of the field of folklore in academia, as well as the field of Mexican American studies. He served as president of the American Folklore Society and was recognized for his leadership internationally. In the United States, he was honored with one of the nation's highest awards for a humanist, the Charles Frankel Prize given by the National Endowment for the Humanities (1989), and in Mexico, the highest award given a foreigner by the Mexican government, the Aguila Azteca (the Aztec Eagle) medal (1991).

Besides publishing numerous research articles, Paredes is the author of *With a Pistol in His Hand: A Border Ballad and Its Hero* (1958), *Folktales of Mexico* (1970), *A Texas Mexican Cancionero* (1976), and *Uncle Remus con chile* (Uncle

Remus with Chile, 1992). He is also the author of two novels, *George Washington Gomez* (1990) and *The Shadow* (1998), both of which were written decades before their publication. The former is today considered a forerunner of Chicano literature for its analysis of the protagonist caught between two cultures and forced to Americanize. The latter won a national award for novel writing in 1954, but Paredes was unable to find a publisher. He is also the author of numerous stories published in newspapers and magazines, some of which were collected in his *The Hammon and the Beans* (1994). Likewise, *Between Two Worlds*, a selection of poetry in Spanish and English that was published in newspapers in the Southwest from the 1930s to the 1960s, was issued in book form in 1991.

Lucy Parsons (Lucía Eldine Parsons González, 1852–1942)

Some biographers have asserted an Afro-American as well as Mexican American identity for the labor activist who came to be known as Lucy Parsons, the widow of the famed martyr Albert Parsons of the historic Haymarket Square riots in Chicago in 1886. Born Lucía González in Johnson County, Texas, just four years after U.S. statehood was conferred on Texas, she married ex-Confederate soldier Albert Parsons in the early 1870s. The couple moved to Chicago around 1873 and became involved in anarchist-led labor organizing in the area. During the height of this movement, Lucy Parsons González began writing for the labor and socialist press and, in 1884, became the editor for *Alarm*, an arm of the International Working People's Association. While her husband and six other anarchist leaders were in jail for the bombings at Haymarket Square, Lucy began a fundraising and speech-making crusade across numerous states that set the tenor for much of the rest of her life. Her editorials, speeches, and testimony in trials are spread throughout newspapers and court documents in the Midwest, and to this day have not been collected.

Lucy Parsons wrote and published two books, *Life of Albert Parsons* (1889) and *Speeches of the Eight Chicago Anarchists* (1910). She continued editing and writing for such periodicals as *Freedom* (1892) and *Liberator* (1905–06), and became associated with many of the progressive causes of her time, including work with Jane Addams, the defense of the Scottsboro Boys, the International Workers of the World, the International Defense League, and the Communist Party of America.

Luis Pérez (1904–1962)

Born in San Luis Potosí, Mexico, Pérez migrated to Los Angeles probably as a teenager during the Mexican Revolution and graduated from Hollywood High School in 1928. He attended Los Angeles City College until 1933 and eventually earned a B.A. from there in 1956. For most of his life, Pérez worked as a Spanish teacher at Los Angeles City College as well as in high schools, and as a translator of Spanish and Italian. Pérez is the author of the first novel of Mexican immigration written in the English language: *El Coyote: The Rebel* (1947), which was issued by mainstream publishing house Henry Holt. In addition, he authored other unpublished novels, stories, and children's works. The novel *El Coyote* is an important contribution to the development of Hispanic literature for its insights into revolution and immigration, two themes that dominate Mexican-American culture. Also, it was written in English and crossed over to the mainstream at a time when such outstanding writers as Jovita González and Américo Paredes were not successful in having their English-language novels published.

Gaspar Pérez de Villagrá (1555–1620)

Born in Puebla, Mexico, and a graduate of the University of Salamanca in Spain, Pérez de Villagrá was a captain in the colonizing mission to New Mexico led by Juan de Oñate in 1598. While participating in founding the first European settlements in what later became the U.S. Southwest, Pérez de Villagrá penned the first epic poem in a European language in that territory—*Historia de la Nueva México* (History of New Mexico)—in 1610, it was published in Alcalá de Henares, Spain, where Villagrá was living in forced exile from Mexico. Thanks to Villagrá's straightforward narrative, many of the historical details, including news of poetry and theatrical performances during the settlers' expedition, have been documented.

Gustavo Pérez-Firmat (1949–)

Pérez-Firmat was born in Havana, Cuba, on March 7, 1949, and relocated with his family to Miami after Castro came to power in Cuba. Pérez-Firmat received most of his formal education in Miami, obtaining a B.A. and an M.A. in Spanish from the University of Miami in 1972 and 1973, respectively. He went on to earn his Ph.D. in comparative literature (1979) at the University of Michigan, but Miami and the life of Cuban Americans remained central to his consciousness, even when he became a professor of Spanish and literature at Duke University in 1978. Pérez-Firmat's basic condition—born in Cuba and transplanted to American soil in his youth—has made him a member of the new Cuban American generation and has led to his theories about the dual perspective held by what he terms a "transitional" generation. For this poet/theorist, Cuban Americans of his generation can be equally at home or equally uncomfortable in both Cuba and the United States. They are cultural mediators, who are constantly translating not only language, but also the differences between the Anglo-American and Cuban/Cuban American world views. Since they have the unique ability to communicate with and understand both cultures, these Cuban Americans have taken on the role of translator not only for themselves but for society at large.

In his groundbreaking book-length essay, *Life on the Hyphen: The Cuban-American Way* (1993), Pérez-Firmat maintains, however, that this is only a transitional stage and that the next generation will follow a path similar to that of the children of European immigrants, who are simply considered ethnic Americans and are more American than they are anything else. Themes of biculturalism are everpresent in Pérez-Firmat's poetry, which is full of code-switching and bilingual-bicultural double entendres and playfulness. While biculturalism forms the framework for Pérez-Firmat's poetry, it is not his sole theme. He is an expansive poet, a poet of love and eroticism, and of the daily, tedious rhythms of life. He chronicles both growing up and growing old, battles with family and battles with illness. In his book-length memoir, *Next Year in Cuba* (1995), Pérez-Firmat documents the tension his generation feels between identifying with other Americans their age and identifying with their parents, who always looked forward to returning to Cuba. True to form, Pérez-Firmat re-created the memoir in Spanish in 1997 as *El año que viene estamos en Cuba. Anything but Love* (2000),

Gustavo Pérez-Firmat.

Pérez-Firmat's latest novel, is a tour de force of culture conflict revolving around love, marriage, and sex roles, all articulated with that inimitable rhapsodic excess that is the author's trademark.

Pedro Pietri (1943–)

Pedro Pietri is famous for the literary persona of street urchin or skid-row bum that he has created for himself. His works are characterized by the consistent perspective of the underclass in language, philosophy, and creative and psychological freedom. Pietri was born in Ponce, Puerto Rico, on March 21, 1943, just two years before his family migrated to New York. He was orphaned while still a child and raised by his grandmother. Pietri attended public schools in New York City and served in the Army from 1966 to 1968. Other than his having taught writing occasionally and participated in workshops, very little else is known about this intentionally mysterious and unconventional figure.

Pietri has published collections of poems and poetry chapbooks: *The Blue and the Gray* (1975), *Invisible Poetry* (1979), *Out of Order* (1980), *Uptown Train* (1980), *An Alternate* (1980), and *Traffic Violations* (1983). Nevertheless, it was his first book of poetry, *Puerto Rican Obituary* (1971), that brought him his greatest fame and a host of imitators, making him a model for the Nuyorican school of literature. In 1973, a live performance by him of poems from this book was recorded and distributed by Folkways Records. In 1980, Pietri's short story *Lost in the Museum of Natural History* was published in bilingual format in Puerto Rico. Pietri has also had numerous unpublished, but produced, plays and one published collection, *The Masses Are Asses* (1984). Always a master of the incongruous and surprising, Pietri has created unlikely but humorous narrative situations in both his poetry and plays, such as that in his poem "Suicide Note from a Cockroach in a Low Income Housing Project" and in a dialog between a character and her own feces in his play *Appearing in Person Tonight—Your Mother*. Pietri's work is a total break with conventions, both literary and social, and it is subversive in its open rejection of established society and its hypocrisies.

Cecile Pineda (1942–)

Born and raised in New York City Pineda moved to the San Francisco Bay Area of California in 1961 and has lived there ever since. She is the author of *Face* (1985), *Frieze* (1986), *Love Queen of the Amazon* (1991), and *Fishlight: A Dream of Childhood* (2001), which was written with the assistance of a National Endowment Fiction Fellowship and named Notable Book of the Year by the *New York Times*. Both *Frieze* and *Face* won gold medals from the Commonwealth Club of California. Prior to her career as a novelist, Pineda worked extensively in theater. In 1970, Pineda received an M.A. degree in theater from San Francisco State University. She founded Theatre of Man, which she directed from 1969 to 1981 as an ensemble poet's theater.

Miguel Piñero (1946–1988)

Miguel Piñero, the most famous dramatist to come out of the Nuyorican school, was born in Gurabo, Puerto Rico, on December 19, 1946. He was raised on the Lower East Side of New York, the site of many of his plays and poems. Shortly after moving to New York, his father abandoned the family, which had to live on the streets until his mother could find a source of income. Piñero was a gang leader and involved in petty crime and drugs while an adolescent; he was a junior high-school dropout, and by the time he was twenty-four he had been sent to Sing Sing Prison for armed robbery. While at Sing Sing, he began writing and acting in a theater workshop there. By the time of his release, his most famous play, *Short Eyes* (published in 1975), had already been prepared in draft form. The play was produced and soon moved to Broadway after getting favorable reviews. During the successful run of his play and afterwards, Piñero became involved with a group of Nuyorican writers on the Lower East Side and became one of the principal spokespersons and models for the new school of Nuyorican literature, which was furthered by the publication of *Nuyorican Poets: An Anthology of Puerto Rican Words and Feelings*, compiled and edited by him and Miguel Algarín in 1975. During this time, as well, Piñero began his career as a scriptwriter for such television dramatic series as "Barreta," "Kojak," and "Miami Vice."

In all, Piñero wrote some eleven plays that were produced, most of which are included in his two collections, *The Sun Always Shines for the Cool, A Midnight Moon at the Greasy Spoon, Eulogy for a Small-Time Thief* (1983), and *Outrageous One-Act Plays* (1986). Piñero is also author of a book of poems, *La Bodega Sold Dreams* (1986). Included among his awards were a Guggenheim Fellowship (1982) and the New York Drama Critics Circle Award for Best American Play, an Obie, and the Drama Desk Award, all received in 1974 for "Short Eyes." Piñero died of sclerosis of the liver in 1988, after many years of hard living and recurrent illnesses as a dope addict.

Mary Helen Ponce (1938–)

Born and raised in the San Fernando Valley of California, Mary Helen Ponce first began writing in grammar school, and in eighth grade wrote a play that was produced. Continuing to envision herself as a writer throughout her education, Ponce received a B.A. and an M.A. in Mexican American studies at California State University in 1978 and 1980, respectively, and eventually a Ph.D. at the University of New Mexico, Albuquerque, in 1988. Throughout these years she developed her literary career and taught at colleges in the Los Angeles area. From her very first self-published collection of stories, *Recuerdo: Short Stories of the Barrio* (1983) to her later books published by a university-based press, Ponce has been faithful to the people she grew up with, especially the women, recording and immortalizing their lives in fine stories and novels. *Taking Control* (1987) followed in the same vein, while *The Wedding* (1989) studied in depth with humor and empathy the community folklore, rituals, and expectations involved in a Chicano wedding. Ponce penned her autobiography, *Hoyt Street: Memories of a Chicana Childhood*, in 1993.

Dolores Prida (1943–)

Dolores Prida is a playwright and screenwriter whose works have been produced in various states and in Puerto Rico, Venezuela, and the Dominican Republic. Born on September 5, 1943, in Caibairén, Cuba, Prida immigrated with her family to New York in 1963. She graduated from Hunter College in 1969 with a major in Spanish American literature. Upon graduation she began a career as a journalist and editor, first for Collier-Macmillan and then for other publishers, quite often using her bilingual skills. In 1977 her first play, *Beautiful Senoritas*, was produced at the Duo Theater. Since then she has seen some ten of her plays produced.

Prida's plays vary in style and format, from adaptations of international classics such as *The Three Penny Opera*, to experiments with the Broadway musical formula, as in her *Savings* (1985), to her attempt to create a totally bilingual play, as in *Coser y cantar* (To Sew and to Sing, 1981). In *Coser y cantar* Prida creates two characters representing, respectively, the Americanized part of a woman's psyche and her "old-country" consciousness to illustrate the tensions and contradictions that need to be resolved by Hispanics everywhere in the United States. In other plays, Prida's themes vary from an examination of the phenomenon of urban gentrification, as in *Savings* (1981), to the generation gap and conflict of culture, as in *Botánica* (1990). Since 1993, *Botánica* (Herb Shop) has won a permanent place in the repertory of Spanish Repertory Theater in New York, which through 1996 was continuing to alternate it on its programs, especially for schools.

Prida's plays, which are written in Spanish or English or bilingually, have been collected in *Beautiful Senoritas and Other Plays* (1991). Prida is also a talented poet who was a leader in the 1960s of New York's Nueva Sangre (New Blood) movement of young poets. Her books of poems include *Treinta y un poemas* (Thirty-one Poems, 1967), *Women of the Hour* (1971), and, with Roger Cabán, *The IRT Prayer Book*. Among her awards are an honorary doctorate from Mount Holyoke College (1989), Manhattan Borough President's Excellence in the Arts Award (1987), and a Cintas fellowship (1976). In 1981 Prida became the first U.S. Hispanic to receive a special award from the Third World Theatre Competition in Caracas, Venezuela, for her play *La era latina* (The Latin Era). Written and first produced in 1980, this bilingual musical comedy toured more than thirty Hispanic neighborhoods in New York City for open-air staging by the Puerto Rican Traveling Theatre.

Roberto Quesada (1962–)

Born in Olanchito, Honduras, Quesada immigrated to the United States in the early 1980s. He has become the humorist of immigrant literature, satirizing both the reasons for Latin Americans to leave their home countries and the reception they receive here in the grand Metropolis. He has been one of the fortunate immigrant writers to have access to English-language publishers in the United States, who have translated his novels into English: *Los barcos* (*The Ships*, 1988), *The Big Banana* (1999), and *Never through Miami* (2002). Quesada has also published works abroad, such as *El humano y la diosa* (The Human Being and the Goddess, 1996), which was published in the Dominican Republic, and *Nunca por Miami* (2001), which was published in Spain. Quesada has also been the editor of the magazine *Nosotros los latinos* (We the Latinos) and in 1986, he founded the literary review *Sobre Vuelo* (On the Wing), both in New York.

Leroy V. Quintana (1944–)

Leroy V. Quintana is one of the most renowned poets to memorialize Hispanic participation in the Vietnam War. Born in Albuquerque, New Mexico, Quintana obtained a B.A. in English in 1969 from the University of New Mexico after serving for two years in the war. In 1974, he obtained an M.A. in English from New Mexico State University and began publishing poems in literary magazines. By 1976, he published his first book, *Hijo del Pueblo: New Mexico Poems*, a highly autobiographical collection of verse. While working as an English instructor in area colleges and universities, Quintana published his next book, *Sangre* (Blood, 1981), which won the Before Columbus American Book Award. Quintana decided to change careers, and after obtaining a master's in counseling from Western New Mexico University he became a psychological counselor in San Diego, California. He continued writing and in 1990 published *Interrogations*, a collection of poems about the Vietnam War, and in 1993 published *The History of Home*, which memorializes growing up in poverty in New Mexico by casting each poem in the voice of a hometown personality. *The History of Home* was Quintana's second American Book Award winner.

Sara Estela Ramírez (1881–1910)

At the age of seventeen, Sara Estela Ramírez came to Laredo, Texas, in 1898, during the period when Mexican teachers were recruited by Mexican Americans in Texas who established their own schools to preserve language and culture, as well as to protect their children from the ravages of segregation and discrimination. During her short, very productive life in the border city, she not only taught class but also founded and edited newspapers, assisted in organizing labor, and became an active member of Ricardo Flores Magón's movement against the dictatorial regime of Porfirio Díaz in Mexico. A sought-after poet whose verses were often published in Laredo's Spanish-language newspapers, Ramírez was equally sought after for her passionate speeches on behalf of labor and liberal causes at organizing meetings for farm workers, miners, industrial workers, and women. Ramírez died of tuberculosis in 1910 before fully developing her potential as a writer.

Manuel Ramos Otero (1948–1999)

Novelist, short story writer, and poet Manuel Ramos Otero was born in Manatí, Puerto Rico, and moved to New York City after graduating from the University of Puerto Rico (1968) to pursue his literary and theatrical career, as well as for the greater freedom accorded gays in the United States. After studying with Lee Strasberg in 1970, Ramos Otero went on to establish his own theater workshop, Aspaguanza, where he worked with experimental Puerto Rican drama. In 1969, he earned an M.A. in Spanish and Latin American literature from New York University and began teaching in New York-area colleges and universities. In 1976, he founded a small literary press, El Libro Viaje, which published several books of poetry and Ramos Otero's own experimental novel *La novela bingo* (The Bingo Novel, 1976). His other books include *El cuento de la mujer y el mar* (The Story of a Woman and the Sea, 1979) and *El libro de la muerte* (The Book of Death, 1985). In 1999, he returned to Puerto Rico, where he died of AIDS the same year.

John Rechy (1934–)

John Rechy is the most famous Chicano cultivator of gay narrative. Born and raised in El Paso, Texas, the son of a Scottish musical composer and a Mexican homemaker, Rechy was a child actor and became a writer in his teens, penning an historical novel, *Time on Wings*, at age seventeen. After graduating from Texas Western College, Rechy relocated to New York to develop his career as a writer, but early rejection sent him to hustle in the streets. In the 1960s, he began publishing fictional recasts of his experiences as a male prostitute, and in 1963 Grove Press issued his passionate, rhapsodic first novel about life in the gay underworld, *City of the Night*. With the publication in 1967 of his second novel, *Numbers*, Rechy was confirmed as a leading gay writer, but not accepted in the literary mainstream. Rechy went on to publish various other works, achieving little attention until 1976, when he published *The Sexual Outlaw: A Documentary* as a protest for gay rights. He soon was in demand as a militant spokesperson for the rights of homosexuals in what he saw as an increasingly fascist national culture. During the 1980s, Rechy moved away from gay-themed novels to publish *Bodies and Souls* (1983), chronicling the lives of young runaways in Los Angeles, and *Marilyn's Daughter* (1988), a fictonalized biography of a woman claiming to be the daughter of Marilyn Monroe and Robert Kennedy. In 1992, Rechy published a very well-received autobiographical novel, *The Miraculous Day of Amalia Gomez.*

Alberto Alvaro Ríos (1952–)

Born in Nogales, Arizona, to a Mexican father and an English mother, Ríos graduated from the University of Arizona with a B.A. in literature and creative writing (1974) and an M.F.A. in creative writing (1979). After establishing a national reputation as a poet and short story writer, Ríos became a tenured professor of creative writing at Arizona State University in 1985, and in 1994 he was appointed a Regent's Professor at the same institution. During his career, he has been a writer in residence at various colleges, including Vassar (1992). Ríos is author of more than ten books of poetry and short fiction, as well as a memoir, *Capirotada* (1999). Among his most important collections of poetry are *Whispering to Fool the Wind* (1982), winner of the Academy of American Poets Walt Whitman Award, and *Teodoro Luna's Two Kisses* (1990), which was nominated by its publisher, W.W. Norton, for the Pulitzer Prize. For his first book of short stories, *The Iguana Killer* (1984), he won the Western States Foundation Award for Fiction. His works were selected for The Best American Poetry, 1996; The Best American Essays, 1999; and The Best American Poetry, 1999. He also bears the distinction of having won Pushcart Prizes in both poetry (1988, 1989, 1995) and fiction (1986, 1993, 2001). He is a fellow of the National Endowment for the Arts and the Guggenheim Foundation.

Tomás Rivera (1935–1984)

Mexican American novelist Tomás Rivera is one of the principal founders of the Chicano literary movement and the author of one of the foundational works of that movement, . . . *Y no se lo tragó la tierra* (. . . *And the Earth Did Not Devour Him*, 1971). Born into a family of migrant workers in Crystal City, Texas, on December 22, 1935, Rivera had to fit his early schooling as well as his college education between seasonal work in the fields. Nevertheless, he achieved an outstanding education and became a college professor and administrator. He became

Chancellor of the University of California–Riverside in 1978, the position he held when he died of a heart attack on May 16, 1984.

Rivera's outwardly simple, but inwardly complex novel . . . *Y no se lo tragó la tierra*, is much in the line of experimental Latin American fiction, demanding that the reader take part in unraveling the story and in coming to his own conclusions about the identity and relationships of the characters, as well as the meaning. Drawing upon his own life as a migrant worker from Texas, Rivera constructed a novel in the straightforward, but poetic, language of migrant workers in which a nameless central character attempts to find himself by reconstructing the overheard conversations and stories, as well as events that took place during a metaphorical year, which really represents the protagonist's entire lifetime. It is the story of a sensitive boy who is trying to understand the hardship that surrounds his family and community of migrant workers; his path is first one of rejection of them only to embrace them and their culture dearly as his own at the end of the book. In many ways . . . *Y no se lo tragó la tierra* came to be the most influential book in the Chicano's search for identity.

Tomás Rivera.

Before his death in 1984, Rivera wrote and published other stories, essays, and poems. Through his essays, such as "Chicano Literature: Fiesta of the Living" (1979) and "Into the Labyrinth: The Chicano in Literature" (1971), and his personal and scholarly activities, he was one of the prime movers in the promotion of Chicano authors, in the creation of the concept of Chicano literature, and in the creation of Chicano literature and culture as legitimate academic areas in the college curricula. In 1989 his stories were collected and published under the title of *The Harvest*, which is also the title of one of his stories, and in 1990 his poems were collected and published under the title of *The Searchers*. In 1990, all of his works were collected and published in *Tomás Rivera: The Complete Works*, the only volume of a Chicano author's complete works published to date. By any account, Tomás Rivera remains the most outstanding and influential figure in the literature of Mexican peoples in the United States, and he deserves a place in the world's canon of Spanish-language literature.

Luis Rodríguez (1954–)

In 1993, Rodríguez's memoir of life on the streets, *Always Running*, became the first Hispanic book to win the Carl Sandburg Award for Non-Fiction. It also won the *Chicago Sun-Times* first prose book award in 1994. Born in El Paso but raised in Los Angeles, where he became a gang member and petty thief, Rodríguez escaped the life on the streets out of sheer force of will and began working in heavy industry as well as keeping journals and writing. By the 1980s while living in Chicago, his articles and stories began to appear in mainstream magazines and newspapers. When he perceived a lack of access to publication for Latino and minority writers, Rodríguez founded Tía Chucha Press in the late 1980s, at first a publisher of chapbooks. He published his own *Poems across the Pavement* with Tía Chucha in 1989. His second book of poetry, *The Concrete River*, won the PEN Oakland/Josephine Miles Award in 1991. When Rodríguez noted that his son was being drawn into street gang life and culture in Chicago, he wrote *Always Running* to document the wasted life and dead-end machismo that awaited his son if he continued on the streets.

Richard Rodríguez (1944–)

Essayist Richard Rodríguez was born on July 31, 1944, in San Francisco, the son of Mexican immigrants. He began school as a Spanish-speaker, but made the difficult transition to English to progress in school. As he recalled in his autobiographical book-length essay, *Hunger of Memory*, Rodríguez came to believe that English was the language of U.S. education and society and that the Spanish language and Hispanic culture were private matters, for the home. Rodríguez had outstanding success in school and eventually received a B.A. in English from Stanford University in 1967 and an M.A. from Columbia University in 1969; he began doctoral work at the University of California, but never completed it because his writing career had begun. In 1981, Rodríguez published the above-mentioned autobiography, which received praise from mainstream critics across the nation for its elegant and passionate prose as well as for its rejection of bilingual education and affirmative action programs. Rodríguez immediately was seen by Hispanics as an Uncle Tom or Tío Taco for having bought success at the price of attacking Hispanic language, culture, and programs aimed to assist Hispanics in education and employment. To this date, despite a successful career as an essayist, television commentator, and opinion writer for newspapers, Rodríguez is not embraced by Hispanic critics as an authentic or valuable voice. His second book, *Days of Obligation: An Argument with My Mexican Father* (1992), which does not have the political content of *Hunger of Memory*, received fewer, but generally good reviews and garnered very little criticism from Hispanic quarters.

Lola Rodríguez de Tió (1843–1924)

On September 14, 1843, Puerto Rican patriot and poet Lola Rodríguez de Tió was born in San Germán, Puerto Rico. She received an education at religious schools and from private tutors, and began to write poetry under the influence of poet Ursula Cardona de Quiñones. In 1865, she married Bonocio Tió, a journalist who shared Rodríguez de Tió's desire for Puerto Rican independence, and they held literary and political meetings regularly at their home in Mayagüez. In 1868, Rodríguez de Tió wrote the nationalist lyrics that would become the Puerto Rican national hymn, "La Borinqueña." In 1877, the government exiled Rodríguez de Tió; she and her family took refuge in Venezuela for three years and then returned to Puerto Rico. In 1889, she was exiled once again, this time to Cuba, where she continued her revolutionary activities until 1895, when she was exiled again. This time she took up residence in New York, continuing to plot with the leading revolutionaries for Puerto Rican and Cuban independence and to publish her writings in Spanish-language periodicals in the metropolis. In 1899 after the Spanish-American War, she returned to a hero's reception in Cuba. She remained in Cuba and began to work on fashioning a new society, one in which women would have greater liberty and opportunity. In 1910, she was elected a member of the Cuban Academy of Arts and Letters. Lola Rodríguez de Tió was a romantic poet, as her three books of poems readily attest: *Mis cantares* (My Songs, 1876), *Claros y nieblas* (Clarities and Cloudiness, 1885), and *Mi libro de Cuba* (My Book about Cuba, 1893). Rodríguez de Tió is celebrated as a beloved patriotic and literary figure, as well as an early feminist, in both Puerto Rico and Cuba. She died on November 10, 1924, in Cuba.

Lola Rodríguez de Tió.

Leo Romero (1950–)

Born in Los Alamos, New Mexico, Romero has become the poet par excellence of rural New Mexican life, his verse inspired by the folklore and folk speech that harkens back to life realtively untouched by Anglo-Americans. In addition, Romero is a talented painter and muralist in the traditional vein who has exhibited his works throughout the state. Widely published in magazines and anthologized, Romero is the author of three collections of poetry: *During the Growing Season* (1978), *Agua Negra* (Black Water, 1981), and *Celso* (1985). The latter, which is a series of narrative poems dealing with the life of the town drunk, was later made into a one-man play and toured nationally by actor-playwright Rubén Sierra. In 1995, Romero published his first book of fiction, a collection of magical realist tales entitled *Rita and Los Angeles.*

María Amparo Ruiz de Burton (1832–1895)

Born in Loreto, Baja California, Ruiz de Burton saw much of her homeland in Baja and Alta, California, transformed with the coming of Anglo-America after the war with Mexico and the admittance of California to the Union. From an upper class ranching family, Ruiz de Burton was able to favorably negotiate the transition to American citizenship and culture as the wife of a captain in the United States Army, but she nevertheless lost lands and patrimony during that transition.

Ruiz de Burton bears the distinction of having written and published the first novel in English by a Hispanic from the United States: *Who Would Have Thought It?* (1872). Originally published anonymously, the novel reconstructs antebellum and Civil War society in the North and engages the dominant U.S. myths of American exceptionalism, egalitarianism, and consensus, offering an acerbic critique of opportunism and hypocrisy as it represents northern racism and U.S. imperialism. The novel is the first by a U.S. Hispanic to address the disenfranchised status of women. In 1885, Ruiz de Burton also produced the first fictional narrative, written and published in English, from the perspective of the conquered Mexican population of the Southwest: *The Squatter and the Don.* Self-published under the pseudonym of C. Loyal in San Francisco, the novel documents the loss of lands to squatters and banking and railroad interests in southern California shortly after statehood. *The Squatter and the Don* is an historical romance that laments land loss and calls for justice and redress of grievances. The novel questions U.S. expansionism, as well as the rise of corporate monopolies and their power over government policy.

Ronald Ruiz (1936–)

Ruiz is one of the most innovative and intellectual Latino writers who explores in depth the themes that are most important to Hispanics: immigration and success in the United States, existence in an underclass here, labor exploitation, and, of course, identity. Born and raised in northern California by Mexican immigrant parents, Ruiz became an outstanding student who achieved distinction in his university and law training. After receiving a B.A. from Saint Mary's College in California (1957) and a law degree from the University of San Francisco (1964), Ruiz practiced law as a defense attorney as well as a prosecutor; today he is the district attorney for San Jose. In much of his career, he has dealt with some of society's most hardened criminals, including many from Hispanic backgrounds. In 1984, Ruiz was named Attorney of the Year by the Mexican American Legal Defense and Education Fund. Ruiz also worked as a lawyer (1975–1976) as well as a board member for the Agricultural Labor Relations Board (1975–1982).

Despite his successful law career, one of Ruiz's first loves was literature and he had been writing since college. In 1994, Ruiz published his first novel, *Happy Birthday Jesus*, the powerful tale of the making of a Latino sociopath, produced by the failure of all the social institutions, from the family and the schools to the church, the courts, and the penal system. Controversial because of its graphic violence and hard-hitting analysis, the novel became a best seller in the West. Ruiz's second novel, *Giuseppe Rocco* (1998), explores the rise and fall of two very American families named Rocco and Martínez, and their will to succeed in the United States through hard labor, scrounging, and saving. In *Big Bear* (2003), Ruiz turned his attention to farm labor within the context of a murder mystery and a lawyer's struggle to come to grips with his own Mexican American identity.

Ronald Ruiz.

Floyd Salas (1931–)

Floyd Salas was born on January 24, 1931, in Walsenburg, Colorado, into a family that traces both its maternal and paternal lines back to the original Spanish settlers of Florida and New Mexico. When he was still very young, the family relocated to California and in pursuit of work opportunities moved around so much that Salas attended six different high schools in four years. One of the most tragic events of his early life was the death of his mother, Anita Sánchez Salas, from a protracted illness during his high school years. Following her death, Salas became a juvenile delinquent and wound up spending 120 days on the Santa Rita Prison Farm; it was a grueling experience that led him to foreswear his delinquent ways to avoid problems with the law. The experience also served as material for his first novel, which graphically depicts prison life. In 1956, Salas won the first boxing scholarship ever given to the University of California, Berkeley, where he discovered literature. A number of writing scholarships and fellowships followed, including a Rockefeller grant to study at the Centro Mexicano de Escritores in Mexico City in 1958. Upon returning to California from Mexico, Salas worked on Bay Area campuses as a creative writing instructor, became active in the campus protest movement and immersed himself in the drug and hippy subcultures. These experiences later became grist for his novels *What Now My Love* (1970) and *State of Emergency* (1996).

Salas' first published book, *Tatoo the Wicked Cross* (1967), was made possible by his winning the prestigious Joseph Henry Jackson Award and a Eugene R Saxton Fellowship, which were awarded based on his early drafts of that novel. *Tatoo the Wicked Cross* is an exposé of the brutality of juvenile jail, as seen by a street youth (Pachuco) who is raped and abused; the brutalized protagonist ends up committing murder. The raw power and passion of Salas' narrative left reviewers believing that Salas had experienced this brutality firsthand, but he actually

Floyd Salas.

based the story on tales he had heard at Preston Reform School. The overwhelming acclaim the novel received from reviewers led Salas into a career as a writer. Salas' next novel, *What Now My Love?* (1970), was of modest proportions; it told the story of the escape of three hippies involved in a drug bust where policemen were shot. The novel follows their flight to Tijuana and their penetration of the border town's drug underworld.

With Salas, life and literature are always closely entwined. His next years were occupied in chasing the drug culture: "I made the world's pot scenes, following the hippy trail from San Francisco to Marakesh, writing a novel about my radical experiences in the Bay Area called *Lay My Body on the Line.*" The novel was eventually published by a small press in 1978 to negligible critical response. His personal battle with drugs, his dysfunctional family, and the break-up of his own marriage led Salas to a long hiatus from publishing. In the early 1990s, through writing his memoir *Buffalo Nickel*, Salas came to terms with his family's dramatic history of widespread drug addiction and suicides (a total of six). The work depicts his own agonizing love-hate relationship with his older brother, a small-time prize-fighter, drug addict, and petty criminal. The memoir leads the reader into the underworld of pimp bars, drugs, and crime, and depicts Salas' struggles to escape the chaos of his family life by becoming a writer. The work was so well received that Salas was awarded a California Arts Council Fellowship for achieving excellence.

Luis Omar Salinas (1937–)

Born in Robstown, Texas, close to the Mexican border, on June 27, 1937, Salinas spent some of his early years in Mexico but by age nine had moved to live with an aunt and uncle in California. He attended public schools and began college at Fresno State University, where he edited the literary magazine *Backwash*, but never received his diploma. At Fresno State in 1966, Salinas took a creative writing course, but his writing education ended when he moved with his family to Sanger, California. During the 1960s, Salinas was hospitalized on various occasions for nervous breakdowns, and these breakdowns have recurred periodically since. His first breakdowns were the result of the combined pressures of his involvement in the Chicano Civil Rights Movement and his teaching Chicano Studies.

In 1970 he published his first book of poetry, *Crazy Gypsy*, a highly artistic work that became an anthem for Chicano activists. Many of the poems were included in the first anthologies of Chicano literature and have become canonized in U.S. Hispanic literature: "Crazy Gypsy," "Aztec Angel," "Nights and Days,"

"Mexico, Age Four," and others. In *Crazy Gypsy* Salinas introduces themes that are evident in all of his works: alienation and loneliness, death, and the defamiliarization of the world around us. Salinas offers a wealth of images in which the stark beauty of language, fed from the grand traditions of both Hispanic and Anglo-American lyric poetry, convinces the reader of the possibilities offered by a synthesis gained from a complete understanding of two or more cultures. In *Darkness under the Trees: Walking behind the Spanish* (1982), and in the works that follow, Salinas heightens the note of sorrow and melancholy as he attempts to rationalize his unjust fate. The themes of love, death, and madness dominate. The second part of the book pays homage to the Spanish Civil War poets who have served as his models, including García Lorca.

Luis Omar Salinas.

Salinas is the most lyrical, most imaginative, deepest, and most humane Chicano/Latino poet. He is, nevertheless, generally overlooked by academe, and often passed over not only by readers but by other Hispanic writers—perhaps because his illnesses have not permitted him to tour and engage in exchanges with editors and other writers, or perhaps because he is shy and has done nothing to promote himself in a field that today quite often demands stellar oral performances and promotional campaigns. Salinas, who has supported himself with a variety of blue-collar jobs, has won some of the most prestigious awards for writing, including the California English Teachers citation, 1973; Stanley Kunitz Poetry Prize (for *Afternoon of the Unreal*), 1980; Earl Lyon Award, 1980; and General Electric Foundation Award, 1983.

Raúl Salinas (1934–)

Born in San Antonio, Texas, Salinas was raised in Austin from age two. In 1957, he moved to Los Angeles, and the next year he was sentenced to 15 years of imprisonment at Soledad State Prison. He spent eleven of those years behind bars in Soledad and other of the most brutal prisons in the United States, during which time he raised his political and social consciousness and discovered poetry as an outlet for his frustrations, the agony of memory, and his political commitment. In Leavenworth penetentiary, Salinas founded and edited two journals: *Aztlán de Leavenworth* and *New Era Prison* Magazine. During this time and after his release, he became one of the most noteworthy self-taught prison poets, even elevating prison to a metaphor in his poetry; appropriately one of his most famous poems (originally published in *Aztlán de Leavenworth* in 1970) and the title of his first book reveal this esthetic: *Un Trip through the Mind Jail y Otras Excursions* (1980). Through assistance from students and professors at the University of Washington,

Salinas was released early and in 1972 took courses at the university, becoming involved in the Chicano and Native American movements. In addition to publishing his work widely in magazines, Salinas is the author of a second book of poems, *East of the Freeway: Reflections de Mi Pueblo* (1994). In 1999, Arte Público Press of the University of Houston reissued *Un Trip* and hailed Salinas as a pioneer of Hispanic literature in the United States. Currently, Salinas is the owner and operator of Resistencia Bookstore in Austin, Texas, and the publisher of Red Salmon Press books.

Ricardo Sánchez (1941–1995)

Ricardo Sánchez was the first Chicano writer to have a book of poetry published by a mainstream commercial publishing house when Anchor/Doubleday issued his *Canto y grito mi liberación* (I Sing and Shout for My Liberation, 1973). It was also the first bilingual poetry book published by a major commercial publisher. Ricardo Sánchez was one of the most prolific Chicano poets, one of the first creators of a bilingual literary style, and one of the first to be identified with the Chicano Movement. He was a tireless and popular oral performer and social activist whose creative power expressed itself in innovative uses of both Spanish and English in poetry, frequently through the creation of interlingual neologisms and abrupt linguistic contrasts. His verse was as overwhelming in sheer power as was his aggressive personality, which was forged in hard prison labor. Ricardo Sánchez was born the youngest of thirteen children in the notorious Barrio del Diablo (Devil's Neighborhood) in El Paso, Texas, on March 29, 1941. He received his early education there and became a high school dropout, an Army enlistee, and later a repeat offender sentenced to prison terms in Soledad Prison in California and Ramsey Prison Farm Number One in Texas. At these institutions he began his literary career before his last parole in 1969.

Much of his early-life experiences of oppressive poverty and overwhelming racism—as well as his suffering in prisons, his self-education, and rise to a level of political and social consciousness—is chronicled in Sánchez's poetry, which although very lyrical, is the most autobiographic among the Hispanic poets. Sánchez always envisioned himself participating, in fact leading, a sociopolitical consciousness-raising movement. His many travels and itinerant lifestyle—always in search of a permanent job in academia—resulted in his functioning as a troubadour-model for the developing Chicano literary movement. His poetry announced and exemplified the authenticity of a bilingual writing style that had roots in oral tradition and community concerns.

José Sánchez-Boudy (1928–)

Born in Havana, Cuba, Sánchez-Boudy was the son of a wealthy Spanish immigrant and the daughter of a Frenchman. Educated in Catholic schools, Sánchez studied for two years in New Hampshire and the University of Detroit but returned to Cuba for a law degree, which he obtained from the University of Havana in 1953. Sánchez became a noted criminal attorney, but in 1961 he abandoned Cuba for Miami and then Puerto Rico after the Castro takeover. In Puerto Rico, he worked as a journalist and professor at the University of Puerto Rico. In 1965, he took his wife and children to Greensboro, North Carolina, where he spent the rest of his career as a professor at the University of North Carolina in Greensboro. Sánchez-Boudy has become one of the most distinguished authors and critics of Cuban exile literature, devoting almost all of his creative work to reliving the Cuban past and the effects of the Cuban Revolution. Included among his most famous works are *Cuentos grises* (Grey Stories, 1966), *Cuentos del hombre* (Stories about Man, 1969), and *Tiempo congelado (Poemario de una isla ausente)* [Frozen Weather (Poetry about an Absent Island, 1979)].

George Santayana (1863–1952)

Philosopher, poet, and novelist George Santayana was born in Madrid, Spain, and moved to Boston with his mother and siblings when he was nine years old. After overcoming the barrier of not speaking English, he became an outstanding student and student poet, and graduated from Harvard summa cum laude in 1886. Santayana went on to study in Germany and England but finished his Ph.D. at Harvard in 1889, after which he embarked on a teaching career at Harvard. Santayana became a prolific poet and later a novelist, in addition to winning respect as an academic philosopher. In 1890, he published his first book of poems, *Lucifer: A Theological Tragedy*. He published his first book on esthetics, *The Sense of Beauty*, in 1896. From 1912 until his death in 1952, Santayana resided in Europe, principally in England, France, Spain, and Italy. In 1927, Santayana was awarded the Gold Medal from the Royal Society of Literature in London. In 1929, he was offered the prestigious Norton Chair of Poetry at Harvard. However, he did not accept the chair because he had given up teaching. In 1935, he wrote the first novel penned by a U.S. Hispanic to be nominated for the Pulitzer Prize: *The Last Puritan: A Memoir in the Form of a Novel*. Included among his many books are *Poems* (1922), *Dialogs in Limbo* (1941), and his autobiography, *Persons and Places* (1944).

Esmeralda Santiago (1940–)

Born in Puerto Rico as the eldest of eleven children, Santiago moved with her family to Brooklyn, New York, when she was thirteen. Despite the poverty of her background, Santiago was able to receive a bachelor's degree from Harvard and an M.A. from Sarah Lawrence. First dedicated to documentary filmmaking, Santiago shifted her artistic career to writing when in 1993 she published her acclaimed memoir of growing up in Puerto Rico and moving to New York: *When I Was Puerto Rican*. In 1998, she published the sequel that covers her maturing in the big city, exploring the immigrant's typical struggle to adapt and establish an identity, as well as the adolescent's fight for independence from a strong-willed mother who still retains the old customs. In these and her novel of immigration,

America's Dream (1997), Santiago revived the 1960s and 1970s themes of culture clash, racial identity, and the culture of poverty, although from a feminist perspective. In addition to these themes, Santiago explores the relationship between mothers and daughters and the cycles of womanhood.

Juan Seguín (1806–1890)

The first autobiography written by a Mexican American in the English language was *The Personal Memoirs of John N. Seguín*, the embattled and disenchanted political figure of the Texas Republic and former mayor of San Antonio. Seguín was born on October 27, 1806, and became a politician and one of the founders of the Republic of Texas. Born into a prominent family of French extraction in San Antonio, Texas, by the age of eighteen he was elected mayor of San Antonio. One of the developers of a nationalist spirit in Texas, Seguín led Texans in opposition to the centrist government of Antonio López de Santa Anna in the 1830s. In the struggle for independence from Mexico, Seguín served as a captain in the Texas cavalry, eventually achieving the rank of lieutenant colonel. After the war of independence, Seguín once again served as the head of San Antonio government, but this time as commander. In 1838, he was elected to the Texas senate, and in 1840 again to the mayoralty of San Antonio. He was active in defending Tejanos against profiteering Anglos rushing into the state to make their fortune at all costs. Unjustly accused of favoring invading Mexican forces and betraying the Santa Fe Expedition to foment revolt in New Mexico against Mexico, Seguín was forced by Anglos to resign as mayor in April 1842. He moved with his family across the Río Grande into Mexico in fear of reprisals. In Mexico, he was jailed and forced to serve in the Mexican army, including in battle against the United States during the Mexican War. In 1848, he once again moved to Texas, only to return to live out his days in Nuevo Laredo, Mexico, from 1867 until his death in 1890. As a figure caught between two cultures, Seguín is considered a forerunner of the bilingual and bicultural literature, as well as one of the first Mexican Americans to express the disillusionment that many Mexican American writers felt after the Anglo-American takeover of the Southwest.

Salomón de la Selva (1893–1959)

Born in León, Nicaragua, de la Selva was a precocious poet, who at the age of twelve was sent to the United States to study on a government scholarship. His first literary language was English, and, in fact, it was in English that he published his first book, *Tropical Town and Other Poems* (1918), a book whose verses were never translated to Spanish despite the author's later residence and renown in his native Nicaragua. At the outbreak of World War I, de la Selva enlisted in the U.S. Army and underwent basic training but was not allowed to serve because he was not a U.S. citizen. He subsequently left for the country of his maternal grandmother, England, and served in the war in the British army. After the war he made his way back to the Americas, and in 1922 published his second poetry book, *El soldado desconocido* (The Unknown Soldier). In 1930, he published *Poemas: Ilustre Familia* (Poems: Illustrious Family). His publications were sparse thereafter, and he did not publish his next book, *Evocación a Píndaro* (Evocation of Pindar) until 1957, after winning the Nicaraguan National Culture Contest for the manuscript. Although he has been canonized in Nicaragua, he remains to this date a poet somewhat lost between cultures: a foreigner in U.S. letters and a Nicaraguan poet whose first literary language was foreign.

Ramón Sender (1901–1982)

One of the most famous exiled writers of the Spanish Civil War, Sender was born in Huesca, Spain. During his university studies in Madrid, Sender began editing a small newspaper; he eventually went on to edit *El Sol* (The Sun), a voice for liberals in Spain, which led to his jailing in 1927. In 1930, Sender published his first novel, *Imán* (Magnet), and left his work at *El Sol*. In 1934, he visited the Soviet Union and at the outbreak of the Spanish Civil War in 1936 he joined the republican forces against fascism; he lost his wife and his brother during the hostilities. In 1939, he left Spain and by 1943 had made his way to the United States, where from 1947 to 1963 he made his living as a professor of Spanish literature at the University of New Mexico. During his long life he opposed fascism and dictatorship in Spain and even became a United States citizen. Most of his very prolific career was developed in the United States, with the production of a vast body of novels, stories, essays, poetry, and theater. He also published more than 600 articles in periodicals throughout the Western Hemisphere.

Emma Sepúlveda (1950–)

Born in Argentina, but raised in Chile, Sepúlveda came to the United States as a Chilean refugee when Salvador Allende was overthrown and assassinated by dictator Augusto Pinochet. Sepúlveda has made a life for herself through political, feminist, and literary struggles in the United States. After receiving her M.A. and Ph.D. in Spanish literature from the University of Nevada (1978) and the University of California, Davis (1976), Sepúlveda began her career as a university professor, and continues today as a full professor at the University of Nevada, Reno. Sepúlveda is a distinguished poet who has published her works in Spanish and English in numerous magazines and anthologies. In 1993, she received the Carolyn Kizer Award for Poetry. Her books include *Tiempo cómplice del tiempo* (Time the Accomplice of Time, 1989), *A la muerte y otras dudas* (*To Death and Other Doubts*, 1996), and *Muerte al silencio* (*Death to Silence*, 1997). While Sepúlveda's poems run the gamut of themes from that of the loss of voice and identity to women's liberation, her work continues to exhibit the feelings of a political exile in its attack on fascism and its feelings of alienation within a new society.

Gustavo Solano (dates unknown)

Salvadoran poet-playwright-journalist Gustavo Solano became persona non grata in various Central American countries and Mexico over a period of some twenty years of activism against dictatorships and pursuit of his dream of a united Central America. Solano first came to the United States as consul for El Salvador in New Orleans, where he founded and edited the bilingual newspaper *La Opinión* and published books of his own poetry between 1911 and 1912. His involvement in politics took him throughout the United States, Cuba, Puerto Rico, and Mexico, and led to his imprisonment in Mexico City in 1916; he was declared persona non grata there and in Central American countries for insulting the government of Guatemala (1918), and accused of running guns in 1924. Despite his adventurous life as a revolutionary, Solana was able to produce numerous comedies and social realist plays for the professional stage. Southern California was his home base throughout the 1920s, where he wrote for the stage and worked as a journalist for the Los Angeles daily *El Heraldo de México* and periodicals in San Diego and northern Mexico. *Sangre* (Blood), Solano's four-act tragedy depicting the crimes and finally the overthrow of Guatemala's bloody dictator Manuel Estrada Cabrera, is a fine example of the theater of exile and probably one of the reasons for Solano's political problems in Central America. But not all of Solano's works were politically engaged; he also wrote romantic poetry, as well as farces, allegories, and comedies of customs. Of all of the Hispanic playwrights in the United States prior to World War II, Solano had the greatest number of works published, issued from publishing houses in the United States, Mexico, and the Netherlands.

Gary Soto (1952–)

Gary Soto is the Chicano poet who is most acclaimed in academic circles in the United States. After winning some of the most prestigious creative writing awards and achieving tenure at the University of California, Soto transformed himself into a highly commercial writer of children's and young adult literature. Born on April 12, 1952, to Mexican American parents in Fresno, California, Soto was raised in the San Joaquin Valley. At California State University he came under the guidance of the renowned poet Philip Levine, who helped Soto launch his career as a poet. In 1976, Soto earned his M. F. A. in creative writing from the University of California, Irvine, and thereafter began teaching at the University of California-Berkeley. While at Berkeley, Soto's fame became well established; he won numerous awards and fellowships and published his poetry books with such prestigious presses as that of the University of Pittsburgh.

All Soto's works, including the fiction that he later cultivated, are highly autobiographical and characterized by a highly polished craft. In his poetry and prose there is also great attention paid to narration and characterization; in prose as in verse, Soto is always conscious of telling a story. Soto is one of the Hispanic writers who concentrate on the universality of themes and literature rather than plumbing the special or particular in his community's experience. Despite his renown, Soto's department turned him down for a full professorship at Berkeley, which contributed to Soto's breaking with academia and dedicating himself to the pursuit of more commercial literature, especially as a writer for children. For his poetry, Soto won the following awards: the Academy of American Poets Prize (1975), the Bess Hopkins Prize (1977), a Guggenheim Fellowship (1979), and the Levinson Award (1984), among others. His short story collections and children's books have also won awards, including the American Book Award (1984) and the Tomás Rivera Award (1998). Soto's poetry books include *The Elements of San Joaquín* (1977), *Where Sparrows Work Hard* (1981), *Black Hair* (1985), and *Who Will Know Us?* (1990), among others. His most famous young adult novel is *Baseball in April* (1990). Among his children's picture books are *Boys at Work* (1995), *Chato's Kitchen* (1997), and *Big Bushy Mustache* (1998).

Pedro Juan Soto (1928–)

Born in Cataño, Puerto Rico, Soto moved to New York City to study medicine after graduating from high school. He left medicine for literature and earned a bachelor's degree from the University of Long Island in 1950. After a short stint in the Army, Soto earned a master's degree at Columbia University in 1953. In 1976, Soto earned a Ph. D. in literature from the University of Toulouse in France. He had been writing all along, but after completing his master's he did so as a professional for *Visión* magazine in New York. Soto began winning prizes for his short stories, including "Los Inocentes" (The Innocents), which depicted life in the Puerto Rican immigrant communities of New York and was recognized with the first prize award from the Ateneo de Puerto Rico in 1954. This is also the period when he wrote his most famous story, "Garabatos" (Scrawlings), the story of a struggling and misunderstood Puerto Rican artist living in poverty in New York. In 1955, Soto returned to Puerto Rico to work in the Division of Publications of the Puerto Rican Department of Education. From then on, he wrote and published a steady stream of short stories and novels, which made him one of the most famous and respected Puerto Rican literary figures.

In 1956, Soto published his definitive collection of stories centering on Puerto Rican life in New York: *Spiks*. Ever attracted by marginality, his first published novel, *Usmail* (1958), portrayed a Puerto Rican mulatto living on the island of Vieques. His other novels include: *Ardiente suelo, fría estación* (Burning Soil, Cold Season, 1961), *El francotirador* (The Sniper, 1969), *Temprada de duendes* (Ghost Season, 1970), and *Un oscuro pueblo sonriente* (A Dark Smiling People, 1982). Pedro Juan Soto teaches literature at the University of Puerto Rico.

Clemente Soto Vélez (1905–1993)

One of the most famous innovators of Puerto Rican poetic style and purpose, Soto Vélez was born in Lares, the seat of a famed rebellion against Spanish rule, and dedicated himself and his poetry to freeing Puerto Rico from U.S. colonial rule. As a journalist and poet in San Juan, in 1929 he was a leader of the iconoclastic "Atalaya de los Dioses" (Watchtower of the Gods) poetry movement which, while mainly esthetic in its innovation, led to political activism. In 1936, Soto Vélez was indicted with other nationalist leaders for inciting the overthrow of the U.S. government; he was found guilty and served seven years imprisonment. Upon release in 1942, he moved to New York, his return to Puerto Rico having been prohibited in his parole. He spent the rest of his life in New York, where he continued his writing and his political activism. In 1954, Soto Vélez published his first book of poetry, *Abrazo interno* (Internal Embrace). Other books followed, including *Arboles* (Trees, 1955), *Caballo de palo* (Wooden Horse, 1959) and *La tierra prometida* (The Promised Land, 1979). In 1976, his importance as a national writer was recognized by the Institute of Puerto Rican Culture with its reprint of *Caballo de palo*.

Virgil Suárez (1962–)

The only son of a pattern cutter and a piecemeal seamstress working the sweatshops, Suárez was born in Cuba in 1962 and raised in the United States beginning in 1974. Suárez is the holder of an MFA in creative writing (1987) from Louisiana State University, where he studied with Vance Bourjaily. He is currently an assistant professor of creative writing at Florida State University in Tallahassee. Although educated in the United States from age eight, Suárez has been preoccupied with the themes of immigration and acclimatization to life and culture in the United States. He arrived in this country as a refugee from communist Cuba; before settling here, he and his parents spent four years in Spain in a refugee community. Suárez is the author of five successful novels and numerous stories, essays, and poems, which have been published in literary magazines. He is also an active book reviewer for newspapers around the country, as well as an editor of anthologies of Latino literature.

Suárez's first novel, *Latin Jazz* (1989), chronicles the experiences of a Cuban immigrant family in Los Angeles by adopting the narrative perspectives of each of the family members. His second novel, *The Cutter* (1991), deals with the desperate attempts of a young sugar cane cutter to leave Cuba and join his family in the United States.

Suárez's collection of short fiction, *Welcome to the Oasis* (1992), portrays a new generation of young Hispanics who

Virgil Suárez.

struggle to integrate themselves into American culture while preserving pieces of their heritage. *Havana Thursdays* (1995) and *Going Under* (1996) are mature novels in which Suárez casts a critical eye at middle-class Cuban-American life in Miami. *Havana Thursdays* brings together a family of exceptional women who are attending a funeral and are in the process of adjusting to their loss. The funeral becomes an occasion for a painful assessment of their lives. Virgil Suárez had this to say about the women: "I wanted to create a garland—a necklace of voices beautiful and lasting. After I finished the book, I spent almost a year being haunted by the voices of these great women." *Going Under* is the chronicle of a Cuban-American yuppy who is sold on the American Dream: He is nervous and energetic and blind to the consequences of his feverish chase up the ladder of success. He loses sight of and control over things of value—family, friends, identity. Virgil Suárez has also compiled two collections of autobiographical essays, stories and poems: *Spared Angola: Memories of a Cuban-American Childhood*, and *Infinite Refuge*. In both books he uses his own life experiences as a refugee and immigrant to ponder universal questions of identity, homelessness, and being the outsider.

Carmen Tafolla (1951–)

Chicana poet Carmen Tafolla was born and raised in San Antonio and came to prominence in the late Chicano Movement of the mid-1970s. Tafolla earned B.A. (1972) and M.A. (1973) degrees from Austin College and a Ph.D. in bilingual education from the University of Texas (1981). Despite her educational accomplishments, Tafolla is an oral poet and performer who bases her work on the bilingualism and biculturalism of working-class Mexican-American neighborhoods. A folklorist at heart, she has preserved many of the folk ways and much of the worldview of common folk in her verse. To date, she has published three books: *Get Your Tortillas Together* (in 1976 with Cecilio García-Camarillo), *Curandera* (1983), and *To Split a Human: Mitos, Machos y La Mujer Chicana* (Myths, Machos and Women, 1985). In 1989, her *Sonnet to Human Beings* won the University of California-Irvine award for Chicano literature, and in 2001 she published a well-reviewed collection, *Sonnets and Salsa*. Tafolla has also written works for children, including *The Dog Who Wanted to Be a Tiger* (1996) and *Baby Coyote and the Old Woman* (*El coyotito y la viejita*, 2000).

Piri Thomas (1928–)

Nuyorican writer Piri Thomas was the author of a foundational work for Nuyorican literature: His memoir, *Down These Mean Streets* (1967), was the first agonizing tale of the search for identity among conflicting cultural, racial, ethnic, and linguistic alternatives presented to Latinos in general and Afro-Hispanic peoples in the United States in particular. Like many autobiographies, it was a personal catharsis for Thomas: "*Down These Mean Streets* was a catharsis for me. I had realized that I could go back in time and live it and feel it—the rage, the anger, the hurt, everything. The walls had my fist prints, cabinets would be smashed. The rage!" It was such a milestone that the Nuyorican and Latino literature that followed either continued its themes or totally rejected its poetic melange of street language and psychodrama as a naive and unsophisticated cry out of the culture of poverty.

Thomas was born John Peter Thomas on September 30, 1928, in New York City's Harlem Hospital to a white Puerto Rican mother and an Afro-Cuban working-class father. In his upbringing he experienced racism in the most intimate of settings, since his siblings' lighter skin was preferred over his obviously dark African inheritance—which, of course, presented one of the principal causes for anguish in his life and in his books. When his family attempted to escape the ills of the city by moving to Babylon, Long Island, again he faced rejection at school and in the neighborhood because of his skin color; in part, this is the subject of his second book, *Savior, Savior, Hold My Hand*, which also deals with the hypocrisy he faced while working with a Christian church when he was out of prison. Thomas grew up on the streets of Spanish Harlem, where he became involved in gang activity and criminality. In 1950, he participated in an armed robbery of a nightclub that left him and a policeman wounded; he was sentenced to and served seven years in jail, the subject of his *Seven Long Times* (1974). While in prison, Thomas became part of the black pride movement, converted to Islam, earned a G.E.D., and began writing. As an ex-convict, he was befriended in 1962 by an editor from Knopf and supported by a grant for five years from the Louis M. Rabinowitz Foundation, with which he was able to produce the modern classic autobiography that forever changed his life and the trajectory of Latino and ethnic literatures in the United States.

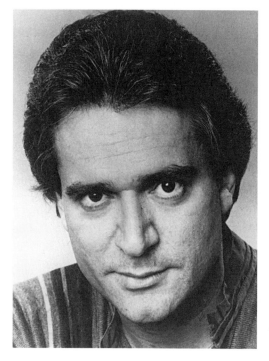

Omar Torres.

Omar Torres (1945–)

Omar Torres is an actor, playwright, poet, and novelist. Born on September 13, 1945, in Las Tunas, Cuba, he immigrated to Miami, Florida, with his family in 1959. There he attended both junior and senior high school. The family then moved to New York, where he attended Queens College for a while, only to drop out to study on his own. Torres has had an active career in radio, television, and movies. In 1972, he co-founded with Iván Acosta the Centro Cultural Cubano, and in 1974 he founded the literary arts journal *Cubanacán* (a nonsense word meaning "Cuba"). From 1972 to 1982, Torres had numerous plays produced at the Centro and on other stages, after which he seems to have made a transition to writing fiction. He is the author of three novels: *Apenas un bolero* (Just a Bolero, 1981), *Al partir* (Upon Leaving, 1986), and *Fallen Angels Sing* (1991). He has also authored five books of poetry: *Conversación primera* (First Conversation, 1975), *Ecos de un laberinto* (Echoes from a Labyrinth, 1976), *Tiempo robado* (Stolen Time, 1978), *De nunca a siempre* (From Never to Always, 1981) and *Línea en diluvio* (Line in the Deluge, 1981).

Estela Portillo Trambley (1936–1999)

Estela Portillo Trambley is one of the first women writers to successfully publish prose in the early male-dominated stages of the Chicano literary movement. Born in El Paso, Texas, on January 16, 1936, she was raised and educated in El Paso, where she attended high school and earned her B.A. degree (1957) and her M.A. degree (1977) from the University of Texas. After graduation from college, she became a high school English teacher and administrator. Since 1979, she has been affiliated with the Department of Special Services of the El Paso Public Schools. From 1970 to 1975, she served as dramatist in residence at El Paso Community College.

Portillo Trambley was the first woman to win the national award for Chicano literature, Premio Quinto Sol, in 1973, for her collection of short stories and the novella *Rain of Scorpions and Other Writings*, which was published in 1975. Besides stories and plays published in magazines and anthologies, Portillo Trambley has written a collection of plays, *Sor Juana and Other Plays* (1981), and a novel, *Trini* (1983). In both her prose and drama, Portillo Trambley develops strong women who resist the social roles that have been predetermined for them because of their sex. In her fiction, women command center stage and achieve a level of self-determination and control over social and cultural circumstances. The culmination of her pursuit of strong women is represented in her exploration of the life of the eighteenth-century poet and essayist Sor Juana Inés de la Cruz in her play *Sor Juana*. The protagonist of her novel, *Trini*, is a fictional character who struggles against poverty and adversity to make her way in life; she eventually leaves Mexico and crosses the border illegally to find the power over her own life for which she has been searching.

Sabine Ulibarrí (1919–)

Short story writer, poet, and essayist Sabine Ulibarrí has had one of the longest and most productive literary careers in Chicano literature. He is a well known and highly respected chronicler of the way things once were in his beloved New Mexico. Born on September 21, 1919, in the small village of Tierra Amarilla, New Mexico, he was raised on a ranch by his parents, both of whom were college graduates. Besides learning the ways of rural life and the rugged countryside, Ulibarrí also experienced firsthand the folk culture of the area, which included not only the full repository of oral literature but also a strong connection to the language and oral literature of Spain and the Spanish-speaking Americas. His early love for the Spanish language and Hispanic literature took Ulibarrí to college and eventually to a Ph.D. degree in Spanish. Over the years he taught at every level,

Sabine Ulibarrí.

from elementary school to graduate school, except during World War II, when he flew thirty-five combat missions as an air force gunner. Today he is a professor emeritus of the University of New Mexico, where he spent most of his academic career as a student and professor.

Among Ulibarrí's awards are the following: Governor's Award for Excellence in Literature (1988), Distinguished Alumni Award and Regents' Medal of Merit, University of New Mexico (1989), and the White House Hispanic Heritage Award (1989). Ulibarrí has had two books of poems published, *Al cielo se sube a pie* (You Reach Heaven on Foot, 1966) and *Amor y Ecuador* (Love and Ecuador, 1966), and the following collections of short stories in bilingual format: *Tierra Amarilla: Cuentos de Nuevo México* (*Tierra Amarillo: Stories of New Mexico*, 1971), *Mi abuela fumaba puros y otros cuentos de Tierra Amarilla* (*My Grandma Smoked Cigars and Other Stories of Tierra Amarilla*, 1977), *Primeros encuentros/ First Encounters* (1982), *El gobernador Glu Glu* (*Governor Glu Glu*, 1988), and *El Condor and Other Stories* (1989).

In his work, Ulibarrí preserves a style, narrative technique, and language that owes much to the oral folk tradition. Through his works he has been able to capture the ethos and the spirit of rural New Mexico before the coming of the Anglo. His works memorialize myths and legends and such distinctive characters of the past as cowboys, sheriffs, folk healers, penitents, and just the common everyday folk. Quite often describing two versions of the same story, in English and Spanish, his works are among the most direct and accessible to broad audiences in all of modern Chicano literature.

David Unger (1950–)

David Unger was born in Guatemala to an Hispanic Jewish family, and he was raised in the United States, where his parents took refuge from the violence in their homeland when David was five years old. Unger is a poet, novelist, and short story writer who writes in both English and Spanish. However, his fame as a creative writer is surpassed by his work as a translator of Nicanor Parra, Roque Dalton, Mario Benedetti, Sergio Ramírez, Luisa Valenzuela, José Agustín, Paco Ignacio Taibo II, and many others. His first and only novel, *Life in the Damn Tropic*, which narrates the life of a Jewish family in Guatemala during the 1980s, is filled with black political comedy.

Luis Valdez (1940–)

Luis Valdez is considered to be the father of Chicano theater—the instigator of the contemporary Chicano theatrical movement and its most outstanding playwright. Valdez has distinguished himself as an actor, director, playwright, and film maker; however, it was in his role as the founding director of El Teatro Campesino, a theater of farm workers in California, that his efforts inspired young Chicano activists across the country to use theater as a means of organizing students, communities, and labor unions. Valdez was born on June 26, 1940, into a family of migrant farm workers in Delano, California. The second of ten children, he began to work the fields at the age of six and to follow the crops. Valdez's education was constantly interrupted; nevertheless, he finished high school and went on to San Jose State College, where he majored in English and pursued his interest in theater. While there, he won a playwriting contest with his one-act play "The Theft" (1961), and in 1963 the drama department produced his play "The Shrunken Head of Pancho Villa." After graduating from college in 1964, Valdez joined the San Francisco Mime Troupe and learned the techniques of agitprop (agitation and propaganda) theater and Italian *commedia dell'arte* (comedy of art), both of which influenced Valdez's development of the basic format of Chicano theater: the one-act presentational *acto* or "act."

In 1965 Valdez enlisted in César Chávez's mission to organize farm workers in Delano into a union. It was there that Valdez brought together farm workers and students into El Teatro Campesino to dramatize the plight of the farm workers. The publicity and success gained by the troupe led to the spontaneous appearance of a national Chicano theater movement. In 1967 Valdez and El Teatro Campesino left the unionizing effort to expand their theater beyond agitprop and farm worker concerns. Since then Valdez and the theater have explored most of the theatrical genres that have been important to Mexicans in the United States, including religious pageants, vaudeville with the down-and-out *pelado* or underdog figure and dramatized *corridos* or ballads. The new type of socially engaged theater that El Teatro Campesino pioneered led to the creation of a full-blown theatrical movement in fields and barrios across the country. For more than three decades, El Teatro Campesino and Luis Valdez have dramatized the political and cultural concerns of Hispanics, initially among workers and their supporters but later among students in universities and the general public through the legitimate stage, television, and film. In establishing the canon of what *teatro chicano* should be, Valdez and El Teatro Campesino published their *actos* (short, one-act agitprop pieces) in 1971 with a preface in which Valdez outlined their theatrical principles: (1) Chicanos must be seen as a nation with geographic, religious, cultural, and racial roots in the Southwest; teatros must further the idea of nationalism and create a national theater based on identification with the Amerindian past; (2) the organizational support of the national theater must be from within and totally independent; (3) "Teatros must never get away from La Raza . . . If the Raza will not come to the theater, then the theater must go to the Raza. This, in the long run, will determine the shape, style, content, spirit, and form of *el teatro chicano*."

Whether Valdez and El Teatro Campesino have strayed from the spirit of this

Luis Valdez.

declaration will be judged by posterity. The fact is that Valdez and his theater did expand their horizons by taking Chicano theater to Broadway and more commercial venues and by moving into commercial cinema and television. During the late 1960s and the 1970s El Teatro Campesino produced many of Valdez's plays, including *Los vendidos* (The Sell-Outs, 1967), *The Shrunken Head of Pancho Villa* (1968), *Bernabé* (1970), *Dark Root of a Scream* (1971), *La Gran Carpa de la Familia Rascuachi* (1974), and *El Fin del Mundo* (1976). In 1978, Valdez broke into mainstream theater in Los Angeles with the Mark Taper Forum's production of his *Zoot Suit*, and, in 1979, with the Broadway production of the same play. In 1986 he had a successful run of his play *I Don't Have to Show You No Stinking Badges* at the Los Angeles Theater Center. In *Bernabé*, one of Valdez's most poetic plays, a young village idiot is transformed by his marriage to La Tierra (The Earth) and his subsequent death. Employing Aztec mythology and symbols in a tale about contemporary barrio characters, the play explores the pre-Columbian heritage of Chicano society. The Mayan theme of death is life and life is death was developed here and continued to appear in Valdez's later works. The writing of *Bernabé* marked the beginning of Valdez's search for the meaning of Aztec and Mayan legends, history, and philosophy and revealed the influence of Spanish playwright Federico García Lorca, who also strove to elevate the country folk to heroic and mythic stature.

Valdez's screenwriting career began with early film and television versions of Corky González's poem *I Am Joaquín* (1969) and his own *Los Vendidos*, and later with a film version of *Zoot Suit* (1982). But his real incursion into major Hollywood productions and success came with his writing and directing of *La Bamba* (the name of a dance from Veracruz), the screen biography of Chicano rock and roll star Ritchie Valens. Other screenplays include *Corridos* (1987) and the successful television movies *La Pastorela* (1991) and *The Cisco Kid* (1993). Valdez's plays, essays, and poems have been widely anthologized. He has published two collections of plays: *Luis Valdez—The Early Works* (1990) and *Zoot Suit and Other Plays* (1992). Valdez's awards include an Obie (1968), Los Angeles Drama Critics awards (1969, 1972, and 1978), a special Emmy Award (1973), the San Francisco Bay Critics Circle for Best Musical (1983), and honorary doctorates from San Jose State University, Columbia College, and the California Institute of the Arts.

Mariano Guadalupe Vallejo (1808–1890)

Mariano G. Vallejo, Californio politician and military leader, was born on July 7, 1808, into an upper class family in Monterey, the capital of Alta, California, under Mexican rule. At age fifteen, Vallejo became a cadet at the Monterey presidio; at age twenty-one he was already a commander and an elected member of the territorial legislature. In his mid-twenties, Vallejo was appointed military commander of all of northern California and administrator of the San Francisco Solano Mission at the time when missions were being secularized. During his tenure in these positions, Vallejo began to believe that the American takeover was inevitable and that it would be advantageous for Californios. During the Bear Flag Revolt, Vallejo was jailed for two months, but afterwards, under American rule, was named to the legislative council. Later he also served as the northern Indian agent. In 1849 he was one of only eight Californios elected to the constitutional convention, and was subsequently elected to the state's first senate. Despite his prominence and influence in California politics, Vallejo lost important lands, including the large Soscol land grant, through court action by squatters and speculators. When he died on January 18, 1890, he owned only 280 acres. Much of Vallejo's life was narrated in a series of memoirs he dictated and wrote. His most important work was *José Mariano Vallejo: Recuerdos históricos y personales tocante a la alta California* (José Mariano Vallejo: Historical and Personal Memories of Alta California, 1875).

Vallejo strove to bring two cultures together that had not achieved an uneasy accommodation even during his late life: "If before I pass on to render an account of my acts to the Supreme Creator, I succeed in being a witness to a reconciliation between victor and vanquished, conquerors and conquered, I shall die with the conviction of not having striven in vain." Although he had lost much with the coming of the Yankees, Vallejo could still pronounce the following: "The inhabitants of California have no reason to complain of the change of government, for if the rich have lost thousands of horses and cattle, the poor have been bettered in condition."

Platón Vallejo (1841–1925)

The only college-educated child of Mariano Guadalupe Vallejo and Francisca Carrillo de Vallejo, parents from distinguished old-line Californio families, Vallejo became a medical doctor and served with honor as a surgeon in the Union Army during the Civil War. After receiving his medical degree from Columbia University in New York, he settled down with a medical practice in Vallejo, California, and devoted himself to intellectual pursuits, including writing sketches of prestatehood Alta, California. In his recollection of the golden years of California's past, Vallejo credited the Hispanic past for the development of California's resources; he also attempted to elevate the status of the Californios by emphasizing the accomplishments of their Spanish ancestors, countering the ethnocentrism of the easterners who had overwhelmed the native population. He did recognize and, somewhat paternalistically, defend the Indians, but often cast them as "noble savages." Both his letters and his dictated "Memoirs of the Vallejos" revealed his efforts to counter official history of California and the West. In the letter to a writer of California history, Vallejo protested the treatment of the Californians by historians.

Erasmo Vando (1896–1988)

Poet, playwright, actor, *cronista*, and political activist, Erasmo Vando was born on June 2, 1896, in Ponce, Puerto Rico, while it was still a colony of Spain. There are no records to indicate that Vando went beyond elementary school in his education. Vando immigrated to the southern United States as a laborer and made his way to New York, where he became a community leader, most notably as the president of the Puerto Rican Brotherhood. In the twenty-seven years that he lived in New York (1919–1945) he was deeply involved in the cultural life of the Puerto Rican community, becoming a founder of and participant in many political and civic organizations. In 1945, Vando returned to his hometown, Ponce, where he was able to earn a living writing for *El Mundo*, a major national newspaper, and the major Ponce local newspaper, *El Día*.

Vando was considered by Bernardo Vega to be the best interpreter of the *jíbaro*, the Puerto Rican campesino, on the stages of New York; and like fellow autodidacts Vega and Jesús Colón Vando always framed his intellectual and artistic pursuits within this working-class perspective. Vando took up the cause of the uprooted and destitute Puerto Rican community in New York and elsewhere in the United States, challenging politicians in Puerto Rico island to tackle the problem of their emigrant brothers. To his dying day, he was a promoter of independence for Puerto Rico.

As a writer, Vando penned numerous *crónicas* and poems published in community newspapers in Brooklyn and Manhattan. His life as an actor also led him to write various short dramatic pieces, which were never published. His poetry was published posthumously by his family in a volume entitled *Amores* (Loves, 1996).

Gloria Vando (1934–)

Gloria Vando is the daughter of two Puerto Rican writers, Anita Vélez Mitchell and Erasmo Vando. Born and raised in New York and educated in the United States (at New York University) and Europe (Amsterdam and Paris), she ultimately received her B.A. from Texas A&M University in 1975. Vando dedicated herself to the literary life, becoming a respected poet of the English language. For many years she dedicated herself to service of the literary field and women's culture, while only occasionally publishing her poems in magazines. In 1977, Vando founded a literary magazine and press, *Helicon Nine*, which published outstanding literary and artistic works by women until 1992. That year, she cofounded with her husband, William Hickok, The Writers Place in Kansas City, Kansas, a venue for writers to come together and discuss their works. The Writers Place emphasizes workshops, book signings, art openings, readings, and theater productions.

While more than fifty anthologies contain her poems, it was not until 1993 that Vando published her first collection of poems, *Promesas: Geography of the Impossible*, which became the first Hispanic book to win the Thorpe Menn Award for literary achievement. In 2002, Vando published her second collection, *Shadows and Supposes*, winner of the 1998 Alice Fay Di Castagnola Award from the Poetry Society of America; the book was also a finalist in the Walt Whitman Poetry Contest. Other awards for her work over the years include the Billee Murray Poetry Prize (1991), the Stanley Hanks Memorial Award (1986), and various fellowships and grants from the Kansas Arts Commission.

Félix Francisco Varela y Morales (1788–1853)

Félix Varela, one of the first Hispanic exile writers in the United States, was born in Havana, Cuba. At age three, Varela was sent to live with his paternal grandfather, a military commander at St. Augustine in the Spanish colony of East Florida. At age fourteen, he entered the San Carlos Seminary in Havana to train for the priesthood. Upon becoming a priest and earning his baccalaureate in 1811, Varela began teaching philosophy at San Carlos. He became known as Cuba's foremost philosopher, which also led to his involvement in politics, and to his election to the Spanish Cortes in 1821. At the Cortes he proposed political autonomy for Cuba, the abolition of slavery, and support for the independence of Spanish America.

Because of his political ideas, Varela had to take refuge in the United States in 1823. In Philadelphia, he founded and published one of the first exile newspapers, *El habanero: papel político, científico y literario* (1823). In 1826, he anonymously published the first historical novel ever written in the Spanish language, *Jicoténcal*, a novel in which the narrator takes the side of the Native Americans in Mexico during the Spanish conquest. Throughout his career as a writer, theologian, and working priest who often tended to the immigrant populations in New York, Varela continued writing philosophical and theological tracts. He also edited *Children's Catholic Magazine* (1838), *Young Catholic's Magazine* (1840), and *The Catholic Expositor and Literary Magazine* (1841). In 1850, Varela retired to the town of his childhood, St. Augustine, where he died.

Bernardo Vega (1885–)

Born in Cayey, Puerto Rico, Bernardo Vega became one of the most famous chroniclers of Puerto Rican life in New York City during the early twentieth century. A self-taught intellectual coming out of a background of cigar factories and union organizing, Vega was at the center of Puerto Rican community events from the time of his migration to New York in 1916 until his retirement in Puerto Rico. In his memoir, *Memorias de Bernardo Vega: Contribución a la historia de la comunidad puertorriqueña* (as *The Memories of Bernardo Vega*, 1979), Vega details the struggles of the Puerto Rican working class in the metropolis, its organizations and the social and environmental conditions in which it had to live. Vega was also a political organizer for Puerto Rican independence, as well as a labor leader, and his memoirs detail the issues and the participants in these movements. The Vega memoirs were edited and published posthumously in 1977 by a friend, César Andreu Iglesias, who eliminated some fictional parts of the narration. It seems that Vega thought it advantageous to publish the work as a novel; however, Andreu and contemporary scholars have verified and appreciated the work as documentary testimony and community history.

Ed Vega (1936–)

Ed Vega is a Puerto Rican fiction writer who bases many of his works on life in New York City's Spanish Harlem. Edgardo Vega Yunqué was born in Ponce, Puerto Rico, on May 20, 1936, where he lived with his family until they moved to the Bronx, New York, in 1949. He was raised in a devout Baptist home, his father having been a minister of that faith; today, Vega and his wife and children have adopted the Buddhist faith. As a child, books were very accessible at home, and he began both his education and writing at an early age in Spanish in Puerto Rico. After moving to New York and going through the public education system, he served in the air force and studied at Santa Monica College in California under the G.I. Bill. In 1963, Vega almost graduated as a Phi Beta Kappa from New York University with a major in political science but he was short three hours of credit and did not actually graduate until 1969. He did not return to finish until that date because he had become disillusioned after personally experiencing racism at the university. From 1963 on, he worked in a variety of social service programs. In 1969, he returned to academic life as a lecturer for Hunter College and thereafter assumed various other lecturing and assistant professor positions at other colleges. From 1977 to 1982, he worked at such community-based education programs as ASPIRA of New Jersey.

Since 1982 Vega has been a full-time writer. He is one of the most prolific Hispanic prose writers, although much of his work remains unpublished. In 1977, his short stories began appearing in Hispanic magazines such as *Nuestro, Maize,* and

Ed Vega.

Revista Chicano-Riqueña. In 1985, his novel *The Comeback*—a rollicking satire of ethnic autobiography and the identity crisis as personified by a half-Puerto Rican, half-Eskimo ice hockey player who becomes involved in an underground revolutionary movement for Puerto Rican independence—was published. In 1987, a collection of interconnected short stories—*Mendoza's Dreams*, narrated by a warmhearted observer of the human comedy, Alberto Mendoza—was published. An additional common thread holding these barrio stories together is their charting of various Puerto Ricans on the road to success in the United States; thus, once again we have a Puerto Rican interpretation of the American Dream. Vega's third book, *Casualty Report* (1991), is just the opposite; for the most part the collection of stories included here chronicle the death of dreams, as characters faced with racism, poverty, and crime succumb to despair in many forms: violence, alcohol and drug abuse, withdrawal, and resignation.

Gloria Velásquez (1949–)

Born in Loveland, Colorado, to migrant worker parents, Velásquez grew up with her studies interrupted at times due to the exigencies of the migrant stream. While working part time, she was able to graduate high school and the University of Northern Colorado (1978). While a university student, she began participating in Chicano literary circles and festivals as a poet. Her interest in literature led her to earn a Ph.D. in Spanish at Stanford University (1985) and to become a professor of Spanish at the California Polytechnic State University in San Luis Obispo. As a poet, Velásquez has published her poems of social and political commitment to women and minorities in numerous literary magazines and anthologies. She published her first and only book of poems, *I Used to Be Superwoman* in 1997. In 1994, Velásquez began the Roosevelt High School Series, a series of young adult novels set among a multiracial group of teenagers at Roosevelt High, who must face such social and cultural issues as child and spousal abuse, racial prejudice, homosexuality, teen pregnancy, and others. To date, she has produced six highly acclaimed books in the series: *Juanita Fights the School Board* (1994), *Maya's Di-*

Gloria Velásquez.

vided World (1995), *Tommy Stands Alone* (1995), *Rina's Family Secret* (1998), *Ankiza's Rainbow* (2000), and *Teen Angel* (2003). Her outstanding sensitivity in interpreting teenage angst and social conditions in the series has made Velásquez a popular speaker at high schools throughout the nation and has led some to call her the "Chicana Judy Blume."

Daniel Venegas (dates unknown)

We know very little about Daniel Venegas, author of one of the most important novels of immigration, *Las aventuras de Don Chipote, o cuando pericos mamen* (*The Adventures of Don Chipote, Or When Parrots Breast Feed*, 1928). A man of letters, albeit a street-wise intellectual, Venegas was very knowledgeable about Mexican working-class life, especially in the Mexican communities in Los Angeles and El Paso. Venegas' name appears in the Spanish-language press of Los Angeles related to performance reviews of his plays and of the vaudeville ensemble, Compañía de Revistas Daniel Venegas, between 1924 and 1933. His theatrical group seemed to always perform in the more modest, working-class houses of the city. This was not always so for the production of his plays: *¿Quién es culpable?* (Who Is to Blame?), which had its debut in 1924; *Nuestro egoísmo* (Our Selfishness), a three-act play which debuted in 1926 and was dedicated "in honor and defense of Mexican women," according to *El Heraldo de México*, October 11, 1926; *Esclavos* (Slaves, 1930), about whose relationship to Mexican labor we can only guess; and the vaudeville reviews *El maldito jazz* (That Darned Jazz), *Revista astronómica* (The Astronomic Review), *El establo de Arizmendi* (Arizmendi's Stable), which celebrated the famed Mexican boxer baby Arizmendi, and the supposedly very popular *El con-su-la-do* (a play on the word "consulate" in Spanish). While these later works were of the musical comedy variety so enjoyed by blue-collar audiences, it is almost certain that *¿Quién es culpable?* and *Nuestro egoísmo* were works of serious drama, especially since the "first lady" of the Mexican theater, Virginia Fábregas, produced both works for the stage in Los Angeles.

From 1924 to 1929, Daniel Venegas wrote, edited, and published a weekly satirical newspaper, *El Malcriado* (The Brat), which poked fun at the customs and politics in the Mexican community of Los Angeles. Venegas himself came to be known as "El Malcriado," for his penchant for taking jabs at community figures through his newspaper. His talent for burlesque was also evident in the cartoons he drew to illustrate the stories in his tabloid. Before founding *El Malcriado*, Venegas had worked for the *El pueblo* newspaper in Los Angeles, and because *El Heraldo de México* published his *Don Chipote* he may have also been a staff writer for that paper, as well. There is no information available as to whether Venegas had any formal education or worked on newspapers in Mexico before immigrating to the United States. However, the April 7, 1927, issue of *El Malcriado* identifies Venegas as president of the Mexican Journalists Association of California.

Whatever else can be constructed of the life of this important author must be gleaned from the autobiographical passages in *The Adventures of Don Chipote*, claiming that the author migrated to the United States as a *bracero*, worked on constructing and maintaining the rail lines in New Mexico and Arizona, and experienced many of the same sufferings as the protagonist of the novel.

Evangelina Vigil-Piñón (1949–)

Vigil-Piñón was born in San Antonio, Texas, on November 19, 1949, the second of ten children of a very poor family that lived for years in public housing. In her later childhood years, Vigil-Piñón lived with her maternal grandmother and uncle, from whom she learned much of the oral lore which has become such an important basis for her poetry; but Vigil-Piñón's mother was also an avid reader who gave her daughter a love of books. From her grandmother, she learned "to observe and listen for words of wisdom which come only with experience." And, indeed, the predominant narrator in her first full-length collection of poems, *Thirty an' Seen a Lot* (1982), winner of the American Book Award of the Before Columbus Foundation, is that of the acute but anonymous observer of the life of working-class people in her beloved West Side barrio of San Antonio, the recorder of their language and diction, their proverbs and music, their joys and sorrows.

Evangelina Vigil-Piñón.

Despite the apparently natural vernacular of her writing, Vigil-Piñón's poetry is the product of great craftsmanship, obtained through extensive reading and self-education as well as through formal study: She obtained a B.A. in English from the University of Houston in 1974 and took post-graduate courses at various institutions afterward. She also has served as an adjunct faculty member for the University of Houston since the mid 1980s. In 1977, Vigil-Piñón became the first Hispanic writer to win the National Literary Contest of the Coordinating Council of Literary Magazines for work published in a small magazine.

Vigil-Piñón is the Chicano poet who has most sensitively portrayed and celebrated working-class culture. She is also one of the leading exponents of bilingual code-switching in poetry–in Vigil-Piñón a transference from English to Spanish and back is as natural as conversation at the kitchen table. Working at the center of U.S. Hispanic literature as the poetry editor for the leading Hispanic literary magazine, *The Americas Review*, Vigil-Piñón has also been a leader in the Hispanic women's movement as an anthologizer, speaker, and host of writers on tour. Vigil-Piñón's second poetry collection, *The Computer Is Down* (1987), explores how common folk must accommodate or become displaced from the modern social and technological landscape. In 2001, Vigil-Piñón published a lyrical first book for children, *Marina's Muumuu*.

Tino Villanueva.

Tino Villanueva (1941–)

Although outside of the Chicano Movement while living in Boston, Tino Villanueva became a celebrated Chicano bilingual poet during the early 1970s. Born in San Marcos, Texas, to migrant farm workers, Villanueva grew up in poverty and discrimination. After serving in the Army, Villanueva studied at Southwest Texas State University, where he began to write poetry, graduated in 1968, and went on to graduate school at Stony Brook and Boston. While studying for his Ph.D. at Boston University, he published his first book, *Hay Otra Voz: Poems* in 1972, in which he experimented with bilingual writing and recalled the migrant farm worker and *pachuco* culture. The book led to his widespread acceptance as a leading Chicano poet, and in this leadership role he was able to compile one of the earliest anthologies of Chicano literature and the first to be published in Mexico: *Chicanos, antología histórica y literaria* (1980). In 1981, Villanueva obtained his Ph.D. and began teaching at Wellesley College but was never able to win tenure at that institution. In 1984, Villanueva founded *Imagine: International Chicano Poetry Journal*, which published authors from widespread cultures in various languages. Also in 1984, Villanueva published his second widely acclaimed book of poetry, *Shaking Off the Dark*. Villanueva's other books include *Scene from the Movie Giant* (1993) and *Chronicle of My Worst Years*, neither of which has had the impact of his earlier works.

José Antonio Villarreal (1924–)

Villarreal published what is considered to be the first Chicano novel in contemporary times, *Pocho* (1959), a developmental novel in which the protagonist has a classic identity crisis. It was also the first Chicano novel to be published by a major commercial house: Doubleday. Villarreal was born in Los Angeles to Mexican immigrant parents who were migrant farm workers. Villarreal became an excellent student and loved reading. After graduating high school and serving three years in the Navy during World War II, he returned to California and earned a B.A. in English from the University of California at Berkeley in 1950. Villarreal took various and sundry jobs to support his wife and children and his writing. He finished *Pocho* in 1956 but was not able to find a publisher until 1959. The novel of immigration remained relatively unknown until the Chicano Movement created a market for such literature and it was reissued by Anchor Books in 1970. Since then, it has become required reading in Chicano and Latino literature classes at universities. Villarreal published his second novel, a tale of the Mexican Revolution, *The Fifth Horseman*, with Doubleday in 1974, but it never achieved the status of *Pocho*. Villarreal became an outspoken critic of the Chicano Movement, its writers, and critics, attacking the very base that had made his first work so popular. Villarreal's third novel, *Clemente Chacón* (1984), is an American Dream tale of a poor Mexican who crosses the border to rise in riches and social success. This latest Villarreal offering was published not by a mainstream house but by Bilingual Press, a small university-based publisher, and is indicative of Villarreal's struggle to please both mainstream publishers and students of Chicano literature.

Victor Edmundo Villaseñor (1940–)

A novelist and screenwriter who has brought the experience of Mexican immigration to the United States to wide audiences through his novel, *Macho!* (1973) and the non-fiction saga of his own family in *Rain of Gold* (1991), Villaseñor was born on May 11, 1940, in Carlsbad, California, the son of Mexican immigrants. Villaseñor was raised on a ranch in Oceanside and experienced great difficulty with the educational system, who started school as a Spanish-speaker and, unknown to his family and teachers, a dyslexic. He eventually dropped out of high school and worked on his family's ranch, in other agricultural fields as a farm worker, and as a laborer in construction. Because of his learning disability and his failure at school, Villaseñor felt compelled to over-compensate precisely for what was most difficult for him: reading and writing. While supporting himself for ten years as a construction worker, he completed nine novels and sixty-five short stories, all of which were rejected for publication. Finally, *Macho!* was accepted and published by the world's largest paperback publisher, Bantam, in 1973. In 1977, another major publisher issued *Jury: The People vs. Juan Corona*, a non-fiction narrative of the life and trial of a serial killer, immigrant Juan Corona.

Victor Edmundo Villaseñor.

Villaseñor's most important work was to come much later, for it took years of research to produce his own family's biography, *Rain of Gold* (1991). It became the very first Chicano best seller. *Rain of*

Gold was so powerful and important a story that it occupied the next years of literary production for Villaseñor, who penned related works. His collection of stories, *Walking Stars* (1994), was a compilation of additional stories from his family's saga, and *Wild Steps of Heaven* (1995) was a "prequel" and *The Thirteen Steps* (2001) a sequel to *Rain of Gold*. There is unanimity among critics and teachers that Villaseñor's works, while attesting to lived experience, are also very poetic and deeply spiritual. *Macho!* tells the tale of a young Mexican-Indian's illegal entry into the United States to find work; it is in many ways a classic novel of immigration, though it departs from the model in that when he returns to his hometown in central Mexico the protagonist has been forever changed. He is unable to accept the traditional social code, especially as it concerns *machismo*. *Rain of Gold* is the nonfiction saga of various generations of Villaseñor's own family, their experiences during the Mexican Revolution, and their eventual immigration to California. The saga is narrated in a style full of spiritualism and respect for myths and oral tradition, derived not only from Villaseñor's own childhood but also from the years of interviews and research that he did in preparing the book.

The popularity of *Rain of Gold* has brought to millions of Americans one family's stories of the social, economic, and political struggles in Mexico that have resulted in widespread Mexican immigration to the United States, a place where new stories of racism, discrimination, and the triumph over these barriers continue to develop in the epic of Mexican-American life.

Marcos McPeek Villatoro (dates unknown)

Born in the Appalachian Mountains of Tennessee to an Anglo father and a Salvadoran mother, McPeek Villatoro has comically elaborated his unusual biography in stand-up comedy routines and in his autobiographical novel, *The Holy Spirit of My Uncle's Cojones* (1999). After studying for the priesthood for a while, McPeek Villatoro married and worked in various relief organizations in El Salvador, Guatemala, and Nicaragua, at times during the heat of civil war conflicts. After returning to the United States and working with Latino immigrant communities in the South, he earned an MFA degree in creative writing from the University of Iowa (1998). After graduating, he moved his wife and four children to Los Angeles and became the Fletcher Jones Endowed Chair in Creative Writing at Mount St. Mary's College. Even before attending the Iowa Workshop, McPeek Villatoro was an accomplished writer, publishing his monumental epic of Salvadoran history, *A Fire in the Earth*, in 1996. His reportage of living and working in Central America, *Walking toward La Milpa: Living in Guatemala with Armies, Demons, Abrazos and Death*, followed in 1996.

A diverse writer, he published a bilingual collection of poems on the themes of identity and Salvadoran culture and politics, *They Say that I Am Two*, in 1997. His first effort after the workshop, *The Holy Spirit of My Uncle's Cojones*, was the finalist in the Independent Publisher Book Award. His most recent novel, the first installment in a series of detective fiction starring a Latina detective, *Home Killings* (2001), was named one of the best books of the year by the *Los Angeles Times*. Shortly after moving to Los Angeles, McPeek Villatoro founded and serves as host for a literary talk show on Pacifica Radio, "Shelf Life."

Helena María Viramontes (1954–)

Viramontes was born on February 26, 1954, in East Los Angeles, one of eight siblings in a working-class family. She graduated from East LA's Garfield High School and, in 1975, graduated from Immaculate Heart College with a B.A. in English. Her love of literature led her to study English and creative writing over the next two decades. Her work as a writer was put on hiatus when she married and became the mother of two children, to whom she devoted most of her time. In 1994, almost a decade after the publication of her first book, she finished her M.F.A. in creative writing at the University of California-Irvine. By the time she had her degree in hand, Viramontes was already a force on the Hispanic literary scene, and her works had been canonized in some of the most important textbooks and anthologies, including those used by academia.

Helena María Viramontes.

Viramontes creates highly crafted tales of women struggling to live their lives in the barrios. However, her imagery, as in *The Moths and Other Stories* (1985), is often classically based, her command of language reveals years of hard study, and her works are the result of numerous drafts. Viramontes's powerful writing is based on politics and is grounded in the sociological reality of working-class Latinas. In her conscious effort to give voice to women through her stories, she is personally battling and subverting patriarchal practices. Viramontes's stories graphically depict the repression of women and the price they pay in challenging a misogynist society. *Under the Feet of Jesus*, Viramontes's first and only novel is an apparently simple and direct narrative that follows the life of a thirteen-year-old migrant worker girl; however, it soon becomes an indictment of corporate agriculture in California and its practices of child labor and pesticide poisoning. The book is narrated from the point of view of the young girl, Estrella, who also questions the limitations placed on her as a female. Reviewers see Viramontes as working in the social realist vein of John Steinbeck and Upton Sinclair. In addition to the brutal disregard for life by the agricultural companies that she portrays in *Under the Feet of Jesus*, her lush, vibrant language vividly depicts the bleak world faced by migrant workers.

Viramontes's awards include the first prize for fiction, from *Statement Magazine*, California State University, Los Angeles, 1977; first prize for fiction, University of California, Irvine Chicano Literary Contest, 1979; National Endowment for the Arts Fellowship, 1989; Sundance Institute Storytelling Award, 1989; Robert McKee Story Structure Award, National Latino Communications Center, 1991; finalist, Women Script Writing Project, Paul Robeson Fund Exchange, 1991; finalist, Chesterfield Film Company, Universal Studios, 1991;

National Association of Chicano Studies Certificate of Distinguished Recognition, 1993.

Jose Yglesias (1919–1995)

Born in the Ybor City section of Tampa, Florida, Jose Yglesias is the first writer with a Cuban-American consciousness. He grew up within the tradition of Cuban cigar rollers, but upon graduation from high school, moved to Greenwich Village in New York City to become a writer. From his early twenties on, he became politically engaged; his politics would initiate him into the groups of writers and artists who militated against fascism in Spain under Franco, who promoted socialism in the United States, and who were the first supporters of Fidel Castro in Cuba. His early journalistic writing in the *Daily Worker* and elsewhere during the late 1940s and early 1950s eventually led to his writing several journalistic books on Spain and Cuba, including *The Goodbye Land* in 1967, *In the Fist of the Revolution: Life in a Cuban Country Town* in 1968, *Down There* in 1970, and *The Franco Years* in 1977.

Jose Yglesias.

But it is Yglesias' work as a novelist that is most enduring, made noteworthy by his very humane narrators, eloquent prose, and sly humor. For more than thirty years, he wrote novels and stories based on Hispanic life in the United States, and he saw them published by some of the largest and most respected publishing houses in the country. Moreover, Yglesias was one of the very first U.S. Hispanic writers to be published by mainstream presses in the United States. His first novel, *A Wake in Ybor City* (1963), based on the Cuban-Spanish community in Tampa, is considered to be a classic of U.S. Hispanic literature. His other novels include *The Kill Price* (1976) and *Tristan and the Hispanics* (1989). Yglesias was a working writer until his death from cancer in 1995. Two important new and highly received novels were published posthumously: *Break-in* (1996), set in Tampa and exploring the theme of race relations, and *The Old Gent* (1996), set in New York and dealing with the final days of an aging novelist. Two of his stories were included in *Best American Stories* and form a part of his posthumous collection, *The Guns in the Closet* (1996). In all, he wrote ten books of fiction, three of which were published posthumously. During his life, Yglesias never achieved the fame that he deserved; however, he did receive such awards as Guggenheim fellowships (1970 and 1976) and a National Endowment for the Arts fellowship (1974).

CHAPTER 4

SIGNIFICANT TRENDS, MOVEMENTS, AND THEMES IN HISPANIC LITERATURE OF THE UNITED STATES

BILINGUALISM IN LITERATURE

Hispanics have the highest retention rate of their ancestral language of any other group in the United States. The reasons for this retention are hotly debated in linguistic circles as well as in the general population. One of the reasons forwarded is that Hispanics who were incorporated into the United States when their lands were conquered or purchased by the United States—i.e., Mexicans in the Southwest as well as Puerto Ricans on the island—did not have to give up their language and identity to become residents or citizens. Another explanation is that because of the closeness of Mexico, the Caribbean, and Central America, travel to and fro has resulted not only in Spanish-language preservation but also renewal, as contact with the Spanish-speaking home countries reinforced and renewed Spanish language usage in the United States. There is also considerable evidence that the minority status and marginalizing of Hispanics in the United States has contributed to their isolation and, therefore, preservation of their language. Finally, there is no doubt that for more than a century and a half, U.S. industries have targeted workers from the Hispanic world as cheap labor, first to replace the liberated slaves and later to alleviate manpower shortages during wars and economic expansion; this industrial and economic policy (supported by the government) has also contributed to isolation of the Spanish-speaking working class, a class that often has been denied education and upward mobility in the labor camps that industry set up.

Despite all these reasons for retaining the Spanish language in the United States, English has never been totally absent; in fact, it has been pervasive in work, education, and the public sphere. In primary and secondary education, in fact, for many years Spanish use was dissuaded. This did not lead to the eradication of Spanish, but to high dropout rates among Hispanics. Since the nineteenth century, most Spanish-speaking communities in the United States have been bilingual or have evolved a bilingual-bicultural existence. Today, it is not uncommon for members of the same household to be dominant in either Spanish or English, or for them to express themselves in a blend of both languages, what linguists call "code-switching." Many linguists have endeavored to unravel the formulas in Spanish-language code-switching, and many critics have attempted to understand code-switching in literature. Despite all this research and appreciation by linguists and other scholars, mixing both languages has often been the target of derision by purists, who defend the use of only a pure, educated English or Spanish. There also seems to be some class differences operating here, where middle- and upper class or educated speakers become embarrassed at what they think of as bastardized expression. Spanish teachers, in particular, have long fought losing battles to separate the languages among their Hispanic students.

The literature of Hispanics in the United States has since the late nineteenth century reflected the blending of as well as the competition between the Spanish and English linguistics systems that exists in Hispanic communities. Research into the publications of Hispanics in the nineteenth century reveals that code-switching was already taking place in poetry, stories, and essays being published, especially in New Mexico. Prior to the English-Spanish blending in literature, in fact, there are poems and songs of the Southwest that reveal a blending of the Spanish and indigenous languages. In the early twentieth century, almost all immigrant newspapers published poetry that incorporated English into the base of its verses. In exile literature beginning in the nineteenth century, it was not uncommon for editors to publish essays side by side in English and Spanish versions, or to translate books to English, in an effort to influence U.S. popular opinion and government action. Some Hispanic authors, such as María Amparo Ruiz de Burton, published their creative literature in Spanish from the nineteenth century on, a trend which has culminated today with a vast array of English-dominant authors writing and publishing their works only in English and using a Spanish word here and there for flavor or emphasis.

Beginning in the mid-1960s, however, the Chicano and Nuyorican literary movements emphasized code-switching, especially in poetry and theater. Prose writers were often too physically removed from their audiences and too mediated by editors and publishers to code-switch extensively, in comparison to labor theater and poets who performed directly for their communities. Code-switching in theater was especially popularized by Luis Valdez and El Teatro Campesino, which toured nationally and inspired a whole improvisational theater movement whose ideology was to create a theater from folklore and popular culture. One of Valdez's famous dictums was, "If the barrio cannot go to the theater, then the theater must go to the barrio." Through example, El Teatro Campesino demonstrated exactly how a grass-roots theater could reflect the code-switching that was common in Hispanic communities. Of course, this led literary critics to assume that the only modus for code-switching in Latino literature was reflecting common everyday speech. But this was a simplification that never really applied to Valdez or most of the successful bilingual writers of poetry and drama. All of these artists were just as creative with code-switching and barrio dialects as they were with plot, structure, characterization, and ideology.

One of the first widely recognized bilingual poets was Alurista, who raised code-switching to the highest level of poetic experimentation. Showcased in the canonizing anthology, *El Espejo* (*The Mirror*) in 1969, from the start and even in his most politically engaged poems, Alurista did not attempt to reproduce everyday speech or dialect in his code-switching; instead he exhibited a highly idiosyncratic style of imaginatively combining the English and Spanish languages in his poems. As a student of pre-Columbian literature, Alurista took code-switching a step further by incorporating Nahuatl words and Aztec referents in his now trilingual poetry, as evident in *Floricanto en Aztlán* (1971), which takes its title from the Aztec concept of poetry (flowers and songs) and *Nationchild Plumaroja* (1972). Alurista culminated his code-switching experiment with the publication of *Spik in glyph?* (1981), when he experimented with using English graphemes to sound out Spanish words and Spanish graphemes to sound out English ones, effectively creating an interlingual language reminiscent of e.e. cummings' experiments with English language syntax.

Another writer, Ricardo Sánchez, not as academically grounded as Alurista, preserved the feeling of common speech in English and Spanish, but nevertheless juxtaposed surprising combinations of words from both languages and freely invented words and phrases that resulted from language blending. His long, rambling verse was often baroque in its sensibility, syntax, and meaning, and very far indeed from daily language usage in the barrios. His famous poem "*Entequila*," in fact, took the philosophical concept of entelechy and elaborated an *ars poetica* that decried how barrio society misunderstands and withholds its support from the artist; he created this within an elaborate code-switching, rambling framework of neologisms that typify his poems.

Alurista.

Another poet whose stance is very close to the common folk, Tato Laviera, also experiments with the juxtaposition of Spanish and English for esthetic effect and not just to capture the ideolect of his characters, such as Juana Bochisme. In "The Song of an Oppressor," for example, Laviera incorporates the theme song from a soap opera, "Simplemente María," and uses it as an ironic leitmotif to emphasize the exploitation of mothers and working people in the barrio. He also incorporates signs from storefronts, such as "Trabajo Chipe (Piss Work): Un Chavo por Cada Veinte Trajes," with the common Spanish adoptions for "cheap" and "piece work," and other such appropriations of the people's language turned against them to exploit them. In other works, Laviera incorporates and builds on the language of *santería*, the Afro-Caribbean syncretic religion, to create a syncretic Hispanic-Anglo-African text. But Laviera's Africanisms in his *santería* poems come from lived experience, while Alurista's pre-Columbian-inspired verses are imaginative glosses on an imagined literary past. Miguel Piñero and Pedro Pietri also recover the Spanish that has been manipulated commercially in the barrio, while Victor Hernández Cruz and Sandra María Esteves explore Africanisms from within the context of *salsa* performance—as does Laviera. Thus, in these writers and others, bilingualism and code-switching in poetry functions as a gateway to the exploration of the multiculturalism (more than bilingualism) in Latino life and art.

One of the few experiments in code-switching in a novel is Rolando Hinojosa's *Mi querida Rafa* (1981). Through his alter ego P. Galindo's introduction to the novel, we learn that it will be narrated, or constructed, using speech patterns as they actually exist in the Rio Grande Valley. Thus, letters, monolog, and dialogs, as well as editorial comment, are compiled by Galindo in a sort of collage of evidence to solve the central mystery of the book. The full gamut of discourse is represented in the book, with characters only speaking in Spanish, others only in English, and still others code-switching—this regardless of their ethnicity, for it seems that in the Valley some Anglos speak good Spanish and some Mexican Americans prefer English. Of course, this is all Hinojosa's elaborate subterfuge, since each and every word is a creative rendition by him in a novel that is ironic and tongue in cheek, undermining all the protestations of veracity given by narrator Galindo. Hinojosa's sophisticated ruse about culture and language really speaks to the question of bilingualism in literature: it is not a tape recording of actual speech but a creative representation of biculturalism, perhaps multiculturalism.

CENTRAL AMERICAN LITERATURE

While Central American writers have individually produced literary works in the United States since the mid-nineteenth century, there was no consistent corpus of work that could be identified as Central American until the last two or three decades, when large waves of political and economic refugees settled in the United States as a result of the disruptions caused by civil wars and U.S. involvement in these wars in Nicaragua, El Salvador, and Guatemala. The majority of the literature produced to date has been of immigrant and exile character, as exemplified by the novels of Mario Bencastro, who at first documented the wars in his El Salvador and now writes novels dealing with why Central American immigrants come to the United States, the economic privation they suffer here, and the problems they have in adjusting to life in the metropolis. There is the beginning of a native literature among the children of immigrants, exemplified by Marcos McPeek Villatoro, who writes about his generation raised in the United States. But clearly there is a larger corpus of works that will emerge in the coming decades.

Marcos McPeek Villatoro.

CHICANO LITERATURE

The term "Chicano" is derived from the very origin of Mexican nationality, ie. "Mechicano," when the *x* in Mexico was pronounced by Spaniards like the *sh* in English. This term for "Mexican" was used it seems for at least two centuries. It did not really appear in written form, in newspapers, until the late nineteenth century. By the 1920s, an immigrant literature had emerged in the Southwest that identified its readers as Chicanos, meaning Mexican immigrant workers. The term was somewhat negative, however, as used by middle- and upper class Mexicans, who were embarrassed by the poverty and lack of schooling of their lower class immigrant compatriots. The term really gained prominence in the 1960s, however, when the children of Mexican immigrants and longstanding Mexican American communities became involved in a widespread civil rights movement; they resuscitated the term "Chicano" and applied it to themselves and their working-class educational and political movement—the Chicano Movement. Scholars agree that the Chicano Movement began with César Chávez's organizing of farm workers in 1965 and spread into other areas of worker and community life, as well as to the schools. As a result of the Great Society programs of president Lyndon Baines Johnson, the late 1960s and early 1970s saw the largest enrollment of Latino students at universities throughout the country. These students would carry the movement into all corners of academia for the next twenty years.

The first writers of Chicano literature in the 1960s committed their voices to the political, economic, and educational struggles. Their works were frequently used to inspire social and political action, quite often with poets reading their verses at organizing meetings, at boycotts, and before and after protest marches. Of necessity, many of the first writers to gain prominence in the movement were the poets who could tap into an oral tradition of recitation and declamation—such as Abelardo Delgado, Ricardo Sánchez, and Alurista—and create works to be performed orally before groups of students and workers, to inspire them and raise their level of consciousness.

While the first works of Chicano literature appeared with the performances of El Teatro Campesino in 1965 and Rodolfo "Corky" Gonzales's epic poem *I am Joaquín* (*Yo soy Joaquín*) in 1967, a type of Chicano literary canon began solidifying with the awards given and books published by Editorial Quinto Sol, beginning in 1970. From 1971 to 1973, Quinto Sol awarded prizes to

Rodolfo "Corky" Gonzales.

Arte Público Press authors at a National Association of Chicano Studies Conference in Austin, Texas: (from left) Ana Castillo, Evangelina Vigil-Piñón, Sandra Cisneros and Pat Mora.

and published three of the foundational novels of Chicano literature: Tomás Rivera's . . . *Y no se lo tragó la tierra* (. . . *And the Earth Did Not Devour Him*, 1971), Rudolfo Anaya's *Bless Me, Ultima* (1972), and Rolando Hinojosa's *Estampas del Valle y otras obras* (*Sketches of the Valley and Other Works*, 1973). It also published a magazine, *El Grito*, and issued editions of an anthology, *El Espejo* (*The Mirror*), featuring some of the models that would become part of the cultural nationalist canon it was constructing—a canon that emphasized the indigenous past of Aztec and Mayan roots, rural culture, bilingualism, and code-switching, as well as working-class culture and resistance to Anglo domination. Both directors of Quinto Sol, Octavio Romano and Herminio Ríos, consistently used these criteria in selecting works to be published, and through their choices also constructed a masculine, phallocentric ideal that retarded the appearance of women authors during the early years of Chicano literature. The growing number of Chicano students and professors in academia helped spread the canon in the courses they created, the ethnic studies departments, and the academic associations where literature was studied. The success of integrating literature into the curricula was also due in part to the large number of writers who were or became university professors, including Alurista, Anaya, Hinojosa, Rivera, and scores of others.

Finally, in the mid–1970s—through magazines such as *Revista Chicano-Riqueña* (later *The Americas Review*), *Bilingual Review*, and *Caracol*, and later through such magazines as *Mango* and *Third Woman* edited by women—Chicanas began to gain access to publishing. By the early 1980s, a whole wave of women writers had become prominent in Chicano literature, including Ana Castillo, Lorna Dee Cervantes, Sandra Cisneros, Pat Mora, Evangelina Vigil-Piñón, and others who, for the most part, were being published by Arte Público Press. In the late 1980s and early 1990s, Cisneros and Castillo led the way into commercial, mainstream publishing with their established works being reprinted and their new works being issued by large commercial publishers. During the 1990s, not only Chicano literature, but the rest of Hispanic ethnic literature, including the literature of men, began making inroads into mainstream commercial publishing. But during this decade, as more and more Hispanics of all backgrounds became part of the national scene and as an increasing number of Mexican Americans took part in professional life and culture (beyond the culture of ethnicity and protest), the term Chicano began to pass from currency, giving rise to such terms as "Hispanic" and "Latino" and "multicultural" literature.

CHILDREN'S LITERATURE

The writing of literature for Hispanic children of the United States is a relatively recent phenomenon. Although from the nineteenth century to World War II, Spanish-language newspapers in the United States did occasionally publish stories and rhymes for children—newspapers published by Protestant sects were more likely to do so—there were very few books published targeting young readers. Two early exceptions were Father Félix Varela, who published Catholic religious magazines for children in the mid-nineteenth century, and José Martí, who published a magazine for children, *La Edad de Oro*, in the 1890s. Also, from the 1930s through the 1960s, a New York City librarian, Puerto Rican Pura Belpré, expanded her children's reading hours to writing stories for her young audiences. She became the most prolific author of children's stories, mostly based on Puerto Rican folklore, and even wrote a young adult novel, *Firefly Summer* (written during World War II, but published posthumously in 1997).

It was during the establishment and promotion of bilingual education in the late 1960s and early 1970s that a need was identified for books in Spanish and/or English to assist Latino children in learning to read. At first, the answer by teachers and librarians was to import children's books from Spain and Spanish America. However, it soon became apparent that the dialects employed in these national literatures and the characters, social and physical environment, and particular cultural referents were not easily recognizable or relevant to Latinos growing up as minorities in the United States. To remedy this, numerous educational publishers had American children's literature translated to Spanish for the classroom, but once again this literature did not represent the lives of Hispanic children and, even worse, was often riddled with stereotypes.

There were some valiant efforts by early Chicano writers, such as Ernesto Gal-

Pura Belpré.

arza, who penned many stories and rhymes directed at children from Spanish-speaking backgrounds, but his talent lay more in writing social scientific work for adults; however, his memoir of growing up, *Barrio Boy*, was a very successful text in reaching young adult readers. Four other writers of the 1970s had adult audiences in mind when they wrote their books about growing up Latino in the United States, but teachers and librarians subsequently found their works very appropriate for young adult and high school audiences. In fact, today this young audience is a substantial readership of the culture conflict and growing pains of the young adult protagonists in Rudolfo Anaya's *Bless Me, Ultima* (1972), Sandra Cisneros' *The House on Mango Street* (1984), Nicholasa Mohr's *Nilda* (1973), and Tomás Rivera's . . . *Y no se lo tragó la tierra* (. . . *And the Earth Did Not Devour Him*, 1971). Later, in the 1980s and early 1990s, such "adult" authors as Gary Soto specifically began to address the young adult audiences with a series of autobiographical novels and pure fiction.

Beginning in the 1990s, Hispanic authors responded on a large scale to the need for a literature that was based on the language, culture, and environment of Hispanic children in the United States. A number of leading adult writers began to write picture books for pre-school and beginning readers: Francisco Alarcón, Sandra Cisneros, Gary Soto, Nicholasa Mohr, and Pat Mora, among others. More recently, best selling authors Julia Alvarez and Victor Villaseñor have also addressed this need. Probably the most interesting of the children's and young adult authors are those who almost exclusively and consistently address young readers. Ofelia Dumas Lachtman, for instance, has created a spunky young protagonist, Pepita, for a continuing series of picture-book adventures based on actual dilemmas in the lives of Latino children—such as always having to translate for the monolingual adults in their homes, schools, and neighborhoods, as exemplified by her *Pepita Talks Twice* (*Pepita habla dos veces*, 1995). The Pepita series is just one of the Piñata Books published by Arte Público Press that function as bridges from the home culture to the schools, with the distinctive format of having the text translated on the same page. Another successful author, Diane Gonzales Bertrand, explores the life of Latino children and teenagers in the inner city by depicting deeper culture as represented by cooking in the family context, as in her picture book, *Sip, Slurp, Soup, Soup/Caldo, Caldo, Caldo* (1997); the *quinceañera*, or fifteen-year coming-out ritual in *The Last Doll* (2000); or struggling to maintain family values while fighting pressure to join gangs, in the young adult fiction series of *Trino's Choice* (1999) and *Trino's Time* (2001).

Diane Gonzales Bertrand.

Today the field of children's literature among Hispanic authors and readers is growing in leaps and bounds, as is the size of the young population of Latinos, who make up more than fifty percent of the public school enrollment of our largest cities. There are literally scores of Latino writers creating books for children and young adults, helping them to forge confident and secure personalities who can speak two languages and relate to most of the cultures of the Americas.

CUBAN EXILE LITERATURE AND CUBAN AMERICAN LITERATURE

Cuban culture and literature in the United States date back to the nineteenth century, when on these shores such exiled writers as Félix Varela penned literary works attacking Spanish colonialism and smuggled them back into Cuba. During the nineteenth and twentieth centuries, longstanding Cuban immigrant communities, such as those of the tobacco workers

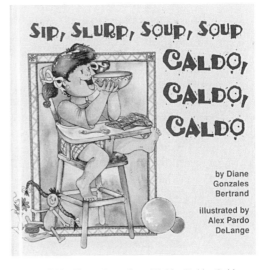

Cover of *Sip, Slurp, Soup, Soup/Caldo, Caldo, Caldo.*

in Tampa, also produced a literature of immigration. But as early as the American Civil War, Cubans, such as Federico L. Cavada, were writing in English from the perspective of a U.S. citizen. However, the largest source of Cuban American literature, that is, a native American literature written by people who were born or raised in the United States and identify themselves as Cuban Americans, is the expression of the children of Cuban exiles from the Cuban Revolution of 1959. Since the beginning of the post-revolution exodus, young writers have developed who are no longer preoccupied with exile or their parents' past in Cuba; instead, they look forward to participating in the English-language mainstream or to creating a literary and cultural expression for the U.S. Cuban and Hispanic communities. Thus, there has developed a definite separation of purpose and aesthetics between the younger writers—Iván Acosta, Roberto Fernández, Cristina García, Oscar Hijuelos (a child of pre-revolution immigration), Gustavo Pérez-Firmat, Dolores Prida, and Virgil Suárez—and the older writers of exile—Lydia Cabrera, Matías Montes Huidobro, José Sánchez Boudy, and so on. Also, there continues to be an influx of exiled writers disaffected by Cuban communism, such as Heberto Padilla, who are young but continue the exile tradition. A middle ground also has arisen among the exiled writers—that of producing a highly abstract literature devoid of direct political reference, as in the works of acclaimed playwright María Irene Fornés, who writes in English for a mainstream audience but whose works would hardly be recognized as Cuban, Cuban American or exile literature.

The literature of the exiled writers almost predominantly attacked the Cuban Revolution, Castro, and Marxism. The novel and the theater of exile, especially the popular farces on Miami stages, became weapons in the struggle. Following the first antirevolutionary novel, *Enterrado Vivo* (Buried Alive), published in Mexico in 1960, were a host of others published in the United States and abroad by minor writers such as Emilio Fernández Camus, Orlando Núñez, Manuel Cobo Souza, Raúl A. Fowler, Luis Ricardo Alonso, and many others. When they were not openly propagandistic and rhetorical, they were nostalgic for the homeland to the point of idealization. Poetry and drama followed the same course, for the most part. Later, political verse would come to form a special genre of its own, what has been called by critic Hortensia Ruiz del Viso prison poetry ("poesía del presidio político"), as in the works of Angel Cuadra, Heberto Padilla, and Armando Valladares.

A key figure in providing a new direction for Cuban literature in the United States has been Celedonio González, who, beginning with *Los primos* (The Cousins, 1971), changed the focus from the Marxist homeland to concentrate on Cuban life and culture in the United States. Later, in *Los cuatro embajadores* (The Four Ambassadors, 1973) and *El espesor del pellejo de un gato ya cadáver* (The Thickness of Skin on a Cat Already a Corpse, 1978), he not only examined culture shock between Cubans and Americans, but he also treated a very taboo topic among Cuban exiles: criticism of the U.S. economic system, especially in its exploitation of Cuban workers. González depicts Cubans who do not consider themselves Americans but who are also conscious that Cuba is no longer theirs.

Ironically, one of the most important writers in forging a Cuban American identity and in breaking new ground in the use of the English language is a professor of Spanish, Roberto Fernández. Through his novels, Fernández not only satirizes all the taboo subjects in the Cuban community of Miami—the counterrevolutionary movement, racism, acculturation, assimilation, etc.—but he also helps the community to take them in a less serious vein and laugh at itself. In his four open-form mosaic-type novels—*La vida es un special* (Life Is on Sale, 1982), *La montaña rusa* (The Roller Coaster, 1985), *Raining Backwards* (1988), and *Holy Radishes!* (1995)—Fernández presents a biting but loving satire of a community transformed by the materialism and popular culture of the United States. He, nevertheless, indicts the community for being paralyzed by the nostalgia for Cuba and the political obsession with its communist government. Fernández's style includes bilingual and bicultural humor, in which the dissonance and irony of parallel customs intersecting shock, surprise, and intrigue the reader.

Roberto Fernández.

Gustavo Pérez-Firmat, on the other hand, has served in his essays, poetry, and novels as a theorist of the Cuban American condition. Pérez-Firmat theorizes that the dual perspective of Cuban Americans born on the island but raised in the United States is "transitional"; they are cultural mediators, who are constantly translating not only language but also the differences between the Anglo-American and Cuban/Cuban American world views. Since they have the unique ability to communicate with and understand both cultures, these Cuban Americans have taken on the role of translator not only for themselves but for society at large. In his groundbreaking book-length essay, *Life on the Hyphen: The Cuban-American Way* (1993), Pérez-Firmat maintains, however, that the next generation will follow a path similar to that of the children of European immigrants, who are simply considered ethnic Americans and are more American than they are anything else. Themes of biculturalism are ever-present in Pérez-Firmat's poetry, which is full of code-switching and bilingual-bicultural double entendres and playfulness. In his book-length memoir, *Next Year in Cuba* (1995), Pérez-Firmat documents the tension his generation feels between identifying with other Americans their age and identifying with their parents, who always looked forward to returning to Cuba. *Anything but Love* (2000), Pérez-Firmat's latest novel, is a tour de force of culture conflict revolving around love, marriage, and sex roles, all articulated with that inimitable rhapsodic excess that is the author's trademark.

Linden Lane, one of the most influential literary magazines of Cuban literature in the United States, was published in Spanish by Heberto Padilla and edited by Belkis Cuza Malé and accommodated the expression of both groups: the exiles and the Cuban Americans. In 1990, the magazine formally announced the advent of a Cuban American literature with its publication of an anthology containing works in both English and Spanish. Entitled *Los Atrevidos: The Cuban American Writers*, the entries were selected and edited by Miami poet Carolina Hospital.

In 1991, Arte Público Press published the first anthology of *Cuban American Theater*, edited by critic Rodolfo Cortina. Both collections drew upon writers dispersed throughout the United States, not just from the Miami and New York-area communities.

Among the new generation of Cuban American writers growing up in the United States there is a substantial representation that has gone through university creative writing programs and has had access to mainstream publishing. A graduate of the important Masters in Creative Writing Program at Louisiana State University, Virgil Suárez has had novels and anthologies published by large commercial houses. His first novel, *Latin Jazz* (1989), is a somewhat different ethnic biographical novel, portraying a Cuban family through alternate chapters devoted to the individual family members. His most recent novel, *Going Under* (1996), however, is a tour de force about the difficulty of assimilation and economic success on American terms for Cuban Americans. His volumes of belles lettres, including *Spared Angola: Memories from a Cuban-American Childhood* (1997) and *Infinite Refuge* (2002), are collections of highly autobiographical stories, essays, and poems that ponder the themes of family, rootlessness, identity and cultural exile.

Probably the most important of the Cuban American writers to come out of the creative writing schools is Oscar Hijuelos, who is not the son of political refugees from the Cuban Revolution but of earlier immigrants (economic refugees) to New York City. Hijuelos' first offering, *Our House in the Last World* (1983), is a typical ethnic autobiography and may be seen as a symbol of Cuban assimilation in that it is one of the few novels that negatively portrays the island culture, as personified by an alcoholic, macho father, while developing the common theme of the American Dream. His novel, *The Mambo Kings Play Songs of Love* (1990), made history; it is the first novel by an Hispanic writer of the United States to win the Pulitzer Prize. It marks the first time that a major publishing house, Simon and Schuster, invested heavily in a novel by an Hispanic writer, bringing it out at the top of its list and promoting the book very heavily. *The Mambo Kings Play Songs of Love* is the story of two musician brothers during the height of the mambo dance music craze in the 1950s. The novel, thus, has an historical background that lends it a rich texture; it allows us to see a portion of American popular culture history through the eyes of two performers very wrapped up in the euphoria of the times and then the waning of things Latino in the United States. The story of the tragic ending of the duo is very touching, but offers hope for the potential of Hispanic culture to influence the mainstream. In fact, Hijuelos' book itself directly influenced popular culture when it was made into a Hollywood feature film.

Following Hijuelos, other Cuban writers have experienced commercial success. Cristina García's *Dreaming in Cuban* was awarded the National Book Award in 1992. Also a child who accompanied her parents into exile in the United States, García studied journalism in college and maintained an interest in politics that led her into the world of writing and the examination of her Cuban American circumstances. Her highly acclaimed *Dreaming in Cuban* was the first novel authored by a Cuban American woman to give insight into the psychology of the generation of Cubans born or raised in the United States and who grew up under the looming myth of the splendors of the island in the past and the evils of

Castro—a generation, however, that never really had first-hand knowledge of their parents' homeland. The novel closely examines women's perspective on the dilemma of living between two cultures as it chronicles three generations of women in the Pino family, and in so doing compares the lives of those who live in Cuba with those living in the United States. The same themes are also revisited in her second novel, *The Agüero Sisters* (1997), which compares the lives of two sisters growing up separately in Cuba and the United States and acclimated to the political and economic cultures of each country.

EXILE LITERATURE

Hispanic exile literature in the United States is the product of the great moments in the political history of the Hispanic World, from the beginning of the nineteenth century on: the Napoleonic intervention in Spain, the movements of the Spanish American colonies for independence from Spain, the French intervention in Mexico, the War of 1898, the Mexican Revolution, the Spanish Civil War, the Cuban Revolution, the recent wars in Central America and the numerous struggles in Spanish America against autocratic regimes and foreign interventions, including the many incursions into the domestic affairs of these countries by the United States. The very act of U.S. partisanship in the internal politics of the Spanish American republics at times directed the expatriate streams to these shores. All of these struggles contributed hundreds of thousands of political refugees to the United States throughout its history. Because of U.S. territorial expansion and Hispanic immigration, the United States gradually became home to large communities of Spanish speakers, which continually received the expatriates. Thus, the refugees found familiar societies where they could conduct business and eke out a living while they hoped for and abetted change in the lands that would someday welcome their return. Much of the literary expression of the exiles has traditionally emerged from their hopes and desires for the political and cultural independence of their homelands, be that from the Spanish empire or from U.S. imperialism. Much of this literature is highly lyrical and idealistic in its poetry and often elegant in its prose. However, it is also characterized by its aggressive and argumentative tone because of its commitment to political change in the homeland.

From the beginning of the nineteenth century, Spanish-speaking political refugees from Spain and the Spanish American countries have as part of their political culture repeatedly taken up exile in the United States to gain access to a free press and thus offer their compatriots uncensored news and political ideology, even if their writings have to be smuggled and passed surreptitiously hand to hand back home. In many cases, the exile press also engages in political fund raising, community organizing, and revolutionary plotting to overthrow regimes in their countries of origin. The raison d'etre of the exile press has always been to influence life and politics in the homeland by providing information and opinion about the homeland, changing or solidifying opinion about politics and policy in the *patria*, and assisting in raising funds to overthrow the current regime.

The freedom of expression available in exile is highly desirable in light of the repression that may exist in the homelands. The historical record is rife with examples of the prison terms, torture, and executions of writers, journalists, publishers, and editors during the struggles to establish democracies in Spanish America in the wake of Spain's colonialism and during autocratic regimes. Numerous exiled authors have suffered torture in prisons and death on battlefields in the Americas. Numerous authors, viewing themselves as patriots without a country, have been forced to live in exile and/or wander from country to country creating their literary works and spreading their political doctrines. This ever-present base for the culture and literature of Hispanic communities in the United States exemplifies how U.S. Hispanic literature is transnational and can never truly be understood solely from within the geographical and political confines of the United States.

The first political books printed in exile by Hispanics were written by Spanish citizens who were protesting the installation of a puppet government in Spain by Napoleon; these exiled writers published poetry and novels in addition to their political treatises. The longest lasting independence movement in the Hemisphere was that of Spain's Caribbean colonies, Cuba and Puerto Rico, and many of their independence struggles were plotted, funded, and written about from U.S. shores. One of Cuba's first and most illustrious exiles was the philosopher-priest Félix Varela, who founded *El Habanero* newspaper in Philadelphia in 1824 and moved it to New York in 1825. *El Habanero* openly militated for Cuban independence from Spain. Varela set the precedent for Cubans and Puerto Ricans of printing and publishing in exile and having their works circulating in their home islands.

Since the writings of Varela and other nineteenth-century expatriates, exile literature has been one of the continuing currents in Hispanic letters and culture in the United States. Many of the writers to follow them have become steeped in that tradition, building on the work of predecessors who used their literary art to promote their political causes. To date, some of the commonplaces of exile literature remain, even among the most recent exile writers from Central America and Cuba. In general, the literature of exile is centered on the homeland, *la patria*, rather than on the fate of the exile community in the United States. Always implicit is its premise of return to *la patria*, and thus there is no question of assimilating into the culture during the temporary sojourn in the States. As return is always impending, however, there is a static vision of the homeland culture that oftentimes does not reflect the evolution of culture in the homeland during the exiles' absence; this literature is nostalgic for the *patria* as remembered before the authors left, and on foreign soil these authors seek through their writing to preserve the language and culture in their communities to facilitate the easy reintroduction into the home culture. The writing does not support the mixing of Spanish and English, as it seeks to emulate the best cultural forms in the elevation of their political ideologies. The stories tend to be epic in nature and heroes larger than life, even in their tragic downfalls. Often, the metaphors that characterize their lives far from home relate to the Babylonian captivity and to "paradise lost"; their fiction and non-fiction writings emphasize the strangeness of the new social environment and the dangers it poses for cultural survival. The nineteenth-century authors engaged in the movements for independence from Spain, often cultivating the "Spanish Black Legend" (propaganda about the Spanish abuses of the Amerindians spread by the English and Dutch in their competition with Spain for

New World colonies) and identifying themselves with the Native Americans suffering the inhuman abuses of the Spanish conquistadors. These exile writers sought to construct their own New World identity: Thus, the literature was not only culturally nationalistic, but often politically as well, in attempting to construct the nation and its identity. The impact of this literature is affected by the fact that many of these writers have been actually engaged in armed revolutionary and political struggles.

Exiles and political refugees have continued to make up an important segment of Hispanic immigrants to the United States. With the Cuban Revolution and the United States fighting much of the Cold War through involvement in the civil wars in Central America and Chile, large-scale immigration of political refugees has continued to the present day, and the dictatorships in these countries and Argentina have arisen as themes in the literature of Hispanic exile. Beginning in 1959, a new wave of refugees from the Cuban Revolution established a widespread exile press as well as a more informal network of hundreds of newsletters. Chileans, Salvadorans, Nicaraguans, and other Spanish American expatriates have all contributed to a literature of exile. What is different today is that many of these exiled voices have been readily translated into English, and the works of such liberal writers as Argentines Luisa Valenzuela, Manuel Puig, and Jacobo Timmerman; Chileans Emma Sepúlveda and Ariel Dorfman; and Guatemala's Arturo Arias are published alongside the more conservative voices of Cuban exiles, such as those of Heberto Padilla and Reinaldo Arenas. As the Hispanic population of the United States continues to grow—estimated to be one-fourth of the total population by 2050—and as the economy of the United States becomes more integrated with those south of the border through such agreements as the North American Free Trade Agreement, United States culture will become even more directly linked to the internal politics of Spanish America.

LITERATURE BASED ON FOLKORE AND WORKING-CLASS ESTHETICS

Folkore is the knowledge of the people, the grass roots of those people and communities situated the farthest away from the official institutions of a society. For the most part, folk literature is the oral expression of the common folk; it maintains its own sense of history, art, and audience. While folk literature arises in pre-literate societies, it can persist and grow within literate societies among communities that have been subjected to colonization, marginalization, and exploitation. Folk literature is important in U.S. Hispanic culture in both its pre-literate and internal colonial and/or minority manifestations. Because North American frontier society was so far from the centers of Spanish colonial administration and because the Spanish crown outlawed the printing press in these northern frontier territories, much of cultural expression in what became the Southwest of the United States was created and passed on orally in the form of personal experience narratives, tales, proverbs and sayings, songs and other poetic genres, dramatic pageants, such as *las posadas*, and plays, such as the *pastorela*. This body of expressive knowledge was cumulative over centuries and became the basis of a Spanish-language literary culture, both when Mexico gained its independence in 1821 and subsequently administered these territories and when these territories came under U.S. rule and Hispanic and indigenous communities were colonized, marginalized, and exploited as human resources of these lands.

As labor recruitment from Mexico and the Caribbean became a federally sanctioned and industrially preferred practice from the late nineteenth century on, United States industrial policy and practice were central to the formation within U.S. borders of large immigrant communities drawn from the poorest and least educated workers in the nearby Latin countries. Cuban, Dominican, Mexican, Panamanian, and Puerto Rican economic refugees also brought along a wealth of oral lore to add to the rich repositories of folk literature already existing in U.S. Hispanic communities. Many of these laborers had lived in pre-industrial societies, far from educational institutions, in their homelands—which had been colonized and administered by Spain, up until the twentieth century in the cases of Cuba and Puerto Rico—and now had become part of broad urban and rural labor camps, segregated from the society at large in the United States. While most of these workers did not have access to education and integration, some specialized workers, such as tobacco rollers, were able to become literate and informally educated through their own efforts of hiring readers to distract them from the boredom of the repetitive jobs. Nevertheless, within their own unions, mutual aid societies and communities, working-class Hispanics were able to develop consistent oral and written expression that served their own needs for cultural sustenance and reflection, developing a true working-class literature with its own sense of esthetics and mission.

Whether it be in the border ballads, or *corridos*, of the Southwest, beginning in the mid-nineteenth century and composed and sung to this day; the *plenas*, *bombas*, and *décimas* of Puerto Rican migrants and their children in the large cities of the East and the Midwest; or the Hispanic women's songs and proverbs related to family and domestic life, a rich corpus of oral literature not only survived, but influenced the development of written literature throughout the twentieth century. Of particular importance is the folk expression in the written literature of immigrants, which has often reproduced the diction, anecdotes, and genres from oral expression. Such is the case not only of the poems, *décimas*, and *corridos* published in immigrant newspapers but also entire novels, such as Daniel Venegas' *Las aventuras de Don Chipote, o cuando los pericos mamen* (1928), which incorporate songs, proverbs, and worker experiences and also employ a narrative voice representative of working-class immigrants. Even *crónicas*—local-color satirical newspaper columns written by elites such as Julio G. Arce and Benjamín Padilla, often to criticize the "uncivilized" and uneducated behavior of immigrant workers—borrowed extensively from the personal experience narratives, language, and perspectives of the immigrant working classes. Then, too, there were working-class *cronistas*, such as Jesús Colón and Alberto O'Farrill, who consciously produced a literature based in immigrant working-class culture that was representative of working-class interests.

Beginning in the mid-1960's with the emergence of university-educated Hispanic writers originally from the working-class communities, Chicano and Puerto Rican literature consciously assumed a working-class stance to reflect the culture from which it sprang and function as a tool to help students and communities analyze their economic, social, and political circumstances. Thus, such foundational Chicano writers of Spanish narrative as Tomás Rivera and Rolando Hinojosa became masters of orality in their works, capturing the nuances of oral speech as well as the ideology and world view behind the folk speech patterns. Of course, the literary genres that are performed orally and are closest to the community through performance, such as drama and poetry reading, depend the most on folk tradition and performance styles, as in the case of such poets as Tato Laviera and Evangelina Vigil-Piñón and Chicano theater in general. These tendencies in written literature continue to this date, even with new wellsprings of oral literature constantly emerging from the grass roots and from immigrant communities.

IMMIGRANT LITERATURE

Hispanic immigrant literature is the literature created orally or in written form by the immigrants from the Hispanic world who have come to these shores since the early nineteenth century. Among its characteristics are: 1) the predominant use of the language of the homeland, in 2) serving a population united by that language, irrespective of national origin, and 3) solidifying and furthering national identity. The literature of immigration serves a population in transition from the land of origin to the United States by reflecting the reasons for emigrating, recording the trials and tribulations of immigration, and facilitating adjustment to the new society, all the while maintaining a link with the old society.

Unlike the literature of European immigrants to the United States, Hispanic immigrant literature generally does not support the myths of the American Dream and the Melting Pot: the belief that the immigrants came to find a better life, implicitly a better culture, and that soon they or their descendants would become Americans and there would no longer be a need for literature in the language of the "old country." While Hispanic authors writing in English since World War II may have subscribed to these notions to get published or to achieve a broad readership, Hispanic immigrant literature in the Spanish language is not about assimilating or "melting" into a generalized American identity. In fact, the history of Hispanic groups in the United States has shown an unmeltable ethnicity, and, as immigration from Spanish-speaking countries has continued steadily since the founding of the United States, there seems no end to the phenomenon at this juncture in history nor in the foreseeable future.

In general, the literature of Hispanic immigration displays a double-gaze perspective: forever comparing the past and the present, the homeland and the new country, and only seeing the resolution of these dual, conflicting points of reference when the author, characters, and/or the audience can return to the *patria*. The literature of immigration reinforces the culture of the homeland while facilitating the accommodation to the new land. While fervently nationalistic, this literature seeks to represent and protect the rights of immigrants by protesting discrimination, human rights abuses, and racism. As much of this literature arises from or is pitched to the working class, it adopts the working-class and rural dialects of the immigrants.

Among the predominant themes in the literature of immigration are the description of the metropolis, often in satirical or critical terms, as is seen in essays by José Martí, Francisco "Pachín" Marín, and Nicanor Bolet Peraza; the description of the trials and tribulations of immigrants, especially in their journey here and, once here, in their being subjected to exploitation as workers and discrimination as foreigners and racial others, as in Daniel Venegas and Conrado Espinosa; the conflict between Anglo and Hispanic cultures, ubiquitous in this literature; and the expression of gender anxieties in nationalist reaction against assimilation into mainstream culture. Immigrant authors often cast their literary discourse in the framework of an imminent return to the homeland or a warning to those back home not to come to the United States and face the disillusionment that the writers and their protagonists have already experienced. This stance of writing to warn their compatriots, when in actuality they are speaking to their immigrant enclave or community here, helps authors to find common cause and solidarity with their audiences, as both writers and readers are rendering testimony to the uninitiated, who are the potential greenhorns destined in the future to suffer as have the protagonists of these immigrant genres. Of course, these formulae and themes depend on the underlying premise of immigrant literature: the return to the *patria*, which necessitates the preservation of language and culture and loyalty to the *patria*. Almost invariably, the narratives of immigration end with the main characters returning to the home soil; failure to do so results in death, the severest form of poetic justice, as illustrated in the first novel of immigration, Alirio Díaz Guerra's *Lucas Guevara* (1914) and, almost half a century later, in René Marqués' play *La carreta* (*The Oxcart*, 1953).

Because of the massive migrations of working-class Mexicans and Puerto Ricans during the twentieth century, much of immigrant literature is to be found in oral expression, folk songs, vaudeville, and other working-class literary and artistic expression. The anonymous Mexican corrido "El lavaplatos" (The Dishwasher) reproduces the same cycle as Daniel Venegas' working-class novel *Las aventuras de Don Chipote, o cuando los pericos mamen*—leaving home to find work in the United States, disillusionment in laboring like a beast of burden here, and eventual return home. The immigrants' songs of uprootedness and longing for the homeland can be heard in the *décima* (a song with ten-line stanzas and a sonnet-like rhyme scheme) "Lamento de un jíbaro." But the ultimate disillusionment and disgrace for the immigrant is deportation, as documented in the plaintive refrains of the *corrido* "Los deportados" (The Deportees) and the outraged newspaper editorials by Rodolfo Uranga. Quite often the setting for this literature is the workplace, be that on the streets walked by Wen Gálvez's door-to-door salesman in his *Tampa: impresiones de un emigrado* (1897), in the factory of Gustavo Alemán Bolaños' *La factoría* (1925), or under the burning sun in the agricultural fields, as in Conrado Espinosa's *El sol de Texas* (1926); but domestic settings are also frequent, even in contemporary plays such as René Marqués's *La carreta* and Iván Acosta's *El super* (1977), both depicting the intergenerational conflict splitting U.S.-acculturated children from their immigrant parents.

In fact, culture conflict of all sorts typifies this work, and from this conflict arise some of its most typical characters, such as the *agringados* (Gringoized), *renegados* (renegades), and *pitiyanquis* (petite Yankees), who deny their own culture to adopt "American" ways. But more than any other archetype of American culture, the predominantly male authors have chosen the American female to personify the eroticism, immorality, greed, and materialism that they perceive in American society. What was an amoral Eve in a metropolis identified as Sodom by Alirio Díaz Guerra evolved into the 1920s flapper in works by Jesús Colón, Daniel Venegas, and Julio B. Arce ("Jorge Ulica"); this enticing but treacherous Eve led unassuming Hispanic Adams into perdition. These authors place the responsibility for preserving Hispanic customs and language and for protecting identity in the hands of their women, and subsequently levy severe criticism at those who adopted more liberal American customs or even dared to behave like flappers themselves. This can also be seen in such contemporary works as René Marqués's *La carreta* and Jaime Carrero's Nuyorican play *Pipo No Sabe Reír* (*Pipo Doesn't Know How to Laugh*).

NATIVE LITERATURE

Native Hispanic literature developed first out of the experience of colonialism and racial oppression. Hispanics were subjected to more than a century of "racialization" through such doctrines as the Spanish Black Legend and Manifest Destiny (racist doctrines that justified the

Poster for the 1954 production of René Marqués' *La carreta*.

appropriation of lands and resources by the English and Anglo-Americans). The Hispanics were subsequently conquered and/or incorporated into the United States through territorial purchase and then treated as colonial subjects—as were the Mexicans of the Southwest, the Hispanics in Florida and Louisiana, the Panamanians in the Canal Zone and in Panama itself, and the Puerto Ricans in the Caribbean. (Also, Cubans and Dominicans may be considered as peoples who developed their identities under United States colonial rule during the early twentieth century.) Added to the base of Hispanics already residing within the United States was the subsequent migration and immigration of large numbers of people from the Spanish-speaking countries to the continental United States over a period of 100 years. Their waves of emigration were often directly related to the colonial administration of their homelands by the United States. Their children's subsequent U.S. citizenship created hundreds of thousands of new natives with cultural perspectives on life in the United States that have differed substantially from those of immigrants and exiles.

Hispanic native literature first developed as an ethnic minority literature among Hispanics already residing in the Southwest when the U.S. appropriated it from Mexico (there are very few extant Hispanic texts from Louisiana and Florida from U.S. colonial and early statehood days). Native Hispanic literature has specifically manifested itself in an attitude of entitlement to civil, political, and cultural rights. From its very origins in the nineteenth-century editorials of Francisco Ramírez and the novels of María Amparo Ruiz de Burton, Hispanic native literature in general has been cognizant of the racial, ethnic, and/or minority status of its readers within U.S. society and culture. The fundamental reason for existence of native Hispanic literature and its point of reference has been and continues to be the lives and conditions of Latinos in the United States. Unlike immigrant literature, it does not have one foot in the homeland and one in the United States; it does not share that double gaze of forever contrasting experience in the United States with experience in the homeland. For native Hispanic peoples of the United States, the homeland *is* the United States; there is no question of a return to their ancestors' Mexico, Puerto Rico, or Cuba.

Thus, this literature exhibits a firm sense of place, often elevated to a mythic status. Chicanos in the 1960s and 1970s, for example, referenced Aztlán, the legendary place of origin of the Aztecs supposedly in today's Southwest, that gave them—as mestizo people—priority over Euro-Americans. In this place, syncretic cultures developed and reigned supreme, as in the Nuyoricans' "Loisaida" (the Lower East Side of New York), so eulogized by poet-playwright Miguel Piñero, and "El Bronx," as in Nicholasa Mohr's *El Bronx Remembered*. This sense of belonging to a region or place or just the *barrio*, where their culture has transformed the social and physical environment, is only one manifestation of the general feeling of newness—that is, of a new culture derived from the synthesis of the old Hispanic and Anglo cultures that had initially opposed one another.

The "Chicanos" and "Nuyoricans" appeared in the 1960s along with the civil rights movement to claim a new and separate identity from that of Mexicans (even from Mexican-Americans) and Puerto Ricans on the island. They proclaimed their bilingualism and biculturalism, mixed and blended the English and Spanish in their speech and writing, and created a new esthetic that was interlingual and transcultural. The construction of this new identity was often explored in literary works that examined the psychology of characters caught between cultures, pondering the proverbial existential questions, as in four foundational works on coming of age: Piri Thomas' autobiography *Down These Mean Streets* (1967), Tomás Rivera's novel written in Spanish . . . *Y no se lo tragó la tierra* (. . . *And the Earth Did Not Devour Him*, 1971), Rudolfo Anaya's *Bless Me, Ultima* (1972), and Nicholasa Mohr's *Nilda* (1973). But the process of sorting out identity and creating a positive place for themselves in an antagonistic society was at times facilitated only by a cultural nationalism that promoted opposition to Anglo-American culture and a strict code of ethnic loyalty. No other artist explored the question of image and identity more than playwright Luis Valdez throughout his career, but most certainly in his allegory of stereotypes *Los Vendidos* (1976), in which he revisited the history of Mexican stereotypes, the products of discrimination and culture clash.

In the 1960s and 1970s, native Hispanic literature was closely associated with the civil rights movements of Mexican Americans and Puerto Ricans in the continental United States. Literary works tended toward the militant, often emphasizing the working-class roots, language dialects, and audiences over the academic and commercial. Today, native Hispanic literature is characterized by academic preparation and readership as well as publication by large commercial publishing houses. In the works published by mainstream publishers, English is the preferred language and university-prepared authors are the most published. Political ideology and working-class culture have been almost entirely eliminated in an attempt to appeal to broader audiences.

NOVEL OF IMMIGRATION

Immigration has been one of the basic realities of life for Latino communities in the United States since the nineteenth century. It has not only been a sociocultural reality but also a powerful determinant of the Latino or Hispanic's vision of the world. The impact of successive generations of immigrants, originating principally in Mexico and the Caribbean but also from Central and South America, has had an indelible mark on the psyche of Hispanic minorities in the United States. These successive waves of immigration have also had the effect of renewing the cultural character of the Hispanic communities in this country. It is no wonder that one of the most important themes in Hispanic literature is immigration and has even given rise to a specific type of narrative.

Like all themes that arise from the grass roots of society and permeate many aspects of daily life, the theme of the Hispanic immigrant in the grand metropolis first arises in oral lore as personal experience narratives and anecdotes and spreads with its characteristic dialectical expression to jokes, songs, and such popular theatrical forms as vaudeville. Long before literary works based on immigrant life appeared in the written literature, Spanish-language newspapers began collecting and printing these jokes, anecdotes, and tales of misfortune of the greenhorns come to the metropolis. It is not surprising that the first Hispanic novel of immigration appeared in New York City in 1914, given that the city was one of the favorite ports of entry of Hispanic immigrants at the turn of the twentieth century. Since the publication of Alirio Díaz Guerra's *Lucas Guevara* in that year, New York and other cities have continued to be the base for the launching of a continuous stream of immigrant literature in Spanish. Included among the many immigrant novels and plays that have appeared throughout the twentieth century are Conrado Espinosa's *El sol de Texas* (The Texas Sun, San Antonio, 1927), *Las aventuras de Don Chipote, o cuando los pericos mamen* (The Adventures of Don Chipote, or When Parrots Breast Feed, Los Angeles, 1928) by Daniel Venegas, *La factoría* by Gustavo Alemán Bolaños (The Factory, published in 1925 in Guatemala, written in New York), *Trópico en Manhattan* (Tropics in Manhattan) by Guillermo Cotto-Thorner (written in New York but published in San Juan, 1951), *La carreta* by René Marqués

Roberto Quesada.

(*The Oxcart*, debuted in New York in 1952), *El super* by Iván Acosta (New York, 1977), *Odisea del Norte* by Mario Bencastro (Odyssey to the North, written in Washington, DC, published in Houston, 1998), and Roberto Quesada's *The Big Banana* (1998) and *Never through Miami* (2001), both written in New York but published in Miami.

All of these works are tales about greenhorn immigrants who come to the big city to improve their lives and seek their fortunes in the land of opportunities. But, in the end, they become disillusioned by what the authors see as the ills of American society: oppression of the working class, racial discrimination, the underworld and the underclass culture, and a capitalism that erodes Hispanic identity and values, including family, religion, machismo, language, and culture. In this way, Spanish-language immigrant literature opposed and deconstructed the myth of the American Dream—as opposed to the reinforcement and celebration of the American Dream that usually occurs in the English-language ethnic autobiography that is written by the children of immigrants, such as Julia Alvarez, Oscar Hijuelos, Esmeralda Santiago, and Victor Villaseñor. In fact, the Spanish-language immigrant novel is written by the immigrants themselves, not their children, and their texts take on an additional historical authenticity, as opposed to stories re-created from inherited family sagas.

Lucas Guevara was the first of these novels and initiates the ethos and structure that will be repeated in many of the works cited above:

1. A naive Hispanic immigrant filled with high expectations and fascinated by the advanced technology and progress of the metropolis ultimately becomes disillusioned with the United States.

2. The greenhorn, not knowing sophisticated city ways, becomes the victim of numerous abuses by the authorities, petty criminals, and hucksters, as well as by the bosses and foremen where he works.

3. The authors or narrators reject the materialism and "superiority" of the metropolis and instead embrace Latino cultural values and identity, which eventually leads to the protagonists returning to their homelands. Those who remain in the metropolis, as in *Lucas Guevara* and *La carreta*, will die, as a form of poetic justice for the betrayal of national values and ideals.

4. Frequently the plot of these immigrant novels and plays is a vehicle for biting criticism of metropolitan culture: the lack of ethical standards, the prevalence of racial discrimination, the rampant sense of superiority to Latinos and their cultures, and a hypocrisy that is endemic among Anglos. The metropolis is seen as Babylon, Sodom and Gomorra, and Anglos are the corruptors of Latino innocence. Their money perverts everything. The technological marvels of their advanced civilization destroy humanism, dignity, and respect. The Hispanic immigrant is considered by them as nothing more than a beast of burden, or *camello* (camel), on whose back the technological marvels are built. The immigrants compare themselves to the slaves of Babylonia, Egypt, and the Old South. Their foremen are "slave drivers."

5. Needless to say, cultural nationalism prevails in these works, and it tends to protect and preserve the Hispanic Catholic religion, the Spanish language, and Hispanic customs threatened with assimilation. At times the severest criticism, however, is reserved for those Latinos who are seen as cultural traitors for having adopted Anglo-American cultural ways. They are denigrated as *agringados* (Gringoized), *renegados* (renegades), *pochos* (no longer Mexicans), and *pitiyanquis* (petite Yankees).

The Adventures of Don Chipote, or When Parrots Breast Feed (1928), by Daniel Venegas, is an immigration novel that seems to have suddenly arisen from the rich wellsprings of oral tradition, where its basic plot already existed, as did the character types and even the specific argot of the Chicanos. All of these had made their way from the anecdotes and lived experience of the *bracero* immigrants into jokes, popular ballads (*corridos*), and vaudeville routines that became so popular in Mexican American culture in the U.S. in the early twentieth century. The character types, as well as their picturesque argot, had developed in oral culture from at least the turn of the century, if not before, and broke into print first in the local-color columns (*crónicas*) of Spanish-language newspapers published throughout the Southwest. In the weekly *crónicas* of such satirists as "Jorge Ulica" (Julio B. Arce), "Kaskabel" (Benjamín Padilla), "Loreley" (María Luisa Garza), "Az T. K." (pseudonym of an unknown author), "El Malcriado" (Daniel Venegas), and so many others, the customs of Mexican immigrants were habitually transformed into literary texts. The written literature of immigration in the Spanish language was not just represented by the *crónicas*; there were also hundreds of books of immigrant literature issued by publishing houses and newspapers. As in *Lucas Guevara*, Venegas' *Don Chipote* also contrasts the United States with the homeland, which is presented as pristine and honest, although unable to afford its native son the education or economic resources to sustain an adequate level of existence at home. The United States, while seen as the seat of great industrial and technological progress, is also a center for corruption, racism, and dehumanization, as in *Lucas Guevara*. Beyond mere local color in these novels is the depiction of the social environment in the United States, which unanimously is portrayed as corrupt and anti-Hispanic.

So far as the folk base of *Don Chipote* is concerned, there is a notable similarity between its plot of coming to the United States "to sweep the gold up from the streets" and that of several *corridos*, including *El lavaplatos* (The Dishwasher); besides coinciding in the narrative structure of immigrating and working on the *traque* (railroad) these works coincide in the attraction that the cinema and theater hold for their respective protagonists, their progressive disillusionment ("Adiós sueños de mi vida"—Good-bye, my life's dreams), and their return to Mexico ("vuelvo a mi patria querida/mas pobre de lo que vine"—I return to my beloved fatherland/poorer than when I left). The message of *El lavaplatos* is just as clear and firm as that of *Don Chipote*: Mexicans should not come to the United States.

Qué arrepentido
qué arrepentido
estoy de haber venido.

Aquél que no quiera creer
que lo que digo es verdad,
Si se quiere convencer
que se venga para acá.

(How regretful
how regretful
I am of having come.

He who won't believe
that what I say is true,
is sure to be convinced
by coming straight
here).

The burlesque tone of *Don Chipote*, so characteristic of this *corrido* as well as of the *crónicas* that Daniel Venegas wrote, serves to entertain the reader and soften the criticism of the socioeconomic–political reality on both sides of the border that forced the poor to leave their homeland and be exploited here by "slave drivers," *coyotes*, ladies of the night, and flappers—all of whom are personifications of the hostile and corrupt metropolitan environment. Daniel Venegas's tragicomic treatment of immigration was developed during years of writing and directing vaudeville reviews for the poorest classes of Mexican immigrants and of writing, illustrating, and publishing his weekly satirical tabloid, *El Malcriado* (The Brat). Díaz Guerra, on the other hand, was a medical doctor and a poet from his early, privileged days among the elite in Colombia. An intellectual and political activist, Díaz Guerra found his way to New York as a political exile, expelled from both Colombia and Venezuela. He avoided the kind of grass roots-based humor characteristic of Venegas to explore the mythic dimensions of exile and Babylonian captivity in New York. While Venegas chose *Don Quijote* as a metatext, Díaz Guerra found his inspiration in the Bible. In *Don Chipote*, the flappers (acculturated but Mexican, after all), represent acculturation and disloyalty to the homeland; in *Lucas Guevara*, the Eves are the American temptresses, personifications of iniquitous Yankee culture, that lure the protagonist into perdition after he turns his back on Latin American religion and morality. While in *Don Chipote* social order is reestablished with Doña Chipota's rescue and the return to Mexico of her straying husband—for she represents the hearth and home and Mexican family and cultural values—Díaz Guerra's Hispanic Everyman cannot be rescued, for there is no salvation possible after having given himself over completely to Eve. Thus Lucas commits suicide by diving from the Brooklyn Bridge, a symbol at that time of Yankee technological and industrial prowess.

Novels and plays of immigration continue to be written today, employing similar formulas to preserve the integrity of the immigrant psyche and culture. The genre will exist as long as Hispanics continue to come to the United States to better their economic circumstances and opportunities, and as long as they wish not to change their identities as the price to be paid for economic betterment.

NUYORICAN LITERATURE

Nuyorican literature is produced by Puerto Ricans born or raised in the continental United States. While the term "Nuyorican" derives from "New York Rican," today the term follows Puerto Ricans wherever they live in a bilingual-bicultural environment outside of the island. (Author Jaime Carrero even promoted the term "Neo-Rican" as a further denotation of bicultural evolution.) Puerto Rican writing in New York dates back to the end of the nineteenth century and Nuyorican creative writing in English dates back to the 1940s, when newspaper columnist Jesús Colón made the transition to English for the *Daily Worker*. This seems to be a rather appropriate beginning for Nuyorican writing and identity, given that Colón was highly identified with the Puerto Rican working class and was staking out a piece of Manhattan as part of Puerto Rican cultural identity, as have many of the writers who followed him and were influenced by his highly regarded book, *A Puerto Rican in New York and Other Sketches* (1961). Unlike the writers of the island of Puerto Rico, who are members of an elite, educated class—many of whom are employed as university professors—the New

York writers who came to be known as Nuyoricans were products of parents transplanted to the metropolis to work in the service and manufacturing industries. These writers are predominantly bilingual in their poetry and English-dominant in their prose; they hail from a folk and popular tradition heavily influenced by roving bards, storytellers, *salsa* music composers, and the popular culture and commercial environment of New York City.

Thus, Nuyoricans are typically the children of working-class Puerto Rican migrants to the city; they are generally bilingual and bicultural, as is their literature. During the search for ethnic roots and the civil rights movement of the 1960s, young Puerto Rican writers and intellectuals began using the term "Nuyorican" as a point of departure in affirming their own cultural existence and history as divergent from that of the island Puerto Rico as that of mainstream America. A literary and artistic flowering in the New York Puerto Rican community ensued in the 1960s and early 1970s as a result of greater access to education and the ethnic consciousness movements. By the early 1970s, a group of poet-playwrights working on the Lower East Side of Manhattan ("Loisaida") gathered in a recitation and performance space, the Nuyorican Poets' Café, and generated exciting performances and publications. Included in the group were Miguel Algarín (the founder of the café), Lucky Cienfuegos, Tato Laviera, and Miguel Piñero, with frequent participation from Victor Hernández Cruz, Sandra María Esteves, Pedro Pietri, and Piri Thomas, all of whom became published writers and literary activists. Three of the core Nuyoricans—Cienfuegos, Piñero and Thomas—were ex-convicts who had begun their literary careers while in prison and associating with African-American prison writers; all three influenced the development of Nuyorican writing by concentrating on prison life, street culture and language, and their view of society from the underclass. Algarín, a university professor, contributed a spirit of the avant-garde for the collective and managed to draw into the circle such well-known poets as Alan Ginsberg; the Nuyorican Poets' Café was often successful at reestablishing the milieu and spirit of the Beat Generation cafés. Tato Laviera, a virtuoso bilingual poet and performer of poetry (*declamador*), contributed a lyrical folk and popular culture tradition that derived from the island experience and Afro-Caribbean culture, but was cultivated specifically in and for New York City.

It was Miguel Piñero's work (and life, which has been memorialized in a Hollywood film, *Piñero*), however, that became most celebrated when his prison drama *Short Eyes*, won an Obie and the New York Drama Critics Circle Award for Best American Play in the 1973–1974 season. His success—coupled with that of fellow Nuyorican Piri Thomas, as well as that of Pedro Pietri, who developed the image of the street urchin always high on mari-

Miguel Algarín.

Miguel Piñero pictured on the cover of his book of poems.

juana—resulted in Nuyorican literature and theater often being associated with crime, drugs, abnormal sexuality, and generally negative behavior. Thus, many writers who, in fact, were asserting Puerto Rican working-class culture did not want to become associated with the movement. Still others wanted to hold onto their ties to the island and saw no reason to emphasize differences; rather, they wanted to stress similarities.

What exacerbated the situation was that the commercial publishing establishment in the early 1970s was quick to take advantage of the literary fervor in minority communities, and issued a series of ethnic autobiographies that insisted on the criminality, abnormality, and drug culture of the New York Puerto Ricans. Included in this array were Piri Thomas' *Down These Mean Streets* (1967, issued in paperback in 1974), his *Seven Long Times* (1974), and *Stories from El Barrio* (1978); Lefty Barreto's *Nobody's Hero* (1976); and a religious variation on the theme, Nicky Cruz's *Run Nicky Run*. So ubiquitous was this type of supposed autobiography that it generated a satire by another Nuyorican writer, Ed Vega, who comments in the introduction to his novel *The Comeback* (1985), as follows:

> I started thinking about writing a book, a novel. And then it hit me. I was going to be expected to write one of those great American immigrant stories, like *Studs Lonigan, Call It Sleep,* or *Father.* . . . Or maybe I'd have to write something like *Manchild in the Promised Land* or a Piri Thomas' *Down These Mean Streets.* . . . I never shot dope nor had sexual relations with men, didn't for that matter, have sexual relations of any significant importance with women until I was about nineteen. . . . And I never stole anything. . . . Aside from fist fights, I've never shot anyone, although I felt like it. It seems pretty farfetched to me that I would ever want to do permanent physical harm to anyone. It is equally repulsive for me to write an autobiographical novel about being an immigrant. In fact, I don't like ethnic literature, except when the language is so good that you forget about the ethnic writing it.

More than anything else, the first generation of Nuyorican writers was dominated by poets, many of whom had come out of an oral tradition and had found their art through public readings. Among the consummate performers of Nuyorican poetry were Victor Hernández Cruz, Sandra María Esteves, Tato Laviera, and Miguel Piñero. Like many of his fellow poets, Cruz's initiation into poetry was through popular music and street culture; his first poems have often been considered jazz poetry in a bilingual mode, except that English dominated his bilingualism and thus opened the way for his first book to be issued by a mainstream publishing house: *Snaps: Poems* (Random House, 1969). It was quite a feat for a twenty-year-old inner city youth. *Snaps* contains the themes and styles that would flourish in his subsequent books; in all of Cruz's poetry, sound, music, and performance are central. His experimentation with bilingualism includes the search for graphic symbols to represent the orality of both languages and music. His next two books were odysseys that take the reader back to Puerto Rico and primordial Amerindian and African music and poetry (*Mainland*, 1973) and across the United States and back to New York, where the poet finds the city transformed by its Caribbean peoples into their very own cultural home (*Tropicalization*, 1976). *By Lingual Wholes* (1982) is a consuming and total exploration of the various linguistic possibilities in the repertoire of a bilingual poet, and *Rhythm, Content and Flavor* (1989) is a summary of his entire career.

Victor Hernández Cruz.

Tato Laviera's bilingualism and linguistic inventiveness have risen to the level of virtuosity. Laviera is the inheritor of the Spanish oral tradition, with all of its classical formulas, and the African oral tradition, which stresses music and spirituality; in his works he brings both the Spanish and English languages together, as he does Manhattan and Puerto Rico—constant dualities in his works. His first book, *La Carreta Made a U-Turn* (1979), uses René Marqués' *La carreta* as a point of departure but redirects Puerto Ricans back to the heart of New York rather than to Puerto Rico, as Marqués had desired; Laviera believes that Puerto Rican culture can flourish in New York. His second book, *Enclave* (1981), is a celebration of diverse heroic personalities, both real and imagined, who have been important for Puerto Rican art and culture. *AmeRícan* (1986) and *Mainstream Ethics* (1988) are surveys of the poor and marginalized in the United States and a challenge for the country to live up to its promises of equality and democracy.

One of the few women's voices to be heard in this generation is a very strong and well-defined one, that of Sandra María Esteves, who from her teen years has been very active in the women's struggle, Afro-American liberation, the Puerto Rican independence movement, and the performance of poetry. In 1973, she joined El Grupo, a New York-based collective of touring musicians, performing artists, and poets associated with the Puerto Rican Socialist Party. By 1980, she had published her first collection of poetry, *Yerba Buena*, which involves the search for identity of a colonized Hispanic woman of color in the United States, the daughter of immigrants from the Caribbean. Her three books—*Yerba Buena*,

Tropical Rains: A Bilingual Downpour, and *Bluestown Mocking Bird Mambo* (1990)—affirm that womanhood is what gives unity to the diverse characterizations of her life.

Nicholasa Mohr is one of the most productive Nuyorican prose writers. Her works include *Nilda* (1973), *El Bronx Remembered* (1975), *In Nueva York* (1986), *Rituals of Survival: A Woman's Portfolio* (1985), and *A Matter of Pride and Other Stories* (1997), in addition to numerous works for children. Her best-known novel, *Nilda*, traces the coming of age of a Puerto Rican girl living in New York during World War II. Highly autobiographical, the novel depicts a girl who gains awareness of the plight of her people and her own individual problems by examining the racial and economic oppression that surrounds her and her family. In *El Bronx Remembered* and *In Nueva York*, Mohr examines through a series of stories and novellas various Puerto Rican neighborhoods and draws sustenance from the power of common folks to survive and still produce art, folklore, and strong families in the face of oppression and marginalization. In *Rituals* and *A Matter of Pride*, Mohr portrays women who take control of their lives, most of them by liberating themselves from husbands, fathers, or families that attempt to keep them confined in narrowly defined female roles. In the 1990s, these themes were revisited in Esmeralda Santiago's memoir, *When I Was Puerto Rican* (1993) and her autobiographical novels, *America's Dream* (1997) and *Almost a Woman* (1999).

A Nuyorican writer who has not benefited from the collective work done by the Nuyoricans is Judith Ortiz Cofer, who grew up in New Jersey and has lived most of her adult life in Georgia and Florida. Cofer is the product of university creative writing programs, and her poetry and prose are highly crafted, capturing some of the magic and mystery of the Latin American boom. Her first book of poems, *Reaching for the Mainland* (1987), is the chronicle of the displaced person's struggle to find a goal, a home, a language, and a history. In *Terms of Survival* (1987), she explores the psychology and social attitudes of the Puerto Rican dialect and how it controls male and female roles; in particular she carries on a dialog with her father. In 1989, Cofer published a critically acclaimed novel of immigration, *Line of the Sun*, and in 1990 an even more highly praised collection of autobiographical essays, stories, and poems, *Silent Dancing: A Remembrance of Growing Up Puerto Rican*. Cofer followed with another highly regarded novel, *The Latin Deli*, in 1994 and a collection of stories for young adults, *The Year of Our Revolution*, in 1999.

ORALITY

Orality in literature is the preservation or reproduction of everyday speech patterns in composing works; it often duplicates local and class dialects and represents the author's identifying himself or herself, consciously or unself-consciously, with the human subjects they write about. Orality is also irrevocably linked to the oral performance of literature. Many writers of Hispanic literature in the United States—perhaps the majority of poets and to a lesser degree, the prose writers—compose their work for oral performance. In one of the examples studied that follow, this performance objective is exclusive; in the others, publication and distribution to a primarily reading audience is the aim. Walter Ong's nine principles of orality, as identified in his book *Orality and Literacy*, help us identify a commonality that Hispanic writers have with poets and storytellers from primary, secondary and residual oral cultures around the world, quite often from cultures emerging from colonialism. As Finnegan has shown in "Literacy and Literature," *Universals of Human Thought: Some African Evidence*, the common denominator of their orality may not be a world view but a need to perform and the physical and social exigencies of performance itself. Furthermore, the need to perform may be determined more by Hispanics' marginal or minority status in the United States than by any other cultural factors, as illustrated below.

Helping understand the phenomenon of orality and performance are four examples of writers who run the gamut from street-corner poet to the novelist who creates in a secluded studio. Regardless of the physical distance of their intended audiences, the oral performance is central to each of these writers. No matter how educated or integrated any of them may be into the society, their need to interact with their audiences and communities and to keep close to the "human life world," to use Ong's terminology, irrevocably forces them to rely on oral modes of presentation.

The first of these is a street bard who many would identify as a folk poet, a minstrel. Jorge Brandon was a Puerto Rican poet who spent much of his life performing in the public plazas of Puerto Rico, Venezuela, Colombia, Central America, and Mexico before settling in New York's Lower East Side. His proud calling was always to be a poet; for him there was no greater rank or position in society. The only function of the poet that he can conceive is to communicate directly, orally, to a public audience. He is perhaps one of a few left in a long line of *declamadores*—performers of their own compositions and those of others, both oral and written, both famous and unknown writers. In fact, part of his repertoire features the works of poets who exist only in the oral tradition, poets he places alongside Cervantes and Rubén Darío. Brandon, who does not allow anyone to see his work written or to publish any of his poems, performs his poems—nothing else; he gestures, acts out the passages, and projects his trained voice, reliving the emotional nuances so deeply that he is sometimes thought to be eccentric. In this, he is emphatic and participatory in the material, criteria identified by Ong. Moreover, his epic poem "El Masacre de Ponce" (The Ponce Massacre), composed from first-hand observation, is one of the unknown masterpieces of Puerto Rican literature in which virtually all of the formulas and characteristics identified by Ong are displayed. Up to this point, I have described the oral poet of any nineteenth-century Spanish American country, roaming the countryside, gracing the town plazas during festivals and feast days, eulogizing heroes, mourning the dead.

Brandon is distrustful of Broadway, Wall Street, and Madison Avenue—the world of entertainment, finance and publishing. He performs his works for money, but fearful that recording and publishing companies may pirate his works, he transcribes his poems in mnemonic patterns. He continually goes over these in memorizing and planning his performances. I have seen his book of codes and I have personally observed him rehearsing. The poet uses a tape recorder to listen to himself and analyze his delivery. He stands on street corners wearing a World

War I army helmet with a sign stating in English and Spanish that he recites the 100 best poems of the Spanish language. As a gimmick to attract an audience, he places a small speaker inside a coconut with a face painted on it and recites his poems into a microphone so that the head appears to be performing ("coconut" is figuratively used to mean *"head"* in Spanish). His pitch is "el coco que habla," the "talking coconut."

Brandon's astonishing memory, his performance style, his commitment to poetry and Art with a capital A inspire the most sophisticated writers. He considers himself to be an artist in the highest sense of the word. His language and diction are impeccable; at the same time, he is a linguistic innovator and creator of neologisms. Although Brandon's English is as elegant as his Spanish, he never mixes the two languages. His favorite poet in the English language is Edgar Allan Poe, probably because of the oral qualities of Poe's works. What most characterizes Brandon's performances, however, is the delight of the public and other poets as well. No festival or public celebration in the Puerto Rican community of the Lower East Side is complete without him.

Tato Laviera, author of several books of poetry and produced plays and composer and lyricist of commercially recorded songs, is an important Hispanic writer in the United States. As Brandon's apprentice, he committed to memory much of that poet's (as well as his own) work and adopted some of Brandon's performance styles. He also considers poetry to be essentially an oral art, one that must be shared in performance with a group or a community—a commitment that comes from his observation of the power of oral poetry to move the listener. To overcome the distance between the individual performer and the group, Laviera believes, the poet must master certain physical and emotional postures and declamatory techniques. As a writer who also depends on published works to reach an unseen audience, he is wary of the physical and intellectual demands of the written tradition in both English and Spanish. But, in Laviera, even the written word is the product of an effort to re-create the oral performance. The process is so evident in his published poems that without the gestures, the enunciation, the physical and oral nuances, and the music that are an integral part of their oral performance many of them lose their essence and their power.

Laviera writes in English, Spanish, and what he calls "Spanglish"—the blending of two European tongues by a poet with roots in the African and American continents. His work is emphatic, situational, and homeostatic, feeding from the "human life world." Contentious, proud, and often "agonistic," as Ong would put it, Laviera is by any account a virtuoso in the use of language. Perhaps relying on the Puerto Rican oral tradition of the *bomba* and the *décima* debates, he is ready to engage anyone in contests of improvisation or presentation. His second work, *Enclave* (1981), is the other side of the agonistic, however; it celebrates such imaginary personalities who embody his community as Tito Madera Smith—half southern Black and half Puerto Rican—and the barrio gossip, Juana Bochisme; he also sings the praises of such real cultural heroes as John Lennon, Miriam Makeba, the Cuban ballet dancer Alicia Alonso, Suni Paz, and the writer Luis Palés Matos. One of the poems in the work, "Jesús Papote," is a modern epic, a long monologue sung by a fetus struggling to be born, on Christmas Day, from the womb of a dying drug addict (*Enclave*, pp. 12–21). The fetus personifies the future of Laviera's people in the United States.

A black Puerto Rican living in New York's Lower East Side, Laviera incorporates themes from several cultures but remains marginalized, like his own community. His poems may speak to his native Santurce in Puerto Rico, to Spanish Harlem, black Harlem, Africa, and to white America and Europe, but always from his particular racial, political, and cultural perspective. Laviera's bilingual poems, like those of Chicano writers Abelardo, Alurista, Ricardo Sánchez, and Evangelina Vigil-Piñón, are obviously aimed at a specialized audience. For the most part, they use the language of the people whose daily lives are articulated through a continuous exchange of Spanish and English. But like Alurista, Sánchez, and Vigil, he goes beyond the simple reproduction of recognizable speech patterns to explore the aesthetic possibilities of contrasting and mixing the sound and sense of the two languages, even stretching both linguistic systems to virtually create a new one. An example of Laviera's blending of popular and standard dialects of both languages and his creating a new poetic experience is his poem "velluda: alliterated y eslembao," in which he demonstrates his alliterative virtuosity while acting out a seduction and consummation of sex.

Cover of Tato Laviera's *Mainstream Ethics.*

Like many black poets whose works incorporate musical structures such as the blues, Laviera has written poems to be sung in part or in full. His inspiration comes from the native *plena* lyric and rhythmic structures of Puerto Rico, which rely on rhymed couplets improvised by a leader and repeated by a chorus or counterpointed by a choral refrain. His purpose is not to discover roots; rather, the *plena* represents a pattern of expression that he has heard in popular music his whole life. The dividing line between song and poetry is elusive to Laviera and, I would think, should be so for poets of residual orality. An example of his sung poetry is "Unemployment Line" (*Enclave*, p. 29), in which phrases are repeated as many as seven times and sung with slightly varying melodic lines.

Miguel Algarín, a poet, playwright, and prose writer, professor of English at Rutgers University, links the worlds of avant-garde American writing and grassroots folklore. He goes from the halls of academia, where he teaches Shakespeare, to poetry festivals in Amsterdam and Rome, to the streets of the Lower East Side, where he lives and runs the Nuyorican Poets Café, a center for the performance of literature. In New York, Algarín has been intimate with Amamu Imiri Buraka, Allen Ginsberg, William Burroughs, and Joseph Papp. He has written for television and screen, translated Neruda and, with Miguel Piñero, compiled the anthology *Nuyorican Poetry*, the first of its kind. Algarín acknowledges the imperative of orality and performance in poetry in his article, "Volume and Value of the Breath in Poetry."

Algarín is a consummate performer, a master of diction, a creator of musical verse, an exposer of the most intimate and shameful corners of the psyche—an exorcist. For all his sophistication, his graduate studies at Princeton, his work at the Jack Kerouac School of Disembodied Poetics of the Naropa Institute, Alagrín is an oral poet. As a writer, his task is to create in his poetry the emotional impact of his oral performance. The way that poetry is understood and taught in English in this country presents the obstacle that Algarín's writing must overcome: he has to sensitize the English reader to the re-creation of the oral performance of the poem. His poetry is alive primarily in performance, as is Laviera's and Brandon's. Algarín's poetic bilingualism is not as extensive as Laviera's, however, partly, I believe, because of his need to address the American literati. His bilingual poems generally use a more standardized language, and they are not as situational as Laviera's, but every bit as agonistic in tone and content.

Algarín's first book, *Mongo Affair* (1979), follows up its bilingual title with a text that creates a linguistic, emotional, and philosophical tension between English and Spanish usage. *On Call* (1980), his second work, is aimed at a national English-speaking and bilingual audience; the last section of the book emerges from his travels in the Southwest. His third book, *Body Bee Calling from the 21st Century* (1982), is Algarín's interstellar exploration of existence in a bionic future; the book, written entirely in a bare-bones English, is the furthest removed from the communal, oral mode, which is partially regained in *Ya es tiempo* (*Time's Now*, 1985), written with separate English and Spanish versions of the same poems in an effort to unite the local with the universal.

The stories and novels of Rolando Hinojosa, celebrated prose writer in Spanish and English, consist predominantly of monologs, dialogs, and first-person narratives, all of which suggest verbal performance by the individual characters. The novels and stories are part of a continuing, complex mosaic of life in a mythical south Texas town, Klail City. Written in Spanish, English, and bilingual text, the hundreds of portraits in the novels are created through the characters' ideolects (personal dialects) in talking about themselves and others. Many of the portraits are, in fact, dramatic monologs similar to the poetic monologs of Tato Laviera's characters in *Enclave* and *AmeRícan* (1985). Hinojosa's *Mi querido Rafa* (1981) departs in structure from his three previous books in that the first half is epistolary and experiments with the graphic representations of speech by the two main characters. However, the second part of the novel uses techniques similar to those in his other books: testimony, interviews, storytelling in bars, gossip—the types of speech of small town social settings, in which people can paint individually inaccurate pictures of characters and events. *Rites and Witnesses* (1982) was his first novel totally written in English. The choice of language was determined by the work's focus on the Anglo-American landowners, the big ranchers, and much of the text is articulated in a dialog style that approaches drama. Following *Rites and Witnesses*, Hinojosa published a re-creation of *Mi querido Rafa*, entitled *Dear Rafe* (1985), and of his prize-winning *Klail City y sus alrededores* (1976), entitled *Klail City* (1987). In the last decade, Hinojosa has continued to write and publish in English in a search for a broader audience.

Klail City y sus alrededores, the pivotal book in Hinojosa's generational series, best exhibits the orality of culture in Hinojosa's novelistic world. The work itself is a mosaic of oral performance styles, including everything from Protestant sermons and hymns to pitches by traveling salesmen, jokes, tales, and *corridos*, or folk ballads. The central performance piece, however, is a speech by an aging patriarch of the Rio Grande Valley that underscores the ideology of Hinojosa's orality and, perhaps, provides insight into that of Hispanic literature in the United States. In the monolog entitled "Echavarría tiene la palabra," critic Yolanda Broyles in "Hinojosa's *Klail City y sus alrededores*: Oral Culture and Print Culture" sees the act of speech granted the status almost of a hallowed rite, comparable in English to the respect shown to the Gospel according to St. John (p. 115). She further states that Echavarría

> is the voice of collective memory. Historical memory is transmitted through verbal performance, not through written materials. Events of significance in the Mexicano community are the guideposts of Echavarría's narrative. His dramatic and emotive narrative in the bar El Oasis recounts the violence perpetrated by the rinches (Texas Rangers) and the gullibility of *raza* (Mexican Americans). It is a subversive history for it contradicts the official Anglo record upheld by the courts and disseminated in history books. (pp. 114–15)

This particular monolog is one of the most popular selections requested of Hinojosa, the performer, the reader of his works in public. Through inflection, subtle facial expressions, and gestures, Hinojosa adopts the character of Echavarría and becomes the official purveyor of that alternative history and worldview that his community embodies.

Unlike Brandon and Laviera, Hinojosa is an academically trained intellectual, with a Ph.D. in literature and experience as a professor in both the Spanish and English departments of major universities. Despite the orality of his works, they are clearly anchored in the Hispanic and Anglo-American written traditions. Ong would probably recognize a residual orality in the works derived from Hinojosa's socialization in the bilingual communities of the Rio Grande Valley, where residual and secondary orality shape popular culture. What Ong would, perhaps, be unfamiliar with is the region's combative folktale and balladry tradition, in which intense feelings of Mexican and Anglo nationalisms clash and are often articulated in the dialectic of English versus Spanish, written versus oral, official institution versus popular culture, Anglo official history and authority versus collective memory and resistance by the Mexican dispossessed. Thus for Hinojosa—despite his academic training and employment—and the other writers studied here, the oral mode is more than just a style, a conditioning from their backgrounds, a romantic attitude, a search for roots. It is the only authentic and, to a great degree, unselfconscious posture for them as creators of the literature of their community.

Were the Hispanic community in the United States to possess the means of production, promotion, and distribution of its literature in printed form, and were it to control its history and image in print, then Hinojosa's and the other writers' works might be more print-bound and less performance-oriented. It is the very marginality of Hispanic communities in the United States and their lack of political and economic power that determine the need for and popularity of orality and performance. Hinojosa, Laviera, and Algarín reach more people through the spoken word than through their books, which are published exclusively by small, noncommercial presses. And their published materials in Spanish are even more marginalized in the United States, where Spanish-language and literature teachers and the book industry snub them in favor of canonical culture from abroad. As is clearly demonstrated by Jorge Brandon, orality and performance are conscious choices, determined by the economics, politics, and culture of the community and the individual artist. All four of these writers are highly literate and most of their audiences are literate. The currency of their exchange, however, is neither the printed page nor the book. It is the spoken word, alive and painfully throbbing as an expression of *communitas*, commonality, communion.

Orality and performance are conscious technical and ideological choices. The writers we have examined are not limited by these modalities but are liberated by them. They are freer to communicate directly with a known audience, to control the destiny and impact of their works. Even prose writers like Hinojosa are con-summate readers and performers of their material. Hinojosa sees the effects of his works, sees the audience react and recognize themselves in his literature, sees his ideas reenter popular culture in a thousand ways.

The complexities of orality and performance are many. I have not mentioned the poets of salsa verse, such as that of Héctor Lavoy, whose commercial record-ings reach millions through the Hispanic world, or Rubén Blades, also a recording star, who has composed two albums of narration in song that deal with three generations of a family; theirs is an attempt to do in music what Gabriel García Márquez has done in *Cien años de soledad* (*One Hundred Years of Solitude*). I have not analyzed poetic works that are recited on commercial recordings between cuts of music, or the continuation of the *corridor* tradition on disks mainly heard on early morning Spanish-language radio broadcasts. The study of prison writers is a task unto itself: the genre and styles, the commitment of large audiences of prisoners to poetry, and the poets, such as the late Miguel Piñero and the late Ricardo Sánchez, who emerged from that oral tradition. There are also the street theaters and the farm worker theaters; the jazz poetry of Victor Hernández Cruz, Ana Castillo, and David Hernández; and many other writers and forms that de-pend on orality and performance. For all of them, orality is a powerful engine for their literature.

TRENDS IN POETRY

Latinos have been writing poetry in these lands that became the United States since the late sixteenth century. Despite their having cultivated all types of written and oral literature during the ensuing centuries of incorporation into the United States through conquest, territorial purchase, and immigration, many of their lit-erary traditions persisted to preserve their cultural identity within an expanding and overwhelmingly aggressive "national" culture that did not recognize Spanish speakers as part of an ever-evolving "America."

Despite the centuries of Hispanic literacy and literary production in the United States and in other lands of origin, such as Puerto Rico, that were incorporated into the United States, it was not until the emergence of a Latino literary movement as part of civil rights struggles in the 1960s that scholars, critics, and writers gained some awareness of Latino poetry, its traditions and practices, albeit only in the poetry that was accessible to them through the English language. The poetry of the social movement was produced in Spanish and English or in a mixture of both. Like the civil rights struggles themselves, the literary movement was highly identified with working-class communities and mores; it was unself-consciously derived from and nurtured by folk literary practices and rituals and, most important, by the tradition of the roving bards and musical performers responsible for the continuation of centuries-old public poetic performance. The "primitivism" and oral performance, above all, seems to have been what was most noteworthy to those observers outside of Hispanic culture, whose only reference for understanding it was jazz poetry or the recitations of the Beat Generation.

The first poets involved in the Chicano Movement hailed from these grass-roots traditions and were not influenced by academic conventions and expectations. Rodolfo "Corky" Gonzales, the author of what has been acknowledged as *the* Chicano epic poem, *Yo soy Joaquín* (*I Am Joaquín*), was a boxer and political activist. I Am Joaquín disseminated a cultural-nationalist esthetic that provided a model for grass-roots and student-activist poets. The poem, self-published bilingually in 1967, summarized Mexican and Mexican American history, reviewed the exploitation of the *mestizos* from colonial times to the present, and shaped a nationalist ideology for activism, using the model of the nineteenth-century social rebel, Joaquín Murieta. The short bilingual pamphlet edition of the poem was literally passed from hand to hand in communities, read aloud at rallies, dramatized by Chicano theaters, and even produced as a slide show on a film with a dramatic reading by the major dramatist/activist of the times, Luis Valdez. All of this spurred further grass-roots poetic creativity and pointed to the poet as a spokesperson for his/her disenfranchised community.

Another community-based poet, Abelardo Delgado, was a Spanish-dominant bilingual writer steeped in the performance styles and the intimate relationship of *declamadores* to their local audiences; instead of performing his works at holiday celebrations, on Mother's Day, and at poetic *debates* (which he was perfectly capable and willing to do), his performances took place at political rallies, strikes, and marches to articulate community perspectives and inspire the community to action. Unlike many a traditional *declamador*, however, Abelardo allowed his poems to be printed and circulated in local barrio newspapers throughout the Southwest, where community folk and activists found them, copied them, and then circulated them by hand. Out of practicality and to spread the word of the Chicano Movement, Abelardo began to self-publish books of his own poetry, such as *Chicano: 25 Pieces of Mexican American Mind* (1969), which became the first bestsellers in the barrios and part of the early ethnic studies courses at universities. The word of the political and social movement, accompanied by artistic expression of all types, from mural painting to street theater, quickly spread to those warehouses of the victims of racism and miseducation: the prisons. From prison cells emerged self-taught voices that again returned to their barrio upbringings for inspiration and passionately declared that their previous violence on society would be redirected to revolution or reform in the name of their community. From behind the bars emerged some of the most lasting and inspiring poets: Ricardo Sánchez, Raúl Salinas, and later Jimmy Santiago Baca. In fact, Salinas made the prison experience the central metaphor for Chicano life in the barrios in his *Un Trip through the Mind Jail* (1973).

The influence and social impact of *I Am Joaquín, Chicano, Trip* and the works of the other poets who wrote for and came from the grass roots in the militant stage of the Chicano Movement is inestimable. This period was one of euphoria, power, and influence for the Chicano poet, who was sought after, almost as a priest, to give his or her blessings in the form of readings at all Chicano cultural and movement events.

In New York and the Midwest, a similar grass-roots movement emerged, also led by poets of the spoken word who were inspired by folk poetry and music, in this case salsa music and performance. From the prisons emerged Piri Thomas, Miguel Piñero, Lucky Cienfuegos, and numerous others. Community bards, such as Jorge Brandon, reciting his poems on corners on the Lower East Side, served as models of artistic and cultural commitment for these writers, as did the Afro-American jailhouse poets. Tato Laviera even apprenticed himself to Brandon, who had traveled the countries rimming the Caribbean basin, reciting his works and collecting the words and styles of other *declamadores* from Colombia to Mexico. A very young Victor Hernández Cruz studied the relationship established by salsa composers and performers with their audiences and emulated their artistry, hoping to reproduce the Afro-Caribbean sounds and ethos of Ray Barreto, Eddie Palmieri, and Tito Puente. In Chicago, David Hernández likewise took street and salsa rhythms and diction and even performed with Afro-Caribbean jazz ensembles.

Ricardo Sánchez. Photo by Rikard Sergei Sánchez.

Nuyorican writing made its appearance in the United States with a definite proletarian identity, emerging from the working-class, urbanized culture of the children of migrants. It arose as a dynamic literature of oral performance based on the folklore and popular culture within the neighborhoods of New York, the most cosmopolitan and post-modern city in the United States. Victor Hernández Cruz's urban jazz poetry, Piri Thomas' black-inflected poetry and prose in the late 1960s, and later Miguel Algarín and Miguel Piñero's Nuyorican Poetry anthology (1975)—all issued by mainstream commercial presses about the same time they were reprinting *I Am Joaquín* and publishing Ricardo Sánchez's *Canto y grito mi liberación* (1971)—led the way toward the establishment of a new cultural and literary Nuyorican identity that was as hip as salsa and as alienated and seethingly revolutionary as shouts from urban labor camps and from prisons, the prisons in which many of the first practitioners of Nuyorican poetry learned their craft. Ex-con and ex-gang leader Miguel Piñero and the Nuyorican group of poets, some of whom were outlaws in the literal as well as figurative sense, embellished the theme of urban marginalization and repression, and made it the threatening dynamic of their bilingual poetry and drama: Piñero was even successful in taking it to the stages of Broadway and to Hollywood films. Their works threatened the very concept of literature cultivated by academia as highly crafted art based on literate models selected from the classical repertoire of Western civilization.

The Nuyorican writers created a style and ideology that still dominates urban Hispanic writing today: working-class, unapologetic, and proud of its lack of schooling and polish—a threat not only to mainstream literature and academe but also, with its insistence on its outlaw and street culture elements, to mainstream society. Poets such as Tato Laviera, Victor Hernández Cruz, Sandra María Esteves, and Pedro Pietri did not seek written models for their work. They were far more attuned to and inspired by urban argot, salsa lyrics and the recitations of the folk poets who had always performed the news, history, and love songs in the public plazas and festivals of small-town Puerto Rico—often in the form of *décimas* and the refrains of *bombas* and *plenas*, the prevalent folk song frameworks on the island. In capturing the sights and sounds of their "urban pastoral," it was an easy and natural step to cultivating bilingual poetry, capturing the bilingual-bicultural reality that surrounded them, and reintroducing their works into their communities through the virtuosity that live perform-

Sandra María Esteves.

ance demands in folk culture. Neighborhood audiences in El Barrio, the Bronx, Loisaida (the Lower East Side), made exigent by the technical sophistication of salsa records and live performance, as well as by television and film, demanded authenticity, artistic virtuosity, and philosophical and political insight, Laviera, Hernández Cruz, Esteves, and Pietri reigned as masters for almost two decades. That they are accessible to far more people through oral performance than publication is not an accident nor is it a sign of lack of sophistication; it was their literary mission, their political and economic stance. It was Miguel Algarín, however, a university-educated poet and professor at Rutgers University also raised in the Puerto Rican barrios, who insisted on the publication of Nuyorican poetry in

¡Aqui se Habla Español!

y otros poemas de protesta . . . y chistes

PEDRO PIETRI

en Casa Puerto Rico

Recording album cover of a live recital by Pedro Pietri.

anthologies, magazines, and through Arte Público Press books. He further showcased Nuyorican performance art at his Nuyorican Poets Cafe in "Loisaida" and took troupes of writers on national tours and poetry slams. Besides authoring outstanding avant garde poetry himself (somewhat indebted to the Beat Generation), Algarín helped to solidify the Nuyorican literary identity and foster its entrance into the larger world of contemporary American avant garde poetics.

The 1970s saw the emergence of the first generation of U.S. Hispanics to have greater access to college, largely due to the Kennedy–Johnson initiatives to democratize education. For Chicano literature, the decade of the 1960s was a time of questioning of all the commonly accepted truths in the society, foremost of which was the question of equality. The grass-roots movement was soon joined by one in academe, with university-educated writers and university-based magazines and publishing houses continuing the development of Latino literature, mostly in the English language. Precedents were set for Algarín founding a Nuyorican Press; Professor Samuel Betances in Chicago founding a journal, *The Rican: Journal of Contemporary Puerto Rican Thought* (1971); professors Nicolás Kanellos and Luis Dávila founding in Indiana the first national literary magazine dedicated to Latino writing in general, *Revista Chicano-Riqueña* (1973); and Professor Gary Keller initiating *The Bilingual Review* (1974), when two University of California-Berkeley social science professors started publishing *El Grito: A Journal of Contemporary Mexican-American Thought* (1967) and their canonizing publishing house, Editorial Quinto Sol. The Berkeley professors—Octavio Romano and Herminio Rios—also issued their own first anthology of bilingual-bicultural Chicano literature, *El Espejo* (*The Mirror*, 1969), which helped to launch the career of the important pioneer and transitional writer, Alurista (Alberto Baltasar Urista), who combined the activism of the grass-roots poet with a literary tradition that went back to Aztec and Maya writers in poems that were trilingual.

Alurista's *Floricanto en Aztlán* (1971) was the first poetry collection to be issued by a university (UCLA's) ethnic studies program, and he later became the greatest experimenter and innovator of bilingual poetry, creating a meta-language of sound and symbol with conflicting connotations and denotations, especially in *Spik in glyph?* (1981). In 1976, the Chicano Studies Program at UCLA followed with a tome of fluid, inventive bilingual poetry, *Hechizospells: Poetry/Stories/Vignettes/Articles/Notes on the Human Condition of Chicanos & Pícaros, Words and Hopes within Soulmind*, by Ricardo Sánchez. Tino Villanueva and Tomás Rivera, professors of Spanish hailing from Texas, also helped the transition to academia with their grounding in contemporary Spanish Peninsular poets while rescuing the migrant-worker argot of their upbringing. However, Rivera is most known for his foundational Chicano novel . . . *Y no se lo tragó la tierra* (1971) and Villanueva for his first book *Hay Otra Voz: Poems* (1972) and his compiling of the first Spanish-language anthology of Chicano literature, *Chicanos: antología histórica y literaria*, published in Mexico in 1980.

As ethnic studies courses and student activism grew during the 1970s, numerous Chicano, Nuyorican, and even Cuban writers developed at universities from coast to coast. In general, they were not educated in creative writing programs, which up until the 1990s remained aloof from and reproving of what their professors believed to be uneducated doggerel. Rather, many of the Latino poets were Spanish majors and, if students of English, their models remained outside the academe, for the most part, including the literate models from Spain and Latin America. Among these politically committed authors making the transition from the activist poetry of the 1960s and the learned university environment were José Antonio Burciaga, Martín Espada, Cecilio García Camarillo, Leroy Quintana, Luis Omar Salinas (whose early works in the 1960s were highly influential in the Movement), Juan Felipe Herrera, Leo Romero, and the first women writers to finally break through what had been a male-dominated and testosterone-fueled movement: Lorna Dee Cervantes, Lucha Corpi (writing only in Spanish), Inés Hernández Tovar, Angela de Hoyos, Pat Mora, Marina Rivera, Carmen Tafolla, Gina Valdés, Alma Villanueva, Evangelina Vigil-Piñón, and Bernice Zamora. Like Sandra María Esteves in New York, who started performing her works with the Puerto Rican independence movement musical company El Grupo, San Antonio's Vigil-Piñón, El Paso's Mora, and Chicago's Ana Castillo emerged in the mid-1970's with strong roots in public performance.

But despite publishing their poems in such Latino literary magazines as Lorna Dee Cervantes's *Mango*, San Antonio's pulp *Caracol* (edited by Cecilio García Camarillo), and *Revista Chicano-Riqueña* (to become *The Americas Review* in 1981 and in 1979 to spawn Arte Público Press), Cervantes, Mora and Vigil-Piñón were not able to publish books until the early 1980s. Cervantes brought to the literature a clear and passionate commitment to human rights born of her own experience of poverty and oppression, along with personal family tragedy. Mora translated within her own clean and spiritual verse the emotions and worldview of border dwellers, very much preserving a sense of spoken Spanish but within an English-language framework. Much like Esteves and Laviera, Evangelina Vigil-Piñón captured the internal history of cultural and linguistic conflict within her bilingual poems that celebrated life in the barrios. Very early on Castillo took up the women's struggle within Latino culture as a dominant theme, while the other writers mentioned pressed their feminism as an orientation for a diverse array of sociopolitical themes. (It was not until the late 1980s and 1990s that a fully developed feminist and lesbian poetics developed in such writers as Gloria Anzaldúa, Alicia Gaspar de Alba, Cherríe Moraga, Aurora Levins Morales, and Luz María Umpierre.) All of these writers served as transitions to the first generation of Latino writers to gain attention from a national culture finally becoming aware of its diversity.

To borrow a term from minority music criticism, the first generation of Latino poets to "cross over" to the English-language academy was in place by the mid-

Gary Soto and Evangelina Vigil-Piñón at the Second National Latino Book Fair in Houston, Texas.

1980s. For the most part, they were the beneficiaries of a democratized university and greater access to Latino models as well as mainstream literary models, and they were predominantly the products of creative writing programs. Something new had occurred in the history of Hispanic literature in the United States: Latinos were going to college and graduate school to become professional writers. Furthermore, a Latino could actually make a living by writing about his or her own cultural upbringing; Latino life was an adequate subject for "high art," or so their creative writing professors had counseled them. Among the ranks of graduates from MFA programs were Alberto Ríos, Julia Alvarez, Denise Chávez, Sandra Cisneros, Judith Ortiz Cofer, Gary Soto, Virgil Suárez, and Helena María Viramontes, among a number of others. To those looking in on Latino literature from the outside, these writers of well-crafted English *were* Latino literature. Most of these authors were to be recognized with some of academe's most prestigious awards, from Walt Whitman prizes and Guggenheims and NEA fellowships to a MacCarther Prize. Many of their books were published by prestigious university presses, including those of Pitt and Georgia, and their prose works were issued or reissued (after first appearing in Latino presses) by the large commercial publishers, including Norton, Random House, and Simon & Schuster. Some of them were able to sustain their writing with faculty positions in creative writing at such prestigious institutions as the University of California-Berkeley, Cornell, and Vanderbilt.

It is the literature of this generation that is most known by non-Latino readers in the United States today and has the greatest possibility of entering and influencing mainstream culture. However, this is also the Hispanic literature that has emerged from and been influenced most by mainstream culture and its institutions; therefore, it is the most accessible to a broad segment of English speakers and has the greatest access to publishing houses and critics. On the other hand, this is the literature of a minority of Hispanic writers (a very select few, indeed), and tends to distance itself from its indigenous communities since the writers often live within university communities and target non-Hispanic readers, especially those that make up the creative writing establishment. Theirs is a contemporary manifestation of a longstanding Latino heritage; it is the very tip of an iceberg whose body is made up of centuries of writing in Spanish as racialized natives of the United States, or as immigrants sought for their cheap labor, or as the children of political exiles. Because more than 80 percent of

Lorna Dee Cervantes.

Latinos in the United States are working-class and without advanced education, members of this elite cadre of poets and writers find themselves today in the position of some of their counterparts in the Third World, where, given the poverty and illiteracy of their countries, they must find their audiences outside of their immediate national communities. However, the history of Latino culture in the United States, even among the working class, has never been one of illiteracy, and Latino audiences have always been accessible to their writers.

Today, all of these trajectories continue to produce poetry, although the fervor and opportunities for politically engaged poetry have abated considerably since the 1970s. Few writers have been able to cross from one writing culture to another in Latino literature. Lorna Dee Cervantes is an exception in her ability to maintain the passion and the craft and to continue to develop her art while finding a permanent place for herself in a creative writing program at the University of Colorado. Others, such as Judith Ortiz Cofer, have attained endowed chairs and prestigious awards while remaining faithful to their bicultural upbringing and culture; Cofer has accomplished this not just through the authenticity and frankness of her voice but also by reaching out to young Latino audiences through young adult literature—without prejudice to the genre.

Distinguished writers outside academe who continue to be a mainstay of the literature include Pat Mora, who has become the most reprinted Latino poet in language arts and high school textbooks. In addition, she has produced poetry

Sarah Cortez.

collections for young adults, such as her *My Own True Name* (2001) and even introduced her poetry in children's picture books. Rafael Campo, who is a physician, has become one of the most distinguished voices of the gay community in his poetry and, in addition, has successfully captured the attention of academe by winning prestigious awards. Somewhat distanced from the Puerto Rican populations in the Northeast and the Midwest, Gloria Vando has produced two outstanding books, collections of poems reflective of imperialism and colonized peoples around the world. Her Thorpe Menn Prize-winning *Promesas: Geography of the Impossible* (1993) is appropriate to read alongside Lorna Dee Cervantes' Patterson Prize-winning *From the Cables of Genocide: Poems of Love and Hunger* (1992). Finally, a new writer has come up through university training but maintained the authentic voice and class standing of her people: police officer-poet Sarah Cortez, whose *How to Undress a Cop* (2001) has attracted significant critical response from *The Hudson Review* and academic journals.

It should be noted that during the last two decades, an important segment of Latino poetry has been created by immigrant writers, who write in Spanish and/or English and deal with feelings of alienation, exile, and uprootedness in American society. Among them are Marjorie Agosin, José Corrales, Isaac Goldemberg, Guillermo Gómez Peña, Carolina Hospital, José Kozer, Rubén Medina, Jaime Montesinos, Heberto Padilla, Gustavo Pérez Firmat, Emma Sepúlveda, Iván Silén (a Puerto Rican writing in New York as an exile), Virgil Suárez, and a number of others. Of these, Guillermo Gómez Peña has been the most experimental and daring, fully exploring the transnationalism of Latinos and other populations around the post-modern world. His poems are part of a multimedia happening that extends to theater, essay, painting, and music in bilingual performance.

I hope that it has become clear that this iceberg called Latino Poetry is not new, runs deep, and has many facets.

WOMEN AND FEMINISM IN HISPANIC LITERATURE

Many Hispanic women writers feature gender relationships and how they are affected by such issues as biculturalism, *mestizo* or mixed-race identity, minority status, and the power relationships that exist in society. Hispanic women writers question the patriarchal structure of past and current societies in the Hispanic and Anglo-European worlds. Feminist critics have been concerned about the lack of Latina access to writing and publishing, as well as the silence and self-censorship in the writings once they do have access.

That these preoccupations are not new in the world of Latino letters is confirmed by texts from the period of Mexican-American identity formation in the nineteenth century. These texts reveal women deconstructing the power, racial, and gender relationships in the United States, as in María Amparo Ruiz de Burton's *Who Would Have Thought It?* (1872), and women exercising self-censorship and silences when testifying before Anglo-male scribes hired by Hubert Bancroft to take the dictations of their life histories, as in María Angustias de la Guerra Ord's 1878 dictations. De la Guerra Ord was more the rule than Ruiz de Burton in that she did not have direct access to publishing. The search for women's writings prior to the mid-twentieth century has led scholars to examine a wide variety of forms that were accessible to women and in which they could express their literary creativity beyond the traditional narrative and poetic genres that were created and dominated by men.

In addition to much oral lore, scholars have found women's literary expression in letters, memoirs, recipe books, and divorce declarations, among various other non-canonical genres. Fabiola Cabeza de Vaca's writings are a case in point; she memorialized folk practices and family recipes in books meant to pass on the traditions of her family in New Mexico. Her reconstruction of these in *We Fed Them Cactus* (1954) laid a base for many subsequent creative writers who experiment with genre, perspective, and style based on women's domestic culture. Such is the case with Roberta Fernández in her stories "Amanda" and "Andrea" in her *Intaglio: A Novel in Six Stories* (1990), which use the women's arts of dressmaking and hair braiding as models for writing stories. Sandra Cisneros has used the weaving of a shawl as the central metaphor for a family history in her novel *Caramelo* (2002). Both of these writers, and many others, are attempting to create a women's literary esthetic by exploring the arts traditionally practiced by women out of the sight of men, often in sites for story telling among women. Judith Ortiz Cofer, in *Silent Dancing: A Partial Remembrance of a Puerto Rican Childhood* (1991), also explores the site of oral storytelling in her grandmother's back yard under a mango tree.

As contemporary women writers strive to analyze the struggles of women within patriarchal societies, of necessity they have turned to the *bildungsroman* and autobiography to revisit their own development and rise to consciousness. Novels of development and autobiographical writings have been the most popular narrative structures among Latinas from the earliest contemporary novels, such as Nicholasa Mohr's *Nilda* (1974) to the later works of Julia Alvarez, Alba Ambert, Judith Ortiz Cofer, Cristina García, Esmeralda Santiago, and Helena María Viramontes. Even in poetry, Lorna Dee Cervantes, Sandra María Esteves, Pat Mora, Luz María Umpierre, Evangelina Vigil-Piñón, among many others, constantly revisit those moments when their gender consciousness was raised and when their sensibility as women writers became acute. However, traditional genres often are not sufficiently open and ample enough to serve as vehicles for women's expression, especially since those genres were formed by and respond to the esthetic, economic and political needs of the patriarchy. Thus, simply adapting women's perspectives and traditional arts to these traditional genres is not valid for many feminist writers, including Gloria Anzaldúa, Cherríe Moraga, Aurora Levins Morales, and others who experiment with combining essay, narrative, and poetry within the same work, as well as freely shifting from English to Spanish.

The writers who focus on feminism in their works, moreover, believe that fundamental questions about class, race, and identity are intimately connected to the definition and relationship of maleness and femaleness in society. In the case of Latinas, these questions become even more acute and pressing because they have to address them from a dual perspective of Hispanic and Anglo traditions and current societal practices and expectations, as well as from the perspective of internalized sexism, or homophobia, among Latinos. These women writers, for the most part, also reject the application of liberal bourgeois feminism as practiced by Anglo theorists and writers in the United States because it reproduces the patterns of exploitation and marginalizing women of color. Two of the greatest exponents of these feminist ideas, as well as of a lesbian poetics, are Cherríe Moraga and Gloria Anzaldúa. After assuming a leadership role among Latina feminists for co-editing *The Bridge Called My Back: Writings by Radical Women of Color* (1981), which promoted a militant poetics of feminism as an alternative to that of Anglos, both went on separately to pen foundational essays, poems, stories, and plays that illustrate this approach. In 1983, Moraga published *Loving in the War Years: Lo que nunca pasó por sus labios*, which effectively illustrated this poetics through her personal exploration of growing up a biracial Chicana lesbian; she accomplished this by weaving genre to message, applying a quilting technique to integrate the multiple genres, in disregard of traditional literary conventions. In *Borderlands (La frontera): The New Mestiza* (1987), Gloria Anzaldúa appropriates the metaphor of the border to advance militant feminist poetics: Latina lesbians will survive only by transgressing borders, definitions, limits. Through the transgression of the political, ethnic, racial, sexual, linguistic, and literary borders, the new Mestiza will go on to create new values, a new literature and a new culture.

While Moraga and Anzaldúa have illustrated the new Mestiza poetics in their multiform literary works, they have been buoyed up by theories and ideologies of such scholars as Norma Alarcón and Emma Pérez, whose essays and books have delved deeply into the intellectual history of Latina feminism and have striven to create a solid ideological base for creative writers, as well as other scholars. Alarcón is also the founder and editor of *Third Woman* magazine, which explores feminist literature and ideology from within the context of Hispanic third-world women in the United States and Latin America. Pérez has illustrated her scholarly explorations with a deeply personal exploration of growing up in small-town Texas through her novel *Gulf Dreams* (1996), published by Third Woman Press. Numerous other writers combine their scholarly work with creative writing in furthering this dynamic literature, including Cordelia Candelaria, Alicia Gaspar de Alba, María Herrera-Sobek, Rosaura Sánchez, and Yvonne Yarbro Bejarano.

Finally, in the creation of a feminist esthetic, women writers have constructed a pantheon of heroes that includes women in history who strove to express themselves in literature, such as Sor Juana Inés de la Cruz for Mexicans, Gertrudis Gómez de Avellaneda for Cubans, and Julia de Burgos for Puerto Ricans. All of these have become canonical figures in their national literatures, but have barely been appreciated for their struggles with the patriarchy. Contemporary Latina writers carry on their tradition and hope to extend the reach of these foundational figures. Other mythological figures, such as Doña Marina or La Malinche in Mexican history—and her parallel folk figure La Llorona, the crying woman who, Medea-like, killed her children—have been appropriated by today's feminist writers to explore how women have been written into religion and national identity as traitors and have given birth to bastard races (mestizos). Such writers as Gaspar de Alba, Ana Castillo, Angela de Hoyos, and Sandra Cisneros have revalidated these women not only as victims but as rebels and iconoclasts.

Ana Castillo.

Two positive mythical figures have also been appropriated from folklore—the Abuela (grandmother or matriarch) and the Adelita (woman soldier, revolutionary)—as models of female nurturing and activism, respectively. Among many other writers, Pat Mora is notable for centering many of these values of strength, will, nurturing, and resistance in the Abuela, while María Herrera-Sobek has used the Adelita to inspire activism among Latinas today.

In summary, Hispanic women writers have constructed a literature rich in a reconstructed tradition and mythology, with its own historical and esthetic antecedents and an ethos of transgressing all types of borders to create a new, empowered place for women in society and a new literature.

CHAPTER 5

PUBLISHING TRENDS

After Mexico gained its independence from Spain in 1821, printing presses were finally allowed in the frontier areas where they had been previously prohibited by the Spanish Crown, and both California and New Mexico obtained presses in 1834. The first California press was a government press while the first New Mexican press was held in private hands by Father Antonio José Martínez, who printed catechisms, law books, and textbooks, as well as New Mexico's first newspaper, *El Crepúsculo*, beginning in 1835. The printing press had already made its way into Texas in 1813 as part of the movement for Mexico's independence from Spain.

Hispanics settling in the thirteen British colonies, however, always had access to printing. In the mid-seventeenth century, the first Spanish-speaking communities were established by Sephardic Jews in the northeast of what would become the United States. They were followed by other Hispanics from Spain, New Spain, and the Caribbean who, by the 1790s, were printing and publishing books in the Spanish language, principally in New York City and Philadelphia but also in Spanish Louisiana. By the 1800s, numerous publishing houses issued not only political and commercial books but original creative literature written principally by Cuban and Spanish immigrants and political refugees. Among the first books written and published by Hispanics here, beginning with Giral de Pino's *New Spanish Grammar* in 1795, were textbooks, Spanish readers, and anthologies, reflective of two cultures coming more and more in contact with each other in the early Republic. This educational publishing soon blossomed into an industry that issued grammars, Spanish-English dictionaries, and textbooks that would institute Spanish language and literature in the curriculum of schools and colleges.

The history of Hispanic literary culture in the United States, however, has existed quite beyond the need for Spanish-language education. By the 1800s, Hispanic communities in the Northeast, South, and Southwest were substantial enough to support trade and communications among themselves and, thus, require printing in the Spanish language. The first Spanish-language newspapers published in the United States were *El Misisipí* (1808) and *El Mensagero Luisianés*

(1809), both in New Orleans; *La Gaceta de Texas* and *El Mexicano* (1813) in Nacogdoches, Texas/Natchitoshes, Louisiana. These were followed by Florida's *El Telégrafo de las Floridas* (1817), Philadelphia's *El Habanero* (1824), New York's *El Mensajero Semanal* (1828) and numerous others in Louisiana, Texas, and the Northeast.

Despite the existence of Spanish-language book publishing during the nineteenth century, the newspaper was the principal publishing enterprise in Hispanic communities in the United States and northern Mexico (most of the West and Southwest as we know it today). Literally hundreds of newspapers carried news of commerce and politics as well as poetry, serialized novels, stories, essays, and opinion both from the pens of local writers as well as reprints of the works of the most highly regarded writers and intellectuals of the entire Hispanic world, from Spain to Argentina. When northern Mexico and Louisiana were incorporated into the United States, this journalistic and intellectual discourse, rather than abate, intensified. The newspapers took on the task of preserving the Spanish language and Hispanic culture in territories and states where Hispanic residents were becoming rapidly and vastly outnumbered by Anglo and European migrants. The newspapers became forums for discussions of rights, both cultural and civil; they became the libraries and memories of the small towns in New Mexico, the *defensores* (defenders) of Hispanics in the large cities, quite often the only Spanish-language textbooks for learning to read and write Spanish in rural areas—and they were excellent textbooks at that. Many of the more successful newspapers grew into publishing houses by the end of the nineteenth century and beginning of the twentieth.

Hispanic newspapers in the United States have had to serve functions hardly ever envisioned in Mexico City, Madrid, or Havana. Most of the newspapers, if not functioning as a bulwark of immigrant culture, have at least had to protect the language, culture, and rights of an ethnic minority within the framework of a larger culture that was in the best of times unconcerned with the Hispanic ethnic enclaves and in the worst of times openly hostile to them. Whether serving the interests of immigrants or an ethnic minority community, it was incumbent on the press to exemplify the best writing in the Spanish language, to uphold high cultural and moral values, and, of course, to maintain and preserve Hispanic culture—a mission often extended to the protection and preservation of the Catholic religion within the larger cultural environment dominated by Protestantism. Quite often, too, Hispanic-owned newspapers took on the role of contestation, challenging and offering alternative views and reports to those published in the English-language press, especially as concerned their own communities and homelands.

From the beginning of the nineteenth century, the literary culture of Hispanics began assuming the expressive functions that have characterized it to the present day. There are predominantly three distinctive types of literary culture: that of the exile, the immigrant, and the native. While there existed a native literary culture in the Southeast and the Southwest since the days of Juan Ponce de León and Juan de Oñate, the exile and the immigrant were the first to have access to the printing press. The world of books, libraries, and education had been introduced by the Spanish to North America, but their banning of the printing press in their frontier territories retarded the development of printing and publishing in what became the Southwest of the United States—the strongest base of native culture.

THE EXILE PRESS

Book and periodical publication by Hispanics began in three cities: New Orleans, Philadelphia and New York. Judging from the number of political books published at the beginning of the nineteenth century, the overwhelming motive for the Spaniards and Cubans in the United States to bear the cost of printing and distribution of their written matter was their desire to influence the politics in their homelands. They established the model of the Hispanic exile community producing publications to be shipped or smuggled back into their homelands or distributed among other expatriate communities in the United States and abroad. Spanish-speaking political refugees from both Spain and the Spanish American countries have as part of their political culture repeatedly taken up exile in the United States to enjoy its protected freedom of expression, including access to a free press. The raison d'etre of the exile press has always been the influencing of life and politics in the homeland: providing information and opinion about the homeland, changing or solidifying opinion about politics and policy in the *patria*, assisting in raising funds to overthrow the current regime, providing the ideological base for that overthrow, but nevertheless maintaining a foreign point of reference. Over time, the exile press eventually made the transition to an immigrant and ethnic minority press as their communities became more permanent in the United States and/or the return to the homeland was no longer feasible or of particular interest.

The first political books printed in exile by Hispanics were written by Spanish citizens who were protesting the installation of a puppet government in Spain by Napoleon. For the most part these early books of protest were typeset and printed in the shops of early American printers such as John Mowry, Thomas and William Bradford, Mathew Carey, J.F. Hurtel, and Thomas and George Palmer. However, by 1822, Hispanics began operating their own presses and publishing houses. One of the first to print his revolutionary tracts on his own press was Vicente Rocafuerte in Philadelphia; by 1825, Carlos Lanuza's press (Lanuza, Mendía & Co.) was operating in New York, printing and publishing political tracts as well as creative literature by Hispanic authors. In the 1830s, they were joined by the Imprenta Española of Juan de la Granja and the press of José Desnoues, both in New York; however, it bears repeating that newspapers such as *El Mensagero*, *El Reflector*, and *El Mundo Nuevo* were also printing and publishing books there. Most of these Hispanic printer-publishers were rather short-lived, but eventually two enterprises appeared with strong enough financial bases and business know-how to last for decades and provide some of the most important books by Hispanics in the nineteenth century: the houses of Cubans Nestor Ponce de León and Enrique Trujillo (to be discussed later).

The longest lasting independence movement in the Hemisphere was that of Spain's Caribbean colonies, Cuba and Puerto Rico, and much of their struggle for independence was to be plotted, funded, and written about from U.S. shores.

One of Cuba's first and most illustrious exiles was the philosopher-priest Félix Varela, who founded the *El Habanero* newspaper in Philadelphia in 1824 and moved it to New York in 1825. Subtitled "political, scientific and literary paper," *El Habanero* openly militated for Cuban independence from Spain. Varela set the precedent for Cubans and Puerto Ricans of printing and publishing in exile and having their works circulating in their home islands. Varela was also among the expatriates who actively translated the American liberalism and governmental organization, as in his 1826 translation and annotation of Thomas Jefferson's *Manual de práctica parlamentaria: para el uso del Senado de los Estados Unidos* (Manual of Practical Parliamentarianism for Use by the Senate of the United States). That Varela would launch *El Habanero* and other Cubans and Puerto Ricans would continue the exile press in New York, Philadelphia, New Orleans, Key West, and Tampa is remarkable, given the scant tradition of newspaper publishing on these islands under Spanish government control and censorship. Licenses to publish in the Spanish colonies had to be obtained directly from the Spanish crown, and materials were subject to review and censorship by both state and religious authorities. As the tide of revolutionary fervor rose in Cuba and Puerto Rico, so, too, did censorship, repression, and persecution of the press, with the intellectuals of both islands often suffering imprisonment, exile, and/or worse: death by garroting.

Following Varela were a host of publishers and printers who relocated to New York, Philadelphia, Tampa, and New Orleans to write and publish political tracts and literary works. One of the most notable Puerto Ricans was Francisco "Pachín" Marín, who brought his revolutionary newspaper *El Postillón* from Puerto Rico, where it had been suppressed by the Spanish authorities, to New York in 1889. In the print shop he set up in New York, Marín published his paper, as well as books and broadsides for the Cuban and Puerto Rican expatriate community. His shop became a meeting place for intellectuals, literary figures, and political leaders. A poet in his own right, he published in New York two volumes of his own verse that are foundational for Puerto Rican letters: *Romances* and *En la arena*. Sotero Figueroa was the president of the Club Borinquen and owner of another print shop, Imprenta América, which provided the composition and printing for various revolutionary newspapers and other publications, including *Borinquen*, a bimonthly newspaper issued by the Puerto Rican section of the Cuban Revolutionary Party. More important, Figueroa worked closely with the Cuban patriot, philosopher, and literary figure José Martí on both his political organizing (Figueroa was the board secretary for the Cuban Revolutionary Party) and his publishing projects. Figueroa provided the printing for one of the most important organs of the revolutionary movement, New York's *Patria*, founded by Martí as the official organ of the Cuban Revolutionary Party. In addition, Imprenta América probably prepared the books and pamphlets that were issued for *Patria*'s own publishing house, Ediciones de *Patria*, as well as for the book-publishing arm of *El Porvenir* (The Future), which issued, beginning in 1890, the monumental five-volume biographical dictionary *Album de "El Porvenir,"* which memorialized the expatriate community and provided it a firm sense of historical mission and national identity.

One of the most active and important publishers was Nestor Ponce de León, the Havana editor and literary figure who was forced into exile in 1869. In New

York, he promptly founded a publishing house. By the mid-1870s, Ponce was publishing a wide variety of books in Spanish, including political tracts, technological dictionaries, histories of Cuba, biographies, medical and legal books, novels, and books of poetry, as well as translations of Moore, Byron, and Heine effected by Antonio and Francisco Sellén, among others. In fact, Ponce was the principal publisher of the most celebrated Cuban poet of the time, the exiled José María Heredia, who has since been canonized as one of the greatest poets of the entire Hispanic world. Ponce also printed some of the leading Spanish-language periodicals in New York and was proprietor of the most important Hispanic bookstore in the Northeast. In 1887, along with José Martí and Colombian immigrant Santiago Pérez Triana, Ponce founded the influential literary club Sociedad Literaria Hispano-Americana de Nueva York that brought together Hispanic literature enthusiasts and writers from throughout the city—except for the Spaniards, who were seen as the enemy. Like the many literary societies

José Martí.

formed by Hispanics from the late nineteenth century to the present, the Sociedad Literaria was the forum where literary works could be read and discussed, speeches could be made, and authors visiting the cities could be received and celebrated.

Enrique Trujillo, on the other hand, was principally a newspaperman who was deported to New York in 1880 in retaliation for his revolutionary activities. After working on various revolutionary newspapers and editing *El Avisador Hispano-Americano* (1889) in New York, Trujillo founded in 1890 what became an immensely influential newspaper, *El Porvenir*, which he printed on his own. Trujillo also participated in laying the intellectual foundations for a Cuban national culture by publishing his biographical magazine, *Album del Porvenir* and *Apuntes históricos* (Historical Notes, 1896), which documented the effort of the expatriate community in the struggle for independence leading up to the Spanish-American War.

Thanks to the four printer-publishers mentioned above, as well as various others such as A. da Costa Gómez, M.M. Hernández, R. De Requenes, Modesto A. Tirado, and Viuda de Barcina, hundreds of books and pamphlets were issued in New York and distributed openly to expatriate communities throughout the United States and to at least ten Spanish American republics, as well as Cuba and Puerto Rico. Within the four years preceding the Spanish-American War, some eighty titles on Cuba alone poured forth from the exile press, located mainly in New York but also represented in Tampa, Key West, Philadelphia, and abroad.

Some of these titles were issued in printings of five and ten thousand copies. When this voluminous outpouring is added to the hundreds of thousands of pages of periodicals produced by the expatriates, as well as the hundreds of books on diverse subjects that were published, one can form a better judgment not only of the passion and intensity of the literary discourse, but also of the commitment to the printed word.

While Cubans and Puerto Rican expatriates had to endure passage by ship and inspections by customs authorities to enter as refugees into the United States, Mexican exiles crossed the border with relative ease to establish their press in exile; they simply walked across a border or over a bridge and installed themselves in the longstanding Mexican-origin communities of the Southwest. In fact, the relatively open border had abetted refuge for numerous personae nongratae from both sides of the dividing line for decades. The Mexican exile press movement began around 1885, when the Porfirio Díaz regime in Mexico became so repressive that scores of publishers and editors were forced north into exile. Publishers such as Adolfo Carrillo, who had opposed Díaz with his *El Correo del Lunes* (The Monday Mail), crossed the border, hoping to smuggle their papers back into Mexico. Carrillo ended up in San Francisco, where he established *La República* in 1885. General Martínez went into exile in Brownsville to launch *El Mundo* in 1885, while organizing insurgent groups from there. An assassin's bullet terminated Martínez's activities in 1891. Paulino Martínez established his *El Monitor Democrático* in San Antonio in 1888 and his *La Voz de Juárez* and *El Chinaco*, both in Laredo, in 1889 and 1890, respectively.

By 1900, the most important Mexican revolutionary journalist and ideologue, Ricardo Flores Magón, had launched his newspaper *Regeneración* in Mexico City and was promptly jailed. After another four stints behind bars for his radical journalism, at times being prohibited from reading and writing in jail, Flores Magón went into exile in the United States. In 1904, he began publishing *Regeneración* in San Antonio, then in Saint Louis in 1905, and in Canada in 1906; in 1907, he founded *Revolución* in Los Angeles, and once again in 1908 revived *Regeneración* there. Throughout these years, Flores Magón and his brothers employed any and every subterfuge possible to smuggle the newspapers from the United States into Mexico, even stuffing them into cans or wrapping them in other newspapers sent to San Luis Potosí, where they were then distributed to sympathizers throughout the country.

Ricardo Flores Magón emerged as one of the major leaders in the movement to overthrow the Díaz regime, founding the Liberal Reformist Association in 1901. What was somewhat different about Flores Magón's approach was that he wedded his ideas about revolution in Mexico to the struggle of working people in the United States, and this in part accounted for his newspapers' popularity among Mexican and Mexican-American laborers engaged in unionizing efforts in the United States. Pursued by Díaz's agents in San Antonio, Ricardo and his brother Enrique moved to St. Louis, but corresponded with a chain of chapters across the Southwest that spread their revolutionary ideology, largely through meetings, fund raising events, and, of course, the publication of newspapers, pamphlets, and books. Numerous Spanish-language periodicals in the Southwest thus echoed the ideas of Flores Magón and were affiliated with the Partido Liberal Mexicano (PLM), including: *La Bandera Roja*, *El Demócrata*, *La Democracia*,

Humanidad, 1810, El Liberal, Punto Rojo, Libertad y Trabajo, and *La Reforma Social*, which were located along the border from South Texas to Los Angeles. Among the most interesting affiliated papers were those involved in articulating labor and gender issues as part of the social change to be implemented with the triumph of the revolution. The most notable were Teresa Villarreal's *El Obrero* (The Worker, 1909), Isidra T. de Cárdenas' *La Voz de la Mujer* (The Woman's Voice, 1907), Blanca de Moncaleano's *Pluma Roja* (Red Pen, 1913–1915), and Teresa and Andrea Villarreal's *La Mujer Moderna* (The Modern Woman).

Ricardo (left) and Enrique Flores Magón.

The Mexican exile press flourished into the 1930s, with weekly newspapers siding with one faction or another, and publishing houses, often affiliated with newspapers, issuing political tracts as well as novels of the revolution. In fact, more than any other literary genre published in book form, the novel of the Mexican Revolution flourished, with more than 100 issuing from such presses as Casa Editorial Lozano in San Antonio. And by no means was the press in the 1920s and 1930s as liberal as the exile press prior to the outbreak of the Revolution. To the contrary, what sprung up was a press founded by exiles of the different warring factions who often opposed those in power in Mexico. Some of them founded newspapers to serve the rapidly expanding community of economic refugees, and their newspapers eventually became the backbone of an *immigrant* rather than an *exile* press, as their entrepreneurial spirit overtook their political commitment to change in the homeland. With the Cristero War (1926–1929), resulting from government persecution of the Catholic Church stemming from the anticlerical tenets of the 1917 Mexican constitution, a fresh batch of political refugees founded newspapers and publishing houses to attack the Mexican government and to serve the needs of the religious community in exile. During the buildup of conflict between church and state in Mexico, such periodicals as *La Guadalupana: Revista Mensual Católica* (The Guadalupan: Catholic Monthly Magazine, 1922) and *El Renacimiento: Semanario Católico* (The Renascence: Catholic Weekly, 1923) were founded in El Paso and *La Esperanza* (Hope, 1924) in Los Angeles. In fact, El Paso became the destination of choice for many Hispanic religious presses, not just for the Catholics but also for the Mexican Baptists, Methodists, and others who took refuge in Texas. The influence of the Cristero refugees was felt in many of the immigrant newspapers, not just in specialized publications; the already conservative counterrevolutionary papers naturally focused on the religious persecution in Mexico and the atrocities committed by the government of *bolche-*

viques. A spate of books appeared defending the church and decrying the atrocities committed on the clergy in Mexico. More important, an Hispanic religious publishing industry, which issued books and periodicals in both Spanish and English, became cemented in El Paso, where it still functions today.

The next large wave of Hispanic political refugees to reach these shores came from across the Atlantic: the liberals defeated by Spanish fascism in the 1930s. The Spanish expatriates were fast to establish their own exile press in Depression-era Hispanic communities that were hotbeds for union and socialist organizing. From Manhattan and Brooklyn alone the expatriate press issued the following titles: *España Libre* (Free Spain, 1939–1977), *España Nueva* (New Spain, 1923–1942), *España Republicana* (Republican Spain, 1931–1935), *Frente Popular* (Popular Front, 1937–1939), and *La Liberación* (The Liberation, 1946–1949). Many of the Hispanic labor and socialist organizations in which Spanish immigrant workers were prominent published newspapers that also supported the Republican cause: the long-running anarchist paper *Cultura Proletaria* (Proletarian Culture, 1910–1959), *El Obrero* (The Worker, 1931–1932), and *Vida Obrera* (Worker Life, 1930–1932). Working-class writers, publishers, and printers were not the only intellectuals to come to these shores as refugees of the Spanish Civil War. A whole cadre of exiled Spanish writers found work at colleges and universities throughout the United States now that Spanish-language courses had become an important part of the curriculum. Included among these were major writers such as Jorge Guillén and Ramón Sender, the latter remaining permanently in the United States and producing the largest body of his work here.

Exiles and political refugees have continued to make up an important segment of Hispanic immigrants to the United States. With the Cuban Revolution and the United States fighting much of the Cold War through involvement in the civil wars in Central America and Chile, large-scale immigration of political refugees has continued to the present day. Beginning in 1959, a new wave of refugees from the Cuban Revolution established a widespread exile press as well as a more informal network of hundreds of newsletters. Along with the political periodicals, such literary magazines as *Linden Lane* have also flourished. The largest and longest lasting publishing house for the Cuban exiles is still very active in Miami: Ediciones Universal. Chileans, Salvadorans, Nicaraguans, and other Spanish-American expatriates have all issued political newspapers and magazines in recent years. The celebrated playwright and novelist Matías Montes Huidobro was a literary leader who founded and edited for many years a publishing house headquartered in Hawaii, where he was a professor, dedicated to the publication of Cuban exile theater. A notable Chilean literary magazine was the *Revista del exilio chileno* (Review of Chilean Exile), founded and edited by Fernando Alegría. In 1990, Alegría and fellow Stanford Professor Jorge Rufinelli compiled and published an important anthology of exile literature entitled *Paradise Lost or Gained: The Literature of Hispanic Exile*. However, perhaps because the United States furthered the Cold War during the 1970s and 1980s, many Cuban, Chilean, Argentine, and Central American writers in the United States did not have to rely on their own exile presses for publication; rather many of them, such as Heberto Padilla, Jacobo Timmerman, and Ariel Dorfman, readily found mainstream U.S. publishers for their works in translation.

THE IMMIGRANT PRESS

Since the mid-nineteenth century, Hispanic immigrants have founded publishing houses and periodicals to serve their enclaves in their native language, maintaining a connection with the homeland while helping the immigrants to adjust to a new society and culture here. (See the Literature of Immigration section in Chapter 4 for more details on the characteristics of this literature.) While *El Mercurio de Nueva York* (The Mercury, 1829–1830) and *El Mensagero Semanal de Nueva York* (The Weekly Messenger, 1828–1831) may have served immigrant populations and functioned somewhat along the lines described above, it was not until much later when larger Hispanic immigrant communities began to form that more characteristic immigrant newspapers were founded. Among these, San Francisco's *Sud Americano* (South American, 1855), *El Eco del Pacífico* (The Pacific Echo, 1856), *La Voz de Méjico* (The Voice of Mexico, 1862), and *El Nuevo Mundo* (The New World, 1864) served a burgeoning community of immigrants from northern Mexico and from throughout the Hispanic world, as far away as Chile, who had been drawn to the Bay Area during the Gold Rush and collateral industrial and commercial development. From the 1850s through the 1870s, in fact, San Francisco supported the largest number, longest running, and most financially successful of the Spanish-language newspapers in the United States. In fact, San Francisco was able to support two daily Spanish-language newspapers during this period: *El Eco del Pacífico* and *El Tecolote* (The Buzzard, 1875–1879). The San Francisco Spanish-language press covered news of the homeland, which varied from coverage of Spain and Chile to Central America and Mexico, and generally assisted the immigrants in adjusting to the new environment. Very closely reported on was the French intervention in Mexico, with various newspapers supporting fund raising events for the war effort and aid for the widows and orphans, in addition to working with the local Junta Patriótica Mexicana, even printing *in toto* the long speeches made at the Junta's meetings. The newspapers reported on discrimination and persecution of Hispanic miners and generally saw the defense of the Hispanic *colonia*, or colony, to be a priority, denouncing abuse of the Hispanic immigrants, as well as of the natives. Hispanic readers in the Southwest were acutely aware of racial issues in the United States and sided with the North during the Civil War, which also was extensively covered in the newspapers.

While San Francisco's Hispanic population was the state's largest in the nineteenth century, it was Los Angeles that received the largest number of Mexican immigrants with the massive exodus of economic refugees from the Revolution of 1910. Thus, Los Angeles in the twentieth century, along with San Antonio and New York, supported some of the most important Spanish-language daily newspapers, periodicals that began as immigrant newspapers. Between 1910 and 1924, some half-million Mexican immigrants settled in the United States; Los Angeles and San Antonio were their most popular destinations. These two cities attracted an entrepreneurial class of immigrants who came with the cultural and financial capital sufficient to establish businesses of all types to serve the rapidly growing Mexican enclaves; they constructed everything from tortilla factories to

Hispanic theaters and movie houses, and through their cultural leadership in mutual aid societies, churches, theaters, and newspapers were able to disseminate a nationalistic ideology that ensured the solidarity and insularity of their community, or market, if you will. The flood of Mexican workers into both cities spurred the founding of numerous Spanish-language newspapers from 1910 until the Depression; both cities supported more Spanish-language newspapers during this period than any other cities in the United States.

El Heraldo de México (The Mexican Herald), founded in Los Angeles in 1915 by owner Juan de Heras and publisher Cesar F. Marburg, was considered a "people's newspaper" because of its focus on and importance to the Mexican immigrant worker in Los Angeles. It often proclaimed its working-class identity, as well as its promotion of Mexican nationalism; through its publishing house it issued in 1928 the first novel narrated from the perspective of a "Chicano," that is, a Mexican working-class immigrant: Daniel Venegas' *Las aventuras de Don Chipote, o cuando los pericos mamen*. With its circulation extending beyond 4,000, it was the most popular Mexican newspaper at this time. Like many other Hispanic immigrant newspapers, *El Heraldo de México* devoted the largest proportion of its coverage to news of the homeland, followed by news directly affecting the immigrants in the United States and a representation of news and advertisements that would be of interest to working-class immigrants. *El Heraldo de México* defended immigrant working-class interests by publishing editorials and devoting considerable space to combating discrimination, mistreatment, and exploitation of immigrant labor. *El Heraldo de México* even went a step further in 1919 by attempting to organize Mexican laborers into an association, the Liga Protectiva Mexicana de California, to protect their rights and interests.

For the Mexican immigrant communities, defense of civil and human rights also extended to protecting Mexican immigrants from the influence of Anglo-American culture and Protestantism. The publishers, editorialists, and columnists were almost unanimous in developing and promoting the idea of a "México de afuera" or a Mexican colony existing outside of Mexico, in which it was the duty of the individual to maintain the Spanish language, keep the Catholic faith, and insulate their children from what community leaders perceived as the low moral standards practiced by Anglo-Americans. Basic to this belief system was the imminent return to Mexico when the hostilities of the Revolution were over. Mexican national culture was to be preserved while in exile in the midst of iniquitous Anglo-Protestants, whose culture was aggressively degrading even while discriminating against Hispanics. The ideology was most expressed and disseminated by cultural and business elites, who exerted leadership in all phases of life in the *colonia* and solidified a conservative substratum for Mexican-American culture for decades to come.

Among the most powerful of the political, business, and intellectual figures in the Mexican immigrant community was Ignacio E. Lozano, founder and operator of the two most powerful and well-distributed daily newspapers: San Antonio's *La Prensa* (The Press), founded in 1913, and Los Angeles' *La Opinión* (The Opinion), founded in 1926 and still published today. Lozano, from a successful business family in northern Mexico, relocated to San Antonio in 1908 in search of business opportunities. With the business training and experience that he received in Mexico, Lozano was able to contribute professionalism and business acumen to Hispanic journalism in the United States, reflected in his hiring of well-trained journalists, starting at the top with his appointment of Teodoro Torres to edit *La Prensa*. The ideas of men like Torres and Lozano reached thousands not only in San Antonio but throughout the Southwest, Midwest, and northern Mexico through a vast distribution system that included newsstand sales, home delivery, and mail. *La Prensa* also set up a network of correspondents in the United States who were able to issue regular reports on current events and cultural activities of Mexican communities as far away as Chicago, Detroit, and even New York. When, around 1920, Mexican President Alvaro Obregón took a more liberal stance toward the expatriate community, *La Prensa* began to circulate freely in northern Mexico, gaining a large readership from Piedras Negras west to Ciudad Juárez. Unlike the publishers of many other Hispanic immigrant newspapers, Lozano also set about serving the longstanding Mexican American population in San Antonio and the Southwest and reaching a broader market and all social classes. He and his staff also sought to bring Mexican Americans within the "México de afuera" ideology. Unfortunately, *La Prensa* did not survive long enough to see the Chicano Movement of the 1960s, the civil rights movement that promoted a cultural nationalism of its own. Unlike Los Angeles, where *La Opinión* still thrives today, San Antonio did not continue to attract a steady or large enough stream of immigrants to sustain the newspaper when the children of the immigrants became English-dominant in the consumption of information.

However, in her day, *La Prensa* was indeed influential. Lozano and many of his prominent writers and editorialists became leaders of the Mexican/Mexican American communities. They shaped and cultivated their market for cultural products and print media as efficiently as others sold material goods and Mexican foods and delivered specialized services to the community of immigrants. The Mexican community truly benefited in that the entrepreneurs did provide needed goods, information, and services that were often denied by the larger society through official and open segregation. And, of course, the writers, artists, and intellectuals provided the high as well as popular culture and entertainment in the native language of the Mexican community that was not offered by Anglo-American society: Spanish-language books and periodicals, silent films with Spanish-dialog frames, and Spanish-language drama and vaudeville, among other entertainment and popular art forms.

Some of the most talented writers from Mexico, Spain, and Latin America earned their living as reporters, columnists, and critics in the editorial offices of *La Prensa*, *La Opinión*, and *El Heraldo de México*. Included among these were such writers as Miguel Arce, Adalberto Elías González, Esteban V. Escalante, Gabriel Navarro, and Daniel Venegas. They and many others used the newspapers as a stable source of employment and as a base from which they launched their literary publications in book form or wrote plays and revues for the theater that was flourishing in Los Angeles and San Antonio. Various newspaper companies, in fact, operated publishing houses, as did both Lozano papers and *El Heraldo de México*. They also imported books and published reprint editions under their own imprints. The largest of these, Ignacio Lozano's Casa Editorial Lozano, advertised in the family's two newspapers books to be sold via direct mail and in the Lozano bookstore in San Antonio; *El Heraldo de México* also operated a bookstore, in Los Angeles. In addition to the publishing houses owned by the large dailies, in the same cities and in smaller population centers there were many other newspapers publishing books, as well.

Without a doubt, however, San Antonio became the publishing center for Hispanics in the Southwest, and housed more Spanish-language publishing houses than any other city in the United States. During the 1920s and 1930s, San Antonio was home to the Casa Editorial Lozano, Viola Novelty Company, Whitt Publishing, Librería de Quiroga, Artes Gráficas, and various others. They unanimously dedicated themselves to both publishing and importing books and printing catalogs for mail order. Lozano and Viola Novelty, which were connected to newspapers, also published book listings in their parent newspapers, *La Prensa*, *La Opinión*, and the satirical *El Fandango*. Those that were proprietors of bookstores, such as Lozano, Quiroga, and Librera Española, of course, had a ready sales outlet. Among the offerings of San Antonio publishers was everything from the practical, such as Ignacio E. Lozano's manual for (male) secretaries, *El perfecto secretario* (The Perfect Secretary), to autobiographies by exiled political and religious figures and sentimental novels and books of poetry. The Whitt Company (exiled publishers from northern Mexico) issued religious plays appropriate for parish Christmas festivities, along with numerous other books of Mexican folklore and legend. The Librería de Quiroga seems to have dedicated itself to supplying the leisure reading for housewives, especially those of the middle class, with such sentimental fare as María del Pilar Sinués' novel *El amor de los amores* (The Love of Loves), Rafael del Castillo's novel *Amor de madre* (A Mother's Love), Joaquín Piña's novel *Rosa de amor* (Rose of Love), Stowe's *La cabaña de Tom* (*Uncle Tom's Cabin*), and Antonio Plaza's poetry collection, *Album del corazón* (Album of the Heart).

A fiction genre that almost all of these houses had in common was the novel of the Mexican Revolution, as numerous expatriate intellectuals fictionalized their personal experiences of the whirlwind that was the Revolution and sought to come to terms with the cataclysm that had disrupted their lives and had caused so many of their readers to relocate to the southwestern United States. The authors represented the full gamut of the revolutionary factions in their loyalties and ideologies, but for the most part the genre was characterized by a conservative reaction to the socialistic change in government and community organization that the Revolution had wrought. One of the first to establish this genre was the now-classic work of Latin American literature, Mariano Azuela's *Los de abajo* (The Underdogs), which first saw the light as a serialized novel in an El Paso Spanish-language newspaper and was later published in book form in that city in 1915. However, the majority of these novels were issued from San Antonio and the house that issued the most titles was Casa Editorial Lozano. In fact, many of the novels were authored by writers employed by Lozano on *La Prensa* and *La Opinión*: Miguel Arce, Julián González, and Teodoro Torres, whose *Pancho Villa, una vida de romance y de tragedia* (Pancho Villa, a Life of Romance and Tragedy, 1924) underwent three editions.

With the flurry of immigrant publishing that existed in the Spanish language prior to World War II, another trend developed that did not survive long after the war: the sporadic and intermittent acceptance of works by Hispanic immigrant authors in English-language mainstream publications. Mexican immigrant author María Cristina Mena, who married American playwright Henry Kellet Chambers and became a protégé of D.H. Lawrence, saw her old-country-based stories published in *Century*, *American*, and *Cosmopolitan*, among others. Nicaraguan immigrant Salomón de la Selva worked his way into Emily Dickinson's circle and saw his poetry published in English. Josephina Niggli saw her novels, stories, and plays issued by mainstream houses in their English originals. Of course George Santayana seems not to have been perceived as an ethnic, embraced as he was by the Northeast establishment and by the nominators for the Pulitzer Prize. A Mexican immigration novel was even published by a mainstream house—Luis Pérez's *El Coyote: The Rebel*, published by Holt in 1947—although Pérez's other literary works remain unpublished to date.

In the Northeast, the large daily and weekly newspapers flourished and also published books, as did small, ephemeral presses. In 1913, José Campubrí founded *La Prensa* in New York City to serve the community of mostly Spanish and Cuban immigrants in and around Manhattan's 14th Street; little did he know then that *La Prensa* would become the nation's longest running Spanish-language daily newspaper in 1962, merging with *El Diario de Nueva York*. One of the main reasons *La Prensa* survived so long was that it was able to expand and adapt to the new Spanish-speaking nationalities that immigrated to the city, especially the Puerto Ricans who migrated from their island en masse during and after World War II and came to form the largest Hispanic group in the city. In 1948, *El Diario de Nueva York* (The New York Daily) was founded by Dominican immigrant Porfirio Domenici, specifically appealing to the Puerto Rican community and giving *La Prensa* competition for this growing readership—*El Diario de Nueva York*'s slogan was "Champion of the Puerto Ricans."

Publisher Domenici hired as its first editor Vicente Géigel Polanco, a well-known journalist and political figure from Puerto Rico; in 1952, he replaced Géigel with José Dávila Ricci, a journalist associated with Puerto Rican Governor Luis Múñoz Marín. Over the years, *El Diario de Nueva York* conducted many campaigns and programs on behalf of the Puerto Rican community. It researched and then published exposés of the abuse and inhuman conditions for Puerto Rican workers and created a counseling and referral center for the community, among many other services.

In 1962, O. Roy Chalk, owner of *El Diario de Nueva York*, purchased *La Prensa* and merged the two journals. From the 1970s to the present, the Hispanic ethnic balance in the city and metropolitan area has shifted repeatedly, with the immi-

Passerby purchasing a copy of *La Prensa* at a newsstand in New York City.

gration of Cuban refugees, then Central Americans and a steady flow of Dominicans, who today form the largest Hispanic group in the city. Following its well-tested formulas, *El Diario–La Prensa* has repeatedly adjusted its focus to embrace the new groups and reflect their concerns and interests.

In 1981, the Gannett newspaper corporation bought *El Diario–La Prensa*; in 1989, it was sold to El Diario Associates, Inc., a corporation founded by Peter Davidson, a former Morgan Stanley specialist in the newspaper industry. In 1990, the Times Mirror Corporation purchased a 50 percent interest in *La Opinión* (San Antonio's *La Prensa* had ceased to exist in 1963). In 1976, the *Miami Herald* founded *El Miami Herald*; in 1987 it was transformed into the new and improved *El Nuevo Herald*. Both the Spanish- and the English-language Miami dailies are subsidiaries of the Knight-Ridder newspaper chain. Thus, today the three major Hispanic dailies are owned and controlled by American (non-Hispanic) multimedia corporations; how this has impacted their functioning in service of the immigrants has not as yet been assessed. There are, however, other smaller dailies which in varying degrees remain independent. Hispanic immigrant publishing houses since the 1950s have been small and rather short-lived, not faring as well as the newspapers, which do not themselves publish literature in any proportion comparable to their predecessors prior to World War II.

Another important facet of immigrant publishing is represented by the cultural magazines that have existed since the nineteenth century. While workers' periodicals obviously served the immigrant working class, Hispanic elites felt the need to reproduce the cultural refinement that was the product of their education and breeding in the homeland. Whether to remain connected to the cultural accomplishments of the greater international Hispanic community or to fill an intellectual void that existed in the foreign land, a number of high-quality periodicals were established in the Northeast and Southwest. Some of them, such as the New York monthlies *El Ateneo: Repertorio Ilustrado de Arte, Ciencia y Literatura* (The Athenaeum: Illustrated Repertoire of Arts, Science and Literature, 1874–77) and *El Americano* (The American, 1892–?), retained the newspaper format, but primarily published literature and commentary, along with illustrations. Others looked much like the cultural magazines being published at the turn of the century, such as *Harper's Magazine* and *Cosmopolitan*. What was most distinctive about them was that they placed the Hispanic immigrant community of the United States on the international cultural map, drawing their selections from essayists, writers of prose fiction and poetry from Spain and Spanish America as well as from the United States. Pan-Hispanism and hemispheric integration, in fact, formed the basis of *El Ateneo*'s and *El Americano*'s ideological stance. Both had a circulation overseas as well as in the United States.

While these two magazines were celebrating the art and culture of the Americas, another New York periodical, *Ambas Américas: Revista de Educación, Bibliografía y Agricultura* (Both Americas: Educational, Bibliographic and Agricultural Magazine, 1867–68), set a task for itself of informing the people and institutions in Central and South America of the educational, scientific, and agricultural advances in the United States so that they would be emulated in the Spanish American countries. From a similarly internationalist perspective developed the most important illustrated Hispanic magazine, *La Revista Ilustrada de*

Nueva York (The Illustrated Revue of New York, 1882–?), which at a subscription price of $3.00 explicitly targeted the middle and upper classes of educated Hispanics in the United States and abroad. Despite its generally positive stance on Anglo-American civilization and the wonders of its science and technology and the stability of its government, the magazine nevertheless called for pan-Hispanic unity in resisting the expansionism of the American empire during a time characterized by American filibustering and interventionism in Spanish America. Thus, despite its elitism, *La Revista* felt it had to protect language, culture, and Hispanic interests just as the working-class Hispanic newspapers did.

Since World War II, book publishing by immigrants has relied on myriad tiny publishers who have often been short-lived. Two of the longest lived, Alejandro Otero and Joseph Otero's Spanish American Printing and Gaetano Massa's Las Américas Publishing House in New York City, published and/or printed a wide variety of books for the Hispanic immigrant community. The former began early in the twentieth century, catering to Hispanic immigrants and Puerto Ricans, and lasted into the 1980s, printing with a subvention from such authors as Puerto Rican José Cuchi-Coll, Peruvian Carlos Johnson, and Puerto Rican Violeta Riomar. Spanish American also did the printing for Las Americas Publishing House and numerous local Spanish-language magazines and Spanish mutual aid societies. Las Américas, on the other hand, survived from the 1940s through the 1980s as an importer of texts for Spanish and Spanish American literature classes and universities on the east coast; it began publishing books when various texts became out of print. It issued some of the important texts of such critics as Pedro Henríquez Ureña, for example, but also published original literature, such as the works of José López Heredia. With the stepped-up migrations that began in the 1970s, many authors from the Caribbean and South America relocated to the United States and needed publishers for their works. Some of these, such as Chilean Hugo Hanriot Pérez and Peruvian Carlos Johnson, established their own houses in the 1980s—New Jersey's SLUSA (Spanish Language Publishing in the United States) and New York's Ediciones Jilguer, respectively—to issue their own works and those of their literary circles. Another active publisher during the late 1970s and 1980s was New York's Senda Nueva de Ediciones, which published some of Marjorie Agosin's first works, and Editorial Mensaje, which published Tino Villaneuva's and Juan Gómez-Quiñones's first books of poetry. A number of Cuban immigrants published their works through Ediciones Universal, which at first was primarily a publisher of exile literature; it is still very much in existence today and continues to publish works that are underwritten by the authors.

A noteworthy magazine issued in New York during the late 1970s and early 1980s was *Areito*, edited by the scholar and creative writer Lourdes Casal and published by Ediciones Vitral Inc.; it was the first publication of the children of exiled Cubans who sought to forge a rapprochement with Cuba and the Castro cultural institutions. Another effort by young Cuban, Puerto Rican, and South American immigrants to forge a literary identity within New York was La Nueva Sangre writers collective and its magazine and book publications, founded and run by such authors as Dolores Prida and Roger Cabán in the late 1960s. For more than ten years beginning in the 1980s, Ediciones del Norte issued works by some of the leading Spanish American exiles and immigrants out of Hanover,

New Hampshire, and was the first press to issue an anthology dedicated to the Latino immigrant writers: *Las paraguas amarillas* (The Yellow Umbrellas), edited by Iván Silén. From the 1980s, Pittsburgh's Latin American Review Press, under Chilean director Yvette Miller, has published a magazine and books dedicated to Hispanic literature translated to English. At the turn of the twenty-first century, Arte Público Press of Houston, the nation's largest Hispanic publisher, was issuing numerous immigrant works by authors of varied Latin ethnicities, quite often publishing the English translation before the Spanish original of a work to introduce their authors to the American buying public and thus establish a track record for institutional buyers such as libraries and schools. At the same time, Arte Público also began issuing works by such Central American immigrant authors as Mario Bencastro and Roberto Quesada, reflecting the changing nature of Hispanic demographics in the United States. In addition to those named above, there have been numerous sporadic and short-lived publishers, including Editorial Persona in Hawaii; Ediciones de la Frontera in Los Angeles; Cruzada Spanish Publications, Editorial Arcos, Editorial SIBI and LS Press in Miami; Contra Viento y Marea in New Jersey; and El Libro Viaje, Libros del Maitén, Peninsula Publishing, and Prisma Books in New York, among many others.

THE NATIVE HISPANIC PRESS

An Hispanic native or ethnic minority perspective developed first among Hispanics already residing in the Southwest when the U.S. appropriated it from Mexico. It has specifically manifested itself in the political realm and in Hispanic attitudes towards civil and cultural rights. The ethnic minority or native press that developed among Hispanics has been cognizant of the racial, ethnic, and/or minority status of its readers within U.S. society and culture. This press has made use of both Spanish and English. It has included immigrants in its readership and among its interests, but its fundamental reason for existence and its point of reference has been its readership's life and conditions in the United States. Unlike the immigrant press, it does not have one foot in the homeland and one in the United States.

Many of the Hispanic newspapers, books, and other publications that appeared in the Southwest after the Mexican War was concluded in 1848 laid the basis for Hispanics throughout the United States seeing themselves as an ethnic minority within this country. While the origins of their journalistic endeavors date well before the all-important signing of the peace treaty between the United States and Mexico, it was the immediate conversion to colonial status of the Mexican population in the newly acquired territories of California, New Mexico, and Texas that made their journalistic efforts a sounding board for their rights first as colonials and later as "racialized" citizens of the United States.

While the printing press was not introduced to California and New Mexico until 1834, the society there, as in Texas, was sufficiently literate to sustain a wide range of printing and publishing once the press was allowed. Newspaper publication in the Southwest of what became the United States originated, it will be recalled, in 1813 with papers published to support Mexico's independence movement from Spain. In 1834 and 1835, almost contemporaneously with the introduction of the press to California and New Mexico, Spanish-language newspapers began to appear in these northern provinces of Mexico: Santa Fe's *El Crepúsculo de la Libertad* (The Dawn of Liberty) and Taos' *El Crepúsculo* (Dawn, 1835–?). Prior to the U.S. conquest, other newspapers were published in New Mexico: *La Verdad* (The Truth, 1844–1845) and its successor, *El Payo de Nuevo México* (The New Mexico Countryman, 1845).

Beginning with the American presence in New Mexico and California during the outbreak of the Mexican War in 1846, many newspapers there began publishing bilingually in English and Spanish; in Texas, numerous newspapers had been publishing bilingually since just before the proclamation of the Texas Republic in 1836, some dating back to as early as 1824. In New Mexico, publishing only in Spanish or bilingually was a necessity for the Anglo owners of the newspapers because the vast majority of the inhabitants of the territory were Spanish speakers. In California, newspapers received a subsidy from the state as well as from some cities for printing laws in Spanish, since the state constitution required laws to be issued in both languages. One can envision how this initial motivation developed into a profitable enterprise once the Spanish-language market was identified and cultivated. Indeed, the Spanish-language section of Los Angeles' *Star* grew into *La Estrella de Los Angeles* and then a separate newspaper, *El Clamor Público* (The Public Clamor, 1855–1859). From San Francisco's *The Californian* (1846–1848), the first Anglo-American newspaper in Alta, California, to New Mexico's *Santa Fe Republican* (1847–?), Brownsville's *La Bandera* (184?–1863?) and *The Corpus Christi Star* (1848–?), the Anglo-established press was a bilingual institution.

After a long scarcity of printing presses during the Spanish and Mexican periods in what became the U.S. Southwest, it was the coming of the Anglo-American with technology and equipment that resulted in printing presses coming into Hispanic hands as never before and facilitating the subsequent founding of an increasing number of Spanish-language newspapers and publishing houses to serve the native Hispanic population of the Southwest. By the 1880s and 1890s, books were also issuing from these presses, although it should be noted that books written in Spanish were printed from the very inception of the printing press in 1834. A native literature in manuscript form had existed since the colonial period, and when the printing press became available, this literature made the transition to print. And when the railroad reached the territories, dramatic changes occurred as a consequence of greater access to machinery and technology as well as to better means of distribution for print products. The last third of the century saw an explosion of independent Spanish-language publishing by Hispanics. During this time also a native literature in book form helped to develop a sense of ethnic and regional identity for Hispanics in the Southwest. Autobiographies, memoirs, and novels appeared, specifically treating the sense of dislocation and uprootedness, the sense of loss of patrimony, and the fear of persecution as a racial minority in the United States. In 1858, Juan Nepomuceno Seguín published his *Personal Memoirs of John N. Seguín*, the first autobiography written by a Mexican American in the English language. Seguín, the embattled and disenchanted political figure of the Texas Republic, was personally persecuted and ultimately experienced great disillusionment in the transformation of his Texas by Anglo-Americans. In 1872, the first novel written in English by an Hispanic of the United States was self-published by María Amparo Ruiz de Burton: her domestic novel *Who Would Have Thought It?*, which critiqued American ideas about race and egalitarianism. In 1885, Ruiz de Burton published another novel, this from the perspective of the conquered Mexican population of the Southwest: *The Squatter and the Don*, which documented the loss of lands to squatters, and banking and railroad interests in Southern California shortly after statehood. In 1881, the first Spanish-language novel written and published in the Southwest was published: Manuel M. Salazar's *La historia de un caminante, o Gervacio y Aurora* (The History of a Traveler on Foot, or Gervasio and Aurora), which created a colorful picture of pastoral life in New Mexico at the time.

As the century ended, numerous native texts found their way into book form. However, as immigration from Mexico increased in the Southwest and from Puerto Rico, Cuba, and Spain in the Northeast and immigrant newspapers and publishing houses were established, the opportunities for establishing large native publishing outlets soon disappeared as the immigrant culture overwhelmed the native Hispanic populations. However, Hispanic native writing persisted and laid the foundation for today's bilingual, bicultural citizenry, although most often native authors either self-published or worked through the immigrant newspapers and publishing houses to see their works into print. While a number of immigrant and exile authors found their way into the mainstream press during these years, an important native writer, Américo Paredes of Brownsville, was unsuccessful in placing his early works in English; his 1936 novel *George Washington Gómez* did not make it into print until 1990. The 1930s Texan writer Jovita González never saw her two novels in print: *Caballero* and *Dew on the Thorn*, were published posthumously in 1995 and 1998, respectively. It was not until the 1960s that such writers as Puerto Rican Nicholasa Mohr, Cuban American Jose Yglesias, and Mexican Americans José Antonio Villarreal (actually Doubleday issued his *Pocho* in 1959) and Floyd Salas saw their works issued by the large commercial houses in New York. The Hispanic civil rights movements and the entrance of a broad sector of Hispanics into universities helped usher in the flourishing of Hispanic American literature in the English language that began in the 1970s and persists today.

New Mexico

Because New Mexico drew comparably fewer Anglo settlers and entrepreneurs than California and Texas and because of its vastly larger Hispanic population, only in there did Hispanics maintain a demographic superiority in the late nineteenth and early twentieth centuries. New Mexico was the territory that first developed a widespread independent native Hispanic press. Hispanics in New Mexico lived in a more compact area and with comparably less competition and violence from Anglo newcomers. The Nuevomexicanos were able to hold onto more lands, property, and institutions than did the Hispanics of California and Texas. Control of their own newspapers and publications became essential in the eyes of Hispanic intellectuals and community leaders in the development of Nuevomexicano identity and self-determination as they adjusted to the new culture foisted upon them during the territorial period. Nuevomexicanos were living under a double-edged sword: they wanted to control their own destiny and preserve their own language and culture while enjoying the benefits and rights of the advanced civilization as a state of the Union. But the Nuevomexicanos immediately became aware of the dangers of Anglo-American cultural, economic, and political encroachment in New Mexico. According to Meléndez (1997, 24–25), many of the intellectual leaders, especially newspaper publishers, believed that the native population would only advance, learn to protect itself, and merit statehood through education; they saw the newspapers as key to the education and advancement of the natives as well as to the protection of their civil and property rights. Nuevomexicanos felt the urgency to empower themselves in the new system— and/or retain some of the power they had under Mexico—while Washington was delaying statehood for more than fifty years in expectation, most historians agree, of Anglos achieving a numerical and voting superiority in the territory.

In the decade following the arrival of the railroad in 1879, native Hispanic journalism increased dramatically in the New Mexico territory, and, according to Meléndez (1997, 26), a true flowering of Nuevomexicano periodicals followed in the 1890s, when some thirty-five Spanish-language newspapers were being published. From 1879 to the year New Mexico was admitted as a state of the Union in 1912, more than ninety Spanish-language newspapers were published in New Mexico (Meléndez, 29). By 1891, native Hispanic journalism had become so widespread and intense that a newspaper association was founded, La Prensa Asociada Hispano-Americana, to set up a network of correspondents, share resources, and facilitate reprinting items from each member newspaper in a type of informal syndication. Thus, in a few short decades, a corps of the native inhabitants of what had been a backwater province under Mexico and a frontier colony under the United States, had been transformed into intellectuals and activists utilizing the written and published word through print and transportation technology; they were taking the lead in ushering their community into the twentieth century and statehood.

In his book, Meléndez proceeds to amply document how the Nuevomexicano journalists set about taking control of their social and cultural destiny by constructing what they saw as a "national" culture for themselves, which consisted of using and preserving the Spanish language and formulating their own version of history and their own literature to ensure their self-confident and proud entrance as a state of the Union. From within the group of newspaper publishers and editors, in fact, sprang a cohesive and identifiable corps of native creative writers, historians, and publishers who elaborated a native and indigenous intellectual tradition that is the basis of much of the intellectual and literary work of Mexican Americans today. In addition, the young journalists and publishers quite often went on to become leaders in New Mexico trade, commerce, education, and politics—a legacy that is still felt today. Thus, the development of the New Mexican Hispanic press at that time followed a very different pattern from that of New York's Hispanic press, which received publishers, writers, and journalists trained abroad and who saw themselves as exiles or immigrants.

The cultural nationalism of these native journalists, of course, sprang from the necessity to defend their community from the cultural, economic, and political onslaught of the "outsiders." Their newspapers were to provide "la defensa de nuestro pueblo y nuestro país" (the defense of our people and our homeland) and "buscar preferentemente el mejoramiento y adelanto del pueblo hispano-americano" (preferably seek the improvement and progress of the Hispanic American people), according to *El Nuevo Mundo* (The New World, 8 May 1897). In keeping with their community leadership, their defense of cultural and civil rights was often issued in front-page editorials that in no uncertain terms made it clear that Nuevomexicanos had to assume a posture of defense to survive, and that part and parcel of the defense was the furthering of education and cultural solidarity.

To combat the American myth of civilizing the West—i.e., subduing the barbarous and racially inferior Indians and Mexicans—that empowered the United States and its "pioneers" to encroach and dispossess Indians and Nuevomexicanos of their lands and patrimony, the Nuevomexicano journalists began elaborating a myth of their own: the glorious introduction of European civilization and its institutions by the Spanish during the Colonial Period. Prior achievement legitimized their claims to land as well as to the protection and preservation of their language and culture. In their rhetoric the Nuevomexicano editorialists were able to turn the tables on the Anglo-American settlers and businessmen who had "invaded" the territory by claiming their own higher breeding and Catholic religion over the low morality, vicious opportunism, and hypocrisy of the Protestant interlopers and adventurers. In the construction of their history, the editors regularly included historical and biographical materials, even in weekly columns, covering the full gamut of Hispanic history, from the exploration and colonization of Mexico, including what became the U.S. Southwest, to the life histories of important historical figures such as Miguel de Hidalgo y Costilla, Simón Bolívar, and José San Martín. They also began to publish history books and biographies documenting their own evolution as a people. Even in their newspapers, biographies became standard fare as they documented the contributions of their own forebearers and even their contemporaries in New Mexico and the Southwest.

One institution stands out in its furthering of the ethnic nationalist goals of the Nuevomexicanos: the *Revista Ilustrada* (The Illustrated Review), which New Mexican Camilo Padilla founded in El Paso, Texas, in 1907 and continued to publish in Santa Fe, New Mexico, from 1917 to approximately 1931. The *Revista Ilustrada* was ahead of its times in identifying and furthering an Hispanic ethnic minority culture in the United States. Unlike New York's *Revista Ilustrada*, which envisioned an international, pan-Hispanic readership, New Mexico's squarely situated itself in the home. In addition to publishing poetry, stories, and history, often graphically illustrated, the magazine offered space to Nuevomexicano intellectuals to ponder the fate of their culture. Among these collaborators were such notables as historian Benjamin M. Read, poet and novelist Eusebio Chacón, and linguist and professor Aurelio M. Espinosa. In its furtherance of the Spanish language and Hispanic culture, Padilla included the works of some of the outstanding Spanish American literary figures of the time and advertised books of European and Latin American literature in Spanish that could be bought directly from the magazine. After 1925, Padilla's cultural work went far beyond the pages of the magazine to the founding and administration of El Centro de Cultura in Santa Fe—a center for cultural, literary and social events, but foremost a place for native art and culture practice (Meléndez 1997, 198).

As Meléndez asserts, the promotion of a "national" literature and history by these editors and writers demonstrates that as early as the late nineteenth century the Nuevomexicanos saw themselves as a national minority of the United States. This idea was furthered by the region-wide Hispanic American Press Association, by the exchanges with newspapers in Texas and California, and by the awareness of dispossession and proletarization of the Mexican-origin population throughout the region. That they recognized the value of their own local history, folklore, and literature and had elevated it to print was a conscious part of the minority identity formation that was taking place.

California

Soon after the influx of Anglo-Americans occasioned by the Gold Rush and statehood in 1850, the native Hispanic population of California became overwhelmed and was quickly converted to minority status. During the post-Civil War years, immigration of Anglos increased dramatically, as did the arrival of the railroads, the breaking up of the Californio ranches, and the conversion of the economy to American capitalism; the native population was quickly converted to a proletarian one as the Californios and Hispanicized Indians were displaced from farms and ranches and assimilated into the new economy as laborers on the railroads, in mines, and in the fields.

Almost as soon as newspaper ownership came into the hands of the native Hispanic population of California, an ethnic minority consciousness began to develop. When Francisco P. Ramírez took over the Spanish section of the *Los Angeles Star* and founded a separate newspaper, *El Clamor Público*, he created a landmark in awareness that Hispanics in California were being treated as a race apart from the Euro-Americans who had immigrated into the area. Even the wealthy Californios who had collaborated in the Yankee takeover saw their wealth and power diminish under statehood. In addition to covering California and U.S. news, *El Clamor Público* also maintained contact with the Hispanic world outside California and attempted to present an image of refinement and education that demonstrated the high level of civilization achieved throughout Hispanism; this, in part, was a defensive reaction to the negative propaganda of Manifest Destiny that had cast Mexicans and other Hispanics as unintelligent and uneducated barbarians incapable of developing their lands and the natural resources of the West, which would justify these lands and resources being wrested from their hands by the superior newcomers. *El Clamor Público* depended on a subsidy from the city of Los Angeles and had strong ties to the Anglo-American business community in the city; in addition, it was aligned with the Republican Party. Ramírez and his paper were also staunch supporters of learning English; not only was it important for business but also for protecting the Californios' rights. These pro-business and Republican Party stances, nevertheless, did not stop Ramírez from leading in the defense of the native population. While Ramírez was also a great supporter of the United States Constitution, his indignation grew as the civil and property rights of the Californios were left unprotected by the Constitution that he loved so much. He became a consistent and assiduous critic, attempting to inspire the

Hispanics to unite in their defense and the authorities to protect the Hispanic residents of California who were being despoiled, even lynched. Ramírez seems to have been the first Mexican American journalist of the West and Southwest to consistently use the press to establish a native perspective and to pursue civil rights for his people.

In the three decades after statehood was established, *El Clamor Público*, *La Crónica* and most of the other Spanish-language newspapers of California insisted on integration into the American education and political system and promoted learning the English language for survival. In doing so, they created a firm basis for the development of an ethnic minority identity, and a bicultural and bilingual citizenry for Mexican Americans—precisely what Hispanics advocate today in the United States.

In California as in Texas and elsewhere in the Southwest, the mass of immigrants that came as economic and political refugees during the Mexican Revolution of 1910 overwhelmed the native populations. The large immigrant daily newspapers, such as *El Heraldo de México, La Prensa*, and *La Opinión* focused most of their attention on serving the needs of the expatriate communities, even while intending to accommodate Hispanic native issues and culture, as was Ignacio E. Lozano's desire. The effect of this overwhelming population shift and the press that served it was that native interests became incorporated or subsumed in the immigrant press, which hindered, to some extent, the development of a separate Hispanic native press, especially in the big cities. Nevertheless, as the community matured and made the transition toward a Hispanic culture in the United States, those same immigrant newspapers also became more oriented to reflecting their communities as national ethnic minorities, not just immigrants who were temporary residents. By the time of the Depression and World War II, more and more Hispanic publications began to be issued in English, and a new generation saw itself as a citizenry, or at least a permanent community, reflected in their pages. These new publications and this new consciousness existed side by side with immigrant and exile publications.

In California, one such periodical was *The Mexican Voice* (1941–1944), a publication of the Mexican American Movement (MAM), the product of youths who had either been born or raised in the United States. *The Mexican Voice* promoted citizenry, upward mobility through education, and active participation in civil and cultural activities outside the barrio. While hesitant to acknowledge racism as a factor hindering success, the magazine did promote pride in the pre-Columbian background and in Mexican *mestizaje*; this it accomplished in part by publishing brief biographies of high-achieving Mexican Americans in Southern California.

The ideas expressed in *The Mexican Voice* were not far from those expressed at that time in the Mexican American civil rights organizations such as the League of United Latin American Citizens (LULAC), and their publications or from those expressed by Chicanos in their movement during the 1960s. In fact, these and similar English-language periodicals formed a vital link to the attitudes that would find expression in the Chicano Movement, which produced a flowering of politically committed newspapers and magazines in the 1960s and 1970s and even scholarly journals based at universities. In California, the founding in 1965 of *El Malcriado*, the organ of the United Farm Workers Organizing Committee, marked the beginning of publications of the modern-day Chicano civil rights movement. The founding of *Con Safos* literary magazine in Los Angeles in 1968 hailed a grass-roots Chicano literary movement, and the founding of the quarterly *El Grito* (The Shout), also in 1968, and of Editorial Quinto Sol in 1970 by University of California-Berkeley professors Octavio Romano-V. and Herminio Ríos, initiated an academic and scholarly movement that continues to this date through a number of journals and publishing houses. In fact, the pressure placed on educational and cultural institutions by the Chicano Movement and the example set by Editorial Quinto Sol and other early Chicano presses led to the founding of numerous other small publishing houses and magazines in the 1970s and 1980s. In Los Angeles, such grass-roots and student collaborative efforts as the *Con Safos* magazine helped writers like Oscar Zeta Acosta come to the fore. The Bay Area gave rise to publishing houses that catered to the diverse Latino groups resident there, but especially to such Chicano-dominated efforts as Casa Editorial, Editorial Pocho Che, and Lorna Dee Cervantes' *Mango* magazine and publications. Later, Alurista, along with graduate students and professors in San Diego, produced Maize Publications, which not only launched such authors as Gina Valdés but also began the work of recovering the literary past with its edition of the *Crónicas Diabólicas de Jorge Ulica*. In the late 1970s, Quinto Sol broke up and gave rise to two other significant presses headed by each of the former partners: Justa Publications and Tonatiuh-Quinto Sol (later rebaptized TQS Publications).

But From the 1980s on, the leadership in Chicano and Latino publishing passed out of California to Arte Público Press in Houston and Bilingual Review Press in Tempe, Arizona. Thanks to the efforts of these long-lived and currently thriving houses, Chicano and Latino authors were not only able to cross over to mainstream commercial presses in the 1990s but also to university presses in Arizona, New Mexico, and Texas, and even to such formerly stodgy publishers as the University of Chicago and Northwestern University. In addition, the 1990s saw myriad small, independent presses around the country begin to issue Chicano and Latino works—from Minneapolis' Coffee House Press to Connecticut's Curbstone Press to Boston's South End Press and Albuquerque's West End Press. Among the many other small and short-lived houses that Chicanos founded in California were Berkeley's El Fuego de Aztlán, Oakland's Floricanto Press, San Diego's Lalo Press and Toltecas en Aztlán, and Santa Barbara's Ediciones Aztlán and Ediciones Xalman. Many of these Chicano presses also published magazines.

Texas

After Texas achieved statehood in 1850 and well into the period of intense Mexican immigration in the twentieth century, a number of newspapers serving Texas Mexicans assumed activist roles in defining Mexican American identity and entitlement. Such newspapers as San Antonio's *El Bejareño* (The Bejar County, 1855–18??) and *El Regidor* (The Regent, 1888–1916) saw protecting the rights of the Texas Mexicans as their duty, but it was the journalist Catarino E. Garza of the border who made their civil rights a crusade. Born on the border in 1859 and raised in and around Brownsville, Garza worked on newspapers in Laredo,

Eagle Pass, Corpus Christi, and San Antonio. In the Brownsville–Eagle Pass area, he became involved in local politics and published two newspapers, *El Comercio Mexicano* (Mexican Commerce, 1886–?) and *El Libre Pensador* (The Free Thinker, 1890–?), which protested the violence against Mexicans and dispossession of their lands. Beginning in 1888, when he confronted U.S. Customs agents for assassinating two Mexican prisoners, Garza became more militant and struck out at authorities on both sides of the border with a band of followers that included farmers, laborers, and former Texas separatists. A special force of Texas Rangers eventually broke up his force of raiders and Garza fled in 1892 to New Orleans. Garza's exploits were followed in detail in the Spanish-language newspapers of the Southwest and helped to coalesce feelings about exploitation and dispossession among the Mexican American population. This process was also abetted by the reprinting of Garza's articles in newspapers throughout the Southwest.

One of the most influential newspapers along the border was Laredo's *La Crónica* (The Chronicle, 1909–?), written and published by Nicasio Idar and his eight children. Idar had a working-class and union background, and he and his family took the forefront in representing the rights of Texas Mexicans through the pages of *La Crónica* and a magazine they also published, *La Revista de Laredo*. Like many Hispanic newspaper publishers and editors who spearheaded social and political causes for their communities, Idar and his family led many liberal causes, including the establishment of Mexican schools for children in Texas as an alternative to subjecting them to segregated schools and prejudice. His daughter Jovita Idar was at the forefront of women's issues and collaborated on a number of women's periodicals. *La Crónica* decried everything from racism and segregation in public institutions to negative stereotypes in Anglo plays and films.

It was Idar's overriding theme that man in general and Mexicans in Texas specifically needed to educate themselves. Only through education would social and political progress come about—and it was the special role of the newspapers to lead the way and facilitate that education. Only through education would Mexicans in Texas lift themselves up from their poverty and misery and defend themselves from the abuse of the Anglo-Texans. Mexican families, therefore, were exhorted to maintain their children in school so that gradually the conditions of Mexicans in the state would improve from one generation to the next (*La Crónica*, 11 October 1910). The Idar family and their publications were as good as their words: they headed up a successful statewide drive to import Mexican teachers, find them space in which to teach children, and support them financially. Through this strategy two social ills began to be addressed: nonadmittance to or segregation of Mexican children in many schools and the stemming of the loss of the Spanish language and Mexican culture among the young.

As mentioned above, while immigrant newspapers dominated the large urban centers, native papers continued to develop in the small cities and towns. One such newspaper was Santiago G. Guzmán's *El Defensor del Pueblo* (The People's Defender, 1930–?), which promoted a Mexican American identity and supported the nascent civil rights organization League of United Latin American Citizens (LULAC). Located in Edinburg, in impoverished South Texas, *El Defensor del Pueblo* became a watchdog over local politics, with a particular eye to political corruption and the disenfranchisement of Mexican Americans. However, the greatest concern of Guzmán and his paper was the development of a Mexican American conscience and the assumption of the responsibilities of citizenship and voting to vouchsafe the liberties and rights authorized by the U.S. Constitution. He envisioned his paper as a guardian of those rights and as a beacon for guiding Mexican Americans in combating racism and shucking off their sense of inferiority to the Anglo. Guzmán called for a national voting bloc of Latinos, and on the local level a reversal of the political structure in South Texas, where a white minority held all of the positions of power and oppressed the Mexican American majority.

In Texas, the process of Mexican Americanization—that is, establishing a firm identity as a U.S. ethnic minority—gave rise to the two most important national civil rights organizations: LULAC, mentioned above, and the American G.I. Forum. Founded in 1929, LULAC at first was made up mostly of middle-class Mexican Americans and only accepted American citizens as members. LULAC early on targeted segregation and unfairness in the judicial system as primary concerns. Its main periodical—various local chapters had their own newsletters— was *LULAC News* (1931–1979), published monthly in English and Spanish for national distribution. The American G.I. Forum was founded in Corpus Christi by World War II veterans to protect the civil rights of returning Mexican American soldiers. It became actively involved in electoral politics and was responsible for creating a voting block within the Democratic Party, one which experts believe was responsible for winning the 1962 presidential election for John F. Kennedy. In 1948, the American G.I. Forum founded its periodical, *The Forumeer*, which still exists to cover civil rights issues.

The types of newspapers and civil rights periodicals described above were not the only publications representing a native perspective in the Southwest. However, while there were no publishing houses that consistently issued books from that perspective, mainly because the Mexican immigrant press dominated the discourse, individual Mexican American writers self-published their works or were successful in having newspapers and immigrant publishers issue them. Such was the case of Alonso Perales, one of the founders of LULAC, who self-published his *El méxico americano y la política del sur de Texas* (The Mexican American and Politics in South Texas) in 1931, but issued his *En defensa de mi raza* (In Defense of My People) with San Antonio's Artes Gráficas in 1937.

These books, as well as *LULAC News* and *The Forumeer*, were predecessors of the hundreds of Chicano Movement publications that were issued in the 1960s and early 1970s. They kept the populace informed of the civil rights struggle and provided an ideological framework from which to consider social and political progress. On the cultural front, the Chicano Movement gave rise to numerous literary and cultural magazines and presses, such as San Antonio's *El Magazín*, Angela de Hoyos's M&A Editions, and Cecilio García Camarillo's *Caracol*, which launched numerous writers including Max Martínez and Evangelina Vigil-Piñón. Student-related publishing activities out of Austin included the magazine *Tejidos* and Place of the Herons Press. Also publishing in Texas during the 1970s and 1980s were Lubbock's Trucha Publications and El Paso's Dos Pasos. The only press of its type (small, regional, and independent) that survives today is El Paso's Cinco Puntos Press. All of these publishing houses reinforced the entitlement of Mexican Americans as citizens of the United States to the rights and benefits of

Cecilio García Camarillo.

American society—without racial, class, and linguistic discrimination. At their root, they were patriotically American, exhibiting great faith in the American Constitution and the Congress and the judicial system to remedy discrimination and injustice. It is interesting to note that in the year 2000 the nation's largest Hispanic publisher, Arte Público Press, located at the University of Houston, has reassumed the function initiated by LULAC and the Chicano Movement presses in the 1960s by establishing two retrospective series: (1) a Civil Rights Series to publish documents, histories, and memoirs of Hispanic civil rights struggles, including biographies of Dr. Hector García, founder of the American G. I. Forum, and memoirs of such Chicano and Puerto Rican activists as Reies López Tijerina and Antonia Pantoja; (2) the Pioneers of Hispanic Literature Series to issue reprint editions of the out-of-print works of such Chicano Movement authors as Lucha Corpi, Cecilio García Camarillo, and Raúl Salinas, among others, as well as such Nuyorican authors as Piri Thomas and Cuban American authors as Jose Yglesias. In its Civil Rights Series Arte Público has also published histories of the Hispanic civil rights struggle from the nineteenth century to the present, as well as histories of individual organizations such as the American G. I. Forum and ASPIRA Inc.

New York

While New York has been the principal port of entry for immigrants from Europe and the Caribbean and has been a center for immigrant publishing and culture, various publications have reflected their communities' evolution towards Americanization and citizenship status. Even *Gráfico*, which in most respects was a typical immigrant newspaper, began to recognize the American citizenship of its readers, mostly Puerto Ricans and Cubans residing in East Harlem, to demand the rights guaranteed under the Constitution, and freedom from discrimination. Because the Jones Act of 1917 extended citizenship to Puerto Ricans, these former islanders did not have to acculturate or assimilate to become citizens; it was automatic. With the advent of the Depression, New York did not experience the massive repatriation of Hispanics that occurred in the Southwest. Instead, the opposite was true. Hard economic times on the island brought even more Puerto Ricans to the city, a trend that would intensify during World War II as northeastern manufacturing and services industries experienced labor shortages and re-cruited heavily in Puerto Rico. The massive influx of Puerto Ricans during and just after the war further intensified the community's identity as a native citizenry. In addition, community members were appealed to as citizens by their local news-papers to organize politically and vote.

As early as 1927, a league was formed in New York City to increase the power of the Hispanic community by unifying its diverse organizations. Among the very specific goals of the Liga Puertorriqueña e Hispana (The Puerto Rican and His-panic League) were the representing of the community to the "authorities," work-ing for the economic and social betterment of the Puerto Ricans and propagating the vote among Puerto Ricans. The Liga founded a periodical in 1927 entitled *Boletín Oficial de la Liga Puertorriqueña e Hispana*, the League's official bulletin, which evolved into much more than a newsletter, functioning more like a com-munity newspaper and including essays and cultural items as well as news in its pages. Mainly supported at first by the Puerto Rican Brotherhood, a mutual aid society, the Liga's goals included providing information and education to the Hispanic community and promoting suffrage among Puerto Ricans. The biweekly was influential in raising the level of awareness of Puerto Ricans as an electorate and their need to associate and form political coalitions with other Hispanic groups for their political and economic betterment.

Pueblos Hispanos: Semanario Progresista (Hispanic Peoples: Progressive Weekly, 1943–1944) was through its director, Juan Antonio Corretjer, affiliated with both the Puerto Rican Nationalist Party and the Communist Party of America. While *Pueblos Hispanos'* main reason for existence was to support national liberation movements throughout Latin America—especially Puerto Rico's independence movement—it voiced many Puerto Rican nativist ideas, such as encouraging po-litical involvement in the Democratic Party of New York by Hispanic citizens and openly endorsing candidates to office, including the reelection of President Frank-lin Delano Roosevelt through front-page editorials. As its name indicated, *Pueblos Hispanos* promoted a pan-Hispanism and a future integration of the Latin Amer-ican countries. Edited by the important Puerto Rican poet and delegate to the Communist Party of America, Juan Antonio Corretjer, the newspaper promoted socialist causes around the globe, ran weekly columns on politics and culture in Russia—as well as on socialist movements in Peru, Ecuador, Brazil, Mexico, Cen-tral America, and elsewhere—and covered Puerto Rican politics on the island and in New York in detail. It may appear as a paradox that *Pueblos Hispanos* was so concerned with safeguarding the civil rights and promoting the political partici-pation of Puerto Ricans in New York and in federal politics while it was also advocating the island's separation from the United States. But this confidence in the safeguards of freedom of the press, freedom of expression, and the right to organize even dissenting political parties only underlines the degree of confidence that the editors and community felt in their status as American citizens. They were exercising their rights fully and openly, assuming stances that were unheard of in immigrant newspapers.

Despite the press for civil rights and the movement among young people to recover and celebrate their Hispanic roots, no significant publisher of native His-panic literature has developed in the New York area since the 1960s. Perhaps this is due in part to the overwhelming, continuous flow of Hispanic immigrants and exiles, with a significant sector of intellectuals, who have dominated Hispanic publishing, especially in the Spanish language. It may also be attributed to New York being the center for U.S. publishing and, for a long time, U.S. television; the publishing and entertainment industries' efforts to reach mass audiences have all but ignored the minority voices in their midst, except for the handful of writers launched by major presses during the height of the civil rights struggles of the late 1960s and early 1970s. Jesús Colón's modest press was silenced well before he died in 1974. The Nuyorican Poet's Café Press only issued one volume, and its effort was continued by Arte Público Press in Houston.

It was not until the 1990s that major publishing houses began opening their doors to Latino writers, first by obtaining rights to and reprinting the books that Arte Público and Bilingual Press had launched into the college market, a lucrative market that the commercial houses were very interested in taking over. Later, as Hispanic demographic growth and consequent market pressure increased, the mainstream presses began issuing new works by such writers as Rudolfo Anaya, Ana Castillo, Sandra Cisneros, and Victor Villaseñor—who had been successful Latino press authors—and then by publishing and promoting some of their own discoveries such as Julia Alvarez, Cristina García, and Richard Rodríguez. As the twenty-first century opened, with projections of Latinos becoming one-fourth of the national population by 2030, such houses as HarperCollins and Random House were establishing their specific Latino publishing lines to encompass both English- and Spanish-language publishing, both fiction and non-fiction. The emphasis among the large commercial houses from the outset has been on assured sellers such as Sandra Cisneros, Oscar Hijuelos, and Victor Villaseñor, as well as new authors who are television, sports, and movie personalities; these presses expand their Latino list with translations of bestsellers and important works of such leading Latin American authors as Carlos Fuentes and Mario Vargas Llosa.

CHAPTER 6

OVERVIEW OF HISPANIC DRAMA

ORIGINS TO 1940

The Southwest

The roots of Hispanic theater in the United States reach back to the dance-drama of the American Indians and to the religious theater and pageants of Medieval and Renaissance Spain. During the Spanish colonization of Mexico, theater was placed at the service of the Catholic missionaries who employed it in their evangelizing of the Indians and their continued instruction of them and their mestizo descendants in the mysteries and dogma of the Church. The seventeenth and eighteenth centuries in Mexico saw the development of a hybrid religious theater, one that often employed the music, colors, flowers, masks, even the languages of the Indians of Mexico to dramatize the stories from the Old and New Testaments. In Mexico and what eventually became the Southwest of the United States there developed a cycle of religious plays that, while dramatizing these stories from the Bible, nevertheless became so secular and entertaining in their performances that Church authorities finally banned them from church grounds and from inclusion in the official festivities during feast days. They became folk plays, enacted by the faithful on their own and without official sanction or sponsorship from the Church.

At the center of this cycle of folk plays that dealt with Adam and Eve, Jesus lost in the desert and other favorite passages of the Holy Scriptures, was the story of the Star of Bethlehem announcing the birth of Jesus Christ to humble shepherds, who then commence a pilgrimage in search of the newborn Christ. On the way to Bethlehem Satan and the legions of hell attempt to waylay and distract the shepherds, and a battle between Good, represented by the Archangel Michael, and Evil takes place. Among the other various dramatic elements in this shepherds' play, or *pastorela*, as it is called in Spanish, are the appearances of a virginal shepherdess, a lecherous hermit, and a comic bumbling shepherd named Bato. Pastorelas, plays presented by the common folk from central Mexico to northern California, are still performed today, especially in rural areas during the Christmas season; even such professional companies as Luis Valdez's El Teatro Campesino perform a pastorela in alternative years with *Las Apariciones de la Virgen de Guadalupe* at the San Juan Bautista Mission in California.

In 1598 Juan de Oñate led his colonizing mission into what is today New Mexico. While the missionaries introduced religious theater Juan de Oñate's soldiers and colonists brought along the roots of secular drama. Oñate's soldiers would entertain themselves by improvising plays based on the experiences of their journey. They also enacted the folk play that has been spread wherever Spaniards have colonized, *Moros y cristianos,* which is the heroic tale of how the Christians defeated the Moors in northern Spain during the Crusades and eventually drove them from the Iberian Peninsula. For many scholars these represent the roots of an authentic secular folk theater that developed in what became the Southwest of the United States and that gave rise to such New Mexican plays in the eighteenth and early nineteenth centuries as *Los Comanches* and *Los Tejanos,* both of which deal with military conflict in an epic manner. As late as the early twentieth century reenactments of *Moros y Cristianos,* even performed on horseback, have been documented in New Mexico, which seems to be the state, because of its rural culture, that has most preserved its Hispanic folk traditions.

But the most important part of the story of Hispanic theater in the United States is not one of folk theater but of the development and flourishing of a full-blown professional theater in the areas most populated by Hispanics: throughout the Southwest, New York, Florida, and even the Midwest. The origins of the Spanish-language professional theater in the United States are to be found in mid-nineteenth-century California, where troupes of itinerant players began touring from Mexico to perform melodramas accompanied by other musical and dramatic entertainments for the residents of the coastal cities that had developed from earlier Franciscan missions—San Francisco, Los Angeles, San Diego. (As early as the 1830s, professional troupes from Cuba also toured to theaters in New Orleans.) These three California cities were more accessible from Mexico than San Antonio, Texas, for instance, because of the regularity of steamship travel up and down the Pacific Coast.

There is evidence of plays being performed as early as 1789; the manuscript copy of a three-act cloak and dagger play, *Astucias por heredar un sobrino a su tío* (The Clever Acts of a Nephew in Order to Inherit His Uncle's Wealth) bears that date and shows evidence of having been toured through the California settlements. Records of professional theatrical performances become more numerous some decades later. In the 1840s various troupes of itinerant players visited the ranches and inns around the San Francisco and Monterey areas of northern California, performing in Spanish for both Spanish- and English-language audiences. During this time at least one semi-professional theater house existed in Los Angeles. In 1848 Antonio F. Coronel, later to become mayor of Los Angeles, opened a theater, Teatro Merced, that seated three hundred. In the following decades various other theaters opened to accommodate both Spanish- and English-language productions: Vicente Guerrero's Union Theater existed from 1852 to 1854, Abel Stearn's Hall from 1859 to 1875, and Juan Temple's Theater from 1859 to 1892. In the 1860s and 1870s the Hispanic community also frequented the Teatro Merced, Teatro Alarcón, and Turn Verein Hall. In the 1880s Spanish-language productions were even held in the Grand Opera House in Los Angeles.

An 1890s company of touring players.

By the 1860s the professional stage had become so established and important to the Spanish-speaking community that companies that once toured the Mexican Republic and abroad began to settle down as resident companies in California. Such was the case with the Compañía Española de la Familia Estrella, directed by the renowned Mexican actor Gerardo López del Castillo, in its choice of San Francisco for its home. The company was typical of those that toured interior Mexico in that it was composed of Mexican and Spanish players, was organized around a family unit into which López del Castillo had married, mostly staged Spanish melodrama, and held its performances on Sunday evenings. Each program was a complete evening's entertainment that included a three- or four-act drama; songs, dances, and recitations; and a one-act farce or comic dialog to close the performance. The full-length plays that were the heart of the program were mostly melodramas by peninsular Spanish authors such as José Zorrilla, Mariano José de Larra, and Manuel Bretón de los Herreros. Productions by this and the other companies that settled in or toured California were seen as wholesome entertainment appropriate for the whole family and a broad segment of the Hispanic community; not just the elite, subscribed and attended.

Among the twelve or fourteen companies that were resident or actively touring California during the 1870s and 1880s, the Compañía Dramática Española, directed by Pedro C. de Pellón, and the Compañía Española de Angel Mollá were two resident companies in Los Angeles that extended their tours to Baja, California and up to Tucson, Arizona; from there they would return to Los Angeles via stagecoach. During this time Tucson boasted two Spanish-language theater houses: Teatro Cervantes and Teatro Americano. In 1878 Pellón established himself permanently in Tucson where he organized the town's first group of amateur actors, Teatro Recreo. Thus, the 1870s mark Arizona's participation in Hispanic professional theater. It is in this decade as well that troupes began to tour the Laredo and San Antonio axis of Texas, first performing in Laredo and then San Antonio in open air markets, taverns, and later in such German American settings as Meunch Hall, Krish Hall, and Wolfram's Garden in San Antonio. At the turn of the century and afterward, companies touring from Mexico began making San Antonio and Laredo their home bases.

The last decade of the nineteenth century experienced a tremendous increase in Mexican theatrical activity in the border states. A growing number of companies that had previously only toured interior Mexico were now establishing regular circuits extending from Laredo to San Antonio and El Paso, through New Mexico and Arizona to Los Angeles, then up to San Francisco or down to San Diego. It was the advent of rail transportation and the automobile that extended the touring companies to smaller population centers after the turn of the century. Between 1900 and 1930, numerous Mexican theaters and halls were established to house Spanish-language performances all along this circuit to entertain the masses of immigrants leaving Mexico, especially during the Revolution. By 1910 even some smaller cities had their own Mexican theaters with resident stock companies. The more mobile tent theaters, circus theaters and smaller makeshift companies performed in rural areas and throughout the small towns on both sides of the Rio Grande Valley.

Theatrical activities expanded rapidly when thousands of refugees took flight from the Mexican Revolution and settled in the United States, from the border all the way up to the Midwest. During the decades of revolutionary upheaval, many of Mexico's greatest artists and their theatrical companies came to tour and/or take up temporary residence; however, some would never return to the homeland. Mexican and Spanish companies and an occasional Cuban, Argentine, or other Hispanic troupe toured the Southwest, but they found their most lucrative engagements in Los Angeles and San Antonio. They at times even crisscrossed the nation, venturing to perform for the Hispanic communities in New York, Tampa, and the Midwest. By the 1920s Hispanic theater was becoming big business, and important companies such as Spain's Compañía María Guerrero y Fernando Díaz de Mendoza had its coast-to-coast tours into major Anglo-American theaters booked by New York agents, such as Walter O. Lindsay. The company of the famed Mexican leading lady Virginia Fábregas was of particular importance in its frequent tours because it not only performed the latest serious works from Mexico City and Europe, but also because some of the troupe members occasionally defected to form their own resident and touring companies in the Southwest. Virginia Fábregas was also important in encouraging the development of

La Sacerdotiza del Arte Celebra Esta Noche su Función de Gala.

Desea El H(
tes, Corres
Bondadoso

¡True translation filed

LOS FRANCESES BC
ODESA.

Con los cañones de un
rra, barrieron a los rc
puerto eslav

ODESA, diciembre :
do una gran batalla en
la ciudad, la que duró
8.000 soldados francese
te en ella. Por la par
grandes cañones de un
rra francés, "Justicia,
bombardeando hasta c
blicano.
    Todavía es imposibl
bajas o determinar el c
de ningún barrio de la c
cepción del frente.

    LONDRES, diciembr
por de guerra inglés C
turado dos destroyers
el Báltico oriental. U
taba empeñado en bom
queño caserío en la vo
val. Fueron hechos j
oficiales y tripulacio
destroyers, sin que en
hayan registrado bajas
t estaba mandado p
bertram S. Thesiger.

SRA. VIRGINIA FABREGAS, distinguida Primera Actriz Mexicana,
que celebra su función de beneficio y despedida en el Lyceum Hall, la noche
del Martes 31 de Dicimbre.

Los Ferroc
cia

Entrevistando a Virginia.

Antes de ayer, en su alojamiento nocía de nombre.   Hablamos tam-

En nuestro número
cuenta brevemente del

Virginia Fábregas.

local playwrights in Los Angeles by buying the rights to their works and integrating the plays into her repertoire.

The two cities with the largest Mexican populations, Los Angeles and San Antonio, became theatrical centers, the former also feeding off the important film industry in Hollywood. In fact, Los Angeles became a manpower pool for Hispanic theater. Actors, directors, technicians, and musicians from throughout the Southwest, New York, and the whole Hispanic world were drawn there looking for employment. Both Los Angeles and San Antonio went through a period of intense expansion and building of new theatrical facilities in the late teens and early twenties. Los Angeles was able to support five major Hispanic theater houses with programs that changed daily. The theaters and their peak years were Teatro Hidalgo (1911–1934), Teatro Mexico (1927–1933), Teatro Capitol (1924–1926), Teatro Zendejas (later Novel; 1919–1924) and Teatro Principal (1921–1929). There were as many as twenty other theaters operating at one time or another during the same time period. San Antonio's most important house was the Teatro Nacional, built in 1917 and housing live productions up through the Depression. Its splendor and elite status were not shared by any of the other fifteen or so theaters that housed Spanish-language productions in San Antonio during this period. While it is true that in the Southwest, as in Mexico, Spanish drama and *zarzuela*—the Spanish national version of operetta—dominated the stage up until the early 1920s, the clamor for plays written by Mexican playwrights had increased to such an extent that by 1923 Los Angeles had developed into a center for Mexican play writing unparalleled in the history of Hispanic communities in the United States. While continuing to consume plays by Spanish peninsular authors such as Jacinto Benavente, José Echegaray, Gregorio Martínez-Sierra, Manuel Linares Rivas, and the Alvarez Quintero brothers, the Los Angeles Mexican community and its theaters encouraged local writing by offering cash prizes in contests, lucrative contracts, and lavish productions. Various impresarios of the Spanish-language theaters maintained this tradition throughout the 1920s, offering at times as much as two hundred dollars in prize money to the winners of the playwriting contests. It was often reported in the newspapers of the time that the Hispanic theaters drew their largest crowds every time they featured plays by local writers.

The period from 1922 to 1933 saw the emergence and box-office success of a cadre of playwrights in Los Angeles composed mainly of Mexican theatrical expatriates and newspapermen. At the center of the group were four playwrights whose works not only filled the theaters on Los Angeles' Main Street, but also had contracts throughout the Southwest and in Mexico: Eduardo Carrillo, an actor; Adalberto Elías González, a novelist; Esteban V. Escalante, a newspaperman and theatrical director; and Gabriel Navarro, poet, novelist, composer, orchestra director, columnist for *La Opinión* newspaper, and editor of the magazine *La Revista de Los Angeles*. There were at least twenty other locally residing writers who saw their works produced on the professional stage, not to mention the scores of authors of vaudeville revues and lighter pieces.

The serious full-length plays created by these authors addressed the situation of Mexicans in California on a broad, epic scale, often in plays based on the history of the Mexican-Anglo struggle in California. Eduardo Carrillo's *El Proceso de Aurelio Pompa* (The Trial of Aurelio Pompa) dealt with the unjust trial and sentencing of a Mexican immigrant; it was performed repeatedly on the commercial stage and at community-based fundraising events. Gabriel Navarro's *Los Emigrados* (The Emigrees) and *El Sacrificio* (The Sacrifice) dealt, respectively, with Mexican expatriate life in Los Angeles during the Revolution and with the history of California around 1846, the date of the outbreak of the Mexican-American War.

By far the most prolific and respected of the Los Angeles playwrights was Adalberto Elías González, whose works were performed not only locally but also throughout the Southwest and Mexico, as well as made into movies and translated into English. His works that saw the light on the stages of Los Angeles ran the

El Autor de 'Ramona'

: de Ramona," ver-
Adalberto Elías Gon-
-ada a la escena por
probablemente la últi-
ro México, el día de
mismo reparto que se
: su triunfal estreno,
de las obras más gus-
tyan puesto en el re-
léxico desde que éste
as al público mexica-
iguiente se le consi-
de los más rotundos
nporada. Como obra
le decirse sin vacila-
sido la mejor.
que durante las tres
s que ya cuenta se ha
de público el éxpre-
amos seguros de que
tecerá en la función
:s son éxitos que con
reflejan en la taqui-
caso, según sabemos,
han separado sus lo-
rosas de que les suce-
epresentaciones ante-
nan podido ganar ac-
:n virtud de que no
btener a tiempo sus

RMACIONES

ho días será ministra-
to de Confirmación a
s mexicanos mayores
hayan hecho su pri-

Irá lugar en la Igle-
Señora de Los Ange-
ñor Obispo de la Dió
ila don José de Jesús
que lo administre, co-
. 3 de la tarde.

**ADALBERTO Elías Gonzá-
lez, autor de "Los Ámores de
Ramona", la ccmedia dramática que tan sonoros éxitos ha
obtenido, y que se representa-
rá mañana, por última vez, en
el teatro México.**

27 de Octubre de 19:
un plantel educativo (
Maravilla Park, a inici
fuerzos del señor Pro
.onio Flores.
    En el lugar esa esc
tado un árbol como
ese acontecimiento y
transladará la comitiv
situada en el cruzami
lles Carmelita y Bro
    Esta escuela, hay
está siendo sostenida
tectora Latina y esta
es la que ha organiza
ción de aniversario.
tes el vice-cónsul de M
Quiñones, el Cónsul (
Manuel Ayulo y el S
Confederación de Soci
nas, así como el conoc
Emeterio Rentería Al
    El programa será e
    1o.—Recepción de S
vitados de honor.
    2o.—Lectura del in
por el Sr. Prof. Flores
    3o.— Número de Can
rita Ofelia de la Cruz.
    4o.— Discurso por (
Rentería Alvarez.
    5o.—Número de bail
Esperanza de la Cruz
piano por su hermanit
    6o.—Presentación de
tantes del Comité Edu
y Honorífica del mism
mo a los niños repre
escuela mexicana de (
    7o.—Poesía recitada
blo Lara.
    8o.—Música.
    9o.— Número a car
Cultural Independiente
es a cargo del mismo
res.
    10 — Recitación por
lón Medina alumno d(
    11 —Número de bail
Adelita Jacobo y la p
tes de Watts.

Adalberto Elías González.

gamut from historical drama to dime-novel sensationalism. The most famous of
his plays, *Los Amores de Ramona* (The Loves of Ramona), was a stage adaptation
of Helen Hunt Jackson's novel about early California, *Ramona: A Story*; it broke
all box-office records when it was seen by more than fifteen thousand people after
only eight performances, and soon it became a regular item in many repertoires

in the Southwest. Two of González's other plays dealt with the life and culture of Mexicans in California: *Los Misioneros* (The Missionaries) and *Los expatriados* (The Expatriates). Probably his second most successful work was the sensationalistic *La Asesino del Martillo o la Mujer Tigresa* (The Assassin with the Hammer or Tiger Woman), based on a real-life crime story reported in the newspapers in 1922 and 1923. A dozen other plays dealt with love triangles and themes from the Mexican Revolution, including *La Muerte de Francisco Villa* (The Death of Francisco Villa) and *El Fantasma de la Revolución* (The Ghost of the Revolution).

Adalberto Elías González and these other authors addressed the need of their audiences to relive their history on both sides of the border and to revive the glories of their own language and cultural tradition. This they did with the decorum and professionalism befitting the type of family entertainment that the community leaders believed served the purposes of reinforcing Hispanic culture and morality while resisting assimilation to Anglo-American culture. With the rise of vaudeville and the greater access of working-class people to theatrical entertainment, vaudeville-type revues and variety shows became increasingly popular and gradually displaced more serious theater. However, Mexican vaudeville and musical comedy did not avoid the themes that were so solemnly treated in three-act dramas. Rather, the Mexican stage had developed the *revista*—a musical revue influenced by the Spanish *zarzuela*, the French *revue*, and vaudeville that had taken on its own character in Mexico as a format for piquant political commentary and social satire. Also, like the zarzuela, which celebrated Spanish regional customs, music, and folklore, the Mexican revista created and highlighted the character, music, dialects, and folkore of the various Mexican regions. Under the democratizing influence of the Mexican Revolution, the *revista* highlighted the life and culture of the working classes. During the Revolution, the *revista política* in particular rose to prominence on Mexico City stages, but later all revista forms degenerated into a loose vehicle for musical and comedic performance in which typical regional and underdog characters, such as the *pelado* (literally, skinned or penniless), often improvised a substantial part of the action.

The Los Angeles stages hosted many of the writers and stars of revistas that had been active during the time of formation of the genre in Mexico, including Leopoldo Beristáin and Guz Aguila. The theatres of Los Angeles and the Southwest staged most of the revistas that were popular in Mexico and that were of historical importance for the development of the genre. Such works as *El Tenorio Maderista* (The Maderist Tenorio), *El País de los Cartones* (The Country Made of Boxes), *La Ciudad de los Volcanes* (The City of Volcanoes), and numerous others were continuously repeated from Los Angeles to Laredo. Such innovators of the genre as Guz Aguila were for a time a perennial attraction at the Los Angeles theaters. Even important composers of scores for the revistas, such as Lauro D. Uranga, graced the Los Angeles Hispanic stages. With their low humor and popular music scores, the revistas in Los Angeles articulated grievances and poked fun at both the U.S. and Mexican governments. The Mexican Revolution was satirically reconsidered over and over again in Los Angeles from the perspective of the expatriates, and Mexican American culture was contrasted with the "purer" Mexican version. This social and political commentary was carried out although both audiences and performers were mostly immigrants and thus liable to deportation or repatriation. The Los Angeles writers and composers were serving a public that was hungry to see itself reflected on stage, an audience whose interest was piqued by revistas relating to current events, politics, and the conflict of cultures that were produced while living in the Anglo-dominated environment. The revistas kept the social and political criticism leveled at the authorities, both Mexican or American, within the light context of music and humor in such pieces as Guz Aguila's *México para los Mexicanos* (Mexico for the Mexicans) and *Los Angeles Vacilador* (Swinging Los Angeles), Gabriel Navarro's *La Ciudad de Irás y No Volverás* (The City of You Go There Never to Return), and Don Catarino's *Los Efectos de la Crisis* (The Effects of the Depression), *Regreso a Mi Tierra* (The Return to My Country), *Los repatriados* (The Repatriated), *Whiskey, Morfina y Marihuana* and *El Desterrado* (The Exiled One).

It is in the revista we find a great deal of humor based on the culture shock typically derived from following the misad-

Gabriel Navarro.

ventures of naive, recent immigrants from Mexico who have difficulty in getting accustomed to life in the big Anglo-American metropolis. Later on in the 1920s, and when the Depression and repatriation take hold, the theme of culture shock is converted to one of outright cultural conflict. At that point Mexican nationalism becomes more intensified as anti-Mexican sentiments become more openly expressed in the Anglo-American press as a basis for taking Mexicans off the welfare rolls and deporting them. In the revista, the Americanized, or *agringado* and *renegado*, become even more satirized and the barbs aimed at American culture become even sharper. It is also in the revista that the raggedly dressed underdog, the *pelado*, comes to the fore with his low-class dialect and acerbic satire. A forerunner of characters like famed movie comic character Cantinflas, the pelado really originates in the humble tent theaters that evolved in Mexico and existed in the Southwest of the United States until the 1950s. With roots in the circus clown tradition, and a costume and dialect that embody poverty and marginality, the pelado was free to improvise and exchange witticisms with his audiences that often embodied working-class distrust of societal institutions and the upper classes. Although the pelado or *peladito*, as he was affectionately called, was often criticized for his low humor and scandalous language, theater critics today consider the character to be a genuine and original Mexican contribution to the history of theater.

The most important author of revistas was Antonio Guzmán Aguilera, who went by the stage name of Guz Aguila. Guz Aguila settled in Los Angeles expressly to become a theater impresario and movie producer. Instead, he became

Los Angeles's El Teatro California. Photo by Francisco Blasco.

a journalist for *El Heraldo de México* newspaper, but still managed to tour his theatrical company as far south as Mexico City and as far west as San Antonio. Guz Aguila had risen to fame in Mexico City as a newspaperman and prolific revista author, but as a result of a falling out with President Alvaro Obregón and subsequent imprisonment, he went into exile in Los Angeles in 1924. Guz Aguila's production has been estimated as high as five hundred theatrical works, none of which were ever published; but it is certain that many of his revistas were reworked, renamed, and recycled to accommodate different current events, locations, and audiences. In Los Angeles in 1924, Guz Aguila was given a contract that paid $1000 per month to write for the Teatro Hidalgo. In a June 7, 1924 interview for *El Heraldo de México*, Aguila stated that the Hidalgo had also formed a company of thirty performers for him and commissioned special scenery and costumes. In the same interview, he revealed that his personal motto was "*corrigat riendo mores*"—that is, customs are corrected through laughter. And an abundance of laughter, color, patriotic symbolism, and naturalism is what Guz Aguila gave his audiences by pulling out and producing his most famous and time-proven revistas: *Alma Tricolor* (Three-Colored Soul), *La Huerta de Don Adolfo* (Don Adolfo's Garden; a reference to President Adolfo de la Huerta), and *Exploración Presidencial* (A Presidential Exploration). After presenting many of his well-known works, Aguila began to produce new revistas based on culture and events in Los Angeles: *Los Angeles Vacilador* (Swinging Los Angeles), *Evite Peligro* (Avoid Danger), and *El Eco de México* (The Echo from Mexico). Guz Aguila returned to the stages of Mexico City in 1927 but never regained the level of success that he had previously experienced there. He continued to tour the republic and the southwestern United States in the years that followed.

Unlike Los Angeles, the stages of San Antonio did not attract or support the development of local playwrights; and while they hosted many of the same theatrical companies and performers as did the California stages, theater in the Alamo city did not support as many resident companies. To be sure, as stated above, there were many Mexican theater houses and various stock and resident companies, many of which used San Antonio as a base from which to launch tours of Texas and both sides of the Rio Grande Valley. While the story of Los Angeles's Hispanic theater is one of proliferation of Spanish-language houses, companies, and playwrights, the story of San Antonio is one that illustrates the persistence of resident companies, actors, and directors in keeping Hispanic drama alive in community and church halls after being dislodged by vaudeville and the movies from the professional theater houses during the Depression. San Antonio's is also the story of the rise of a number of vaudevillians to national and international prominence. Finally, San Antonio also became a center for another type of theater, one that served an exclusively working-class audience: tent theater.

In San Antonio, Los Angeles, and throughout the Southwest, the Great Depression and the forced and voluntary repatriation of Mexicans not only depopulated the communities but also the theaters. Theater owners and impresarios could no longer afford to present full companies, accompanied by orchestras and technicians; the economic advantage of showing movies was devastating to live theater. After receiving the triple blow of Depression, repatriation, and cinema, the Hispanic theater industry continued to writhe and agonize from 1930 until the middle of the decade, when only a few hardy troupes acquiesced to entertaining briefly between films, donated their art to charity, toured rural areas in tent theaters, struck out to perform for New York's growing Hispanic population, or simply returned to Mexico. Many were the artists from Los Angeles to the Midwest who stubbornly continued to perform—only now their art was staged in church and community halls for little or no pay in the service of community and church charities, which were especially numerous during the Depression.

There was no more heroic battle waged anywhere than that of the San Antonio resident directors and their companies to keep their art alive and in service of the communities. Directors Manuel Cotera, Bernardo Fougá, and Carlos Villalongín, along with such stars as Lalo Astol and María Villalongín, continued to present the same theatrical fare in the same professional manner in church and neighborhood halls throughout San Antonio and on tour to Austin, Dallas, Houston, Laredo, and smaller cities and towns during the 1930s. At the same time, to fill the vacuum that had been created with the return of many performers to Mexico and the cessation of tours from there, amateur theatrical groups began to spring up and proliferate, often instructed and directed by theater professionals; frequently these groups also used the church halls and auditoriums for their rehearsals and performances. It is worth reemphasizing that most of the professional and community groups did not exist to present religious drama; but church facilities and church sponsorship were often offered because the theater and most of the serious plays presented were seen as wholesome entertainment and instruction in language and culture for the youth of the community, which was even more cut off during the Depression from the culture of interior Mexico.

Besides providing the environment for this important community theater movement, San Antonio was also the center for the Hispanic circus and tent-theater industry in the United States. Circus and theater had been associated since colonial days in Mexico, but during the nineteenth century there developed a humble, poor man's circus that traveled the poor neighborhoods of Mexico City and the provinces. It would set up a small tent, or *carpa*, to house its performances; later these theaters were called carpas by extension of the term. It was in the carpa during the Revolution that the Mexican national clown, the pelado, developed; in general, besides offering all types of serious and light theatrical fare, the carpa came to be known for satirical revistas that often featured the antics and working-class philosophy and humor of the pelado. The carpas functioned quite often as popular tribunals, repositories of folk wisdom, humor, and music, and were incubators of Mexican comic types and stereotypes. They continued to function in this way in the Southwest, but particularly in San Antonio, which had become, especially after the outbreak of the Revolution, a home base and wintering ground for many of the carpas.

Probably because of their small size, bare-bones style, and organization around a family unit, the carpas could manage themselves better than large circuses or theatrical companies. Furthermore, they were able to cultivate smaller audiences in the most remote areas. The carpas became in the Southwest an important Mexican American popular culture institution. Their comic routines became a sounding board for the culture conflict that Mexican Americans felt in language usage, assimilation to American tastes and lifestyles, discrimination in the United States, and *pocho*, or Americanized status, in Mexico. Out of these types of conflicts in popular entertainment arose the stereotype of the *pachuco*, a typically Mexican American figure. Finally, the carpas were a refuge for theatrical and circus people of all types during the Depression, repatriation, and World War II. More important, their cultural arts were preserved by the carpas for the post-war generation that was to forge a new relationship with the larger American culture.

From the turn of the century through World War II, San Antonio was home to many a carpa. Two of the most well-known resident tent shows of San Antonio were the Carpa García and the Carpa Cubana, whose descendants still reside in the Alamo city. The Carpa García was founded by Manuel V. García, a native of Saltillo, Mexico. He relocated his family to San Antonio in 1914, after having performed with the Carpa Progresista in Mexico. Featured in his Carpa García was the famed *charro* (Mexican-style cowboy) on the tightrope act. One of the comic actors of the Carpa, Pedro González González ("Ramirín"), later had a successful career in Hollywood westerns. Other members of the family performed magic, ventriloquism, song and dance, and comedy. The highlight of the show was the *peladito* Don Fito. As played by Manuel's son Rodolfo, Don Fito became a typical wise guy from the streets of West Side San Antonio, speaking an urban Mexican American dialect, or *caló*. He also satirized the language of Mexicans and pachucos and often engaged audiences in repartee. The Carpa García at times also hosted Don Lalo (Lalo Astol) and the famous singer Lydia Mendoza and her family of performers. Daughter Esther García, an acrobat, went on to the center ring of the Barnum and Bailey Circus. By 1947 the Carpa García decided to retire after a final run-in with the fire department about making its tents fireproof.

In Latin American and U.S. circus history, the Abreu name appears frequently at the end of the nineteenth century and beginning of the twentieth. The Abreu company, directed by Virgilio Abreu, owned and operated the Carpa Cubana— also known as the Cuban Show and the Circo Cubano—that made San Antonio its home base in the 1920s and 1930s. But before that, various members of the family had appeared as acrobats, tumblers, and wire walkers with such famous shows as Orrin, Barnum and Bailey, Ringling Brothers, John Robinson, and Sells-Floto. In San Antonio, the Cuban circus included trapeze artists, rope walkers, jugglers, clowns, dancers, and its own ten-piece band. Although based in San Antonio, the company toured as far as California and central Mexico by truck and train, but mostly limited its tours to the Rio Grande Valley in the south and Austin to the north during the 1930s. Virgilio Abreu and his wife Federica owned a home on the west side of San Antonio but lived in tents with the rest of the company when on the road. The company would tour for four or five months in the spring until summer heat set in and then not leave San Antonio again until the fall, returning home for the Christmas season. The members of the company would also do variety acts in the local San Antonio cinemas.

New York City

It was during the 1890s in New York that regular amateur and semi-professional shows began as the Hispanic immigrant community, made up mostly of Spaniards and Cubans, grew in size—reflecting once again the patterns of economic disruption and internal conflict in the homeland and immigration to the United States that would be repeated time and again during the development of U.S. Hispanic communities and culture. Of course, the diaspora brought on by the Mexican Revolution (1910) more than any other factor characterized the theater in the Southwest during the first half of the twentieth century. In the second half of the nineteenth century, New York became an organizing and staging center for Cuban and Puerto Rican expatriates seeking the independence of their homelands from Spain. Later in the century heavy migration of Puerto Ricans, now U.S. citizens, and the Puerto Rican nationalist movement in pursuit of independence from the U.S. would also manifest itself on the city's Hispanic stages, as would the efforts by exiled Spanish Republicans fighting fascism during the Spanish Civil War in the mid-thirties.

Documentary evidence of the Hispanic stage in New York begins in 1892 with the *La Patria* newspaper reporting on the dramatic activities of actor Luis Baralt and his company. Until 1898, the year of the Spanish-American War, this newspaper, published by José Martí to support the Cuban revolutionary movement, occasionally covered performances by Baralt and his troupe, which included both amateurs and actors with professional experience. The company had an irregular performance schedule in such auditoriums and halls as the Berkeley Lyceum and the Carnegie Lyceum, where it would present standard Spanish melodramas as well as Cuban plays such as *De lo Vivo a lo Pintado* (From Life to the Painted Version) by Tomás Mendoza, a deceased hero of the revolutionary war, and *La Fuga de Evangelina* (The Escape of Evangelina) by an unknown author, the dramatization of the escape from prison by a heroine of the independence movement. The last performance reported took place at the Central Opera House on January 16, 1899; funds were raised for the sepulcher of the great Cuban philosopher-poet and revolutionary, José Martí. After this last performance there is no further mention in surviving newspapers of theatrical performances in Spanish until the advent of a truly professional stage some seventeen years later in 1916. (It bears mention that the Spanish-language presses of New York had been publishing plays, both locally written and imported, since the 1830s, but there is as yet insufficient information about their staging.)

Unlike the theatrical experience of Los Angeles, San Antonio, and Tampa, in the mid-teens of the new century, the New York Hispanic community could not claim any theaters of its own. Rather, a number of impresarios would rent available theaters around town, but mainly those located in the Broadway area, from midtown Manhattan up to the eighties: Bryant Hall, Park Theater, Amsterdam Opera House, Leslie Theater, Carnegie Hall, etc. The first impresario to lead companies on this odyssey through New York theater houses was a Spanish actor-singer of zarzuelas who had made his debut in Mexico City in 1904: Manuel Noriega. Noriega was a tireless and enthusiastic motivator of Hispanic theater and, for a number of years, had practically the sole responsibility for maintaining Spanish-language theatrical seasons. Noriega's genius as a comic actor could always be relied upon to bring in audiences during difficult financial straits. Noriega found his way to New York in 1916 from the Havana stage to perform at the Amsterdam Theater. That very same year he founded the first of his many theatrical companies, Compañía Dramática Española, which performed at the Leslie Theater from June to September and then went on to other theaters in the city. In Noriega's repertoire was the typical fare of Spanish comedies, zarzuelas and comic afterpieces. During the first two years, Noriega had difficulty in getting the Hispanic community out to the theater, so much so that a community organization, the Unión Benéfica Española, had to have a fundraiser for his poverty-stricken actors. It was in 1918 at the Amsterdam Opera House that Noriega's company began finding some stability, performing each Sunday, with an occasional special performance on Thursdays. By November of that year the company was so successful that it added matinee showings on Sundays, and by December it began advertising in the newspaper for theatrical artists. As Noriega hired more actors—mostly Cuban, Spanish, and Mexican—the nature of the company began to change, at times highlighting Galician or Catalonian works, at others Cuban blackface comedy. In 1919 Noriega formed a partnership with Hispanic, Greek, and Anglo-American businessmen to lease the Park Theater and make it the premier Hispanic house, rebaptizing it El Teatro Español. After a short performance run, all the parties concerned bailed out of the bad business deal; the Noriega company went on to other theaters to perform in its usual manner until 1921, when Noriega slipped from sight.

The 1920s saw a rapid expansion of the Hispanic stage in New York, which was now regularly drawing touring companies from Cuba, Spain, Mexico, and the Southwest and which had also developed many of its own resident companies. Most of the companies followed the pattern of renting theaters for their runs and relocating afterward to different neighborhoods or to Brooklyn, Bayonne, Jersey City, or even Philadelphia. Beginning in 1922, the Hispanic community was able to lay claim to a number of houses on a long-term basis, at times even renaming the theaters in honor of the Hispanic community. The first two theaters that began to stabilize Hispanic theater culture in New York were the Dalys and the Apollo theaters. After 1930, the Apollo no longer offered Hispanic fare; the baton then passed in 1931 to the San José/Variedades, in 1934 to the Campoamor, and finally in 1937 to the most important and longest-lived house in the history of Hispanic theater in New York: El Teatro Hispano.

As in the Southwest, these houses also experienced the same evolution of Hispanic theater: melodrama and zarzuela reigned at the beginning of the 1920s to be gradually displaced by musical revues and vaudeville, while in the 1930s artists of serious drama took refuge in clubs and mutualist societies—rarely in church auditoriums, as in the Southwest. However, the kind of musical revue that was to reign supreme in New York was not the Mexican revista, but the *obra bufa cubana,* or Cuban blackface farce, which featured the stock character types of the *negrito* (blackface), *mulata,* and *gallego* (Galician) and relied heavily on Afro-Cuban song and dance and improvised slapstick comedy. Like the revistas, the *obras bufas cubanas* often found inspiration in current events, neighborhood gossip, and even politics. The most famous of all the bufos, Arquímides Pous, who played in New York in 1921, was the creator of more than two hundred of these short works, many of which were kept alive by his followers after his death in Puerto Rico in 1926. Pous, who always played the negrito, was famous for his social satire and especially his attacks on racism. The bufo genre itself had been influenced in its development during the second half of the nineteenth century by the *buffes parisiennes* and the Cuban circus. Under the Spanish in Cuba, the bufos were particularly repressed for being native Cuban, causing many of them to go into exile in Puerto Rico, Santo Domingo, Mexico, and the United States.

Beginning in 1932 the Mt. Morris Theater (inaugurated in 1913) began serving the Hispanic community under a series of impresarios and names, first as the Teatro Campoamor, then the Teatro Cervantes, and, on August 19, 1937, finally metamorphosing into El Teatro Hispano, which would live on into the 1950s. A somewhat mysterious Mexican impresario who never used his first names, Señor del Pozo surfaced at the head of a group of backers made up of Hispanic and Jewish businessmen. Del Pozo administered the theater and directed the house orchestra. Under Del Pozo, besides movies, the Teatro Hispano offered three daily shows at 2:00, 5:30, and 9:00 P.M., except Sundays when four shows were given. To maintain the interest of his working-class audiences, Del Pozo instituted a weekly schedule that included bonuses and surprises: on Tuesdays and Fridays bunco was played at the theater and prizes were awarded, Wednesday audiences participated in talent shows that were broadcast over radio WHOM, on Thursdays gifts and favors were distributed to audiences, and on Saturday mornings there was a special children's show. There were also occasional beauty contests, turkey raffles, and such. Weekly programs changed on Friday evenings and were billed as debuts. Del Pozo used the radio, his weekly playbills, and personal appearances to promote the theater as a family institution and himself as a great paternal and kindly protector of the community.

Upon El Teatro Hispano's opening in August 1937, Del Pozo immediately began to elaborate the formula of alternating shows relating to the diverse Hispanic nationalities represented in the community. For one week he played to the Puerto Ricans with the revue *En las Playas de Borinquen* (On the Shores of Puerto Rico); he followed in September with an Afro-Caribbean revue *Fantasía en Blanco y Negro* (Fantasy in Black and White) and then *De México Vengo* (I Come from Mexico), then the Compañía de Comedias Argentinas, then a week celebrating Puerto Rico's historic proclamation of independence, El Grito de Lares. By the

New York's El Teatro Hispano.

end of September Del Pozo was again announcing Cuban week, featuring a *Cuba Bella* (Beautiful Cuba) revue. Each week a movie was shown to coincide with the country featured in the revue or plays.

In the months and years that ensued, numerous revues and an occasional zarzuela were staged, always balancing out the ethnic nationality represented. The Puerto Rican negrito Antonio Rodríguez and the Cuban negrito Edelmiro Borras became very popular and were ever-present. The cast at the Teatro Hispano was constantly being reinforced by refugees from the Spanish Civil War, such as Rosita Rodrigo of the Teatro Cómico de Barcelona, and artists from the failing stages of the Southwest, such as La Chata Noloesca. By 1940 the Teatro Hispano had fixed its relationship to the predominantly working-class community, which by now was becoming Puerto Rican in majority.

The Teatro Hispano and the other theaters did not sponsor playwriting contests nor support the development of a local dramatic literature as did the theaters in Los Angeles. While the dramatic activity was intense in New York City, the Big Apple did not support a downtown center where five or six major Hispanic houses located side by side competed with each other on a daily basis, as did the theaters in Los Angeles. The community of Hispanic immigrants in New York was not cognizant of a resident Hispanic tradition, as were the communities in the Southwest. And, while the relationship between journalism and playwriting had been well established in Mexico and the Southwest, this does not seem to have been the case in Cuba, Puerto Rico, or Spain. Also, many playwrights had been drawn to Los Angeles to work in the Hispanic film industry. Furthermore, the New York Hispanic public was not as large as Los Angeles' during the 1920s and could not support so large a business as the theater represented in the City of Angels.

By far the most productive playwrights and librettists in New York were the

Cubans, especially those riding the crest of popularity of the irreverent, bawdy, satirical *obras bufas cubanas*. Of these, the most prolific and popular were Alberto O'Farrill and Juan C. Rivera. The former was a successful blackface comic and literary personality, who edited the weekly *Gráfico* newspaper, and produced a number of zarzuelas and *obras bufas cubanas* based on Afro-Cuban themes. All of them debuted at the Apollo Theater. Juan C. Rivera was a comic actor who often played the role of the *gallego* and is known to have written both melodramas and revistas. Only a few of the works by these authors are known by name; it is assumed that they produced a considerable body of work to be staged by the companies in which they acted.

While it is true that Cubans and Spaniards made up the majority of theater artists in New York City and that their works dominated the stages of the times, it is also true that Puerto Rican drama emerged at this time and, it seems, accounts for a more serious and substantial body of literature. Two of the first Puerto Rican playwrights appear to have been socialists whose dramas supported the Spanish Republican cause and working-class movements: José Enamorado Cuesta (1892–1976) and Franca de Armiño (a pseudonym). Of the former, all that is known is that *La Prensa* on May 22, 1937, called him a revolutionary writer when it covered his play *El Pueblo en Marcha* (The People on the March). Of Franca de Armiño, all we have is her published drama *Los Hipócritas* (The Hypocrites), whose notes and introduction reveal that she was the author of various other plays, essays, and poems, and that *Los Hipócritas* was first staged in 1933 at the Park Palace Theater. The play itself, which begins with the stock market crash, sets a Romeo-and-Juliet story to the background of the Spanish Civil War and the foreground of conflict between the workers and management at a shoe factory. While full of propaganda, Marxist theory, and stereotyped characters, *Los Hipócritas* is a gripping and entertaining play that reflects the tenor of the times.

While Franca de Armiño and José Enamorado Cuesta were calling for a workers' revolution, Gonzalo O'Neill was championing Puerto Rican nationalism and independence from the United States. Immediately upon graduation from Puerto Rico's Instituto Civil, O'Neill moved to New York, where he became a very successful businessman and somewhat of a protector and godfather to newly arrived Puerto Rican migrants. A published poet and literary group organizer as a youth in Puerto Rico, he continued his literary vocation in New York by writing poetry and plays, some of which he published. From his very first published dramatic work, *La indiana borinqueña* (The Indians of Puerto Rico, 1922), O'Neill revealed himself to be intensely patriotic and interested in Puerto Rican independence. His second published play, *Moncho Reyes* (1923), was a three-act biting satire of the current colonial government in Puerto Rico. Although both of these works enjoyed stage productions, it was his third play, *Bajo una sola bandera* (Under Just One Flag, 1928), which debuted at the Park Palace Theater in New York in 1928 and at the Teatro Municipal in San Juan in 1929, that deserves the greatest attention for its artistry and thought, making it a popular vehicle for the Puerto Rican nationalist cause. In *Bajo una sola bandera*, the political options facing Puerto Rico are personified in down-to-earth flesh-and-blood characters. The plot deals with the daughter of a middle-class Puerto Rican family residing in New York who must choose between a young American second lieutenant—the personification of the United States and military rule—and a young native

Puerto Rican, whom she really loves. Both of her parents oppose each other in their preferences. Of course, the Puerto Rican youth wins the day and the play ends with sonorous, patriotic verses that underline the theme of independence for Puerto Rico. Although O'Neill is sure to have written other plays, the only other title that is known, *Amoríos Borincanos* (Puerto Rican Episodes of Love), appeared at the Teatro Hispano in 1938; O'Neill was one of the investors in the Hispano.

Most of the other Puerto Rican and Hispanic playwrights of New York were minor in comparison to these and to the highly productive writers in Los Angeles. The true legacy of the New York Hispanic stage was its cosmopolitan nature and its ability to represent and solidify an ethnically diverse Hispanic community.

Tampa

In the late nineteenth century the Tampa area witnessed the transplant of an entire industry from abroad and the development of an Hispanic enclave that chose the theater as its favorite form of art and culture. To remove themselves from the hostilities attendant on the Cuban war for independence from Spain, to come closer to their primary markets and avoid import duties, and to try to escape the labor unrest that was endemic to this particular industry, various cigar manufacturers from Cuba began relocating to Tampa. In the swampy, mosquito-infested lands just east of Tampa, Ybor City was founded in 1886. By the 1890s the Spanish and Cuban tobacco workers had begun establishing mutual-aid societies and including theaters as centerpieces for the buildings they constructed to house these societies. Many of these theaters eventually hosted professional companies on tour from Cuba and Spain, but, more important, they became the forums where both amateurs and resident professionals would entertain the Hispanic community for more than forty years without interruption. These theaters were also the training grounds where numerous tobacco workers and other community people developed into professional and semiprofessional artists, some of whom were able to make their way to the Hispanic stages of New York, Havana, and Madrid. Also, Tampa played a key role in one of the most exciting chapters of American theater history: it was the site of the Federal Theater Project's only Hispanic company under the Works Progress Administration.

Unlike Los Angeles, San Antonio, and New York, there was very little truly commercial theatrical activity in the Tampa-Ybor City communities. The six most important mutual-aid societies—Centro Español, Centro Español de West Tampa, Centro Asturiano, Círculo Cubano, Centro Obrero, and Unión Martí-Maceo—each maintained a *comisión de espectáculos*, or show committee, to govern the use of their theaters, a task which included renting the theater to touring companies and others, scheduling events, hiring professional directors, scenery painters, and technicians, and even purchasing performance rights to theatrical works. Along with this committee, which obviously took on the theater management role, most of the societies also supported a *sección de declamación*, or amateur theatrical company, made up mostly of the society's members. For a good part of each year the company would rehearse on week nights and perform on

Tampa's El Centro Asturiano.

Sundays. For the most part, the audiences were made up of tobacco workers and their families. The tobacco workers prided themselves on their literary and artistic tastes; they were considered an intellectual or elite labor class that had gained an informal education from the professional *lectores*, or readers, they hired to read aloud to them from literary masterpieces, newspapers, and other matter while they rolled cigars. Neither the demanding audiences nor the managing committees would be satisfied by strictly amateurish renditions, especially since they could compare performances with those of the professional companies that often visited their theaters. It therefore became the custom to recruit and hire professional actors and directors from Havana to train and direct the resident *sección de declamación*, which was paid for its performances. Over the years numerous professional artists either settled in Tampa or were recruited to become part of the companies. Tampa's Hispanic societies also prepared such important actors as Manuel Aparicio, Cristino R. Inclán, and Velia Martínez, who later abandoned the cigar factories to dedicate themselves completely to the world of the footlights and marquees. By the 1920s a good number of the local artists considered themselves professionals and demanded reasonable salaries for their performances.

Of the six societies, the Centro Asturiano was the most important and the longest lived; in fact, it is still functioning today as a theater, hosting theater and even opera companies. While the Centro Español of Ybor City was the oldest society—it was founded in 1891, the Asturiano in 1902—and for a time the most prestigious, the Asturiano held the distinction of hosting in its 1200-seat, first-class auditorium some of the greatest names in Hispanic theater in the world and even opera companies from New York and Italy during the period before World War II. In addition, it was to the Centro Asturiano that Spain's first lady of the stage, María Guerrero, took her company in 1926. That was a stellar year in which, besides producing the works of its own stock company directed by Manuel Aparicio, the Asturiano also hosted the Manhattan Grand Opera Association. The

Tampa's Círculo Cubano.

socially progressive, even liberal, Centro Asturiano—it extended its membership to all Latins, even Cubans and Italians—held the further distinction of housing the only Spanish-language Federal Theater Project.

It was during the tenure of the Federal Theater Project (FTP), for eighteen months in 1936 and 1937, that the Centro Asturiano made American theater history by housing the only Hispanic unit of the WPA's national project. It is a chapter in which the two theatrical traditions, the Hispanic and the Anglo-American, which had existed side by side for so long, finally intersected to produce at times exciting theater but also examples of cultural misunderstanding. From the start the FTP administration's attitude seems to have been a model of condescension and, ultimately, the Hispanic unit had to disband because of the xenophobia in the U.S. Congress.

A unique theatrical experience was that of the Unión Martí-Maceo, Tampa's Afro-Cuban mutual-aid society, whose very existence resulted from the doubly segregationist forces of the Jim Crow South and Cuba's own racism. While the Unión hosted many of the same theater companies touring to Tampa and also sponsored performances by its own and the other society's *secciones de declamación*, the Unión's theatrical and cultural activities were rarely covered in the press, rarely attracted audiences from the Hispanic "white" population, and, on the whole, were hardly integrated into the social life of the Hispanic, the Anglo-American, or black communities. In the archives of the Unión, however, are plays and fragments of plays that provide some interesting glimpses into the nature of the theatrical performances of this society. Two of these works, a one-act play, *Hambre* (Hunger), and the obra bufa cubana, *Los Novios* (The Betrothed), are notable for their relevance to the social and economic ambience of the Martí-Maceo. *Hambre* is a gripping and angry social drama that protests the poverty and hunger suffered by the working class while the rich enjoy the life of luxury. *Los Novios*, a much lighter and more entertaining play with mistaken identities and ridiculously complex love triangles, also deals with the supposed trespassing of race and class barriers and miscegenation. A buffoon of a Galician servant and a negrito spread mistaken information about the landowner having illicitly fathered a mulata and the landowner's daughter being caught embracing a black. The play also includes a number of asides that elaborate on race relations; throughout, the negrito and the mulata maintain the greatest dignity in the play, with the upper class whites shown to be the most bungling and prejudiced. In the end, order is restored when everyone finds his rightful place and his rightful partner to marry. But the social satire from a black perspective is unmistakable.

Another society that offered a unique theatrical experience was the Centro Obrero, the headquarters for the Union of Tampa Cigarmakers, which served as a gathering place for workers and workers' culture. Through its various classes, workshops, publications, and activities, the Centro Obrero promoted unionism and, quite often, socialism. While the Centro Obrero also hosted touring and local companies and even frivolous shows of *obras bufas cubanas*, it is within its halls and auspices that plays were developed and shown that promoted workers' interests, using their dialect and ideology. In the Centro's weekly newspapers, *El Internacional* and *La Federación*, various of these plays were published, including *Julia y Carlota* (Julia and Carlota), in which Julia exhorts Carlota to break the bonds of family and religion that are meant to keep women in their place, oppressed, and divorced from politics so that they do not help to reform evil laws. Probably written by the most renowned feminist in Puerto Rican history, Luisa Capetillo, who worked and organized workers in the Tampa factories, the play is much like her other work, which appropriates an abbreviated melodramatic format to illustrate through dialog the solutions presented by anarchism and women's liberation. She self-published many of her plays in her book *La influencia de las ideas modernas* (The Influence of Modern Ideas). Other works were clearly agitational and propagandistic, attempting to inspire workers to action. Finally, the Centro Obrero went all out to support the Republican cause in the Spanish Civil War. It sponsored numerous fundraising performances of such plays as *Milicianos al Frente* (Militia to the Front), *Abajo Franco* (Down with Franco), and *Las Luchas de Hoy* (The Struggles of Today, 1916), all of unknown authorship.

There are many parallels that can be drawn between the Tampa Hispanic stage and the Hispanic theater as it flourished in the Southwest and New York: the relationship of the theater to politics and to patterns of immigration; the dominance of the Spanish zarzuela and melodrama, eventually ceding to more popular forms, such as the revista and the obra bufa cubana; the effects of the Depression; the role theater played in protecting Hispanic cultural values and the Spanish language and in the education of the youth; the isolation of Hispanic culture and theater from the larger society, etc. But Tampa's Hispanic theatrical experience was unique in that it provided a successful example of deep and lasting community support for theater arts, so deep and so strong that private enterprise could not compete with the efforts of the mutual aid societies. And because the Hispanic stage had become such a symbol of achievement, that legacy lives on today in the memory of the Tampeños and in the Hispanic theatrical groups that still exist there.

HISPANIC THEATER IN THE UNITED STATES: POST-WAR TO THE PRESENT

The Southwest

The postwar period in the Southwest has seen the gradual restoration of the amateur, semiprofessional, and professional stages in the Hispanic communities of the Southwest. From the 1950s on, repertory theaters have appeared through-

La Chata Noloesca (center).

out the Southwest to produce Latin American, Spanish, and American plays in Spanish translations. In San Antonio, the extraordinary efforts of such actors as Lalo Astol, La Chata Noloesca, and her daughter Velia Camargo were responsible for keeping plays and vaudeville routines alive in the communities, even if they had to be presented for free or at fundraisers. Actors like Lalo Astol made the transition to radio and television, usually as announcers, at times as writers and producers. Astol even wrote, directed, and acted in locally produced television drama during the 1950s and 1960s. Almost continuously during the war and through the 1960's, veteran actor-director Rafael Trujillo-Herrera maintained a theater group in Los Angeles made up of his drama students and professionals, who quite often performed at a small theater house that he bought, El Teatro Intimo.

While there are a few stories of valiant theater artists managing to keep Hispanic theater alive during the war and post-war years, in most cases the tale is of theater houses that once housed live performances becoming cinemas, or at least phasing out live performances during the war and through the 1950s by occasionally hosting small troupes of vaudevillians or subscribing to the extravagant *caravanas de estrellas*, or parades of recording stars, that were syndicated and promoted by the recording companies. Through these shows promenaded singers and matinee idols, with *peladitos* and other vaudevillians serving as masters of ceremonies and comic relief. Vestiges of this business strategy still survive today in the shows of Mexican recording and movie stars of the moment, which are now produced not at movie houses but at convention centers and sports and entertainment arenas of large capacity.

The most remarkable story of the stage in the Southwest, however, is the spontaneous appearance in 1965 of a labor theater in the agricultural fields under the directorship of Luis Valdez, and its creation of a full-blown theatrical movement that conquered the hearts and minds of artists and activists throughout the country. Under the leadership of Luis Valdez's El Teatro Campesino, for almost two decades Chicano theaters dramatized the political and cultural concerns of their communities while crisscrossing the states on tour. The movement, largely student- and worker-based, eventually led to professionalism, Hollywood and Broadway productions, and the creation of the discipline of Chicano theater at universities. In 1965 the modern Chicano theater movement was born when aspiring playwright, Luis Valdez, left the San Francsico Mime Troupe to join César Chávez in organizing farm workers in Delano, California. Valdez organized farm workers into El Teatro Campesino in an effort to popularize and raise funds for the grape boycott and farm worker strike. From the humble beginning of dramatizing the plight of farm workers, the movement grew to include small agitation and propaganda theater groups in communities and on campuses around the country and eventually developed into a total theatrical expression that would find resonance on the commercial stage and screen.

By 1968, Valdez and El Teatro Campesino had left the vineyards and lettuce fields in a conscious effort to create a theater for the Chicano nation, a people which Valdez and other Chicano organizers of the 1960's envisioned as working-class, Spanish-speaking or bilingual, rurally oriented, and with a very strong heritage of pre-Columbian culture. By 1970, El Teatro Campesino had pioneered and developed what would come to be known as *teatro chicano*, a style of agit-prop theater that incorporated the spiritual and presentational style of the Italian Renaissance *commedia dell' arte* with the humor, character types, folklore, and popular culture of the Mexican, especially as articulated earlier in the century by the vaudeville companies and tent theaters that had toured the Southwest.

Almost overnight, groups sprang up throughout the United States to continue along Valdez's path. In streets, parks, churches, and schools, Chicanos were spreading a newly found bilingual-bicultural identity through the *actos*, one-act pieces introduced by Valdez that explored all of the issues confronting Mexican Americans: the farm worker struggle for unionization, the Vietnam War, the drive for bilingual education, community control of parks and schools, the war against drug addiction and crime, and so forth.

El Teatro Campesino's *Los Vendidos* (The Sell-Outs), a farcical attack on political manipulation of Chicano stereotypes, became the most popular and imitated of the actos; it was performed by diverse groups from Seattle to Austin. The publication of *Actos by Luis Valdez y El Teatro Campesino* in 1971, which included *Los Vendidos*, placed a ready-made repertoire in the hands of

Scene from Luis Valdez's *El Fin del Mundo*, performed by El Teatro Campesino.

community and student groups and also supplied them with several theatrical and political canons:

1. Chicanos must be seen as a nation with geographic, religious, cultural, and racial roots in Aztlán. *Teatros* must further the idea of nationalism, and create a national theater based on identification with the Amerindian past.

2. The organizational support of the national theater would be from within, for "the *corazón de la Raza* (the heart of our people) cannot be revolutionized on a grant from Uncle Sam."

3. Most important and valuable of all was that "The *teatros* must never get away from La Raza. . . . If the Raza will not come to the theater, then the theater must go to the Raza. This, in the long run, will determine the shape, style, content, spirit, and form of *el teatro chicano*."

El Teatro Campesino's extensive touring, the publicity it gained from the farm worker struggle, and the publication of *Actos* all effectively contributed to the launching of a national teatro movement. It reached its peak in the summer of 1976 when five teatro festivals were held to commemorate the Anglo bicentennial celebration. The summer's festivals also culminated a period of growth that saw some of Campesino's followers reach sufficient esthetic and political maturity to break away from Valdez. Los Angeles's Teatro Urbano, in its mordant satire of American heroes, insisted on intensifying the teatro movement's radicalism in the face of the Campesino's increasing religious mysticism. Santa Barbara's El Teatro de la Esperanza was achieving perfection, as no other Chicano theater had, in working as a collective and in assimilating the teachings of Bertolt Brecht in their plays *Guadalupe* and *La víctima* (The Victim). San Jose's El Teatro de la Gente had taken the corrido-type acto, a structure that sets a mimic ballet to traditional Mexican ballads sung by a singer/narrator, and perfected it as its innovator, El Teatro Campesino, had never done. El Teatro Desengaño del Pueblo from Gary, Indiana, had succeeded in reviving the techniques of the radical theaters of the 1930's in their *Silent Partners*, an exposé of corruption in a local city's construction projects.

The greatest contribution of Luis Valdez and El Teatro Campesino was their inauguration of a true grass-roots theater movement. Following Valdez's direction, the university students and community people creating teatro held fast to the doctrine of never getting away from the *raza*, the grass-roots Mexican. In so doing they created the perfect vehicle for communing artistically within their culture and environment. At times they idealized and romanticized the language and the culture of the mexicano in the United States. But they had discovered a way to mine history, folklore, and religion for those elements that could best solidify the heterogeneous community and sensitize it as to class, cultural identity, and politics. This indeed was revolutionary. The creation of art from the folk materials of a people, their music, humor, social configurations, and environment, represented the fulfillment of Luis Valdez's vision of a Chicano national theater.

While Campesino, after leaving the farm worker struggle, was able to experiment and rediscover the old cultural forms—the carpas, the corridos, the pastorelas or shepherd's plays, the Virgin of Guadalupe plays, the peladito—it never fully succeeded in combining all of the elements it recovered and invented into a completely refined piece of revolutionary art. *La gran carpa de la familia Ras-cuachi* (The Tent of the Underdogs) was a beautiful creation, incorporating the spirit, history, folklore, economy, and music of *la raza*. However, its proposal for the resolution of material problems through spiritual means (a superimposed construct of Aztec mythology and Catholicism) was too close to the religious beliefs and superstitions that hampered *la raza*'s progress, according to many of the more radical artists and theorists of people's theater.

The reaction of critics and many Chicano theaters playing at the fifth Chicano theater festival in Mexico was so politically and emotionally charged that a rift developed between them and El Teatro Campesino that has never been healed. El Teatro Campesino virtually withdrew from the theater movement, and from that point on the Chicano theaters developed on their own, managing to exist as agitation and propaganda groups and rag-tag troupes until the end of the decade. The more successful theaters, such as El Teatro de la Esperanza, administered their own theater house, created play-writing workshops and took up leadership of TENAZ, the Chicano theater organization, while taking over El Teatro Campesino's former role as a national touring company. Other groups, such as Albuquerque's La Compañía, set down roots and became more of a repertory company. The decade of the 1980s saw numbers of Chicano theater groups disbanding, as some of their members became involved in local community theaters, with their own performance spaces and budgets supplied by state and local arts agencies. Thus, such companies as Houston's Teatro Bilingüe, San Antonio's Guadalupe Theater, and Denver's Su Teatro began serving their respective communities as stable, repertory companies. Other former Chicano theater artists successfully made the jump to television and movies, such as Luis Valdez himself. In fact, Valdez's play *Zoot Suit* had a successful two-year run in mainstream theaters in Los Angeles and made its way to a Broadway and a film version. Valdez followed up with stage and television productions of his play *Corridos* (Ballads) and then the overwhelming box-office success of his movie *La Bamba*. In 1994, Valdez also made a successful incursion into commercial television with his made-for-television movie, *The Cisco Kid*. Since then, Valdez has had numerous showings of his plays at mainstream regional theaters, such as Chicago's Goodman and San Diego's Globe, and El Teatro Campesino has continued to produce works by up-and-coming playwrights in their playhouse in San Juan Bautista. Other former Chicano theater directors, such as Jorge Huerta, became university professors of theater and directors of productions in such mainstream organizations as San Diego's Globe Theater. Thus, while the 1980s saw a disappearance of the grass-roots, guerrilla, and street theater movement among Chicanos, these were the years when greater professionalism took place and greater opportunity appeared for Chicano theater people to make a living from their art in community theaters, at universities, and even in the commercial media—the latter facilitated, of course, by the great rise of the Hispanic population and its spending power.

The decade of the 1980s also saw the emergence of a corps of Chicano and Latino playwrights in communities from coast to coast, as the repertory theaters in the Southwest, New York, and Miami began clamoring for works dealing with Hispanic culture and written in the language of Hispanics in the United States. Numerous playwriting labs, workshops, and contests, such as Joseph Papp's Festival Latino in New York, sprang up from New York to Los Angeles. In the mid-

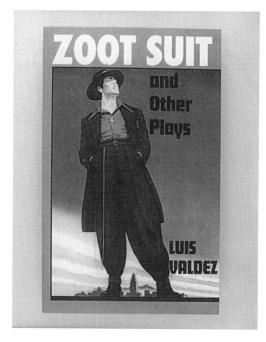

Cover of *Zoot Suit and Other Plays*, by Luis Valdez.

1980s a major funding organization, the Ford Foundation, took official interest in Hispanic theater and began funding the theater companies in a very significant way in an effort to stabilize them (including El Teatro de la Esperanza); Ford also began supporting efforts by mainstream companies and theaters, such as the South Coast Repertory Theater and the San Diego Repertory Theater, to produce Hispanic material and employ Hispanic actors. Furthermore, the Ford Foundation even funded the nation's leading Hispanic press, Arte Público Press, to publish a line of Hispanic play anthologies and collections of works by the leading Hispanic playwrights. By 1991 Arte Público Press had produced a new anthology of plays by Luis Valdez, Milcha Sánchez Scott, Severo Pérez, and others (*Necessary Theater: Six Plays of the Chicano Experience*, edited by Jorge Huerta), as well as anthologies of Hispanic women's plays, Cuban American plays, Puerto Rican plays, and collections by Luis Valdez, Dolores Prida, Edward Gallardo, Iván Acosta, and Carlos Morton. It also reissued its historic (1979) anthology that had been out of print for a decade: *Nuevos Pasos: Chicano and Puerto Rican Theater*, edited by Nicolás Kanellos and Jorge Huerta.

While the 1990s saw the stabilization of theater houses and companies in the Southwest—thanks to such funding agencies as the Ford Foundation as well as local and state arts councils that now recognized Hispanic arts—another outgrowth of Chicano theater became prominent: commercially viable improvisational theater companies. Two such Chicano companies, Culture Clash and Latins Anonymous, appeared in California to resounding success, with Culture Clash even sustaining a television series by the same name for two seasons in the early 1990s. Both groups, with seasoned veterans from El Teatro Campesino and other Chicano theaters, based their improvised comic sketches on satirizing stereotypes of Hispanics and poking fun at politics and current events. Latins Anonymous, with lead playwright Rick Najera, also satirized Hispanic media personalities (there were now enough Hispanic personalities in entertainment and national television for impressions of them to be recognized). Najera and a new breed of stand-up comedians were also increasingly appearing on television and even in their own HBO specials. Nevertheless, since very few playwrights have been able to achieve productions of their plays, a number of them, including Najera, Denise Chávez, and Ruby Nelda Pérez, have taken to the road to present one-man or one-woman shows.

Today only a vestige of *teatro chicano* survives among university groups. Most theater activity among Mexican Americans—as among Puerto Rican, Cubans, and other Latinos—revolves around the production of plays from the entire Hispanic world in Spanish and/or English, as well as the production of original plays by individual Latinos. Only Valdez has remained somewhat true to the *acto* form, but he has expanded and deepened it to hold an audience for two hours, as in his most recent play, *Mummified Deer* (2002). While most other playwrights also continue to confront social and political issues that are important to Latinos, most of them do it through the conventional forms canonized by commodity theater in conventional playhouses.

New York

During the war years and following, serious theater in the Hispanic community waned, as first vaudeville productions drove it from such commercial stages as the Teatro Hispano; then, as in the Southwest, the movies and the caravans of music recording stars even began to drive vaudeville from the stages. Under the leadership of such directors as Marita Reid, Luis Mandret, and Alejandro Elliot, full-length melodramas and realistic plays were able to survive in mutual aid societies, church halls, and lodges during the 1940s and 1950s, but only for smaller audiences and for weekend performances. With such attractions as La Chata Noloesca's Mexican company and Puerto Rican vaudevillians, including famed recording star Bobby Capó, vaudeville survived into the early 1960s, playing to the burgeoning working-class audiences of Puerto Ricans. One notable and valiant effort was represented by Dominican actor-director Rolando Barrera's group Futurismo, which for a while during the 1940s was able to stage four productions a year of European works in Spanish translation at the Master's Auditorium. Beginning in 1950, Edwin Janer's La Farándula Panamericana staged three and four productions a year of classical works, as well as contemporary Spanish, Puerto Rican, and European works at the Master's Auditorium and the Belmont Theater.

In 1953, a play was staged that would have the most direct and lasting impact of any theatrical production in New York's Hispanic community. A young director, Roberto Rodríguez, introduced to a working-class audience at the Church of San Sebastian *La carreta* (The Oxcart) by an as yet unknown Puerto Rican writer, René Marqués. The play, which deals with the dislocation of a family of mountain folk from their farm and their resettling in a San Juan slum and then in New York City, effectively dramatized the epic of Puerto Rican migration to the United States in working-class and mountain dialect. René Marqués went on to celebrity and many more plays and productions in Puerto Rico and the continental United States; however, his *La carreta* became a key for building a Puerto Rican and Hispanic theater in New York in that it presented serious dramatic material based on the history, language, and culture of the working-class communities. Roberto Rodríguez joined forces with stage and screen actress Miriam Colón to form El Nuevo Círculo Dramático, which was able to administer a theater space in a loft, Teatro Arena, in midtown Manhattan. Although there were other minor and short-lived companies, it was El Nuevo Círculo Dramático, along with La Farándula Panamericana, that dominated the New York Hispanic stage into the early 1960s, when two incursions were made into the mainstream: In 1964 Joseph Papp's New York Shakespeare Festival began producing Shakespearean works in Spanish and in 1965 there was an off-Broadway production of *La carreta*, starring Miriam Colón and Raúl Juliá.

LA FARÁNDULA PANAMERICANA

presenta a

Marita Reid

directamente de Broadway—donde triunfó en
la obra teatral "In the Summer House" junto
a Judith Anderson

Mercedes Varnez   Luis Mora

en

"*Los Árboles Mueren de Pie*"

Viernes hasta domingo — — 2, 3, 4 de abril de 1954
a las 8:30 P. M. (Domingo, 4 de abril-matinée a las 2:30 P. M.)

TEATRO MASTER

Calle 103 y Riverside Drive
(7th Avenue Subway)

Poster for a production by *La Farándula Panamericana*, starring Marita Reid.

The 1960s also saw the introduction of improvisational street theater similar to Latin American people's theater and Chicano theater, which attempted to raise the level of political consciousness of working-class Hispanics. Among the most well-known, although short-lived, groups were the following ensembles, which usually developed their material as a collective: El Nuevo Teatro Pobre de las Américas (The New Poor People's Theater of the Americas), Teatro Orilla (Marginal Theater), Teatro Guazabara (Whatsamara Theater), and Teatro Jurutungo. But the most interesting of the improvisational troupes, and the only one to survive to the present, has been the Teatro Cuatro, named so for its first location on Fourth Avenue in the Lower East Side and made up at first of a diverse group of Puerto Ricans, Dominicans, and other Latin Americans. Under the directorship of an Argentine immigrant, Oscar Ciccone, and his Salvadorean wife, Cecilia Vega, the Teatro Cuatro was one of the most serious troupes, committed to developing a true radical art and bringing together the popular theater movement of Latin America with that of Hispanics in the United States. As such Teatro Cuatro became involved with TENAZ and the Chicano theater movement and with *teatro popular* in Latin America, and sponsored festivals and workshops in New York with some of the leading guerrilla and politically alternate theatrical directors and companies in the hemisphere. During the late 1970s Teatro Cuatro became officially associated with Joseph Papp's New York Shakespeare Festival and began to organize the biennial Festival Latino, a festival of Hispanic popular theater. Today, Ciccone and Vega manage the Papp organization's Hispanic productions, including the festival and a playwriting contest, while the Teatro Cuatro has gone its own way, functioning as a repertory company in its own remodeled firehouse theater in East Harlem.

The type of theater that has predominated in New York's cosmopolitan Hispanic culture since the 1960s is that which more or less follows the patterns established by the Nuevo Círculo Dramático and the Farándula Panamericana mentioned above, in which a corps of actors and a director of like mind work as a repertory group in producing works of their choosing in their own style. Styles and groups have proliferated, so that at any one time over the last twenty to twenty-five years at least ten groups have existed with different esthetics and audiences. Among these theaters, many of which have their own houses today, are INTAR, Miriam Colón's Puerto Rican Traveling Theater, Teatro Repertorio Español, Nuestro Teatro, Duo, Instituto Arte Teatral (IATE), Latin American Theater Ensemble (LATE), Thalia, Tremont Arte Group, and Pregones. In addition

The Puerto Rican Traveling Theater's "Pagador de Promesas," performed in New York City streets.

to New York having over one million Hispanic inhabitants, another reason that so many organizations are able to survive—although many of them do not flourish—is that the state, local, and private institutions that provide financial support for the arts have been generous to the theaters. Compared to other cities and states, the financial support for the arts—and theater in particular—in the capital of the U.S. theater world has been excellent.

The three most important theater companies have been the Puerto Rican Traveling Theater, Teatro Repertorio Español, and INTAR (International Arts Relations). The PRTT, founded in 1967 by Miriam Colón, takes its name from its original identity as a mobile theater that performed in the streets of the Puerto Rican neighborhoods. At first it performed works by some of the leading Puerto Rican writers such as René Marqués, José Luis González, and Pedro Juan Soto, alternating Spanish-language performances with English-language ones. The company also produced Latin American and Spanish works and in the early 1970s pioneered productions of works by Nuyorican and other U.S. Hispanic authors, including those of Jesús Colón and Piri Thomas. In addition to its mobile unit, the theater maintained a laboratory theater and children's theater classes. Its most important development came in 1974 when it took over and remodeled an old firehouse in the Broadway area, on 47th street, and opened its permanent theater house. To this day, the PRTT provides the stage, audience, and developmental work for New York-based Hispanic playwrights such as Jaime Carrero, Edward Gallardo, Manuel Ramos Otero, Pedro Pietri and Dolores Prida.

Founded in 1969 as an offshoot of Las Artes by exiled members of Cuba's Sociedad Pro Arte, the Teatro Repertorio Español has grown into the only Hispanic theater in the nation specializing in the production of both classical Spanish works, such as Calderón's *La Vida Es Sueño* (Life Is a Dream) and Zorrilla's *Don*

Juan Tenorio, and works by contemporary authors from Latin America. It is also one of the few companies in the nation to also stage nineteenth-century zarzuelas. Operating today out of the Gramercy Arts Theater, which has a tradition of Spanish-language performances that goes back to the 1920s, the Teatro Repertorio Español caters both to educational and community-based audiences with productions in both Spanish and English. The Teatro Repertorio Español is the only New York Hispanic Theater to tour regularly around the country. This is possible because the Teatro Repertorio Español is the only major Hispanic company in New York still working basically as an ensemble; the others are production companies that hold open auditions for all of their parts.

INTAR was founded in 1967 as ADAL (Latin American Art Group) dedicated to producing works by Latin American authors. By 1977, under the name of INTAR, the company had achieved equity status as a professional theater. After converting a variety of structures into theater spaces, they currently occupy a theater on West 42nd Street near the Broadway theater district. Under the direction of Max Ferra, the company has offered workshops for actors and directors, staged readings for playwrights, and instituted a children's theater. Today INTAR is known for its production of classical works in new settings and innovative directing, for the likes of María Irene Fornés's *La Vida Es Sueño* (Life Is a Dream) and Dolores Prida's *Crisp,* based on Jacinto Benavente's *Los Intereses Creados* (Vested Interests). INTAR also presents works in English, including some standard non-Hispanic fare. INTAR has been particularly instrumental in developing Hispanic playwriting through its playwright's laboratory and readings, quite often following up with full productions of plays by local writers. Today, both Fornés and Prida are the leading Hispanic playwrights of New York and for more than two decades have produced award-winning plays. Fornés has won more Obie awards than any other Hispanic playwright, cultivating a style in English that is abstract and quite often devoid of Hispanic context, while Prida has continuously experimented with adapting the conventional forms of commodity theater to Hispanic culture in plays written in Spanish or English or bilingually. In fact, her most famous play splits the psyche of her protagonist into two characters, one speaking English and being assimilated into U.S. culture and the other speaking Spanish and paralyzed with nostalgia for Prida's birthplace, Cuba.

Scene from Dolores Prida's *Beautiful Señoritas.*

While the Hispanic theatrical environment in New York has been of necessity cosmopolitan, lending itself to the creation of companies with personnel from all of the Spanish-speaking countries, there have been groups that have set out to promote the work and culture of specific nationalities, such as the Puerto Ricans, Cubans, Dominicans, and Spaniards. Most notable, of course, has been the Puerto Rican Traveling Theater. But the Centro Cultural Cubano also was instrumental in the 1970s in developing Cuban theatrical expression, most significantly in producing the work of Omar Torres and Iván Acosta. Acosta's play, *El Super* (1977), has been the biggest hit ever to come out of an Hispanic company and even led to a prize-winning film adaptation. In general, Cuban American theater is well represented in almost all of the Hispanic companies of New York, with Dolores Prida, Iván Acosta, Manuel Martín, María Irene Fornés, and Omar Torres included among the most successful playwrights.

Puerto Rican playwriting is also well represented in most of the Hispanic companies, but during the 1960s an important new focus developed among New York Puerto Ricans that had long-lasting implications for the creation of theater and art in Hispanic working-class communities; this was the Nuyorican works that emerged from the artists born or raised among New York's Puerto Rican working classes. While not a specific form of theater per se, Nuyorican theater has included theatrical genres that vary from collectively created street theater to works by individual playwrights produced in such diverse settings as the Puerto Rican Traveling Theater, the Henry Street Settlement's New Federal Theater, Joseph Papp's New York Shakespeare Festival, and on Broadway itself. Although the term was first applied to literature and theater by playwright-novelist Jaime Carrero in the late 1960s, and finds some stylistic and thematic development in his plays *Noo Jall* (a play on the Spanish pronunciation of "New York" and "jail") and *Pipo Subway No Sabe Reír* (Pipo Subway Doesn't Know How to Laugh), it was a group of playwright-poets associated with the Nuyorican Poets' Café and Joseph Papp that first defined and came to exemplify Nuyorican theater. Included in the group were Miguel Algarín, Lucky Cienfuegos, Tato Laviera, and Miguel Piñero, all of whom focused their bilingual works on the life and culture of working-class Puerto Ricans in New York. Two members of the group, Lucky Cienfuegos and Miguel Piñero, were ex-convicts who began their writing careers while incarcerated and chose to develop their dramatic material from prison, street, and underclass culture. Algarín, a university professor and proprietor of the Nuyorican Poets' Café, created a more avant garde aura for the collective, while the virtuoso bilingual poet Tato Laviera, contributed lyricism and a folk and popular culture base.

It was Piñero's work (and life), however, that became most celebrated. His prison drama *Short Eyes* won an Obie and the New York Drama Critics Best American Play Award for the 1973–74 season. His success, coupled with that of fellow Nuyorican writers, ex-convict Piri Thomas and street urchin Pedro Pietri, often resulted in Nuyorican literature and theater becoming associated with a stark naturalism and the themes of crime, drugs, abnormal sexuality, and generally aberrant behavior. This led to a reaction against the term by many writers and theater companies that were in fact emphasizing Puerto Rican working-class culture in New York. Today there is a new generation of New York Puerto Rican playwrights who were nurtured on the theater of Piñero and the Nuyoricans and who have also experienced greater support and opportunities for developing their work. They quite often repeat and reevaluate many of the concerns and the style and language of the earlier group, but with a sophistication and polish that has

Nuyorican playwrights: Lucky Cienfuegos (with Afro hairdo), Miguel Algarín (center) and Miguel Piñero (right).

come from drama workshops, playwright residencies, and university education. Among these are Juan Shamsul Alam, Edward Gallardo, Federico Fraguada, Richard Irizarry, Yvette Ramírez, and Cándido Tirado, most of whom have had their works included in the historic anthology, *Recent Puerto Rican Theater: Five Plays from New York* (1994), edited by John Antush.

Florida

Today Hispanic theater still finds one of its centers in Florida. However, most of the theatrical activity in Tampa has disappeared, and only the Spanish Repertory Theater continues to perform in the old playhouses (Centro Asturiano) with a fare that varies from the standard *zarzuelas* to Broadway musicals in Spanish. With the exodus of refugees from the Cuban Revolution of 1959, Hispanic theater in Florida found a new center in Miami, where the Cuban expatriates—many from middle-class or upper class backgrounds who were used to supporting live theater in Cuba—founded and supported theater companies and laid fertile ground for the support of playwrights. During the last thirty years, the type of theater that has predominated in Miami has produced standard works from throughout the Spanish-speaking world and from the theater of exile, which is burdened with attacking communism in Cuba and promoting a nostalgia for the pre-Castro past.

While the Cuban playwrights of New York, many of whom have been raised and educated in the United States, have forged an avant garde and openly Cuban *American* theater, the Miami playwrights have been more traditional in form and content and, of course, more politically conservative. Most frequent in the exile theater is the form and style inherited from the theater of the absurd, from theatrical realism, and, to some extent, from the comic devices and characters of the *teatro bufo cubano*; however, the predominant attitude among Cuban exile playwrights is the intellectual one, the creation of a theater of ideas. The exile playwrights whose works have been most produced in Miami are Julio Matas, José Cid Pérez, Leopoldo Hernández, José Sánchez Boudy, Celedonio González, Raúl de Cárdenas, and Matías Montes Huidobro. An effort to bring them together with some of the newer voices such as that of Miami's Miguel González Pando is Rodolfo Cortina's important anthology, *Cuban American Theater* (1991), in which the exile theater is considered as part of the total Cuban American experience and esthetic.

However, overall, the theatrical fare in Miami is eclectic, with audiences able to choose from a variety of styles and genres, from vaudeville to French-style bedroom farce, serious drama, Broadway musicals in Spanish, and Spanish versions of classics such as Shakespeare's *Taming of the Shrew* and *Othello*. The theater

Cover of the first anthology of Hispanic women's plays, *Shattering the Myth: Plays by Hispanic Women.*

companies offering the most "serious" fare have included the Teatro Bellas Artes, the Teatro La Danza, Grupo Ras, and Pro Arte Gratelli. Among the longest lasting theaters in Miami are the two locations of Salvador Ugarte's and Ernesto Cremata's Teatro Las Máscaras, which for the most part produce light comedy and vaudeville for mostly working-class audiences. Two of impresario Ernesto

Capote's three houses, the Martí Theater and the Essex Theater, have a steady lineup of comedies and vaudeville; his third house, the Miami Theater, provides an eclectic bill, including such hard-hitting dramas as *The Boys in the Band* in Spanish. The Teatro Miami's stage also serves for the taping of soap operas for television. The theaters that play more to the working classes in Miami, exemplified by some of the theaters named above and by some that use movie houses after the showing of the last films, produce a type of reincarnation of the *teatro bufo cubano* that uses working-class language and culture as well as the comic style and characters from the *bufo* tradition to satirize life in Miami and Cuba under Castro. Here, comic characterizations of Fidel and his brother Raúl (Raúl Resbaloso—Slippery Raúl) join some of the traditional character types, such as Trespatines (Three Skates) and Prematura (Premature). This type of theater is the most commercially successful Cuban theater, while the other more artistically elite and intellectual theater often begs for audiences and depends on grants and university support for survival.

100 Essential Hispanic Literary Works

This is an alphabetical list by author of recommended titles (books and anthologies) for a library of multicultural literature. Titles are listed first by language of the original; titles in both languages mean the book is available in both. The first date listed is for the first edition, the second for the first translation.

BOOKS

1. Acosta, Iván. *El super* (1982).
2. Acosta, Oscar Zeta. *The Autobiography of a Brown Buffalo* (1972).
3. Alurista. *Floricanto en Aztlán* (1971).
4. Alvarez, Julia. *How the García Girls Lost Their Accents* (1991).
5. Anaya, Rudolfo. *Bless Me, Ultima* (1972).
6. Anónimo. *El laúd del desterrado* (1856).
7. Anzaldúa, Gloria. *La frontera/Borderlands: The New Mestiza* (1987).
8. Arenas, Reinaldo. *Antes que anochezca/Before Night Falls* (1993, 1994).
9. Bencastro, Mario. *Odisea del norte/Odyssey to the North* (1999, 1999).
10. Cabeza de Vaca, Alvar Núñez. *La relación/The Account* (1542, 1993).
11. Capetillo, Luisa. *Influencia de las ideas modernas* (1916).
12. Cervantes, Lorna Dee. *Emplumada* (1981).
13. Cervantes, Lorna Dee. *From the Cables of Genocide* (1992).
14. Cisneros, Sandra. *The House on Mango Street* (1984).
15. Cofer, Judith Ortiz. *Silent Dancing: A Partial Remembrance of a Puerto Rican Childhood* (1990).
16. Cofer, Judith Ortiz. *Terms of Survival* (1987).
17. Colón, Jesús. *Lo que el pueblo me dice* (2001).
18. Colón, Jesús. *A Puerto Rican in New York* (1961).
19. Corpi, Lucha. *Palabras de mediodía/Noon Words* (1980).

20. Cotto-Thorner, Guillermo. *Trópico en Manhattan/The Tropics in Manhattan* (1951).

21. Cruz, Victor Hernández. *Rhythm, Content and Flavor: New and Selected Poems* (1989).

22. Díaz, Junot. *Drown* (1996).

23. Díaz Guerra, Alirio. *Lucas Guevara* (1914, 2003).

24. Espada, Martín. *Trumpets from the Islands of Their Eviction* (1987).

25. Esteves, Sandra María. *Bluestown Mockingbird Mambo* (1990).

26. Fernández, Roberto. *Raining Backwards* (1988).

27. Ferré, Rosario. *La casa de la laguna/The House on the Lagoon* (1996).

28. García, Cristina. *Dreaming in Cuban* (1992).

29. García, Lionel. *To a Widow with Children* (1994).

30. Gómez Peña, Guillermo. *Warrior for Gringostroika: Essays, Performance Texts and Poetry* (1994).

31. González, José Luis. *En Nueva York y otras desgracias* (1973).

32. Gonazález, Jovita. *Dew on the Thorn* (1997).

33. Hijuelos, Oscar. *The Mambo Kings Play Songs of Love* (1989).

34. Hinojosa, Rolando. *Estampas del Valle y otras obras/ Sketches of the Valley and Other Works* (1973).

35. Hinojosa, Rolando. *Mi querido Rafa/Dear Rafe* (1981, 1985).

36. Laviera, Tato. *Enclave* (1981).

37. Laviera, Tato. *La Carreta Made a U-Turn* (1979).

38. Levins Morales, Aurora. *Getting Home Alive* (1986).

39. Limón, Graciela. *The Memories of Ana Calderón* (1994).

40. Limón, Graciela. *Song of the Hummingbird* (1996).

41. Marín, Francisco "Pachín." *Romances* (1892).

42. Marqués, René. *La carreta/The Oxcart* (1961, 1969).

43. Martí, José. *Versos sencillos/Simple Verses* (1895).

44. Mena, María Cristina. *The Stories of María Cristina Mena* (1997).

45. Méndez, Miguel. *Peregrinos de Aztlán/Pilgrims in Aztlán* (1974).

46. Mohr, Nicholasa. *Nilda* (1973).

47. Mohr, Nicholasa. *El Bronx Remembered* (1975).

48. Mora, Pat. *Borders* (1986).

49. Mora, Pat. *Chants* (1984).

50. Mora, Pat. *Communion* (1991).

51. Moraga, Cherríe. *Loving in the War Years* (1983).

52. Morales, Alejandro. *The Brick People* (1988).

53. Morales, Alejandro. *The Rag Doll Plagues* (1991).

54. Paredes, Américo. *George Washington Gomez* (1990).

55. Paredes, Américo. *The Hammon and the Beans and Other Stories* (1994).

56. Pérez de Villagrá, Gaspar. *Historia de la conquista de la Nueva México/History of the Conquest of New Mexico.* (1610, 1933).

57. Pérez Firmat, Gustavo. *Next Year in Cuba/El año que viene estamos en Cuba* (1995, 1997).

58. Pietri, Pedro. *Puerto Rican Obituary* (1971).

59. Piñero, Miguel. *Short Eyes* (1975).

60. Piñero, Miguel. *The Sun Always Shines for the Cool* (1983).

61. Prida, Dolores. *Beautiful Señoritas and Other Plays* (1991).

62. Rechy, John. *Cities of the Night* (1963).

63. Ríos, Alberto. *Whispering to Fool the Wind: Poems* (1982).

64. Rivera, Tomás. . . . *Y no se lo tragó la tierra/And the Earth Did Not Devour Him* (1971).

65. Rivera, Tomás. *La cosecha/The Harvest* (1989).

66. Rodríguez, Luis. *Always Running* (1993).

67. Ruiz, Ron. *Happy Birthday, Jesús* (1994).

68. Ruiz de Burton, María Amparo. *The Squatter and the Don* (1885).

69. Ruiz de Burton, María Amparo. *Who Would Have Thought It?* (1872).

70. Salas, Floyd. *Buffalo Nickel* (1992).

71. Salinas, Luis Omar. *Afternoon of the Unreal* (1980).

72. Sánchez, Ricardo. *Canto y grito mi liberación* (1973).

73. Soto, Gary. *Baseball in April* (1990).

74. Soto, Gary. *The Elements of San Joaquín* (1977).

75. Soto, Pedro Juan. *Spiks* (1956).

76. Soto Vélez, Clemente. *Caballo de palo* (1959).

77. Suárez, Virgil. *Going Under* (1996).

78. Suárez, Virgil. *Spared Angola: Memories from a Cuban American Childhood* (1997).

79. Thomas, Piri. *Down These Mean Streets* (1967).

80. Valdez, Luis. *Luis Valdez–The Early Works* (1990).

81. Valdez, Luis. *Zoot Suit and Other Plays* (1992).

82. Vega, Bernardo. *Memorias de Bernardo Vega/The Memories of Bernardo Vega* (1979, 1984).

83. Venegas, Daniel. *Las aventuras de Don Chipote, o cuando los pericos mamen/ The Adventures of Don Chipote, or When Parrots Breast Feed* (1928, 2000).

84. Vigil-Piñón, Evangelina. *Thirty an' Seen a Lot* (1982).

85. Villarreal, José Antonio. *Pocho* (1959).

86. Villaseñor, Victor. *Rain of Gold* (1991).

87. Villegas de Magnón, Leonor. *The Rebel* (1994).

88. Viramontes, Helena María. *The Moths and Other Stories* (1985).

89. Yglesias, Jose. *The Guns in the Closet and Other Stories* (1996).

90. Yglesias, Jose. *A Wake in Ybor City* (1963).

ANTHOLOGIES

91. Antush, John, ed. *Recent Puerto Rican Theater: Five Plays from New York* (1994).

92. Chávez, Denise, ed. *Shattering the Myth: Plays by Hispanic Women* (1992).

93. Cortina, Rodolfo J. *Cuban American Theater* (1992).

94. Fernández, Roberta, ed. *In Other Words: Literature by Latinas of the United States* (1994).

95. Huerta, Jorge, ed. *Necessary Theater: Six Plays about the Chicano Experience* (1989).

96. Kanellos, Nicolás, ed. *En otra voz: antología de la literatura hispana de los Estados Unidos* (2002).

97. Kanellos, Nicolás, ed. *Herencia: The Anthology of Hispanic Literature of the United States* (2002).

98. Kanellos, Nicolás, ed. *Short Fiction by Hispanic Writers of the United States* (1993).

99. Rebolledo, Tey Diana, and Eliana S. Rivero, eds. *Infinite Divisions: An Anthology of Chicana Literature* (1993).

100. Suárez, Virgil, and Delia Poey, eds. *Little Havana Blues: A Cuban American Literature Anthology* (1996).

SELECTED BIBLIOGRAPHY

Acosta-Belén, Edna, ed. *The Puerto Rican Woman*. New York: Praeger, 1986.

Alarcon, Norma. *Chicana Critical Issues*. Berkeley: Third Woman Press, 1993.

Algarín, Miguel, and Miguel Piñero. *Nuyorican Poetry*. New York: Morrow, 1975.

Almaguer, Tomás. *Racial Fault Lines: The Historical Origins of White Supremacy in California*. Berkeley: University of California Press, 1994.

Antush, John, ed. *Recent Puerto Rican Theater: Five Plays from New York*. Houston: Arte Público Press, 1991.

Aparicio, Frances, and Susana Chavez-Silverman. *Tropicalizations: Transcultural Representations of Latinidad*. Hanover, NH: Dartmouth College, 1997.

Arce, Julio G. (Jorge Ulica). "Treinta años de galeras . . . periodísticas, 1881–1911." Manuscript, Chicano Studies Collection, University of California-Berkeley, s.d.

Argudín, Yolanda. *Historia del periodismo en México desde el Virreinato hasta nuestros días*. Mexico City: Panorama Editorial, 1997.

Babín, María Teresa. *Panorama de la cultura puertorriqueña*. New York: Las Américas Publishing Company, 1958.

Balderrama, Francisco E., and Raymond Rodríguez. *Decade of Betrayal: Mexican Repatriation in the 1930s*. Albuquerque: University of New Mexico Press, 1995.

Boswel, T. D., and J.R. Curtis. *The Cuban American Experience*. Totowa, NJ: Rowan and Allenheld, 1984.

Bruce-Novoa. "*La Prensa* and the Chicano Community." *The Americas Review* 17.3–4 (Winter, 1989): 150–56.

Burunat, Silvia, and Ofelia García. *Veinte Años de Literatura Cubanoamericana*. Tempe: Bilingual Press/Editorial Bilingüe, 1988.

Calcagno, Francisco. *Diccionario biográfico cubano*. New York: Imprenta y Librería de N. Ponce de León, 1878.

Calderón, Hector, and José David Saldívar, eds. *Criticism in the Borderlands. Studies in Chicano Literature, Culture and Ideology*. Raleigh-Durham, NC: Duke University Press, 1991.

Campa, Arthur L. *Hispanic Culture in the Southwest*. Norman: University of Oklahoma Press, 1979.

Carrasco Puente, Rafael. *La prensa en México: Datos históricos*. Mexico City: Universidad Nacional Autónoma de México, 1962.

Castañeda, Carlos E. *The Beginning of Printing in America*. Austin, TX: University of Texas Latin American García Library, s.d.

Castillo, Lillian. *Women's Voices From the Borderlands*. San Francisco: Touchstone Books, 1995.

————. *Our Catholic Heritage in Texas, 1519–1936*. New York: Arno Press, 1976.

Chabrán, Rafael. "Spaniards." In *The Immigrant Labor Press in North America, 1840s–1970s*, edited by Dirk Hoerder, 151–190. Westport, CT: Greenwood Press, 1987.

Chacón, Ramón D. "The Chicano Immigrant Press in Los Angeles: The Case of 'El Heraldo de México,' 1916–1920." *Journalism History* 4.2 (Summer 1977): 48–50, 62–4.

Chamberlin, Vernon A., and Ivan A. Shulman, eds. *La Revista Ilustrada de Nueva York: History, Anthology and Index of Literary Selections*. Columbia, MO: University of Missouri Press, 1976.

Chipman, Donald E. *Spanish Texas, 1519–1821*. Austin: University of Texas Press, 1992.

Cockroft, James D. *Intellectual Pioneers of the Mexican Revolution, 1900–1913*. Austin: University of Texas Press, 1968.

Colón, Jesús. *A Puerto Rican in New York and Other Sketches*. 2d edition. New York: International Publishers, 1982.

————. *The Way It Was and Other Writings*. Edited by Edna Acosta-Belén and Virginia Sánchez Korrol. Houston: Arte Público Press, 1993.

Cortina, Rodolfo J. *Cuban American Theater*. Houston: Arte Público Press, 1991.

Dolan, Jay P., and Allan Figueroa Deck. *Hispanic Catholic Culture in the United States: Issues and Concerns*. Notre Dame, IN: University of Notre Dame, 1994.

Dolan, Jay P., and Gilberto M. Hinojosa. *Mexican Americans and the Catholic Church, 1900–1965*. Notre Dame, IN: University of Notre Dame Press, 1994.

Fabre, Genvieve, ed. *European Perspectives on Hispanic Literature of the United States*. Houston: Arte Público Press, 1989.

Fernández Roberta, ed. *In Other Words: Literature by Latinas*. Houston: Arte Público Press, 1994.

Fincher, E.B. *Spanish Americans as a Political Factor in New Mexico, 1912–1950*. New York: Arno Press, 1974.

Fitzpatrick, Joseph P. "The Puerto Rican Press." In *The Ethnic Press in the United States: An Historical Analysis and Handbook*, edited by Sally M. Miller, 303–14. Westport, CT: Greenwood Press, 1987.

Flores, Juan. *Divided Borders*. Houston: Arte Público Press, 1993.

Florida Department of State. *Florida Cuban Heritage Trail*. Tallahassee: Florida Department of State, Division of Historical Resources, 1995.

Fontana, Bernard L. *Entrada: The Legacy of Spain and Mexico in the United States*. Albuquerque: University of New Mexico Press, 1994.

Fornet, Ambrosio. *El libro en Cuba*. Havana: Editorial Letras Cubanas, 1994.

Foster, David, and Manuel Hernández, eds. *Literatura Chicana, 1965–1995: An Anthology in Spanish, English, & Calo*. New York: Garland Publishing, 1997.

Gallegos, Bernardo P. *Literacy, Education, and Society in New Mexico, 1693–1821*. Albuquerque, NM: University of New Mexico Press, 1992.

García, Mario. *Desert Immigrants: The Mexicans of El Paso, 1880–1920*. New Haven: Yale University Press, 1981.

García Naranjo, Nemesio. *Memorias de Nemesio García Naranjo*. 9 vols. Monterrey, Mexico: Talleres de "El Porvenir," s.d.

Goff, Victoria. "Spanish-Language Newspapers in California." In *Outsiders in 19th-Century Press History: Multicultural Perspectives*, edited by Frankie Hutton and Barbara Straus Reed, 55–70. Bowling Green, OH: Bowling Green State University Popular Press, 1995.

Gómez-Quiñones, Juan. *Roots of Chicano Politics, 1600–1940*. Albuquerque: University of New Mexico Press, 1994.

———. *Sembradores, Ricardo Flores Magón y El Partido Liberal Mexicano: A Eulogy and Critique*. Los Angeles: UCLA Chicano Studies Research Center Publications, 1977.

Gonzales-Berry, Erlinda, ed. *Paso Por Aqui: Critical Essays on the New Mexican Literary Tradition, 1542–1988*. Albuquerque: University of New Mexico Press, 1989.

———, and Chuck Tatum. *Recovering the U.S. Hispanic Heritage*, Vol. II. Houston: Arte Público Press, 1996.

Griswold del Castillo, Richard. "The Mexican Revolution and the Spanish-Language Press in the Borderlands." *Journalism History* 4.2 (Summer 1977): 42–7.

Gutiérrez, Félix. "Spanish-Language Media in America: Background, Resources, History." *Journalism History* 4:2 (Summer 1977): 34–41, 65–7.

Gutiérrez, Ramón, and Genaro Padilla, eds. *Recovering the U.S. Hispanic Literary Heritage*, Vol. I. Houston: Arte Público Press, 1993.

Gutiérrez-Witt, Laura. "Cultural Continuity in the Face of Change: Hispanic Printers in Texas." In *Recovering the U.S. Hispanic Literary Heritage*, Vol. II. Edited by Erlinda Gonzales-Berry and Chuck Tatum, 260–78. Houston: Arte Público Press, 1996.

Henderson, Ann L., and Gary R. Mormino. *Spanish Pathways in Florida*. Sarasota: Pineapple Press, 1991.

Hernández Tovar, Inés. *Sara Estela Ramírez: The Early Twentieth Century Texas-Mexican Poet*. Houston: University of Houston Dissertation, 1984.

Herrera-Sobek, María. *Beyond Stereotypes The Critical Analysis of Chicana Literature*. Tempe: Bilingual Press/Editorial Bilingüe, 1985.

———. *Reconstructing a Chicano Hispanic Colonial Literature of the Southwest*. Tucson: University of Arizona Press, 2001.

———, and Virginia Sánchez-Korrol. *Recovering the U.S. Hispanic Literary Heritage*. Houston: Arte Público Press, 1998.

Horn, Calvin. *New Mexico's Troubled Years: The Story of the Early Territorial Governors*. Albuquerque: Horn and Wallace, 1963.

Huerta, Jorge. *Chicano Theater: Themes and Forms*. Tempe, AZ: Bilingual Review Press, 1982.

———, ed. *Necessary Theater: Six Plays about the Chicano Experience*. Houston: Arte Público Press, 1989.

Jamieson, Stuart. *Labor Unionism in American Agriculture*. New York: Arno Press, 1976.

Kanellos, Nicolás, with Helvetia Martell. *Brief History and Comprehensive Bibliography of Hispanic Periodicals in the United States, 1808–1960*. Houston: Arte Público Press, 1999.

———, ed. *En otra voz: antología de literatura hispana de los Estados Unidos*. Houston: Arte Público Press, 2002.

———, and Claudio Esteva-Fabregat, eds. *Handbook of Hispanic Cultures in the United States*. 4 vols. Houston: Arte Público Press, 1994–95.

———, ed. *Herencia: The Anthology of Hispanic Literature of the United States*. New York: Oxford University Press, 2002.

———. *A History of Hispanic Theatre in the United States: Origins to 1940*. Austin: University of Texas Press, 1990.

———, and Jorge Huerta, eds. *Nuevos Pasos: Chicano and Puerto Rican Theater*. Gary, IN: Arte Público Press, 1979.

———. *Thirty Million Strong: Reclaiming the Hispanic Image in American History*. Boulder: Fulcrum Press, 1998.

———, ed. *Short Fiction by Hispanic Writers of the United States*. Houston: Arte Público Press, 1993.

Kloss, Heinz. *The American Bilingual Tradition*. Rowley, MA: Newbury House, 1977.

Knippling, Alpana Sharma, ed. *New Immigrant Literatures in the United States: A Sourcebook to Our Multicultural Heritage*. Westport, CT: Greenwood Press, 1996.

Kushner, Sam. *Long Road to Delano: A Century of Farmworkers' Struggle*. New York: International Publishers, 1975.

Langham, Thomas C. *Border Trials: Ricardo Flores Magón and the Mexican Liberals*. El Paso: Texas Western Press, 1981.

Larson, Robert W. *New Mexico's Quest for Statehood*. Albuquerque, NM: University of New Mexico Press, 1968.

Lerner Sigal, Victoria. *Algunas hipótesis generales a partir del caso de los mexicanos exilados por la Revolución Mexicana (1906–1920)*. University of Chicago Center for Latin American Studies Mexican Studies Program, Working Papers Series No. 7, 2000.

———. *Mexicanos en Estados Unidos: su actitud hacia México, sus líderes y su situación (1915–1930)*. El Paso, Texas: Center for Inter-American and Border Studies, No. 12, June 1944.

Lomas, Clara. "The Articulation of Gender in the Mexican Borderlands, 1900–1915." In *Recovering the U.S. Hispanic Literary Heritage*. Edited by Ramón Gutiérrez and Genaro Padilla, 293–308. Houston: Arte Público Press, 1993.

———. *Dictionary of Literary Biography: Chicano Writers*. Vol. 82. Detroit: Gale Research, 1989.

———. "Resistencia cultural o apropiación ideológica: Visión de los años 20 en los cuadros costumbristas de Jorge Ulica." *Revista Chicano-Riqueña* 6.4 (otoño 1978): 44–9.

Lomelí, Francisco, and Rudolfo Anaya. *Aztlan Essays on the Chicano Homeland*. Albuquerque: University of New Mexico Press, 2001.

Lomelí, Francisco, and Carl R. Shirley, eds. *Dictionary of Literary Biography: Chicano Writers*. Vols. 122 and 128. Detroit: Gale Research, 1992, 1994.

Lomelí, Francisco, and Carl Shirley. *Chicano Writers: Second Series*. Detroit: Gale Research, 1992.

López, Adalberto, ed. *The Puerto Ricans: Their History, Culture and Society*. Cambridge, MA: Schenkman, 1980.

Lutrell, Estelle. *Newspapers and Periodicals of Arizona, 1859–1911*. Tucson: University of Arizona Press, 1950.

MacCurdy, Raymond R. *A History and Bibliography of Spanish-Language Newspapers and Magazines in Louisiana, 1808–1949*. Albuquerque: University of New Mexico Press, 1951.

MacLachlan, Colin M. *Spain's Empire in the New World. The Role of Ideas and Social Change*. Berkeley: University of California Press, 1988.

McWilliams, Carey. *North from Mexico: The Spanish-Speaking People of the United States*. Philadelphia: Lippincott, 1949.

Martinez, Julio, and Francisco Lomelí. *Chicano Literature: A Reader's Encyclopedia*. Westport, CT: Greenwood, 1985.

Medeiros, Francine. "*La Opinión*, A Mexican Exile Newspaper: A Content Analysis of Its First Years, 1926–1929." *Aztlán* 11.1 (Spring, 1980): 65–87.

Meier, Matt S., and Feliciano Rivera. *Dictionary of Mexican American History*. Westport, CT: Greenwood Press, 1981.

Meléndez, Gabriel. *So All Is Not Lost: The Poetics of Print in Nuevomexicano Communities, 1834–1958*. Albuquerque, NM: University of New Mexico Press, 1997.

Meyer, Doris. *Speaking for Themselves: Neomexicano Cultural Identity and the Spanish-Language Press, 1880–1920*. Albuquerque, NM: University of New Mexico Press, 1996.

Monsiváis, Carlos. *A ustedes les consta: Antología de la crónica en México*. México City: Ediciones Era, 1980.

Montes-Huidobro, Matías, ed. *El laúd del desterrado*. Houston: Arte Público Press, 1995.

Moraga, Cherríe, and Gloria Anzaldúa, eds. *This Bridge Called My Back*. Albany, NY: Kitchen Table/Women of Color Press, 1983.

Munguía, Rubén. "*La Prensa*: Memories of a Boy . . . Sixty Years Later." *The Americas Review* (Fall-Winter 1989): 3–4.

Neri, Michel C. "A Journalistic Portrait of the Spanish-Speaking People of California, 1868–1925." *Historical Society of Southern California Quarterly* 55 (Summer 1973): 193–208.

Ong, Walter. *Orality and Literacy: The Technologies of the Word*. London: Methuen, 1982.

Paredes, Américo. *Folkore and Culture on the Mexican American Border*. Austin: University of Texas Press, 1995.

———. *With His Pistol in His Hand: A Border Ballad and His Hero*. Austin: The University of Texas Press, 1958.

Park, Robert E. *The Immigrant Press and Its Control*. New York: Harper & Brothers, 1922.

Pérez-Firmat, Gustavo. *Life on the Hyphen*. Austin: University of Texas Press, 1993.

Pitt, Leonard. *The Decline of the Californios: A Social History of the Spanish-Speaking Californians, 1846–1890*. Berkeley: University of California Press, 1966.

Poyo, Gerald E. *"With All, and for the Good of All." The Emergence of Popular Nationalism in the Cuban Communities of the United States, 1848–1898*. Durham: Duke University Press, 1989.

Rebolledo, Tey Diana, and Eliana S. Rivero. *Infinite Divisions: An Anthology of Chicana Literature*. Tucson: University of Arizona Press, 1993.

Rice, William B. *The Los Angeles Star, 1851–1864*. Berkeley: University of California Press, 1951.

Ríos-McMillan, Nora. "A Biography of a Man and His Newspaper." *The Americas Review* 17.3–4 (Fall-Winter 1989): 136–49.

Rodríguez, Juan. *Crónicas diabólicas de "Jorge Ulica"/Julio B. Arce*. San Diego: Maize Press, 1982.

Rodríguez de Laguna, Asela, ed. *Images and Identities: The Puerto Rican in Two World Contexts*. New Brunswick, NJ: Transaction Books, 1985.

Romano-V., Octavio, and Herminio Ríos, eds. *El espejo/The mirror*. Berkeley: Editorial Quinto Sol, 1969.

Rosales, F. Arturo. *Chicano! The History of the Mexican American Civil Rights Movement*. Houston: Arte Público Press, 1996.

Rosario, Rubén del, Esther Melón de Díaz, and Edgar Martínez Masdeu. *Breve enciclopedia de la cultura puertorriqueña*. San Juan: Editorial Cordillera, 1976.

Ruoff, A. La Vonne Brown, and W. Jerry Ward. *Redefining American Literary History*. New York: Modern Language Association of America, 1990.

Saldívar, José David. *Border Matters: Remapping American Culture Studies*. Berkeley: University of California Press, 1997.

———, ed. *The Rolando Hinojosa Reader*. Houston: Arte Público Press, 1994.

Saldívar, Ramón. *Chicano Narrative: The Dialectics of Difference*. Madison: University of Wisconsin Press, 1990.

Sánchez, Rosaura. *Telling Identities: The Californio Testimonios*. Minneapolis: University of Minnesota Press, 1996.

Sánchez Korrol, Virginia. *From Colonia to Community: The History of Puerto Ricans in New York City, 1917–1948*. Westport, CT: Greenwood Press, 1983.

Serrano Cabo, Tomás. *Crónicas: Alianza Hispano Americana*. Tucson: Alianza Hispano Americana, 1929.

Sheridan, Thomas E. *Los Tucsonenses: The Mexican Community in Tucson, 1854–1941*. Tucson: University of Arizona Press, 1986.

Shirley, Carl, and Paula Shirley. *Understanding Chicano Literature*. Columbia: University of South Carolina Press, 1988.

Shular, Antonia Castañeda, Tomás Ybarra-Frausto, and Joseph Sommers, eds. *Literatura chicana: Texto y contexto*. Englewood Cliffs, NJ: Prentice-Hall, 1972.

Silén, Iván, ed. *Las paraguas amarillas: Los poetas latinos en Nueva York*. New York: Ediciones de Norte, 1983.

Smith, Michael M. "The Mexican Immigrant Press beyond the Borderlands: The Case of *El Cosmopolita*, 1914–1919." *Great Plains Quarterly* 10 (Spring, 1990): 71–85.

Stefano, Onofre di. " 'Venimos a Luchar': A Brief History of *La Prensa's* Founding," *Aztlán* 16.1–2 (1985): 95–118.

Stratton, Porter A. *The Territorial Press of New Mexico, 1834–1912*. Albuquerque, NM: University of New Mexico Press, 1969.

Suárez, Virgil, and Delia Poey, eds. *Little Havana Blues: A Cuban American Anthology*. Houston: Arte Público Press, 1996.

Tatum, Charles. *Chicano Literature*. Boston: Twayne, 1982.

———. *Chicano Popular Culture: Que Hable el Pueblo*. Tucson: University of Arizona Press, 2001.

———. *Mexican American Literature*. New York: Holt, Rinehart and Winston, 1990.

———. *New Chicana/Chicano Writing 1*. Tucson: University of Arizona Press, 1992.

———. *New Chicana/Chicano Writing 1*. Tucson: University of Arizona Press, 1994.

Treviño, Roberto. *Becoming Mexican American: The Spanish-Language Press and Biculturation of California Elites, 1852–1870*. Stanford: Stanford University History Department, Working Paper Series No. 27, 1989.

Trujillo, E. *Album de "El Porvenir."* Vols. 1–5. New York: Imprenta de "El Porvenir," 1890.

———. *Apuntes históricos*. New York: Imprenta del "El Porvenir," 1896.

Velasco Valdés, Miguel. *Historia del periodismo mexicano (apuntes)*. Mexico City: Librería de Manuel Porrúa, s.d.

Venegas, Daniel. *The Adventures of Don Chipote, or When Parrots Breast Feed*. Edited by Nicolás Kanellos. Houston: Arte Público Press, 2000.

Wagner, Henry R. "New Mexico Spanish Press." *New Mexico Historical Review*. 12.1 (January, 1937): 1–40.

Wallace, John Melton. *Gaceta to Gazette: A Check List of Texas Newspapers, 1812–1846*. Austin, TX: University of Texas, Department of Journalism Development Program, 1966.

Weber, David. *The Mexican Frontier, 1821–1846: The American Southwest under Mexico*. Albuquerque: University of New Mexico Press, 1982.

———. *Myth and History of the Hispanic Southwest*. Albuquerque: University of New Mexico Press, 1988.

———. *The Spanish Frontier in North America*. New Haven: Yale University Press, 1992.

Wynar, Lubomyr R., and Anna T. Wynar. *Encyclopedic Directory of Ethnic Newspapers and Periodicals in the United States*. 2d edition. Littleton, CO: Libraries Unlimited Inc., 1976.

Ybarra-Frausto, Tomás, and Joseph Sommers. *Twentieth Century Interpretations of Modern Chicano Writers: A Collection of Critical Essays*. Englewood Cliffs, NJ: Prentice Hall, 1979.

Zamora, Emilio. "Sara Estela Ramírez: Una Rosa Roja en el Movimiento." In *Mexican Women in the United States: Struggles Past and Present*, edited by Magdalena Mora and Adelaida R. del Castillo, 163–78. Los Angeles: University of California, Chicano Studies Research Publications, 1980.

Zavala, Iris M., and Rafael Rodríguez. *The Intellectual Roots of Independence: An Anthology of Puerto Rican Political Essays*. New York: Monthly Review Press, 1980.

TITLE INDEX

SUBJECT INDEX

About the Author

NICOLÁS KANELLOS is the Brown Foundation Professor of Spanish at the University of Houston. Recognized for his scholarly achievements, Dr. Kanellos is the recipient of the 1996 Denali Press Award of the American Library Association, the 1989 American Book Award—Publisher/Editor Category, the 1989 award from the Texas Association of Chicanos in Higher Education, the 1988 Hispanic Heritage Award for Literature presented by the White House, as well as various fellowships and other recognitions. Dr. Kanellos is the director of a major national research program, Recovering the U.S. Hispanic Literary Heritage of the United States, whose objective is to identify, preserve, study, and make accessible tens of thousands of literary documents of those regions that have become the United States from the colonial period to 1960. In 1994 President Bill Clinton appointed Dr. Kanellos to the National Council on the Humanities.